Transnational Italian Studies

Transnational Modern Languages

Transnational Modern Languages promotes a model of Modern Languages not as the inquiry into separate national traditions, but as the study of languages, cultures and their interactions. The series aims to demonstrate the value – practical and commercial, as well as academic and cultural – of modern language study when conceived as transnational cultural enquiry.

The texts in the series are specifically targeted at a student audience. They address how work on the transnational and the transcultural broadens the confines of Modern Languages; opens an extensive range of objects of research to analysis; deploys a complex set of methodologies; and can be accomplished through the exposition of clearly articulated examples.

The series is anchored by *Transnational Modern Languages: A Handbook*, ed. Jennifer Burns (Warwick) and Derek Duncan (St. Andrews), which sets out the theoretical and conceptual scope of the series, the type of research on which it is based and the kinds of questions that it asks. Following on from the *Handbook*, the series includes a text for the study of the following Modern Languages:

Transnational French Studies, ed. Charles Forsdick (Liverpool) and Claire Launchbury (Leeds)

Transnational German Studies, ed. Rebecca Braun (Lancaster) and Ben Schofield (KCL)

Transnational Spanish Studies, ed. Catherine Davies (IMLR) and Rory O'Bryen (Cambridge)

Transnational Italian Studies, ed. Charles Burdett (Durham) and Loredana Polezzi (Cardiff)

Transnational Portuguese Studies, ed. Hilary Owen (Manchester/Oxford) and Claire Williams (Oxford)

Transnational Russian Studies, ed. Andy Byford (Durham), Connor Doak (Bristol) and Stephen Hutchings (Manchester)

Transnational Italian Studies

edited by
Charles Burdett and Loredana Polezzi

LIVERPOOL UNIVERSITY PRESS

First published 2020 by
Liverpool University Press
4 Cambridge Street
Liverpool
L69 7ZU

Copyright © 2020 Liverpool University Press

The right of Charles Burdett and Loredana Polezzi to be identified as the
editors of this work has been asserted by them in accordance with the
Copyright, Designs and Patents Act 1988.

British Library Cataloguing-in-Publication data
A British Library CIP record is available

ISBN 978-1-78962-137-2 (HB)
ISBN 978-1-78962-138-9 (PB)

Typeset by Carnegie Book Production, Lancaster
Printed in the UK by CPI Group (UK) Ltd, Croydon CR0 4YY

Contents

Part Two: Spatiality

Part Three: Temporality

Part Four: Subjectivity

List of Figures

List of Contributors

Serena Bassi is Postdoctoral Associate at the Yale Translation Initiative and Lecturer in Italian Language and Literature at Yale University. She obtained her PhD in Italian Studies from the University of Warwick. She was research fellow at the Warwick Institute for Advanced Studies and Leverhulme Early Career Fellow at Cardiff University. Her research focuses on contemporary Italian literature and cultural studies, translation studies, LGBTQ history and queer studies. She is also currently at work on *The Handbook of Translation and Sexuality*, co-edited with Brian Baer (Kent State University). Her writing has appeared in the journals *Translation Studies*, *Comparative Literature Studies*, *Gender/Sexuality/Italy* and *Modern Languages Open*.

David Bowe is an Irish Research Council Government of Ireland Postdoctoral Fellow at University College Cork, where his research focuses on the representation of feminine voices in medieval Italian texts. He previously held a Victoria Maltby Junior Research Fellowship at Somerville College, University of Oxford. He works on lyric and other literature from the thirteenth to the fifteenth century, including the works of Dante, as well as their international and cross-medial receptions. His publications include: *Poetry in Dialogue in the 'Duecento' and Dante* (Oxford University Press, 2020); 'Versions of a Feminine Voice: The Compiuta Donzella' in *Italian Studies*, 73.1 (2018); and 'Text, Artefact and the Creative Process: The Sad Bewildered Quills of Guido Cavalcanti' in *MHRA Working Papers in the Humanities*, 9 (2015). He is also editing the first publication of Rachel Owen's *Inferno Illustrations* for Bodleian Library Publishing.

Charles Burdett is Professor of Italian at the University of Durham. The principal areas of his research are literary culture under fascism, travel writing, the Italian colonial presence in Libya and East Africa and its legacy, theories of intercultural contact and the representation of Islam and the Islamic world in recent Italian literature and culture. His books include *Journeys through Fascism: Italian Travel Writing between the Wars* (Berghahn, 2007) and *Italy, Islam and the Islamic World: Representations and Reflections from 9/11 to the Arab Uprisings* (Peter Lang, 2016). He was principal investigator of the collaborative research project 'Transnationalizing Modern Languages: Mobility, Identity and Translation in Modern Italian Cultures' (2014–17). Developing from his work on colonial discourse under fascism and on the aftermath of the Italian occupation of Ethiopia, he is currently working on a study of the memory of the Italian empire.

Jennifer Burns is Professor in Italian Studies at the University of Warwick. Her research engages with contemporary Italian literature and culture, primarily with narratives by migrant and mixed-ethnicity writers in the Italian language (*Migrant Imaginaries*, Peter Lang, 2013). Both independently and as co-investigator in the collaborative research project 'Transnationalizing Modern Languages' (2014–17), her most recent work explores the shared spaces of language, creativity and everyday cultural practice which challenge the notion of discrete and bounded national cultures and reveal the complex relationality of human experience in subnational localities as well as in transnational spaces and communities. This in turn has informed her engagement with initiatives to rethink the disciplinary framework and practices of research and teaching in modern languages for the present and future.

Fabio Camilletti is Associate Professor and Reader in Italian Studies at the University of Warwick. His main specialism is nineteenth-century literature and culture from a comparative perspective. His research investigates phenomena of fracture, transformation and continuity in the Western cultural tradition between the eighteenth and the twentieth centuries; the reception of Dante; the intersections between literature and psychoanalysis; and Gothic, horror and supernatural fiction from the eighteenth to the twenty-first century. His recent publications include the monographs *Italia Lunare. Gli anni Sessanta e l'occulto* (Peter Lang, 2018) and *The Portrait of Beatrice: Dante, D.G. Rossetti, and the Imaginary Lady* (Notre Dame University Press, 2019), as well as *Guida alla letteratura gotica* (Odoya, 2018). He edited the first complete edition of J.-B.B. Eyriès's 1812 anthology of ghost stories *Fantasmagoriana* (Nova Delphi, 2015) and the two-volume set *Villa Diodati Files* (Nova Delphi, 2018–19).

Alessandra Diazzi is Lecturer in Italian Studies at the University of Manchester. Her PhD, awarded from Cambridge University in 2015, examined the reception of psychoanalysis in post-1945 Italian literature and culture. Her research revolves around the controversial relationship between psychoanalytic culture and political commitment in Italy. She has also worked on René Girard's mimetic theory. She has written on Italian modern and contemporary literature (Italo Svevo, Italo Calvino, Alberto Moravia and Giorgio Manganelli) and cinema (Gianni Amelio). Among her recent publications is *The Years of Alienation in Italy: Factory and Asylum between the Economic Miracle and the Years of Lead* (edited with Alvise Sforza Tarabochia, Palgrave Macmillan, 2019). She co-edited, together with Pierpaolo Antonello, *Mimesi e pensiero: saggi su filosofia e letteratura*, a collection of essays by René Girard (Transeuropa, 2019).

Clorinda Donato holds the George L. Graziadio Chair for Italian Studies at California State University, Long Beach, and directs the Clorinda Donato Center for Global Romance Languages and Translation Studies. She works on eighteenth-century knowledge transfer in encyclopaedic compilations, and on gender in medical and literary accounts. Recent publications include *Fanny Hill Now*, a special issue of *Eighteenth-Century Life* (co-edited in 2019 with Nicholas Nace); *Enlightenment Spain and the 'Encyclopédie Méthodique'* (Voltaire Foundation, 2015), co-edited with Ricardo López; *Gender, Science and Sensationalism in Eighteenth-Century Italy and England: The Life and Legend of Catterina Vizzani* (Voltaire Foundation, 2020) and *John Fante's Ask the Dust: A Joining of Voices and Views*, co-edited with Stephen Cooper (Fordham University Press, 2020).

Derek Duncan is Professor of Italian at the University of St Andrews. He has published extensively on modern Italian culture, particularly on intersections of sexuality/gender and of race/ethnicity in a transnational framework. He has been instrumental in the development of Italian Colonial and Postcolonial Studies and Italian Queer Studies. He was founding editor of the 'Cultural Studies' issue of *Italian Studies*, and edits Liverpool University Press's acclaimed series Transnational Italian Cultures. He is also co-editor of *Transnational Modern Languages: A Handbook* (Liverpool University Press, forthcoming). He has organized numerous conferences in the UK and elsewhere. He is currently interested in exploring Italian cultural production as a set of vernacular material practices extending beyond the peninsula itself and in the multiple legacies of migration from Italy. He is increasingly engaged with developments in the creative humanities and in the fusion of academic research and creative practice.

Teresa Fiore holds the Inserra Endowed Chair in Italian and Italian American Studies at Montclair State University (New Jersey, USA). The recipient of several fellowships (De Bosis, Rockefeller and Fulbright), she has been Visiting Assistant Professor at Harvard University, NYU and Rutgers University. Her book *Pre-Occupied Spaces: Remapping Italy's Transnational Migrations and Colonial Legacies* (Fordham University Press, 2017) received the 2017 AAIS Book Prize and the 2019 Gadda Prize (Runner Up). She edited the 2006 issue of *Quaderni del '900*, devoted to John Fante, and co-edited a special section about the migration 'crisis' in the Mediterranean (*Journal of Modern Italian Studies*, 23.4, 2018). Her articles on migration to and from Italy linked to twentieth- and twenty-first-century Italian literature, theatre, music and cinema have appeared in both journals and edited collections (Routledge, Palgrave, Bompiani, Le Monnier-Mondadori). She directs a programme of interdisciplinary events about Italian culture in a transnational perspective: montclair.edu/inserra-chair.

Donna Gabaccia is Professor Emerita at the University of Toronto and a past director of the Immigration History Research Center at the University of Minnesota. She is the author of 14 books and dozens of articles on immigrant class, gender and food studies in the United States, on Italian migration around the world and on migration in world history. Her books have received awards from the American Sociological Association and the Immigration and Ethnic History Society. She is currently the General Editor for the Cambridge History of Global Migrations. In 2018 she received a Lifetime Achievement Award from the Immigration and Ethnic History Society.

Nathalie Hester is Associate Professor of French and Italian and Director of European Studies at the University of Oregon. She is the author of *Literature and Identity in Italian Baroque Travel Writing* (Routledge, 2008) and has published studies on early modern travel writing, seventeenth-century French and Italian women writers, and Italian epic poems on the Americas. Recent publications include an essay on Italian travel writing in *The Cambridge History of Travel Writing* (Cambridge University Press, 2019) and a study of Girolamo Graziani's *Conquisto di Granata* in *The New World in Early Modern Italy*, edited by Elizabeth Horodowich and Lia Markey (Cambridge University Press, 2017). She is currently working on a book entitled *Inventing America in Baroque Italy: Columbus, Vespucci, and New World Epic*, for which she has received a 2019–20 NEH Individual Fellowship.

Monica Jansen is Assistant Professor in Italian Literature at the Department of Languages, Literature and Communication (TLC) of Utrecht University.

Her research interests include modernism and postmodernism, on which she wrote *Il dibattito sul postmoderno in Italia. In bilico tra dialettica e ambiguità* (Franco Cesati, 2002). More specifically, she investigates cultural representations of socially relevant topics such as religion, precarity, youth and migration from an interdisciplinary, transmedial and transnational perspective. Some of her most recent publications include the co-edited volumes and themed issues *The History of Futurism: The Precursors, Protagonists, and Legacies* (Lexington Books, 2012), with Geert Buelens and Harald Hendrix; *Le culture del precariato. Pensiero, azione, narrazione* (Ombre Corte, 2015), with Silvia Contarini and Stephania Ricciardi; and *Televisionismo. Narrazioni televisive della storia italiana negli anni della seconda Repubblica* (Edizioni Ca' Foscari, 2015), with Maria Bonaria Urban. She is an editor of the Moving Texts series (PIE Peter Lang) and of the journals *Annali d'Italianistica* and *Journal of Italian Cinema & Media Studies*.

Tristan Kay is Senior Lecturer in Italian at the University of Bristol. He specializes in Dante and early Italian literature, with a particular focus on medieval theories of love and desire and vernacular culture. He has published widely on Dante and medieval Italian culture and is the author of the monograph *Dante's Lyric Redemption: Eros, Salvation, Vernacular Tradition* (Oxford University Press, 2016) and co-editor of the volume *Desire in Dante and the Middle Ages* (Legenda, 2012). He is also interested in Dante's modern reception and has written essays on the use of the poet in the writing of Primo Levi and Cesare Pavese. With the support of the Leverhulme Trust, he is currently exploring the ways in which the figure of Dante has been used and exploited to construct and articulate different forms of Italian national identity since the process of unification in the nineteenth century.

Giuliana Muscio (PhD UCLA) is Professor Emerita of Cinema Studies at the University of Padua, Italy. She has been a visiting professor at UCLA and at the University of Minnesota. Her books include the monographs *Hollywood's New Deal* (Temple University Press, 1996) and *Napoli/New York/ Hollywood* (Fordham University Press, 2019), and the co-edited anthology *Mediated Ethnicity: New Italian-American Cinema* (John D. Calandra Italian American Institute, 2010) in English; and, in Italian, *Hollywood/Washington* (Cooperativa Libraria Editrice degli Studenti dell'Università, 1977), *Lista nera a Hollywood* (Feltrinelli, 1979), *Scrivere il film* (Savelli, 1981), *La Casa Bianca e le Sette Majors* (Il Poligrafo, 1990), *Alle porte di Hays* (Fabbri, 1991), *Piccole Italie, grandi schermi* (Bulzoni, 2004). She participated in the European programme 'Changing Media, Changing Europe' and is a member of several international networks including 'Women and the Silent

Screen', Inter-American Studies (IAS) and International American Studies Association (IASA). She has written extensively in both Italian and English on classic Hollywood cinema, film relations between the USA and Italy, documentary and screenwriting.

Eugenia Paulicelli is Professor of Italian, Comparative Literature and Women's Studies at Queens College and The Graduate Center, CUNY. She is the founder and director of the Concentration of Fashion Studies and of the partly digital project *The Fabric of Cultures: Systems in the Making* (http://fabricofcultures. qwriting.qc.cuny.edu). She is the author, editor and co-editor of several books: *Parola e Immagine. Sentieri della scrittura in Leonardo, Marino, Foscolo, Calvino* (Cadmo, 1996); *Fashion under Fascism: Beyond the Black Shirt* (Berg, 2004); *Moda e Moderno* (Meltemi, 2006); *The Fabric of Cultures: Fashion, Identity and Globalization* (Routledge, 2009), co-edited with Hazel Clark; *Writing Fashion in Early Modern Italy: From Sprezzatura to Satire* (Routledge, 2014 and 2016); *Rosa Genoni. La moda è una cosa seria. Milano Expo e la Grande Guerra* (bilingual edition, Deleyva, 2015); and *Italian Style: Fashion & Film from Early Cinema to the Digital Age* (Bloomsbury, 2016 and 2017). She is working on fashion and temporality and its implications with aesthetic labour, the arts and film, social justice and the history of women.

Loredana Polezzi is Professor of Translation Studies in the School of Modern Languages, Cardiff University. Her research interests combine translation studies and Italian studies. She has written extensively on Italian travel writing, colonial and postcolonial literature, translingualism and migration. Her current work focuses on how geographical and social mobilities are connected to the theories and practices of translation, self-translation and multilingualism. She has specialist interests in Italian American studies and in memory, translation and the visual arts. With Rita Wilson, she is co-editor of leading international journal *The Translator* and is the current president of the International Association for Translation and Intercultural Studies (IATIS). She was a co-investigator in the research projects 'Transnationalizing Modern Languages' and 'Transnationalizing Modern Languages: Global Challenges', funded by the Arts and Humanities Research Culture's Translating Cultures theme and Global Challenges Research Fund.

Andrea Rizzi is Cassamarca Associate Professor of Italian at the University of Melbourne. A former Australian Research Council Future Fellow (2014– 18), Harvard I Tatti Center Fellow (2010–11) and Associate Investigator for the Australian Centre of Excellence for the Study of the History of Emotions (2015–18), his most recent books are *What Is Translation History?*

A Trust-Based Approach (Palgrave Macmillan, 2019), co-authored with Birgit Lang and Anthony Pym; *Vernacular Translators in Quattrocento Italy: Scribal Culture, Authority, and Agency* (Brepols, 2018); *Trust and Proof: Translators in Renaissance Print Culture* (Brill, 2019); and *City, Court, Academy: Language Choice in Early Modern Italy* (Routledge, 2018), co-edited with Eva Del Soldato.

Barbara Spadaro is Lecturer in Italian History and Culture at the University of Liverpool, UK. The principal areas of her research are the history of Italians from North Africa, colonial and postcolonial migration, transcultural memory and the cultural mediation of history, notably in comics. She has published a monograph and articles on the history of women in the Italian empire, ideas of Italian whiteness and the transcultural trajectories of Italian Jews from Libya. A member of the 'Transnationalizing Modern Languages' research project since 2014, she contributed, with Takoua Ben Mohamed, to the exhibition *Beyond Borders: Transnational Italy*, shown in Rome, London, New York, Melbourne, Addis Ababa and at the Italian Cultural Institute of Tunis (2016–18).

Stefania Tufi is Senior Lecturer in Italian Studies at the University of Liverpool, UK. Her main research interests lie within sociolinguistics, in particular minority and regional languages (including migrant languages), language policy, social dialectology and the linguistic landscape. She is the co-author of *The Linguistic Landscape of the Mediterranean: French and Italian Coastal Cities* (Palgrave Macmillan, 2015) and has also published on variationist sociolinguistics, language policy and ideology and Italian dialectology. Most recently, she has worked on borderscapes, language and memory, and linguistic constructions of identity in transnational spaces. Her most recent publication is the co-edited volume *Reterritorializing Linguistic Landscape: Questioning Boundaries and Opening Spaces* (Bloomsbury, 2020), with David Malinowski.

Naomi Wells is a postdoctoral research associate in translingual communities and digital humanities at the Institute of Modern Languages Research (School of Advanced Study, University of London) on the UK Arts and Humanities Research Council project 'Cross-Language Dynamics: Reshaping Community' (part of the Open World Research Initiative). Her current research focuses on London's Latin American communities and on digital practices of communication and representation. She was previously a research fellow on the Arts and Humanities Research Council-funded 'Transnationalizing Modern Languages' project, where her work and publications focused on the linguistic and cultural practices of contemporary and historic migrant communities to and from Italy.

Introduction

Charles Burdett and Loredana Polezzi

Approaching Italian Studies

Constructing narratives about past and present experience is a distinctive trait of human communities. National histories are a powerful example of how such narratives can act as an essential element for the creation of a shared sense of identity. Academic disciplines, on the other hand, can also be described as historical constructs, with their own narratives, boundaries and communities. Combining both of these dimensions, the field of modern languages is structured by multiple layers of well-established narratives. Its subset of disciplines is largely organized according to national distinctions which follow geographic, historical and linguistic boundaries and which are, for the most part, modelled on nineteenth- and early twentieth-century maps of the world: French studies, German studies, Italian studies and so on. These are traditionally Eurocentric (with a few strategic additions), dominated by national and at times imperial logics, and based on a strong, homogenizing association between nation, territory, language and culture. All of these assumptions have come under intense scrutiny and are, if not outdated, at least under pressure in a world characterized by globalization, by increasing geographic and social mobility, by greater as well as faster connectivity across physical and virtual spaces, by the need to decolonize the curriculum, and by environmental concerns which transcend any geographic or political border. The present volume aims to address the need to rethink the discipline of Italian studies by asking key questions about the field, its specificities and its broader significance. What does 'Italian studies' stand for in this transforming world? What does it mean to 'study Italian' in today's academic context? And how can we define 'transnational Italian studies'?

The study of Italian at university level involves acquiring not only the ability to communicate with a high level of proficiency in the language: it also requires the ability to move between different linguistic and cultural codes. In most cases, the programme requires, therefore, an understanding of what is referred to as 'Italian culture'. In the majority of cases, as we will see, this is achieved through the study of history and the exploration of works of literary and artistic creation. Through engagement with cultural products and possibly also through periods of study abroad, the programme generally also requires the integration of what is learnt through academic study with a first-hand knowledge and experience of the reality of contemporary Italy, as well as an awareness of Italian culture outside the country itself. This exercise in adopting multiple perspectives involves the imagination as much as the intellect and requires an increasingly critical understanding of the constructed nature of what one considers to be one's own culture. Like any form of learning – if it is to be truly successful – these are processes with a marked meta-cognitive dimension which necessitates constant reflection on the skills that are being acquired, on the purpose of their acquisition and on their likely application both within the period of study and beyond it.

Furthermore, that which constitutes the object of study and the lens through which we see it do not stay still. In fact, they can change quite rapidly. Italian culture itself is in constant evolution – as are our perceptions of what we define as 'Italian culture' and how and in what context we use the term. The position we occupy informs our perspective. Are we looking at Italian culture from the viewpoint of an insider or an outsider? From a position of cultural and geographical proximity or distance (whether real or perceived)? Do we identify with it, directly or indirectly (for instance, through family heritage and personal connections), or not? New critical and methodological approaches also emerge and change our definition of what constitutes culture and how we examine cultural phenomena. The development, for example, of what is quite often loosely defined as cultural studies (discussed below) has had an enormous impact on the way in which researchers think about the nature of modern languages as a disciplinary field, and of Italian studies within that field. Similarly, the current emphasis of the link between linguistic and cultural translation is beginning to make itself felt in how we conceptualize and organize the study of cultural production and circulation. Thirdly, gradual changes in the patterns of cultural production and consumption can reduce the perceived topicality of a form or medium (literature, for instance, or, within that, a specific genre such as lyrical poetry) which was once deemed of unquestioned importance. Fourthly, changes within the structure of educational institutions such as universities, the role that they perform within society, and their funding mechanisms inevitably affect the way in which they organize knowledge, produce research and deliver education. In the past, for example, Italian departments tended to be independent units and a large percentage of their students concentrated on Italian as a single or main subject of study. Increasingly, however, Italian studies forms part of larger units, such as schools of modern languages, and learners opt for degree programmes which combine multiple subjects.[1]

Growing stress is placed by universities on mobility, global citizenship and intercultural skills as key outcomes of higher education. This should, at least in theory, make linguistic and cultural knowledge more valuable and its acquisition less narrowly restricted to specialist programmes.[2] Similarly, there is greater emphasis than before on employability as a goal of education and this demands new ways of thinking about the nature of university courses and the preparation they offer for the world beyond the academy. At a time when it is necessary for subjects in the arts and humanities to explain their value to as wide a public as possible, modern languages finds itself in a peculiar position: on the one hand, the skill set it offers, principally in terms of language proficiency, may be easier to identify and quantify than those provided by other humanities subjects. On the other, this view promotes a limited, instrumental image of the field which often decouples linguistic abilities from cultural knowledge and subordinates the desirability of a language to its currency in a perceived global hierarchy of 'usefulness'. English vastly dominates that list at present, leading to its popularity among learners worldwide, but also to the false perception that familiarity with other languages does not constitute a desirable qualification, especially in the Anglophone sphere.[3] As for other languages, such as Italian, their value and appeal vary over time, often in relation to the relative cultural and economic capital associated

---

[1] See Clodagh Brook and Giuliana Pieri, 'Italianistica in Gran Bretagna: tra inter-disciplinarità e tradizione', *La Rassegna della letteratura italiana*, 120.1–2 (2016), 207–16.

[2] On this subject, see The Salzburg Statement for a Multilingual World, https://www.salzburgglobal.org/multi-year-series/education.html?pageId=8543 [accessed 21 March 2019]. See also the policy report 'Transnational Modern Languages: Reframing Language Education for a Global Future', https://www.bristol.ac.uk/policybristol/policy-briefings/transnationalizing-modern-languages/ [accessed 5 May 2019].

[3] For evidence to the contrary, see for instance François Grin et al., eds, *The Economics of the Multilingual Workplace* (New York: Routledge, 2010); Gabrielle Hogan-Brun, *Linguanomics: What Is the Market Potential of Multilingualism?* (London: Bloomsbury, 2017).

with the nations with which they are ostensibly affiliated. Hence Italian is often promoted as a high-prestige subject with a long and distinguished cultural history, but it struggles to hold its place against languages which are maintained to have a more prominent global profile, including ex-imperial ones such as French or Spanish, or those associated with growing economic powers, such as Chinese. A number of these assumptions require examination and are specifically called into question if we adopt different perspectives on both the nature of Italian culture and that of Italian studies.

The Development of Italian Studies

As with many other areas within modern languages, the principal object of research and teaching in Italian departments has, over a long period of time, been literature in Italian. In a study charting the development of the discipline within the UK, David Robey focuses on the subject association, the Society for Italian Studies, and its journal, *Italian Studies* (the first issue of which appeared in 1937).[4] He charts how the subject, establishing itself at university level, initially sought to emulate classics and concentrate on the language and literature of the past. While referring to the different currents within the growing subject area and the strength, but also the complexity, of its relationship with the study of Italian culture as constituted and carried out in Italy, Robey demonstrates the enduring centrality of literature as the primary object of study, whether addressed through critical, literary-historical or philological approaches. The path pursued by scholarship is closely reflected in the establishment of a curriculum which, though it has been substantially modified, still acts as a core structure, underlying the teaching of many, if not most, programmes in Italian. This 'traditional' curriculum stretches from the medieval period to the present and is based, more or less, on the study of the works of writers who are considered to belong to the canon of Italian literature. In other words, it focuses on the work of those writers who are believed to have exerted most influence on the direction that literary culture has taken.[5] Thus, in the medieval and Renaissance periods, it is the work of Dante, Petrarch, Boccaccio, Machiavelli, Tasso, Ariosto and, recently, also Caterina da Siena or Vittoria Colonna which occupies centre stage, while

---

[4] David Robey, '*Italian Studies*: The First Half', *Italian Studies*, 67 (2012), 287–99. The website of the Society for Italian Studies, with links to the journal, is at: http://italianstudies.org.uk/the-society/.

[5] For a brief introduction to Italian literature, see Peter Hainsworth and David Robey, *Italian Literature: A Very Short Introduction* (Oxford: Oxford University Press, 2012).

in the modern period the canon has proved more flexible, incorporating the work of Ugo Foscolo, Giacomo Leopardi and Alessandro Manzoni in the nineteenth century and, in the twentieth century, the poetry of Eugenio Montale and Giuseppe Ungaretti, the plays of Luigi Pirandello and the fiction of a wide array of writers including Leonardo Sciascia, Natalia Ginzburg, Elsa Morante and Italo Calvino.[6]

While spanning a chronology which far exceeds the history of the nation state, this canon embraces the dominant post-Risorgimento narrative of the Italian nation through a celebration of its long and prestigious literary tradition, embodied in its founding fathers and their successive heirs (most of them also notably male). It is significant that, despite the markedly pluri-lingual nature of the Italian peninsula and of its literary production, the canon outlined above firmly privileges writing in Italian, the language of the future (and eventually present) nation, over all other forms of expression, including 'dialects' or minority languages. The emergence of Italian literature and of the Italian language are thus inescapably linked in what becomes a teleological storyline culminating in national unification and linguistic standardization. Yet, at the same time, both the epistemological construction and labour distribution associated with this configuration of the discipline of Italian studies promote a sharp distinction between cultural knowledge and language skills, as well as the teaching of them. A collateral (yet significant) effect of this organization of power and knowledge is the exclusion of trans-lation from the study of literature and its relegation to a purely linguistic practice meant to assist the teaching of 'grammar'. Reading literature in translation is discouraged, translated texts are considered derivative and inferior to the original, and the powerful role of translation as a form of cultural production and dissemination is downplayed in favour of a vision of national literature which emphasizes internal continuities and the making of a national tradition (even *ante litteram*, before the historical advent of the Italian nation).

Within this national framework, the aim of the critical study of literature and of its history is to add both to our knowledge of the evolution of the work of a writer or group of writers and to our understanding of how their work has reflected, commented on and – in certain instances – changed the culture of which they were, or are, a part. This is to allow us to understand how aesthetic experiences are generated and the effects that they can exert both within the intellectual, emotional and imaginative life of the individual and, more

---

[6] For an introduction to the modern period, see Robert Gordon, *Introduction to Twentieth-Century Italian Literature: A Difficult Modernity* (London: Bloomsbury, 2005).

broadly, within society as a whole, creating the sense of a shared culture and, in the case of a national literature, a tradition which sustains the identification with the nation. The purpose of research on literature is not, however, only to convey new knowledge about the works of individual writers or literary movements, it is also to explore the means through which we attain that knowledge. An inquiry into the conceptual tools that we rely on to explore works of literature was, as Robey indicates, given considerable impetus with the development of literary theory from the late 1960s onwards.[7] Almost all courses are now accompanied by a strong theoretical component. Research should explore its own methodology, comment on the framework in which it is situated and seek to refine the series of analytical operations that lie at the core of that disciplinary framework. It should not only suggest new objects of study but new ways of studying, contributing to the range of questions that we can ask of texts and how, through critical scrutiny, they can reveal to us the forces that are at play in defining how people act, feel, think and behave in the world at a given time or in a given place.[8]

A disciplinary framework founded on the study of literature in Italian and which is set up to explore how that body of literature has developed over centuries, making an indisputable contribution to world culture, has a very strong appeal, both within Italy itself and elsewhere. It is an entirely coherent model in which the object of teaching and research is clearly identifiable, delimited and relatively easily accessible. It is based on the study of the multiplicity of strategies that texts deploy in order to convey a complex of interrelated meanings. And it promotes a 'marketable', prestigious image of Italy, its history, its cultural heritage, its contribution to knowledge and artistic creation. Closely associated with the study of the Italian language, the discipline, thus constituted, promotes an acute awareness of the intricacies of communication and how they can be manipulated. It shows us how we can see an individual utterance as revealing some of the deepest patterns of the cultural context to which it belongs. It also allows us to examine how a text has been received within a culture and to explore how its meaning changes according to the types of analysis to which it is subjected. The study of a literary corpus that stretches across centuries not only allows for moments of the past to come into focus, it also enables us to see how the way in which people experience and make sense of their lives depends on their performance of the roles and practices of their time and on their appropriation of

---

[7] See Robey, 'Italian Studies', p. 294.

[8] On the importance of theory in literary analysis, see Andrew Bennett and Nicholas Royle, *An Introduction to Literature, Criticism and Theory* (Harlow: Pearson Longman, 2009).

the evolving set of concepts according to which their society was, has been, or is, structured.

Though it continues to underlie the teaching structure of many courses, this model has undergone a great deal of change over recent years. This is partly due to the nature of the model itself and the questions that one can pose of the coverage that it offers. The concentration on the major works of a literary corpus can be exclusionary, since the inclusion of a period or cultural phenomenon within the framework depends on whether that moment in the historical development of a culture has produced works deemed to be of note. By imposing strict standards of literary quality, we are also excluding from consideration large areas of less distinguished, but potentially highly revealing, cultural production. It is also true that cultural artefacts are both generated and consumed through a much wider variety of media, and we may wonder whether there is an overemphasis on literature within this kind of curriculum. Finally, as we have already noted, changing attitudes and priorities within the educational sector and society as a whole may also lead to questions about the value of humanities programmes (including modern languages degrees) and whether the training they provide could be more demonstrably attuned to the social and professional realities that students are likely to encounter upon leaving university.

Italian Cultural Studies

The desire to address issues arising from a disciplinary framework centred on the examination of literature, to expand complex textual analysis to new spheres of cultural production (including those associated with the notion of popular culture) and to explore the dynamics of that production in a way that is less intent on according an exceptional status to a work of creative writing, accounts in part for the development of cultural studies in language departments over recent decades.[9]

In the 1990s, Oxford University Press published a series of texts aimed at defining the meaning and approaches of cultural studies across modern languages. In their contribution to the series, the editors of the Italian volume, David Forgacs and Robert Lumley, set out to explore the different meanings that

---

[9] On the development of cultural studies, see Stuart Hall, *Culture, Media, Language: Working Papers in Cultural Studies, 1972–79* (London: Unwin, Hyman, 1980) and Lawrence Grossberg, Cary Nelson and Paula Treichler, eds, *Cultural Studies* (Abingdon and New York: Routledge, 1992). With specific reference to Italian studies, see Derek Duncan, 'Editorial. *Italian Studies: Cultural Studies*', *Italian Studies*, cultural studies issue, 65.3 (2010), 308–09.

the term 'culture' has assumed both within Anglophone and Italian academic contexts.[10] They pointed to how the term can be taken to mean, narrowly, a range of intellectual/artistic activities or, more broadly, a much more 'extensive range of practices characteristic of a given society, from its mode of material production to its eating habits, dress codes, celebrations and rituals'.[11] An essential point in their argument was that the nature of a particular branch of academic studies will, to a large extent, depend on the interpretation of the term 'culture'. Rather than suggesting that cultural studies is an academic discipline with a specific object of research and which follows a distinct set of interpretative procedures, they defined this area of academic study more as a cluster of disciplines that include the consideration of literature, social history, media studies, human geography, cultural geography and which are linked to a common set of concerns. Among these concerns, they enumerated: an approach to culture as a 'set of signifying practices and symbolic social forms', an endeavour to address a wide variety of cultural materials in a way that avoids pre-existing value judgements and the intention to bring new theoretical insights to our understanding of the meaning of culture.[12]

Italian Cultural Studies succeeded in demonstrating how questions concerning geography, identity, media, culture and society can be addressed through a range of disciplinary approaches that share a similar set of preoc-cupations. In showing the broad spectrum of new approaches to the study of Italian society and culture, the volume reflected the way in which the object of disciplinary enquiry has widened over a fairly lengthy period of time. This broadening of disciplinary inquiry is also reflected in an important institu-tional development: it is now common for specialists in Italian studies to be experts not just in literature but also in film studies, history, area studies – as well as linguistics, which has always occupied a firmly established position. There is now a greater diversity of courses on offer than ever before and students of Italian can derive enormous benefit from this range of topics and from the diversity of approach to which they are exposed.[13] Italian studies is a porous academic field in which distinct methods of inquiry are continually in contact with one another, suggesting new avenues of research

---

[10] *Italian Cultural Studies: An Introduction*, ed. by David Forgacs and Robert Lumley (Oxford: Oxford University Press, 1996).

[11] David Forgacs and Robert Lumley, 'Introduction: Approaches to Culture in Italy', *Italian Cultural Studies*, p. 2.

[12] Forgacs and Lumley, 'Introduction', p. 1.

[13] See Pieri, 'Teaching Italian Studies in the 21st Century'. The report is available under 'Higher Education Academy report on the Teaching of Italian Studies in UK and Irish HEIs (Dec 2014)' at http://italianstudies.org.uk/wp-content/uploads/2012/07/Teaching-Italian-Studies.pdf [accessed 1 March 2019].

and teaching. This porosity of inquiry is fundamental to teaching as well as research and has become one of the basic conditions for very valuable forms of interdisciplinarity which sustain and demonstrate the openness of the field to developments across the humanities and social sciences.

The very diversity of the range of individual courses that are now on offer within Italian studies also poses some questions, however. In programmes founded upon the study of literature, the object of inquiry is clear and individual courses, linked by a similarity of approach, illuminate one aspect or another of a recognizable continuum. Where the nature of the material and the analytical framework in which it is considered differ from one module to another, it is less easy to draw connections. Or rather, it is less easy to see how the insights gained from one field of study can be sharpened when applied to another. It becomes more difficult to see how the accumulation of courses contributes to the development of an integrated system of critical operations that one can apply both to the immediate object of one's studies and to the reality in which one lives, works and, in whichever way, attempts to make a difference.

Though a diversity of approach without doubt opens windows onto many areas of human experience, there is a risk that, unless it is strongly coordinated, it can become confusing. It is perfectly possible to encounter students of modern languages who are highly appreciative of the depth and explanatory power of the individual courses they have studied, but who struggle to articulate the nature of the intellectual preparation offered by the programme *as a whole*. In a context in which programmes in the arts and humanities are under pressure, it is very important for the framework of a course to be clear and for students to be able to define – immediately and robustly – the underlying principles of their studies to their peers, to their future employers and, above all, to themselves.

At the same time, and despite this broadening of objects and methodology, programmes of study built on the Italian literary or cultural studies model retain an attachment to the national narrative. The field, in all its variety, continues to privilege the space of the nation and its internal channels of cultural production and distribution, associated with Italian as the national language. It is in fact largely the underpinning provided by the twin notions of national culture and national language that provides homogeneity and coherence to programmes in Italian. In recent years, however, this territorial emphasis and the associated stress on linguistic homogeneity have been challenged by the emergence of new voices and perspectives, especially in areas such as colonial, postcolonial and migration studies, as well as by the increasing attention paid to transnational and translational dimensions of sociocultural phenomena.

The National, the Transnational and the Italian Case

There are compelling intellectual, historical and institutional reasons for rethinking the epistemological and educational foundations of modern languages and the role of national cultures within them. And while some of those reasons can be broadly applied to any one of the individual disciplines within the field, others relate to the specificities of the cultures under examination, their histories and their internal as well as external sets of interconnections. The goal of such a reformulation is not to erase existing disciplines, traditions and approaches, replacing them with alternative ones, but rather to integrate those paradigms with new critical perspectives which both foreground the significance of the study of languages and cultures in today's world and underscore the intellectual cohesiveness of the field. In the case of Italian studies, this means substantially rethinking the subject's association with the space, time and language of the nation, and repositioning it in relation to both national and transnational processes of cultural production, circulation and consumption.

At institutional level – within higher education, within modern languages and within Italian studies – there is clearly a need to indicate the intellectual rationale of our programmes and how they promote a diversity of approach while allowing students to apply a range of connected interpretative strategies to the world in which they live. Articulating the specific set of competencies which we aim to develop is crucial in order to respond to the pressure to decouple linguistic and cultural knowledge and to promote a study of culture which does away with the hard work of language acquisition on the one hand and, on the other, the reduction of language learning to a predetermined and restricted set of decontextualized communication skills. Assumptions about the purely instrumental value of language competence go hand in hand, in the public domain, with the perception of linguistic diversity as a problem to be resolved, whether through the increasing dominance of a lingua franca such as international English or through technological advances which are meant to relegate translation to an instantaneous and mechanical operation. In an environment in which many people assume that it is possible to study a language independently of the cultural context in which it is embedded and which it also constructs and articulates, it is similarly imperative to demonstrate how courses in the Italian language interact, at every level, with learning that addresses themes of a cultural, linguistic or historical nature. Similarly, if one studies cultural phenomena without due attention to the language in which they are encoded, one risks embedding a form of chauvinism at the very heart of one's inquiry. The separation between the study of language and the study of culture remains pervasive within modern languages, but it is detrimental both within the academic context and within public perception. It continues to sustain a negative representation of both linguistic and cultural diversity, promoting a vision of society in which difference is both hard to grasp and problematic, while globalization becomes closely associated with homogenization (with all the inequalities and power asymmetries this entails). This is a position which is out of step with contemporary reality and also with its most pressing concerns, from the relationships between global capital, mobility and social cohesion to the local *and* global dimensions of the environmental crisis.

Beyond institutional structures and disciplinary logics, there are powerful intellectual and historical imperatives which make desirable a restructuring of Italian studies beyond its traditional boundaries. These go hand in hand with contemporary reflections on the nature of the nation and of nationalism as both organizing philosophical principles and historical phenomena. A critical appreciation of the nation state is both a crucial and an inescapable component of Italian studies. In the conventional organization of the discipline, as we have seen, the object of research and teaching is Italian culture, mostly understood through its manifestation in literature written in Italian or through the events and processes that have shaped the geographical area that we refer to as Italy. In studying the historical events that occurred and the literary/artistic works that were produced before the creation of the Italian nation state in the mid-nineteenth century, however, one develops an understanding of the multiplicity of linguistic communities, regional power relations, modes of religious observance and locally determined practices that were brought together within the territorial, conceptual and administrative boundaries of Italy. When we come to the modern, post-unification period – whether one is working on literary or cultural studies – the elements which come into focus include such issues as the formation of the institutions of the state and their impact on people's lives, the friction or conflict between regionally based loyalties/practices and the imposition of an homogenized national model, the role that religion continues to play at local as well as national level, the range of movements and forms of political hegemony which have emerged in the country, the operation of power and the tension between different elements of society – and how all of these are both informed by and reflected in cultural products and practices. Far from appearing as a harmonic and homogeneous space, the Italian nation then becomes the locus of tensions articulated through political systems (from the liberal state to fascism and post-war democracy), linguistic policies (relating to a complex and constantly changing map of dialects, spoken and written standards, minority languages) or cultural practices (from neorealist cinema to the fashion industry).

In studying the specificities of Italian cultural history we are, therefore, also investigating the more abstract qualities that define the phenomenon of the nation: the ways in which, to paraphrase Benedict Anderson, the nation, as an 'imagined political community', appropriates elements of the cultural systems that preceded its creation, develops an extremely powerful intellectual and emotional legitimacy, and serves as a means through which the functioning of the world is apprehended.[14] Phenomena such Italy's late unification, its short-lived foray into colonial and imperial expansion, its turbulent political landscape, its complex economic and linguistic composition, or its history of internal and external emigration as well as immigration are unique (and have even led to the identification of an 'Italian exceptionalism'),[15] yet they also point to the intrinsically transnational nature of cultural practices. Though we may construe them as national – fashioning powerful narratives of alterity and belonging, exclusion and inclusion in the process – cultural phenomena are never entirely contained within the frontiers of the state. Cultural processes exceed both the physical boundaries associated with territorial borders and more intangible ones, such as linguistic frontiers or the mapping of individual and collective memory.

This is not to deny the enduring power of the nation both as an organizational structure and as a force within the collective imaginary, but the study of a culture restricted by a geographical area and by the concept of the nation/national identity is becoming increasingly difficult to justify both on a theoretical level and in relation to contemporary social phenomena. If we make the assumption that cultures are contained within national boundaries, we are necessarily, though perhaps unwittingly, accepting a series of narratives of national belonging rather than exposing these narratives to critical scrutiny. We risk, further, becoming guilty of what Andreas Wimmer and Nina Glick Schiller have defined as 'methodological nationalism'[16] and of implying that the condition of being monocultural (as well as, in close association, that of being monolingual) is the norm.[17] If the national is too solidly entrenched as the principle around which we organize our teaching

[14] Benedict Anderson, *Imagined Communities: Reflections on the Origins and Spread of Nationalism* (London and New York: Verso, 1983).

[15] Simon Parker, 'The End of Italian Exceptionalism? Assessing the Transition to the Second Republic', *The Italianist*, 19.1 (1999), 251–83.

[16] Andreas Wimmer and Nina Glick Schiller, 'Methodological Nationalism and Beyond: Nation-State Building, Migration and the Social Sciences', *Global Networks*, 2.4 (2002), 301–34.

[17] See David Gramling, *The Invention of Monolingualism* (London: Bloomsbury, 2016) and Yasemin Yildiz, *Beyond the Mother Tongue: The Postmonolingual Condition* (New York: Fordham University Press, 2012).

and research, then we are clearly ill-equipped to address the phenomenon and consequences of mobility, the pressures of globalization and the potential meanings of the post-national. By opting for a perspective which focuses on the nation and treats national cultures as self-contained, we also render invisible (or at least dramatically underestimate) the fundamental porosity of knowledge and of human practices: the way in which they are constituted and disseminated through creation and recreation, through exchange and appropriation, through complex networks of communication which are intrinsically translational. It is through forms of linguistic as well as cultural translation that, in Homi Bhabha's words, 'newness enters the world',[18] just as it is through translation (or the denial of it) that states often (and mostly unsuccessfully, at least in the long term) attempt to exercise censorship, police the boundaries of the national culture, and restrict what is allowed to travel in or out of it.[19]

Italian studies – in common with other subjects within modern languages – faces the challenge of how a focus on the national can be combined with the study of the transnational and how the framework of the discipline can be more finely attuned to practices of human mobility and cultural exchange. However powerful the concept of the nation may be in defining how we see the world and our place within it, it is only part of a vastly more complicated reality. We live within economic, cultural and religious systems or, to use Clifford Geertz's term, 'webs of signification' that stretch back, in many instances, across millennia.[20] The need to consider the transnational encourages us to think in terms of longer temporalities and to perceive the entanglement of cultures, to become aware of forms of connection stretching across the boundaries of apparently stable imagined communities,[21] to see ideas – with their material consequences – circulating in different directions and to interpret cultures, to paraphrase Tzvetan Todorov,[22] as alluvial plains that are traced by the intermingling of the multiplicity of practices that is the inevitable consequence of human mobility.[23] The emphasis on

[18] Homi Bhabha, 'How Newness Enters the World: Postmodern Space, Postcolonial Times, and the Trials of Cultural Translation', in *The Location of Culture* (London and New York: Routledge, 1994), pp. 212–35.

[19] On this topic see Naoki Sakai, *Translation and Subjectivity: On Japan and Cultural Nationalism* (Minneapolis, MN: University of Minnesota Press, 1997).

[20] See Clifford Geertz, *The Interpretation of Cultures: Selected Essays* (New York: Basic Books, 1973).

[21] Benedict Anderson, *Imagined Communities: Reflections on the Origin and Spread of Nationalism* (London: Verso, 1983).

[22] Tzvetan Todorov, *The Fear of Barbarians: Beyond the Clash of Civilizations*, translated from French by Andrew Brown (Cambridge: Polity, 2010).

[23] For an analysis of the increasing attention towards the transnational within

practices is crucial here: as noted by Patricia Clavin, transnationalism is 'first and foremost about people: the social spaces they inhabit, the networks they form and the ideas they exchange'[24] – so paying attention to the transnational dimension of cultural life is to focus on what people do, not on normative or idealized notions of identity and belonging. Whether it addresses manifold forms of translation, the sharing of values across borders or the existence of multiple processes within the same space, academic inquiry of this kind emphasizes how the world that we create through our everyday activity – and which at the same time continually acts back on us – is defined by the inseparability of the national and the transnational.[25]

It is important to note that these two dimensions, national and transnational, are not mutually exclusive, or antithetical. As noted by Ulrich Beck, the national order was constructed on the opposition between 'national' and 'international'. In that model, space 'was divisible into a clearly defined inside and outside, at the centre of which the nation state rules and keeps order' while 'the international, located in the external sphere of experience, corresponded to the image of "multiculturalism", in which the national self-perception is reflected and confirmed in the distinction from and exclusion of strangers'. The notion of the transnational, on the other hand, 'blows open this entire framework of meanings from the inside', showing that 'national and international cannot be clearly differentiated, nor can they serve to separate homogenous entities from one another'. These orders are not exclusive but exist in tension, in 'an uneasy co-existence of transition, a new form of the simultaneity of the non-simultaneous'.[26] To engage with the transnational does not mean to ignore the importance of the national, or to relegate it to the past, reaffirming a teleological vision of historical progress. Rather, it is to acknowledge the open, dynamic dialogic and relational nature of cultural forms and of our engagement with them.

If we place the inquiry into the way in which cultures continually shift and change as they come into contact with one another at the heart of the disciplinary field, then we are arguing that in studying Italian one is looking at an instantiation of the mixing of cultural practices.[27] In fact, we

Italian studies, see Emma Bond, 'Towards a Trans-national Turn in Italian Studies?', *Italian Studies*, cultural studies issue, 69.3 (2014), 415–24.

[24] Patricia Clavin, 'Defining Transnationalism', *Contemporary European History*, 14.4 (2005), 421–39 (p. 422).

[25] See Chiara De Cesari and Ann Rigney, 'Introduction', in *Transnational Memory: Circulation, Articulation, Scales* (Berlin: De Gruyter, 2014), pp. 1–25 (especially, pp. 3–7).

[26] Ulrich Beck, 'The Cosmopolitan State: Redefining Power in the Global Age', *International Journal of Politics, Culture, and Society*, 18.3–4 (2005), 143–59 (p. 148).

[27] The endeavour to explore the interrelation of cultures lies at the heart of

could suggest – because of its position at the centre of the crossroads of the Mediterranean,[28] its physical proximity to Africa and to the Islamic world, its long history as a site of imperial activity, its relatively recent constitution as a nation state – that what we refer to as 'Italy' represents a highly concentrated space of intercultural contact and for that reason an object of study of indisputable relevance and importance. Moreover, if we develop an approach that seeks to ease the rigidity of the association between culture and territory, and if we focus on the history of Italian mobility or rather on Italy's many diasporas – to quote the title of Donna Gabaccia's influential volume[29] – we can explore the composition and working of communities throughout the northern and southern hemisphere, the continuities and discontinuities of their connection with Italy, the pace at which they develop new forms of cultural expression. Unmooring Italian culture from its rigid association with the national also means opening up Italian studies to cultural phenomena which emerge and circulate not only in other spaces but also in different languages, whether these are the national idioms of host communities as in the case of Italian American authors writing in English, the multiple dialects often used by both regional and emigrant writers, or the learnt variants of Italian which have become the elective tongue of numerous contemporary translingual authors (and, increasingly, film-makers). The study of Italian culture, when seen from this perspective, becomes a means of examining the modalities and the consequences of intercultural exchange on a global scale.

The Aims of the Volume

In the context of widespread change within university education and of disciplinary innovation across the arts and humanities, it is clear that we are at a crucial juncture in the development of Italian studies. We need a resilient yet flexible framework which can encompass the range of approaches that have emerged within the discipline, and provide a series of critical strategies that will both ensure the coherence of the subject and maintain its dynamic dialogue with other fields. An approach that focuses on the dialogic

the research project 'Transnationalizing Modern Languages: Mobility, Identity and Translation in Modern Italian Cultures'. On this subject, see also Teresa Fiore, *Pre-Occupied Spaces: Remapping Italy's Transnational Migrations and Colonial Legacies* (New York: Fordham University Press, 2017) and Cristina Lombardi-Diop and Caterina Romeo, eds, *Postcolonial Italy: Challenging National Homogeneity* (Basingstoke: Palgrave Macmillan, 2012).

[28] The allusion is to Graziella Parati, ed., *Mediterranean Crossroads: Migration Literature in Italy* (Madison, NJ and London: Associated University Presses, 1999).

[29] Donna Gabaccia, *Italy's Many Diasporas* (London: UCL Press, 2000).

interaction between national and transnational perspectives, stressing the dynamic tension between the two, will allow us to make visible how cultures operate and evolve, in the past and the present, how they interact and how they define being human in the world. It will also foreground the translational nature of cultural practices and the constitutive role played by translation processes in the production, circulation and consumption of cultural goods. In the process, such an approach will also encourage greater integration between the study of language and culture, insisting on (but also evidencing and instantiating) the intrinsic connection and largely coextensive nature of the two. In a world of ever-increasing mobility and global interaction we need to combine the study of the national with the study of the transnational and, in the process, to demonstrate how inquiry into linguistic and cultural translation can form a basis of our branch of study as well as its core contribution to understanding the world we live in.

The aim of the present volume is to trace the underlying framework of this kind of transnational Italian studies, to show the interdependence of its various methodologies and to articulate a sense of its relevance and purpose in today's world. The work is part of the Transnational Modern Languages (TML) series, whose volumes collectively participate in redefining 'the disciplinary framework of Modern Languages, arguing that it should be seen as an expert mode of enquiry whose founding research question is how languages and cultures operate and interact across diverse axes of connection'.[30] The present volume is intended to be read with close reference to *Transnational Modern Languages: A Handbook*, edited by Jennifer Burns and Derek Duncan, which provides an essential introduction to the series as well as an extended and indispensable glossary of key terms and definitions.[31] Along with the other volumes in the series, *Transnational Italian Studies* is structured around a set of key organizational principles: it addresses the working of cultural and transcultural processes by focusing on four overlapping areas of inquiry, all of which centre on practices that are crucial to the way in which life is collectively structured and individually experienced and performed. The first section looks at language, translation and multilingualism as constitutive elements of cultural production and exchange; the second at the set of practices that make up a sense of location and of belonging to a geographically determined site; the third at the notions of temporality that obtain within and between cultures; the final section looks at how we can explore modes of

---

[30] For further information about the series, see https://www.liverpooluniversity press.co.uk/series/series-13275/ [accessed 14 November 2019].

[31] Jennifer Burns and Derek Duncan, eds, *Transnational Modern Languages: A Handbook* (Liverpool: Liverpool University Press, forthcoming 2020).

understanding subjectivity and alterity, together with the complex layering of their interrelations.

The contributors work across a range of countries and institutions, but all identify in some form with the field of Italian studies. The essays, deliberately, do not follow a rigidly determined pattern; underlying every contribution, however, is an attempt to address a set of connected questions that are of crucial importance in a volume that is primarily, though not exclusively, intended for a student readership. These questions include the following: How does one approach a given area of study, demonstrating the importance and intellectual excitement of pursuing a specific line of research? What are the issues of most pressing concern within that area of inquiry? How can one demonstrate the modes of inquiry that lie at the base of one's study? What types of approach bring the unfolding of transnational or transcultural processes most sharply into focus? In confronting these questions by drawing on their own research and experience, every author in the collection shows how we can develop and apply a closely related range of methodologies that allow us to consider Italian culture(s) of the past and the present in a transnational perspective.

A volume such as this cannot claim to offer a comprehensive introduction to a field that is as wide as Italian studies. Its ambition is rather to play a part within a growing economy of resources, all of which provide essential information and propose varying means of approaching what is an exceptionally rich, complex and dynamic object of study. What the volume does aim to do is to offer an account of the questions that lie at the heart of the study of Italian culture – understood as a current within world culture – as well as of the kind of approaches that students will pursue in the individual courses they study. The overriding consideration in the preparation of the volume has been, as indicated above, to demonstrate how the close connection between the different elements of such a course does not have to lead to a fully integrated and homogeneous approach to a field of academic inquiry, but rather to the acquisition of a powerful lens, or a theoretical and methodological toolkit through or with which one can see how cultural interaction, in all its forms and multiplicity of viewpoints, determines how people experience their environment, how they perceive both the past and the future, how they think of commonality and alterity, and how they develop a sense of self. The volume aims to show how distinct methodological strategies converge in the analysis of an extended range of objects of research, allowing deep-laid historical and cultural processes that function at a local, national and global level to come into focus. In attempting to train as sharp a light as possible on the densely interwoven network of critical operations that researchers employ in reading and deconstructing cultural exchange, from the medieval to the contemporary period, the volume sets out, lastly, to provide a necessary statement of the value and purpose of Italian studies in the third millennium.[32] In the age of global capital, technological revolution and climate change, understanding how cultures are constructed through dialogical practices and how homes are built on the move is an increasingly vital ability – and one which modern languages can embrace and foster as a crucial skill.

The first section of *Transnational Italian Studies*, 'Language', begins with a chapter by Loredana Polezzi on the role of translation in the formation and circulation of Italian culture. Using examples which range from Dante's reception in nineteenth-century Britain to contemporary Italian American and Italophone writing, the essay charts the multiple journeys of images and ideas of Italy which take place in and through translation, tracing a map which is at once regional, national and transnational. In the following chapter, Andrea Rizzi continues to focus on translation, discussing Renaissance translators as agents of 'intertraffique', understood as the transnational exchange of ideas across Europe and beyond. He shows how the linguistic and cultural mediation of individuals such as Cola de Jennaro or Pietro Lauro, as well as their geographic mobility, affected the circulation of culture and fed a transnational trade in translations.

Shifting attention to the contemporary period, Stefania Tufi discusses the Linguistic Landscape of contemporary Italian cities. Using evidence gathered from urban settings in Italy as its empirical basis, the chapter exemplifies the construction of transnational identities in Italian public spaces, illustrating their multilingual, multimodal and multicultural dimensions and reading them against traditional understandings of citizenship and national identity. In the last chapter of this section, Naomi Wells uses fieldwork conducted with migrant communities in Bologna to illustrate how an interdisciplinary approach which combines ethnographic methodologies and linguistic analysis can illuminate contemporary migration patterns and the ensuing forms of societal multilingualism in today's Italy. The chapter addresses the challenges of studying language in an age of intensified cultural flows, explaining how this has led to the development of new sociolinguistic concepts such as 'translanguaging'.

The second section, 'Spatiality', opens with a chapter by Nathalie Hester on two representations of early modern Italian travel, the *Viaggi* (1650–63) by Pietro della Valle and *L'America* (1650) by Girolamo Bartolomei. Both works reflect on local belonging and identity while offering compelling responses

---

[32] See also Charles Burdett, Loredana Polezzi and Barbara Spadaro, eds, *Transcultural Italies: Mobility, Memory and Translation* (Liverpool: Liverpool University Press, forthcoming).

to imperial expansion, both geopolitical and religious, and Italy's role in that process. In the following chapter, Clorinda Donato applies the lens of trans-nationalism to the polycentric sites of knowledge production of the Italian eighteenth century. She explores how horizontal networks of erudition, sociability, fraternalism, travel, scientific exchange and friendship replaced the circumscribed loci of Renaissance courts and their entrenched systems of patronage with fluid, cosmopolitan, 'citizen of the world' mentalities and lifestyles. Moving towards the end of the nineteenth and the beginning of the twentieth century and to one of the key sites of the Italian diaspora, Giuliana Muscio discusses the significant impact of Italian immigrant actors, musicians and directors – and the southern Italian stage traditions they embodied – on the history of Hollywood cinema and American media in the silent era. Exploring the perspective of the performers themselves, the chapter analyses transnational communication between American and Italian film industries, media or performing arts as practised in Naples, New York, San Francisco and Los Angeles.

In the latter part of this section, Teresa Fiore looks at the shift from a national to a transnational model in the field of Italian studies as part of a recognition of Italy's intrinsic history and culture of mobility. Offering an overview of transnational forms of mobility, she addresses the pivotal role of cultural texts (literature, music, film, etc.) in connecting stories of outbound and inbound migration as well as colonialism. In the final chapter of the section, Jennifer Burns considers the ways in which spaces identified as 'home' by transnational individuals and communities connect multiple geographical locations to provide at once a stable reference point and an expression of mobile national, cultural and linguistic belongings. Analysing the objects and practices which structure the homing activity of migrants and mobile communities, and the narratives of home spaces assembled through fictional writing, accounts of community (print and digital) and cherished objects, her chapter brings to light the experience of being at once settled and unsettled that is articulated when homes become mobile.

The third section of the volume, 'Temporality', opens with David Bowe's chapter on how an understanding of time can inform our analysis of literary culture in premodern Italy and on the role of prenational texts in shaping a transnational reading of Italian culture. Focusing on the transition from the medieval to the early modern period and on key works by Guittone d'Arezzo, Dante Alighieri and Francesco Petrarca, Bowe argues that the unstable and non-linear representation of time in the works in question undermines any straightforward narrative of the self. In her chapter, Eugenia Paulicelli argues that along with the process of imagining nations and national identity, a language of fashion was elaborated within sixteenth-century Italy.

Concentrating on the costume books by Cesare Vecellio (1590 and 1598) and Giacomo Franco (1610) and their relation to works of conduct literature such as *The Book of the Courtier* by Baldassare Castiglione, she argues that costume books testify to the crucial role that visual and material culture played in considering both micro and global history.

Moving to the modern period, Donna Gabaccia investigates the challenge to the governments of both the United States and Italy caused by the movement of millions of migrants between 1880 and 1960. She analyses how, since many record keepers had limited or no knowledge of other languages, translation became an everyday dimension of record-keeping. The chapter focuses on the emerging bureaucratic languages of translation by examining records of mobility for 3,700 migrants who travelled between Sambuca di Sicilia and the United States between 1880 and 1960. In the following chapter, Charles Burdett argues that any consideration of the transnational has to take account of the colonial past and the extent to which the spectre of that past continues to haunt the world we inhabit. Looking at the course of Italian expansionism and at the period following the formal end of colonialism, the chapter concludes by exploring how works of fiction by contemporary writers have attempted to address the manifold legacies of the colonial past. In the final chapter of the section, Barbara Spadaro addresses how comics enable multimodal processes of cultural translation in a world of multiple memories and languages. She provides an introduction to the comics medium and to the thriving scene of the Italian *fumetto* by focusing on graphic journalism. The chapter concentrates on the work of two authors – Zerocalcare and Takoua Ben Mohamed – who help us to understand key aspects of Italian memory in the twenty-first century, namely its multilingualism, transnational dimension and production mechanisms through transcultural acts of mediation-translation.

The last section of the volume, 'Subjectivity', starts with a chapter devoted to Dante and his most well-known work, the *Divine Comedy*. In his analysis, Tristan Kay contrasts Dante's image as the 'father' of the Italian language and one of the pivotal symbols of national identity with a reading of his work (which emerged from a heterogeneous, fragmented and multilingual cultural and political reality) and of its subsequent fortune that is at once prenational and transnational. In the next chapter, Fabio Camilletti and Alessandra Diazzi turn to psychoanalysis, showing how Italian culture and Italian literature assimilated a theoretical model and a discipline coming from outside the nation, while at the same time challenging them and redefining them in line with established notions of 'Italian subjectivity'. This process of adaptation, they argue, is linked to the tension between regional identities and national unity, between political agency and civil responsibility, between the sphere of the private and political commitment.

Turning to cinema, Derek Duncan analyses Daniele Gaglianone's 2013 film *La mia classe* and its dramatization of how transnational mobility is experienced on a local, individual level. The film is set in the outskirts of Rome and focuses on an Italian language teacher (played by a professional actor) and his class of non-Italian language learners (who are played by non-professionals). Duncan draws on Mieke Bal's concept of 'migratory aesthetics' to investigate how the accented voice of the migrant is used to explore and expand our understandings of what is 'Italian' and also of what it means to be 'a citizen'. Monica Jansen then examines notions of post-national citizenship in relation to the violent events which took place in Genoa in 2001, while the Italian city was hosting that year's G8 summit. She juxtaposes three different documents – Christian Mirra's graphic novel *Quella notte alla Diaz* (2010), Carlo Bachschmidt's documentary *Black Block* (2011) and Daniele Vicari's film *Diaz – Don't Clean Up This Blood* (2012) – to show how the G8 events and their memory have come to constitute a watershed moment for the construction of a transnational and transgenerational subjectivity. Finally, in the last chapter of the volume, Serena Bassi applies a transnational approach to the field of queer Italian studies. Her essay takes us back to notions of translation and translingualism, examining the linguistic practices of members of the Italian Gay Liberation Movement in the 1970s. She recasts gay liberation activists as 'queer translanguagers', who resisted both heteronormativity and the notion of a standardized national language. In doing so, she also proposes an approach to translation as queer translingual practice and to queer Italian studies as a transnational object of enquiry.

This volume – and, in many ways, the whole Transnational Modern Languages series – would not have been possible without the help of the Arts and Humanities Research Council and its 'Translating Cultures' theme, which supported the project 'Transnationalizing Modern Languages: Mobility, Identity and Translation in Modern Italian Cultures'.[33] We wish to thank the AHRC as well as Liverpool University Press for their invaluable support.

We would like to thank Kirsty Adegboro for the preparation of the index of the volume.

---

[33] For further information on the project, see https://www.transnationalmodern languages.ac.uk/.

Part One

Language

1

Translation and Transnational Creative Practices in Italian Culture

Loredana Polezzi

Paul Klee famously described a drawing as a line going for a walk. Translation can also be thought of as a way of taking words and cultural objects for a walk, though, as translator and translation scholar David Johnstone has suggested: 'when the translator takes that line for a walk through languages and cultures, the result is not a line drawing a fixed relation between empty meanings but rather a kind of provisional cartography of the complex task of living'.[1] The image of translation as a way of taking culture for a walk as well as taking a walk through culture is a suggestive metaphor which echoes the etymological meaning of the term: both the English 'translation' and the Italian *traduzione* are derived from Latin words – *translatio* and *traductio*, respectively – which foreground the notion of movement and transfer from one location to another. In the Western tradition and imagination, translation is thus closely connected to notions of movement. It is therefore unsurprising that it should have gained particular prominence, both as a concept and as a practice, in a contemporary world where mobility is an increasingly common and salient feature of social interaction. Susan Bassnett, one of the scholars associated with the creation of the discipline of translation studies, directly links contemporary mobility and translation:

[1] David Johnston, 'Prólogo', in Maria Carmen África Vidal Claramonte, *'Dile que le he escrito un* blues'. *Del texto como partitura a la partitura como traducción en la literatura latinoamericana* (Madrid and Frankfurt: Vervuert Iberoamericana, 2017), pp. 11–14 (p. 11); the English version is quoted in Maria Carmen África Vidal Claramonte, 'Violins, Violence, Translation: Looking Outwards', *The Translator*, 25.3 (2019), 218–28 (p. 220).

The twenty-first century is the great age of translation. Millions more people are moving around the planet than at any time in history [...] And as those millions move around, taking their own languages with them, they encounter other languages, other cultural frameworks and other belief systems, hence are compelled, whether consciously or not, to engage in some form of translation. [...] Translation today is an increasingly common human condition, and the rapid rise of electronic media has also served to heighten the awareness of the importance of communicating across cultures.[2]

Approaching that same connection between translation and spatial mobility from the perspective of ethnography, James Clifford noted that thinking in terms of travel and translation also calls into question 'the fallacy "culture (singular) equals language (singular)"' which is implicit in nationalist ideas of culture and hides 'the wider global world of intercultural import-export in which the ethnographic encounter is always already enmeshed'.[3] Translation, like other forms of mobility and diversity, is always already here: it is a fundamental component of the way in which culture is produced, articulated, mediated and remediated.

Understood in this way, translation, while remaining primarily a language practice, is also and just as importantly a cultural process. The act of translating is not limited to producing a target text written (or, at times, spoken) in a target language so that this can be considered a faithful equivalent of an original or source text, written in a source language. Instead, translation becomes a mode of cultural production, circulation and consumption, a creative and productive process in its own right. This broadening of the notion of translation allows us to apply it beyond verbal language, to other media and modes of communication such as music or the visual arts. At the same time, the stress on the productive, creative (or manipulative) nature of translation points to its continuity with rewriting, adaptation, localization, or to practices of self-translation, all of which play an important role in cultural traffic.[4] As

---

[2] Susan Bassnett, *Translation* (Abingdon and New York: Routledge, 2014), p. 1.

[3] James Clifford, *Routes: Travel and Translation in the Late Twentieth Century* (Cambridge, MA and London: Harvard University Press, 1997), pp. 21–22.

[4] In the 1990s a 'cultural turn' took place in the field of translation studies, with scholars stressing precisely the inherently cultural nature of translation processes and practices. On this topic, see Susan Bassnett and André Lefevere, eds, *Translation, History and Culture* (London: Cassell, 1990); Mary Snell-Hornby, *The Turns of Translation Studies: New Paradigms or Shifting Viewpoints?* (Amsterdam: John Benjamins, 2006). On rewriting and adaptation, see the seminal work of André Lefevere, *Translation, Rewriting, and the Manipulation of Literary Fame* (London

such, translation can also be seen as a method or an approach to the study of culture: a lens through which we can analyse the commerce between people across both space and time, follow the articulation between local traditions and global trends, and trace the complex texture which characterizes cultural practices in any one location and moment in time, foregrounding the intrinsic dynamism and creativity of human interaction.

The history of Italy and of what we term 'Italian culture' is marked by multiple, enduring and substantive forms of mobility. The notion of Italy itself as well as the physical boundaries of the nation have varied over time, with the 'idea of Italy' notably preceding the existence of the Italian state. Migration has also been a core feature of Italy's history, especially (though not by any means exclusively) in its post-unification phase. This has taken the form of internal migration (from south to north, or from rural to urban areas), as well as emigration (with a range of motivations, from political exile to economic advancement, and destinations stretching across the globe) and immigration (most notably in recent decades). Social mobility has transformed Italian society over time, its patterns often intersecting those of migratory movements. Mobility across and between languages also features prominently in the Italian landscape, as the emergence of a national language is marked by the constant interplay with the prominence and resilience of local dialects, regional variants or minority languages.

These and related factors mean that Italian culture is internally diverse and polycentric and, at the same time, deeply enmeshed with the development of transnational movements and trends. Translation, both as a set of objects and a method of analysis, can be particularly useful in studying such a complex cultural fabric. It will allow us – to return to Klee's metaphor – to take Italian culture for a walk both inside the confines of the nation and beyond them, tracing the relationship between the national and the transnational dimensions of cultural phenomena. In the process, it will help us to answer some key questions about how 'national culture' is constructed and how its boundaries are policed; about the relationship between what qualifies as 'Italian culture' and 'Italian language'; and about the notion of translation itself, especially in relation to self-translation and multilingualism, on the one hand, and to notions of cultural translation, on the other.

and New York: Routledge, 1992). On self-translation, see Anthony Cordingley, ed., *Self-Translating: Brokering Originality in Hybrid Culture* (London: Bloomsbury, 2013) and the special issue devoted to the topic by the journal *Orbis Litterarum*, 68.3 (2013).

Translation and the Making of the Italian Nation

Long before the country's unification and its constitution as a nation state in the second half of the nineteenth century, Italy existed not only as 'a geographical expression' (following the famous quip attributed to Austrian statesman Klemens von Metternich) but also as a cultural entity. The construction of a notion of Italian culture was supported by multiple processes of linguistic and cultural translation whose direction takes us both outwards and inwards: from inside the peninsula to transnational artistic, intellectual and political networks stretching across Europe (and to a certain extent beyond it) and vice versa. Before and during the Risorgimento, the circulation of ideas, images and stereotypes of Italy was influenced by translation practices both in the narrower sense which refers to the transfer of Italian texts into other languages, and in the wider sense in which forms of intercultural representation can be said to translate and manipulate one culture for the benefit and consumption of another.[5]

It is as a result of such processes, for instance, that at a crucial moment in the Risorgimento Matthew Arnold could write 'England and the Italian Question' (1859), an essay in which he defended the country's right to independence by arguing that Italy had already been a nation, in all but political status, for a number of centuries.[6] Arnold argued that the process of national unification had started in Italy during the twelfth century and that, despite subsequent interruptions, the country's claims to the principle of nationality were still legitimate because of the cultural prestige associated with Italian culture:

> No other country, not even the great powers such as Russia, Austria, and Prussia, could cry with such just humiliation and despair in undergoing a foreign rule, *'Unde lapsus!'* What is the past of these three nations, what their elements for a national pride to feed upon, what their history, art, or literature, compared with those of Italy? – of a people, which, besides having been the most brilliant in Europe in the middle ages and at the Revival of Letters, has in addition, to swell

---

[5] For classic and influential treatments of these themes, see Jacques Le Goff, 'L'Italia fuori d'Italia: L'Italia nello specchio del Medioevo', in *Storia d'Italia*, 6 vols (Turin: Einaudi, 1972–76), II, pp. 1933–2088; Franco Venturi, "L'Italia fuori d'Italia", in *Storia d'Italia*, III, pp. 985–1481.

[6] Matthew Arnold, 'England and the Italian Question', now in *On the Classical Tradition*, ed. by R. H. Super (Ann Arbor: University of Michigan Press, 1960), pp. 65–96 (p. 72).

its consciousness of its gifts and grandeur, all the glories of the Roman Empire.[7]

Arnold concluded his argument by stating that it was the moral and historical duty of 'the Englishman' to 'desire the establishment of a great and free Italy'.[8] The prestige attached to the Italian past, stretching all the way to classical Rome, thus extended its aura beyond the boundaries of literature and the arts, allowing Arnold to forge a direct connection between the prestige of Italian culture and the discourse of politics and international relations.

It is significant that 'On translating Homer', Arnold's famous essay on the importance of translation and its role in the establishment of Britain as the modern heir of the Western cultural tradition, was written in 1860–61, that is shortly after his defence of Italy. In the same period, Arnold also wrote a lecture in praise of Dante.[9] Locating Arnold's defence of Italy in this context sheds some light on the complex links connecting past, present and future cultural prestige, and their relationship with translation. On the one hand, translation is for Arnold (and for the British cultural establishment of his time) both the route to the appropriation of a great tradition of 'universal human genius', in which the Italian Dante stands side by side with the Greek Homer or the English Shakespeare, and a way to affirm the hegemonic role of contemporary Britain and its culture. On the other, by granting access to the past glories of Italian letters and incorporating them into present British cultural achievements, translation provides both a rationale for the existence of a national Italian culture and an imperative to assert its greatness (since it makes such an appropriation desirable).

Such influential representations of Italian culture did not only circulate in Britain but also travelled further afield. The revival of Dante, for instance, spread to the United States, where Longfellow, Norton, Lowell and others created the Harvard 'Dante Club' – and in 1867 Longfellow became the first American translator of the *Divine Comedy*.[10] The importance of the cultural

---

[7] Arnold, 'England and the Italian Question', p. 72.

[8] Arnold, 'England and the Italian Question', p. 94.

[9] *On Translating Homer: Three Lectures Given at Oxford* (London: Longman, Green, Longman, and Roberts, 1861); the lecture on Dante, entitled 'The Modern Element in Dante', was delivered in Oxford in 1862. It is now included in Matthew Arnold, *Lectures and Essays in Criticism*, ed. by R. H. Super (Ann Arbor: University of Michigan Press, 1962), pp. 3–11.

[10] On the Harvard 'Dante Club' and its members, see for instance David Wallace, 'Dante in English', in *The Cambridge Companion to Dante*, ed. by Rachel Jacoff (Cambridge University Press, 1993), pp. 237–58 (pp. 249–50).

dynamics set in motion by translation becomes even more evident if we consider that images of Italy established outside its boundaries also travelled back to their point of origin, influencing mechanisms of self-representation and providing a prestigious model for the construction of a national Italian identity. Books dedicated to Italy and its ancient history by foreign authors are frequently found in Italian libraries and were often translated into Italian during the unification period. Edward Gibbon's *The History of the Decline and Fall of the Roman Empire* (first published 1776–88), for instance, was translated in 1820–24 and published in Milan as *Storia della decadenza e rovina dell'Impero Romano di Edoardo Gibbon*. This was followed by another Italian edition published in Lugano in 1841. From the point of view of translation, however, an even more significant presence in the literary panorama of the recently unified Italy is that of Thomas Carlyle's Dante. Carlyle's lecture on 'Dante and Shakespeare' was published as part of the volume *On Heroes, Hero-Worship and the Heroic in History* in 1841, two decades before Arnold's essays, for which it constitutes an important antecedent.[11] Dante had not always been popular in Britain and the attention devoted to the *Divina commedia* and his other works had been limited until well into the eighteenth century,[12] with translations largely confined to isolated passages, mostly taken from the 'Inferno'.[13] Yet all this changed with the advent of the Romantic age, when the Italian poet became a much-revered, and translated, figure. The first substantial attempts at translating the *Commedia* into English date from the late eighteenth century. The first complete translation, by the Irish cleric Henry Boyd, appeared in 1802, but the version which established Dante as one of the great poets of the Western canon was that by H. F. Cary, published in 1814.[14] Carlyle's interpretation of Dante and his comparison between the Italian poet and Shakespeare must be read within this rediscovery of the Florentine poet. Yet that rediscovery and,

[11] Thomas Carlyle, *On Heroes, Hero-Worship and the Heroic in History* (London: Fraser, 1841); all references are to the 1904 Chapman and Hall edition.

[12] On the *fortuna* of Dante's work, see Robert Hollander, 'Dante and his commentators', *The Cambridge Companion to Dante*, ed. by Rachel Jacoff (Cambridge University Press, 1993), pp. 226–36; the classic Paget Toynbee, *Dante in English Literature from Chaucer to Cary (c. 1380–1844)*, 2 vols (London: Methuen, 1909); and Michael Caesar, ed., *Dante: The Critical Heritage* (London and New York: Routledge, 1989). See also Tristan Kay, 'Dante and the Transnational Turn', in this volume.

[13] For details of English translations of Dante, see Wallace, 'Dante in English'.

[14] On Dante's fortune among the English Romantics, see Wallace, 'Dante in English'; Steve Ellis, *Dante and English Poetry: Shelley to T. S. Eliot* (Cambridge: Cambridge University Press, 1983); and Ralph Pite, *The Circle of Our Vision: Dante's Presence in English Romantic Poetry* (Oxford: Clarendon Press, 1994).

more specifically, Carlyle's essay on Dante also have strong Italian connections: one of the major influences on 'Dante and Shakespeare' is the Italian poet Ugo Foscolo who, as an exile in Britain, published first two articles on Dante in the *Edinburgh Review* (1818) and then a *Discourse on the Text of the Divine Comedy* (1825). The latter was republished in 1842, in a volume collected and edited by Giuseppe Mazzini, one of the leading figures of the Italian Risorgimento, who was also an exile in London, where he became a friend of Carlyle.[15]

For Carlyle, Dante is a universal figure, since 'The *Divina Commedia* is of Dante's writing; yet in truth *it* belongs to ten Christian centuries, only the finishing is Dante's'.[16] Carlyle's Dante, however, is also firmly Italian. His and Shakespeare's role as national poets is crucial to the fortunes of their respective countries: if asked whether they would rather give up their Indian empire or Shakespeare, the English, according to Carlyle, should not hesitate in choosing to keep the latter.[17] As for the Italians, the final paragraph of the essay leaves no doubt about the importance they should attribute to Dante:

Yes, truly it is a great thing for a Nation that it get an articulate voice; that it produce a man who will speak-forth melodiously what the heart of it means! Italy, for example, poor Italy lies dismembered, scattered asunder, not appearing in any protocol or treaty as a unity at all; yet the noble Italy is actually *one*: Italy produced its Dante; Italy can speak! The Czar of all the Russias, he is strong, with so many bayonets, Cossacks and cannons; and does a great feat in keeping such a tract of Earth politically together; but he cannot yet speak. Something great in him, but it is a dumb greatness. He has had no voice of genius, to be heard of all men and times. He must learn to speak. He is a great Dumb monster hitherto. His cannons and Cossacks will have rusted into nonentity, while that Dante's voice is still audible. The Nation that has Dante is bound together as no dumb Russia can be.[18]

---

[15] On these figures and their complex relationships, see E. R. Vincent, *Ugo Foscolo: An Italian in Regency England* (Cambridge: Cambridge University Press, 1953), especially pp. 159–62; Francesco Viglione, *Ugo Foscolo in Inghilterra* (Pisa: Nistri, 1910), pp. 208–50; Fred Kaplan, *Thomas Carlyle: A Biography* (Cambridge: Cambridge University Press, 1983). Substantial extracts from Foscolo's two *Edinburgh Review* articles and his *Discorso* can be found in *Dante: The Critical Heritage*, pp. 447–63 and pp. 483–89, respectively.

[16] Carlyle, *On Heroes*, p. 91.

[17] Carlyle, *On Heroes*, p. 105.

[18] Carlyle, *On Heroes*, pp. 105–06.

Carlyle's essay on Dante and Shakespeare travelled back to Italy in 1896, shortly after the end of the Risorgimento, at a time when the new Italian state was already facing internal political crisis. Significantly, the lecture on Dante and Shakespeare was the only section of *On Heroes, Hero-Worship and the Heroic in History* to be selected for translation in a volume included in the series 'Biblioteca Critica della Letteratura Italiana' (a series devoted to Italian literature, rather than to foreign authors in translation). The copy held by the Biblioteca Nazionale of Florence bears visible traces of the Italian reception of the translated essay in the form of handwritten notes, in two different though equally old-fashioned hands, added at the bottom of the last page. Just after the closing paragraph (quoted above), an Italian reader inscribed the following words:

> Carlyle con questo ha saputo penetrare nell'anima del nostro poeta, mentre da noi, e ciò fa vergogna, si dilungano all'infinito per interpetrare il 'pape satan' ed altro, in che avrà voluto dire Dante.

> [Carlyle in saying this managed to penetrate the soul of our poet, while here among us – and this is to our shame – they are forever trying to interpret the 'pape satan' and other such things, as to what Dante might have meant]

Just below this sentence, a second reader added a further, approving note: 'Bravo! e Molto bene!' [Bravo! and Well done!].[19]

In these emotionally charged comments, we see how Italian readers reacted to images of their nation as a unified country and a long-lived cultural entity which were produced elsewhere and 'brought back home' by translation. Initially designed to be consumed by an audience which did not identify as Italian, but was invited to feel a connection to Italian culture and its achievements as well as the plight of the Italian nation-in-the-making, these images were themselves informed by previous acts of translation. Some of these acts took the form of what Roman Jakobson called 'interlingual translation or translation proper',[20] exemplified here by transpositions of Dante's poetry into English. Others correspond to what translation scholar André Lefevere called 'rewriting',[21] as in the case of essays on Dante produced

---

[19] 'Pape satan' is a reference to one of the *Divine Comedy*'s most cryptic prophecies (Inferno, VII, 1).

[20] Roman Jakobson, 'On Linguistic Aspects of Translation', in *On Translation*, ed. by Reuben A. Brower (Cambridge, MA: Harvard University Press, 1959), pp. 232–39 (p. 233).

[21] See Lefevere, *Translation, Rewriting, and the Manipulation of Literary Fame*.

by Italian political exiles, in English and for the British public. These multiple forms of translation played a role in the context of nineteenth-century Britain (their target culture), sustaining an internal narrative which saw it as the ultimate heir of a great Western tradition. However, that was not the end of the story. Far from being a simple binary process which merely takes a text, message or image from A to B, from source to target language and culture, translation forms much more complex networks. In this case, translation-informed British narratives of Italian culture also travelled further afield and made their way back to Italy. Here they played a part in the process of construction of post-unification Italian national identity, creating a series of refracted mirror images which are still visible in the way Italy represents itself and its cultural heritage today, starting with the tendency to privilege a lingering myth of the past over the modern reality of the country.

Translation and the Borders of the Nation

Translation thus can be seen to play a role in the formation of the Italian nation and of notions of Italian culture, in a complex circulation of texts, images and ideas which has both internal and external dimensions. Within the nation state, processes of translation also shape and regulate the borders of national culture, while maintaining their porosity: they help to construct hierarchies of canonicity, are instrumental to attempts at policing what cultural products get imported and exported, and are intrinsically linked to debates about national identity and national language.

Translation is often associated with the opening up of cultures to new ideas, ways of thinking and forms of creativity. However, it can also function as a mode of censorship and/or assimilation. This often happens in historical contexts marked by strong nationalist ideologies (as in Naoki Sakai's analysis of how a 'regime of homolingual address' has supported the ideology of the nation in modern Japan, for instance), or by hegemonic, ethnocentric tendencies (as discussed by Lawrence Venuti in relation, in particular, to translation trends in the United States).[22] In the case of Italy, the most direct, prominent and well-documented case of attempted control over translation by the state relates to the years of the fascist dictatorship.[23] At the height of

---

[22] Naoki Sakai, *Translation and Subjectivity: On Japan and Cultural Nationalism* (Minneapolis and London: University of Minnesota Press, 1997); Lawrence Venuti, *The Translator's Invisibility: A History of Translation* (London and New York: Routledge, 1995/2008).

[23] On this subject see, for instance, Francesca Billiani, *Culture nazionali e narrative straniere: Italia 1903–1943* (Florence: Le Lettere, 2007); Francesca Billiani, ed., *Modes*

fascism, translations were subject to official processes of censorship before and/or after publication. Between 1938 and 1940, the so-called *bonifica libraria* led to a systematic examination of both Italian and translated volumes. At least partly as a result of the controls imposed by the regime, the number of translations fell from 912 in 1936 to 555 in 1941.[24] The procedure applied not only to literature but also to cinema, where the practice of dubbing allowed the erasure of the original dialogue and the control of information as well as register and other features of linguistic expression.[25]

While fascist censorship certainly attempted to impose official regula-tions on the circulation of cultural products, it was not a clear-cut system in which the state censors were trying to thwart the efforts of publishers, editors and translators to keep the frontiers of Italian culture open. Rather, it was a complex nexus of cultural regulations and negotiations, in which the various agents continuously tested the boundaries of what was acceptable, furthering their respective political, intellectual and economic interests and agendas. While never entirely effective, the system thus also exceeded its apparent limits, by creating the conditions for forms of self-censorship, adjustment and (re)calibration.[26] Perhaps the most notable example of the operation of fascist censorship on translated material is that of the literary anthology *Americana*. The volume was planned by one of Italy's major publishing houses, Bompiani, as a prestigious project which would import and showcase the best of American writing. It involved prominent intellectuals, such as Elio Vittorini (who led the initiative), Cesare Pavese, Emilio Cecchi and others, many of whom were also prolific translators. The anthology included extracts from 33 writers and followed the evolution of American literature, including contemporary authors such as Hemingway and Steinbeck. At the beginning of 1941, however, with the volume almost ready to go into print and Italy now officially at war, the fascist Ministry of Public Culture (Ministero della cultura popolare, or MinCulPop, active between 1937 and 1944) denied permission to publish it. Subsequent negotiations between Bompiani and the fascist

of Censorship and Translation: National Contexts and Diverse Media (Manchester: St. Jerome, 2007); Guido Bonsaver and Robert Gordon, eds, *Culture, Censorship and the State in Twentieth-Century Italy* (Oxford: Legenda, 2005); Christopher Rundle, 'The Censorship of Translation in Fascist Italy', *The Translator*, 6.1 (2000), 67–86; Christopher Rundle and Kate Sturge, eds, *Translation under Fascism* (Basingstoke and New York: Palgrave Macmillan, 2010).

[24] Billiani, *Culture nazionali*, p. 211.

[25] See Rundle, 'The Censorship of Translation in Fascist Italy' and also Carla Mereu Keating, *The Politics of Dubbing: Film Censorship and State Intervention in the Translation of Foreign Cinema in Fascist Italy* (Oxford: Peter Lang, 2016).

[26] Billiani, *Culture nazionali*, p. 217.

authorities led to the eventual publication of the anthology in 1942, with a new preface written by Emilio Cecchi which was intended to reorient the collection, playing down the praise for American culture and taking a more neutral stance towards it. That revised edition remained in circulation well after the end of the Second World War and the fall of fascism. It was only in 1968 that Bompiani finally published a new version, reinstating Vittorini's original plans.[27]

The example of *Americana* shows how translation is a contested territory for the control of cultural production and cultural influence, but it also highlights the complexities of the system regulating it, which involves not just direct censorship but also the internal policing of boundaries through strategies of self-censorship and negotiation on the part of publishers, editors and translators. These strategies may affect the selection of the texts to be translated, as well as the way in which they are presented, starting from the inclusion of prefaces and other paratextual material which frame the translation and invite specific forms of reading and interpretation. And while such cases are particularly evident under regimes such as fascism, they are by no means limited to them. In each historical context, we can illuminate the relationship between cultures and the internal operations of a specific system by asking key questions about translation: what is selected for translation and what is excluded? Who polices the boundaries of the national culture, how and how effectively? And what mechanisms of compliance or resistance are put in place by other agents in the system?

We may also invert the perspective and look at how translation functions as a regulatory mechanism when the products of a national culture are being exported. In this case, a key role is played by notions of canon and canonicity, which regulate the position occupied by cultural objects in a perceived (yet, at least to an extent, also effective) hierarchy of value. Literary canons, in particular, occupy an important role in defining national cultures and asserting or consolidating their prestige. As we have already seen through the example of Dante's fortune in Britain, claiming a long cultural tradition (and singular cases of outstanding achievement within that) can be a way of legitimizing the narrative of the nation, especially when those claims are endorsed both from within a culture and by powerful external voices, in a mutually reinforcing chain of translational acts. The category of world literature is constituted precisely through this double inscription: from Goethe's

---

[27] Billiani, *Culture nazionali*, pp. 218–19; Guido Bonsaver, 'Fascist Censorship on Literature and the Case of Elio Vittorini', *Modern Italy*, 8.2 (2001), 165–86. Documentation on the case can also be found at http://www.apice.unimi.it/mostre/decennale/percorso_editoria_americana.html [accessed 3 May 2019].

notion of *Weltliteratur* to today's reincarnations of the concept, translation plays a key role in taking a text beyond the nation while, at the same time, reaffirming its internal cultural capital. On the one hand, the fact that a work has been widely translated proves its quality and supposedly universal value, so much so that David Damrosh recently stated that 'World literature is writing that gains in translation'.[28] On the other, texts which acquire world literature status in translation also see their own position within a national canon confirmed and, by extension, contribute to reinforcing the prestige and cultural capital of that tradition.

Yet translation also works in more subtle and less predictable ways, not just reiterating but often altering the position of specific works and authors, or entire genres, within a canon or a cultural system. Both systemic theories and sociological approaches have pointed out the way in which translation can introduce new cultural objects and also reposition them.[29] In the case of Italy, recent literary exports provide excellent examples of such cultural dynamics. The two single most successful cases of translation from the Italian of the past few years are Andrea Camilleri's series of detective novels centring on the fictional character of Inspector Montalbano and Elena Ferrante's *Neapolitan Quartet*, both of which have been translated into a large number of languages.[30] Significantly, both sets of texts at least initially occupied a middlebrow position in the Italian literary system and enjoyed a mixed critical reception in their home country.[31] Camilleri's Montalbano novels (as well as their TV adaptations, produced by the Italian state company RAI) belong to the *giallo* genre.[32] This form of popular fiction entered the Italian

[28] David Damrosh, *What Is World Literature?* (Princeton and Oxford: Princeton University Press, 2003), p. 281.

[29] On systemic theories of translation, see Theo Hermans, *Translation in Systems: Descriptive and System-Oriented Approaches Explained* (Manchester: St. Jerome, 1999) and Gideon Toury, *Descriptive Translation Studies and Beyond* (Amsterdam: John Benjamins, 1995); on the sociology of translation, see Michaela Wolf and Alexandra Fukari, eds, *Constructing a Sociology of Translation* (Amsterdam and Philadelphia: John Benjamins, 2007); and the special issue of *The Translator* edited by Moira Inghilleri and devoted to 'Bourdieu and the Sociology of Translation and Interpreting', 11.2 (2005).

[30] For details on Camilleri in translation; see http://www.vigata.org; on Ferrante http://elenaferrante.com/ [both last accessed 3 May 2019].

[31] Elisa Segnini, 'Andrea Camilleri's Montalbano and Elena Ferrante's *L'amica geniale*: The Afterlife of Two "Glocal" Series', *The Translator* (2018), doi: 10.1080/13556509.2018.1502607.

[32] There is a vast literature on Italian detective fiction. For a brief history of the genre and its recent popularity, see also the BBC documentary 'Italian Noir: The Story

system through translation and has now come full circle, becoming one of the country's most visible export products. Under the label of 'Mediterranean noir', the trend has also been credited (together with Scandinavian or Nordic noir) with giving new impulse to translation in the Anglophone publishing industry, which is notoriously impervious to foreign imports.[33] Mediterranean and Scandinavian noir are both transnational genres, linked to areas which do not directly correspond to a specific national culture. In Italy, however, Camilleri is known for his use of (real and imaginary) Sicilian dialect and is strongly associated not just with a national but with a regional dimension which, while not entirely erased, is at least partly downplayed in the reception of his works in translation. The overall result of this double shift from *giallo* and regional identity to Mediterranean noir is to reposition Camilleri's work within a transnational landscape in a way which is substantially different from the space he occupies in Italy. Elena Ferrante's *Neapolitan Quartet*, meanwhile, has also undergone a shift in position through translation. Initially, the novels received a mixed reception in Italy, with popular attention concentrating on the mysterious identity of the author who, throughout her career, has been known to write under a pseudonym. The success of the books in translation has transformed the quartet into a global phenomenon. In the Anglophone market, Ann Goldstein's version of the tetralogy has enjoyed a positive critical reception, marking a shift in the positioning of the books and identifying them as literary bestsellers.[34] The English translations were published by Europa Editions, which was founded in 2005 by the owners of Rome-based Edizioni E/O (who are also the original publishers of Ferrante's work in Italian) with the declared intention to capitalize on their 'deep roots in European publishing to bring fresh international voices to the American and British markets and to provide quality editions that have a distinct look and consistently high levels of editorial standards'.[35] The international success of the translations has also led to a highly visible TV adaptation of Ferrante's quartet, co-produced by a group of international companies, including Italy's RAI and the American HBO. In turn, the TV adaptation is increasing the visibility of the books, both within and outside Italy. In both Camilleri's

---

of Italian Crime Fiction' (2010), now available at https://www.youtube.com/watch?v=-ggN-rgeezk [accessed 3 May 2019].

[33] Venuti, *The Translator's Invisibility*, pp. 153–54.

[34] Segnini, 'Andrea Camilleri's *Montalbano* and Elena Ferrante's *L'amica geniale*'; in the same special issue, see also 'Gigliola Sulis Speaks to Ann Goldstein: Writing Locally, Translating Globally', *The Translator* (2018), doi: 10.1080/13556509.2019.1578549.

[35] For this and related information, see https://www.europaeditions.com/about-us [accessed 3 May 2019].

and Ferrante's cases, then, translation has produced significant shifts in the perception of these authors' works, in and out of Italy. A combination of translation, adaptation and popular as well as critical reception also creates an echo chamber which makes it increasingly difficult, if not impossible, to isolate the Italian texts from their global image and circulation.

Translation, Self-Translation and Migration

So far, we have been tracing the relationship between Italian culture and translation by following, mostly, the journeys undergone by texts as they move in and out of the Italian language and the literary system associated with the Italian nation. However, as noted in the opening section, people move, too, and Italy's history is inscribed with a particularly rich tapestry of migrant experiences and trajectories. These exceed the boundaries of the nation and connect Italian culture to a transnational landscape. As noted by Emma Bond, 'the Italian case is, perhaps, at once peculiarly trans-national and trans-nationally peculiar: historically a space characterized by both internal and external transit and movement, Italy itself can be imagined as a hyphenated, in-between space created by the multiple crossings that etch its geographical surfaces and cultural depths'.[36]

Exploring the connection between migration and the trans-nation takes us even further away from a binary model of translation based on self-contained source and target texts written in homogeneous source and target languages. In their place, we find intricate networks of self-translation, multilingualism and hybridization, which also demand that we call into question the notion of national language and its association with national culture. In spite of what David Gramling has defined as 'the invention' and the enduring resilience of 'the myth of monolingualism',[37] translation, if understood in the inclusive sense noted above, makes visible the diversity of language and cultural practices at any one moment and in any one place, as well as the interconnectedness which characterizes them across time and space. Rethinking the Italian cultural system from the standpoint of mobility and migration makes these networks visible while interrogating the notion of 'Italian'. In doing so, it also grants renewed space and attention to forms of internal linguistic

---

[36] Emma Bond, 'Towards a Trans-national Turn in Italian Studies?', *Italian Studies*, 69.3 (2014), 415–24 (p. 421).

[37] David Gramling, *The Invention of Monolingualism* (London and New York: Bloomsbury, 2016), especially pp. 187–96. On mono- and multilingualism, see also Yasemin Yildiz, *Beyond the Mother Tongue: The Postmonolingual Condition* (New York: Fordham University Press, 2012).

and cultural heterogeneity, such as the long history of creative production in regional languages and dialects across the peninsula. Is 'Italian' coextensive with 'Italophone'? Can Italian culture express itself in a language other than Italian? And who can produce Italian culture, where and when?

Since the 1990s, mobility and migration have received increased attention within political as well as critical discourse.[38] In the Italian context, the last three decades have been marked by growing immigration phenomena but also, at least in part, by a renewed interest in the long and ongoing history of Italian emigration and, in some cases, in the relationship between the two.[39] In terms of the literary production linked to migration phenomena and the effects of translation, we can also start from an intuitive distinction between import and export, yet any neat separation between these vectors soon gives way to more complex maps. The growing corpus of work produced by contemporary writers whose personal experiences and literary production are associated with immigration towards Italy and who have elected to write in Italian has been described through a variety of labels, including 'Italophone writing', 'Italian migration literature', 'postcolonial Italian literature'.[40] The difficulty in naming the phenomenon is indicative of the complexity of the Italian cultural landscape, as well as of the enduring blind spots in approaches to the connection between language, territory and nation. Many of the writers in question, for instance, use a range of languages, whether in succession or within a single individual work; and their linguistic mobility or 'translingualism'[41] may be associated with multiple geographic movements, as they migrate to other places and, in many cases, start writing in other languages.

[38] Kevin Hannam, Mimi Sheller and John Urry, 'Editorial: Mobilities, Immobilities and Moorings', *Mobilities*, 1.1 (2006), 1–22.

[39] Key texts in these areas include Jennifer Burns and Loredana Polezzi, eds, *Borderlines: Migrazioni e identità nel Novecento* (Isernia: Cosmo Iannone Editore, 2003); Teresa Fiore, *Pre-Occupied Spaces: Remapping Italy's Transnational Migrations and Colonial Legacies* (New York: Fordham University Press, 2017); Donna Gabaccia, *Italy's Many Diasporas* (Seattle: University of Washington Press, 2000); Cristina Lombardi-Diop and Caterina Romeo, eds, *Postcolonial Italy: Challenging National Homogeneity* (Basingstoke and New York: Palgrave Macmillan, 2012); Pasquale Verdicchio, *Bound by Distance: Rethinking Nationalism through the Italian Diaspora* (Madison, NJ: Fairleigh Dickinson University Press, 1997).

[40] See Jennifer Burns, *Migrant Imaginaries: Figures in Italian Migration Literature* (Oxford: Peter Lang, 2013); Armando Gnisci, ed., *Nuovo Planetario Italiano: Geografia e antologia della letteratura della migrazione in Italia e in Europa* (Troina: Città Aperta, 2006); Graziella Parati, *Migration Italy: The Art of Talking Back in a Destination Culture* (Toronto, Buffalo and London: University of Toronto Press: 2005).

[41] Steven G. Kelmann, *The Translingual Imagination* (Lincoln, NE and London: University of Nebraska Press, 2000).

Attempting to contain their production within a single language creates artificial boundaries and fragmentation. On the other hand, foregrounding the transnational nature of their writing[42] and the processes of translation and self-translation which inform it allows us to follow the individual and collective journeys traced by these authors and to appreciate the links they forge between different spaces, languages and communities.

An eloquent example of these journeys is that of Shirin Ramzanali Fazel and her first book, *Lontano da Mogadiscio*.[43] The author, who describes herself as 'una scrittrice italiana di origini somalo-pakistane' [an Italian writer of Somali-Pakistani origins], was born and grew up in Mogadishu, attending an Italian school. She moved to Italy in 1971 and in 1994, with the publication of her autobiographical narrative, became one of the first postcolonial voices in Italian. Her book was read and classified as one of the key texts of the emerging category of 'migrant writing'. The author underlined her choice to write in Italian and for an Italian public, but she also inscribed the text with traces of the Somali language. Those traces are accompanied by notes for the Italophone reader, making explicitly visible the process of linguistic and cultural translation which informs the writing and reminding us that this is a book born in and out of translation: it would not exist if it were not for the co-presence of languages and histories, and for the layers of experiences and memories associated with them. Processes of self-translation, therefore, are built into the writing from its inception, rather than being added to it *a posteriori*, as when an existing piece of writing is translated into a new language.

Lontano da Mogadiscio has had a complex editorial history. It was first published by a small Italian company, Datanews, which also reprinted it and produced a second edition during the 1990s. In 2013, another small publisher, Laurana, launched an e-book which contained both an extended version of the Italian text and a translation into English, produced by the author herself who, in the meantime, had moved to the United Kingdom and had started to write in English, as well as continuing to produce works in Italian. A new layer of translation and a different kind of self-translation were therefore added to what was already a translation-rich original. This bilingual edition has since also been transformed into two independent, self-published, volumes: *Far from Mogadishu* (2016) and *Lontano da Mogadiscio* (2017). The choice to

---

[42] In *Migrant Imaginaries*, Burns proposes the term 'transnational (Italian) literature' (pp. 206–07).

[43] Shirin Ramzanali Fazel, *Lontano da Mogadiscio* (Rome: Datanews: 1994). For a detailed exploration of the equally complex case of Amara Lakhous, see also Rainier Grutman, 'Translation That Dare Not Speak Its Name: Amara Lakhous as an Ambivalent Self-Translator', *The Translator* (2018), doi: 10.1080/13556509.2018.1527119.

self-translate was partly motivated by necessity, given the limited receptivity of the Anglophone publishing industry to translations, especially in the case of text and authors who do not carry substantial cultural capital. Yet that choice also prompted Ramzanali Fazel to re-create her book, rewriting some sections and adding new chapters which were devised in parallel, in Italian and English. Following a pattern common to many translingual writers, she embraced translation as a fluid, continuous and circular process in which languages and cultures intersect and dialogically inform each other.[44] The proximity between Italian and Somali language (memory, experience, ...), which was already visible in the first edition of the text, is now enriched by the additional dimension of English, and by the presence of both Italian and Somali in the English version (where we find sentences such as 'I have lived in Manhattan, considered *l'ombelico del mondo*, but I could not smooth out the nostalgia for my Mogadishu').[45] However, where boundaries between languages were made explicit in the 1994 edition through the addition of separate glossary notes, now any processes of translation are built directly – and sparingly – into the text. This approach to translation reflects the personal trajectory of the writer, for whom 'la cultura italiana e quella somala si sono sempre mescolate [e] i due idiomi non [hanno avuto] linea di confine' ['Somali and Italian culture have always been mixed together (and) the two idioms do not (have) border lines'].[46] Translation, in this kind of multi- and translingual writing, does not lead to the substitution or replacement of an original. Rather, it makes visible the layering of personal and collective history, of subjectivity and memory, through the traces left by languages, their fluidity and their articulation on the page.

The writing of Italian emigration follows equally complex itineraries. Here, too, questions of language, place and belonging play a prominent role in how authors and their works are perceived and positioned. And here, too, translation can help us to trace the intricate weaving of cultural production,

---

[44] See in particular Ngugi wa Thiongo's description of his practices of writing/self-translating/rewriting in 'Translated by the Author: My Life between Languages', *Translation* Studies, 2.1 (2009), 17–20.

[45] *Lontano da Mogadiscio/Far from Mogadishu*, bilingual electronic edition (Milan: Laurana), p. 246. The Italian version is found on p. 56: 'Ho vissuto a Manhattan, *l'ombelico del mondo*, ma non sono riuscita a placare la profonda nostalgia che ho per la mia *Hamar*, Mogadiscio'. Here the presence of another idiom is signalled by the Somali toponym 'Hamar'. In both cases, italics are used in the original and contribute to foreground the weaving of different idioms together.

[46] Shirin Ramzanali Fazel, cited in Simone Brioni, 'Postfazione', in *Lontano da Mogadiscio/Far from Mogadishu* (Milan: Laurana), pp. 168–89 (p. 179). The English version, also by Brioni, appears on p. 373.

circulation and reception. What is the position of forms of diasporic Italian culture? How does the production emerging from a field such as Italian American writing, for instance, relate to Italian (or, for that matter, American) culture? And how does translation operate in the case of Italian American authors, the works they produce and their further, subsequent travels? It is indicative that many of the authors who are today recognized as the leading lights of Italian American literature occupy a liminal or entirely external position when it comes to the Italian canon. John Fante, probably the most prominent among these authors, was significantly included in *Americana*, the anthology of translated American literature discussed above in relation to the fascist censorship. Another member of that generation, Pietro di Donato, has been alternatively classified as a migrant, an Italian American and a proletarian writer, both in the United States and in Italy.[47]

Fante and di Donato were second-generation migrants who wrote either entirely or predominantly in English and this automatically excludes them from definitions of Italian literature which centre on the use of the Italian language. The case of Giose Rimanelli, however, is much harder to classify and he has been variously defined as an Italian, an Italian American or a regional writer. Rimanelli was born in Casalcalenda, in the Molise area of Italy, in a family with a long history of migration. His maternal grandfather, Antonio Minicucci, also known as Tony 'Slim' Dominick or 'nonno Dominick', had grown up in New Orleans and spent a number of years in the United States and Canada, before returning to Italy. His mother, Concettina 'Squeeze' Minicucci, was born in Montreal, then lived in Italy, and eventually instigated the family's return to North America after the Second World War.[48] Giose also migrated from his native Molise, first across Italy and Europe, then to Canada and the United States, where he settled in 1960. His writing career started in Italy, in the immediate post-war period, and his early novels were influenced by the neorealist aesthetic of the period. He met Italian writers such as Jovine, Pavese and Alvaro and his connections included influential international figures such as Boris Vian. Even after moving to the United States, Rimanelli continued to publish mostly in Italian. Eventually, however, he switched not just to English, but to idiosyncratic forms of polylingual writing which mirrored his personal trajectory and incorporated dialect, standard Italian, English (often in non-standard and experimental varieties)

---

[47] Loredana Polezzi, 'Of Migrants and Working Men: How Pietro di Donato's *Christ in Concrete* Travelled between the US and Italy through Translation', in *Perspectives on Literature and Translation: Creation, Circulation, Reception*, ed. by Brian Nelson and Brigid Maher (London: Routledge, 2013), pp. 161–77.

[48] Giose Rimanelli, *Familia: Memoria dell'emigrazione* (Isernia: Iannone, 2000).

and also Latin, Provençal, Spanish and other idioms. He produced poetry, novels, autobiographical and critical writing, as well as translations and self-translations which increasingly mixed and hybridized both genres and languages, creating work which is perhaps best defined as a form of trans-languaging – that is, the use of multiple linguistic codes within a single, multilingual repertoire.[49]

Perhaps unsurprisingly, given his complex individual trajectory and artistic profile, the reception of Rimanelli's writing tends to be divided into separate compartments. His early works and especially his first novel, *Tiro al piccione*,[50] were well-received in Italian literary circles and some were also translated into English, as part of post-war Italian production. After his move to America, Rimanelli's connections with the Italian literary establishment quickly faded and when his name reappeared in the United States it was as part of the emerging field of Italian American studies. It is within this context that his most well-known English work, the experimental novel *Benedetta in Guysterland*, has been read as the first postmodern Italian American masterpiece.[51] A further critical line connects Rimanelli's work to a regional context and to the revival of dialect literature in Italy. His poetry collections, in particular, combine Italian, *molisano* dialect, English and a variety of other languages, including classical ones, through strategies of linguistic as well as cultural translation and self-translation. Often multiple versions of original and translated poems are placed side by side on the page in composite arrangements, creating a patchwork effect which invites the reader to blur not only geographical limits but also temporal and historical ones. By privileging the position of dialect over that of national standards, additionally, Rimanelli defies traditional hierarchies of power and prestige among languages.

Both Rimanelli's biography and his literary production place him on the margins of any canon. Imposing a national, regional or even ethnic (as in 'Italian American') perspective on his work inevitably results in

---

[49] Ofelia Garcia and Li Wei, *Translanguaging: Language, Bilingualism and Education* (Basingstoke: Palgrave Macmillan, 2014), p. 12.

[50] Giose Rimanelli, *Tiro al piccione* (Milan: Mondadori, 1953; new edn Turin: Einaudi, 1991).

[51] Giose Rimanelli, *Benedetta in Guysterland: A Liquid Novel* (Montreal and New York: Guernica, 1993). On the genesis of the novel and its critical reception, see Anthony Julian Tamburri, '*Benedetta in Guysterland*: Postmodernism [Pre-]Visited', in *Rimanelliana: Studi su Giose Rimanelli/Studies on Giose Rimanelli*, ed. by Sebastiano Martelli (New York: Forum Italicum, 2000), pp. 223–40; Fred Gardaphé, 'Parody at the Border: Giose Rimanelli as Trickster, *Benedetta* as Missing Link', Introduction to Rimanelli, *Benedetta in Guysterland: A Liquid Novel* (Montreal and New York: Guernica, 1993), pp. 11–25.

fragmentation, foregrounding parts of it while at the same time creating blind spots and areas of exclusion. We can tell a different tale, however, if we place Rimanelli within a transnational perspective and pay attention to his constant processes of personal and artistic self-translation. This allows us to see the continuities rather than the discontinuities in his work. Rimanelli's familiarity and connections with American literature, for instance, can be backdated to his early years of apprenticeship in the post-war Italy of Pavese and Vittorini, who, as we have seen, where championing American authors and their translation into Italian even during the years of fascism. Jazz is also a frequent presence in Rimanelli's work and some of his poems have actually been set to jazz scores.[52] One might imagine that this was a musical taste he acquired during his years in the United States. However, his interest was already present during his Italian youth and has markedly transnational and 'migrant' roots. In the post-war years, for instance, we find Rimanelli's friendship with Boris Vian, whose work is also closely associated with jazz music,[53] and in 1959 Giose's novel *Una posizione sociale* was published with an accompanying record which contained four of his own compositions in Dixieland style.[54] Ultimately, the connection can be traced back to Rimanelli's childhood in Casalcalenda and to his grandfather, Dominick, with his New Orleans youth and his inseparable trumpet. His story is told in a chapter of the autobiographical book *Familia: Memoria dell'Emigrazione* entitled 'Nonno Jazz: Emigrazione come Ricordo', which explicitly connects memory, language, music and migration.[55] Following Rimanelli's transnational and translational routes, then, would also take us beyond literature, towards other forms of cultural production, such as music, in which translation and transnational circulation play just as important a part, tracing even more complex routes and roots.

Conclusion

Reading cultural practices through the lens of translation has taken us to multiple locations and highlighted the complex map of Italian culture. As both a set of objects and a method of analysis, translation allows us to 'take

---

[52] A recording of a jazz version of the poem 'Pàtreme', written in *molisano* dialect, can be found at: http://userhome.brooklyn.cuny.edu/bonaffini/DP/rimanelli.htm [accessed 3 May 2019].

[53] Sebastiano Martelli, 'Introduzione', in Rimanelli, *La stanza grande* (Rome: Avaglione, 1996), pp. 7–19 (p. 16).

[54] Rimanelli, *Familia*, p. 26 (footnote).

[55] Rimanelli, *Familia*, pp. 17–67.

the line for a walk' and explore the boundaries of the (Italian) nation, the relationship between language and culture, and the dynamic circulation of texts, forms and ideas on which all cultural production is predicated. The itineraries we uncover through this process are far from simple journeys from one location to another. They entail multiple movements, refractions, remediations, across both space and time. In the process, languages are not just replaced but also juxtaposed and mixed, memories are made and circulated across geographic and generational boundaries, a sense of self and of community is produced, reinforced, manipulated or transformed – all thanks to the porosity of culture and the pervasive presence of translation.

Following the interconnected paths of Italian culture has brought to the fore a continuum of linguistic and cultural practices which include interlingual translation, but also self-translation, translanguaging, adaptation and other forms of rewriting and cultural transfer which go beyond verbal expression and can also take us, as we have just seen, towards other media such as music. While the focus of the analysis has been primarily on written (and largely literary) texts, the approach taken here is equally pertinent when applied to a range of cultural objects or modes of cultural production. And while some of the itineraries we have followed are inherently linked to the specificities of Italy and its history, the perspectives they open up go well beyond any definition of 'Italian culture', however mobile and transnational. Prioritizing mobility and translation and placing them at the centre of our analysis does not (and must not) lead to renewed forms of a 'great narrative' about the global reach of Italian culture or the prestige of any supposed 'Italian genius'. Beyond the enduring tension between the national and the transnational, which translation, as we have seen, continues both to embody and to make visible, we can thus glimpse further perspectives. In an age dominated by debates about the global and the local, about individual agencies and environmental perspectives, translation reminds us that, in the words of Michael Cronin, we need to view 'languages in their connectedness not in their isolation'.[56]

---

[56] Michael Cronin, *Eco-Translation: Translation and Ecology in the Age of the Anthropocene* (London and New York: Routledge, 2017), p. 152.

2

Renaissance Translators, Transnational Literature and *Intertraffique*

Andrea Rizzi

'Intertraffique' is a word coined by late sixteenth-century English poet and historian Samuel Daniel to describe the safe passage from Paris to London of Michel de Montaigne's celebrated *Essays*. They had first been published in French in 1580–88, and Daniel contributed a prefatory poem to John Florio's translation of the collection into English, which was published in 1603.[1]

'Intertraffique' is perhaps one of the earliest descriptions of transnational literature. Daniel's poetic phrase 'th'intertraffique of the minde' celebrates translation as a crucial means of exchanging ideas. By itself, the term 'intertraffique' also conjures up the business of book printing and selling, the materiality of texts, the agency of translators and the dissemination of knowledge in the European vernaculars. Indeed, the example of *The Essayes [...] of Lo: Michaell de Montaigne [...] now done into English* shows an English-born son of an Italian (and 'bilingued') refugee playing an important role as a transnational and transcultural mediator for the English court: Florio was the first to translate Montaigne into English.

The flamboyant figure of Florio recalls that for centuries translators have crossed cultural and linguistic frontiers in exchange for material and social gains. Italian Renaissance studies (and European Renaissance studies more broadly)[2] has only recently begun to investigate the role played by early

---

[1] Enza De Francisci and Chris Stamatakis, eds, *Shakespeare, Italy, and Transnational Exchange: Early Modern to Present* (New York and London: Routledge, 2017), pp. 3–5. See also Warren Boutcher, 'Intertraffic: Transnational Literatures and Languages in Late Renaissance England and Europe', in *International Exchange in the Early Modern Book World*, ed. by Matthew McLean and Sara K. Barker (Leiden and Boston: Brill, 2016), pp. 343–45 (p. 343).

[2] In this chapter I use 'early modern' and 'Renaissance' interchangeably. Since the

modern translators in the dissemination of early modern culture across city states and nations.[3] To date, scholars have tended to focus on specific centres (such as Florence, Venice and Rome) as well as individual translators. As such, the field of Italian studies is yet to bring a transnational perspective to the consideration of early modern translators as cultural intermediaries who worked across political and linguistic boundaries.[4] In this contribution, I examine a selection of statements written by fifteenth- and sixteenth-century translators in which their transnational mobility emerges strongly – as does the relational context for their work, and their self-awareness as agents of knowledge and culture.

Some further statements indicate ways in which Renaissance vernacular translators working in the Italian peninsula contributed to the development of 'Italian' as a transnational literary language with currency that extended into city states and courts throughout Europe. As I seek to show in the following pages, Renaissance translators negotiated cultural, linguistic, political and economic frontiers, while positioning themselves within the transcultural system of their time and states.

My overall aim is to address a challenging methodological question. How do we twenty-first-century scholars of Italian studies negotiate *our* disciplinary borders – so as to think about literary and translation history in both their local and transnational dimensions? Recent literary history contributions have suggested interdisciplinarity as the way forward.[5] In this chapter,

---

Italian Renaissance is commonly believed to cover the period 1400–1600 and the early modern era 1500–1800, both terms are representative of the period under consideration here (1450–1600).

[3] See, for example, Michael Wyatt, *The Italian Encounter with Tudor England: A Cultural Politics of Translation* (Cambridge and New York: Cambridge University Press, 2005); Anne E. B. Coldiron, *Printers without Borders: Translation and Textuality in the Renaissance* (Cambridge: Cambridge University Press, 2014); Federico M. Federici and Dario Tessicini, eds, *Translators, Interpreters and Cultural Negotiators: Mediating and Communicating Power from the Middle Ages to the Modern Era* (New York: Palgrave Macmillan, 2014).

[4] For recent, more global approaches to late medieval and early modern translators in the Italian peninsula see, for example, Andrea Rizzi, *Vernacular Translators in Quattrocento Italy: Scribal Culture, Authority, and Agency* (Turnhout: Brepols, 2017) and Alison Cornish, *Vernacular Translation in Dante's Italy* (Cambridge: Cambridge University Press, 2011).

[5] See the discussion that followed the contribution by Karin Littau, 'Translation and the Materialities of Communication', *Translation Studies*, 9 (2016), 82–96; see also Guyda Armstrong, 'Coding Continental: Information Design in Sixteenth-Century English Vernacular Language Manuals and Translations', *Renaissance Studies*, 29 (2015), 78–102 (pp. 78–79). A call for an interdisciplinary approach to the study

I follow a similar direction, arguing the need for collaborative approaches to transnational literature that overcome the dichotomy between global, 'distant' reading on the one hand, and nation-based, intertextual reading on the other.

Multiple *Patrie*

Early modern translators were not 'merely' translators. That is, more often than not – like their medieval predecessors – they worked as teachers, diplomats, personal secretaries or administrators for rulers and oligarchies of the 'Italian' peninsula. Most of these translators belonged to an elite community of highly educated men and women who were connected to trans-state political, cultural and social networks of peers, patrons and publics. Certainly, in Renaissance Europe the sense of 'national' community had a narrow basis. Nevertheless, the ruling communities of late medieval and early modern Italian city states developed the 'cultural building-blocks of the later devotion to a national community, or "patriotism"'.[6] *Patria* did not simply refer to a birthplace. Frequently the term also indicated 'the point of origin for an individual's public manifestation of personal traits'.[7] Several literary texts from the Italian Renaissance make specific references to *patria* as the author or translator's place of origin.[8]

Early modern artists, authors and translators often left their *patria* to acquire specialized training and experience in other places. In an early modern peninsula divided into numerous locales, mobility of labour and expertise was almost inevitable. The production of culture in the Renaissance therefore almost always involved the confluence of goods, knowledge and labour from different states, even different continents. This confluence followed both global and local patterns or routes. The routes by which early modern literature was disseminated trace a map that encompasses the localized *patria* where an author or teacher was born or trained, the several pathways taken by authors and translators in the course of their careers, and

---

of early modern women writers is made in Julie D. Campbell and Anne R. Larsen, eds, *Early Modern Women and Transnational Communities of Letters* (Abingdon: Routledge, 2009), pp. 20–21. On 'distant' reading, see Franco Moretti, *Distant Reading* (London and New York: Verso, 2013), pp. 48–49.

[6] Anthony D. Smith, *The Nation Made Real: Art and National Identity in Western Europe, 1600–1850* (Oxford: Oxford University Press, 2013), p. 28.

[7] David Young Kim, *The Traveling Artist in the Italian Renaissance* (New Haven and London: Yale University Press, 2014), p. 83.

[8] See for instance Annibal Caro et al., *Apologia degli Academici di Banchi di Roma contra M. Lodovicho Castelvetro da Modena. In forma d'uno spaccio di Maestro Pasquino* (Parma: Seth Viotto, 1558), USTC 819038.

a global chart of trade and translation. The latter encompasses the sourcing of paper, ink, print technology, texts and finance, as well as the production, distribution and reception of manuscripts or printed texts. To be able to follow all of these routes one needs to take multiple approaches. Like a GPS – which is based on multiple global perspectives (satellite signals) and a local system – the literary scholar needs to process coordinates and localized data from a range of different viewpoints: economic, political and historical, among others.

David Wallace's literary history of Europe demonstrates that late medieval and early modern texts and literary figures followed intricate routes of cultural trade and exchange, locally and beyond their *patria*.[9] Sometimes the distances travelled were short. At other times they were long, as exemplified by Pier Paolo Vergerio the Younger, who was born in the Venetian Republic but settled in Tübingen as a religious refugee; Petruccio Ubaldini and Michelangelo Florio, who were Tuscan-born but worked in early modern England; the missionary priest Giovan Battista Sidotti, who was imprisoned in Japan; Jesuit missionaries and translators who travelled to Japan and China; Hasan al-Wazzan (Leo Africanus) and Michel Angelo Corai, both diplomats and translators, who landed on the Italian peninsula from North Africa and Syria, respectively. These well-known cases signal a complex, multidirectional trade of knowledge and skills, as well as goods.[10]

---

[9] David Wallace, *Europe: A Literary History*, 2 vols (Oxford: Oxford University Press, 2016).

[10] On Italian intellectuals, diplomats and teachers during Tudor England, see Wyatt, *The Italian Encounter*. On European translators in early modern Japan, see Rebekah Clements, *A Cultural History of Translation in Early Modern Japan* (Cambridge: Cambridge University Press, 2015). On Jesuit missionaries and translators in early modern China, see Ronnie Po-Chia Hsia, *Matteo Ricci and the Catholic Mission to China, 1583–1610: A Short History with Documents (1583–1610)* (Indianapolis: Hackett, 2016). For an assessment of Europe-China transcultural relationships in the early modern era, see Mingjun Lu, *The Chinese Impact upon English Renaissance Literature: A Globalization and Liberal Cosmopolitan Approach to Donne and Milton* (Farnham: Ashgate, 2015). On Ubaldini see, for example, Andrea Rizzi, 'English News in Translation: The *Comentario del Successo dell'Armata Spagnola* by Petruccio Ubaldini and its English Version', *Spunti e Ricerche*, 22 (2007), 89–106 and Wyatt, *The Italian Encounter*, pp. 127–28. On Hasan al-Wazzan, see Natalie Zemon Davis, *Trickster Travels: A Sixteenth-Century Muslim between Worlds* (London: Faber & Faber, 2007). On Corai, see Federico M. Federici, 'A Servant of Two Masters: The Translator Michel Angelo Corai as a Tuscan Diplomat (1599–1609)', in *Translators, Interpreters and Cultural Negotiators: Mediating and Communicating Power from the Middle Ages to the Modern Era*, ed. by Federico M. Federici and Dario Tessicini (New York: Palgrave Macmillan, 2014), pp. 81–104.

A Transnational Italian Renaissance

In 2014 Emma Bond described Italy as a case 'perhaps, at once peculiarly trans-national and trans-nationally peculiar', because historically the space of the Italian peninsula has been characterized by external and internal movement.[11] The key problem with this assessment for medieval and early modern Italy is the fact that, as mentioned, no pan-Italian nation state existed. Precisely because Italy did not exist politically, linguistically and economically, 'trans-nationalism' can be called a condition inherent to the Renaissance, and thus one firmly established in the lives and work of Renaissance men and women.[12] Even as political, linguistic, cultural and economic boundaries separated different Italian Renaissance communities, linguistic differences were not insurmountable. And by the early sixteenth century these were diminished by the adoption of the Tuscan vernacular as a standard literary language alongside Latin.[13] Moreover, contracts and other notarial agreements between artists and patrons demonstrate that there were only minor linguistic and legal differences between Italian *signorie*, city states and kingdoms.[14]

Dominant powers asserted their difference by means of arts, social behaviour and language. In the course of the fifteenth century, several ruling families and governments actively supported the production of histories aimed at underscoring differences between states, thereby potentially harming the reputation of other rulers.[15] During the relatively peaceful period

[11] Emma Bond, 'Towards a Trans-national Turn in Italian Studies?', *Italian Studies*, 69 (2014), 415–24 (p. 421).

[12] Among the extensive literature on transnational exchange and communities in early modern Italy and Europe, see at least De Francisci and Stamatakis, *Shakespeare, Italy*; Christopher H. Johnson, David Warren Sabean, Simon Teuscher and Francesca Trivellato, eds, *Transregional and Transnational Families in Europe and Beyond: Experiences Since the Middle Ages* (New York and Oxford: Berghahn Books, 2011); Campbell and Larsen, *Early Modern Women*.

[13] There is a vast literature on the so-called 'questione della lingua'. See at least Mirko Tavoni, *Latino, Grammatica, Volgare. Storia di una questione umanistica* (Padua: Antenore, 1984) and Brian Richardson, *Print Culture in Renaissance Italy: The Editor and the Vernacular Text, 1470–1600* (Cambridge and New York: Cambridge University Press, 1994).

[14] This was in great part thanks to the persistence of ancient Roman protocols for work contracts; see Michelle O'Malley, 'Subject Matters: Contracts, Designs, and the Exchange of Ideas between Painters and Clients in Renaissance Italy', in *Artistic Exchange and Cultural Translation in the Italian Renaissance City*, ed. by Stephen J. Campbell and Stephen Milner (Cambridge: Cambridge University Press, 2004), pp. 17–37 (p. 19).

[15] The publication of Leonardo Bruni's first instalment of the *History of the*

that followed the peace treaty of Lodi (1451), several states continued to experience domestic and transnational unrest. Nevertheless, the comparative peace before the Italian wars at the turn of the sixteenth century provided governments and rulers with the opportunity to develop common historical memories and values by means of literature and history writing.[16] Intellectuals and translators (serving, for example, as teachers and diplomats) offered their skills to furnish updated narratives intended to cement a sense of common or shared heritage within a given community. These 'professionals of the pen' are commonly referred to as 'humanists'.

The term 'humanism' was invented in the nineteenth century to describe a widespread cultural movement that celebrated classical antiquity and involved a charismatic elite of literary scholars focused on Latin texts, translators rendering materials from Greek into Latin and supporters of the growing vernacular culture of the fifteenth and sixteenth centuries. This cultural movement was in constant flux. Notwithstanding traditional interpretations of 'humanism', the makers of this movement frequently crossed linguistic and cultural boundaries – these itinerant scholars were not just 'Italian'. After the fall of Constantinople in 1453, several Greek scholars, teachers and merchants were forced to leave and find a *patria* in one the many 'Italian' centres. The Italian peninsula was also a destination for Jewish communities following their expulsion from Spain in 1492.[17]

The rise of print culture increased the possibilities for transnational communities in Europe. German Johannes of Spira was authorized to introduce printing technology to Venice, and Johannes de Colonia (Cologne) became the first successful entrepreneur in the newly established Venetian print industry. Peter Ugelheimer, originally from Frankfurt, set up a remarkable network of 'transnational and interregional commerce in Venetian books'.[18] Over the sixteenth century, German printers tended to entrust their book trade in Venice to local Venetian book merchants and

---

Florentine People (1428) raised concerns from humanist Bartolomeo della Capra that it would harm the reputation of the Duke of Milan. See Gary Ianziti, *Writing History in Renaissance Italy: Leonardo Bruni and the Uses of the Past* (Cambridge, MA: Harvard University Press, 2012), pp. 91–92.

[16] On 'common historical memories', see Anthony D. Smith, *National Identity* (London: Penguin, 1991), p. 21.

[17] Fiona Cassen, *Marking the Jews in Renaissance Italy: Politics, Religion, and the Power of Symbols* (Cambridge: Cambridge University Press, 2017), pp. 98–99. See also Hans Lamers, *Greece Reinvented: Transformations of Byzantine Hellenism in Renaissance Italy* (Leiden: Brill, 2016).

[18] Angela Nuovo, *The Book Trade in the Italian Renaissance*, trans. by Lydia Cochrane (Leiden and Boston: Brill, 2013), pp. 21–36 (p. 31). On German printers in

entrepreneurs, or to those from France.[19] Perhaps the most famous printer from Renaissance Italy, Aldo Manuzio (*c.* 1452–1515) moved to Venice later in his life, most likely because he was attracted to the thriving community of Greek scholars and the growing print industry.[20] 'Merchant-capitalists' did not confine their business activities to only one city or centre.[21] Several established family printing businesses had agents and headquarters in a number of locales. For instance, the distinguished Giolito publishing house operated in Trino, Lyon and Venice; from the Gabiano dynasty, Baldassarre, Giovanni Bartolomeo, Lucimborgo and Francesco da Gabiano in turn established their family business in Lyon, with operations also in Asti, Trino and Venice.[22]

In point of fact, there were Renaissance printers and agents who established multiple companies for the production and distribution of books. These enterprises took advantage of social relations spread widely across different cities and states. Several languages would have been spoken to facilitate transactions. Key figures in these intercultural businesses were prospective buyers (including wholesalers and booksellers); patrons, business partners and agents; printers, authors, editors and translators. Translators moved in search of patrons and printers who would support and promote their intellectual skills, while printing firms actively sought out the expertise of multilingual scholars. For translators, as for other early modern professionals, mobility was a cultural practice that entailed 'displacement, either voluntary or unwilling, from a homeland; confrontation with and work within an alien environment; and finally, the reception of that mobility by both foreign counterparts and compatriots'.[23] Of course such mobility did not suddenly develop at the turn of the fifteenth century. Whether as exiles or by choice, four of the 'five crowns' of late medieval Italian literature (Dante, Petrarch, Boccaccio and Catherine of Siena) had travelled across the

---

Venice, see Marino Zorzi, 'Stampatori tedeschi a Venezia', in *Venezia e la Germania: Arte, politica, commercio, due civiltà a confronto* (Milan: Electa, 1986), pp. 115–40.

[19] Nicolaus Jenson, Vincenzo Valgrisi (Vincent Valgrise), Antonio Gardano (Antoine Gardane) and Giovanni Griffio (Gryphe) were among the most active French book printers and traders in Renaissance Venice.

[20] On Aldo Manuzio il Vecchio, see most recently Guido Beltramini, *Aldo Manuzio: Il rinascimento di Venezia* (Venice: Marsilio, 2016).

[21] Jane A. Bernstein coined 'merchant capitalists' to describe printers, booksellers, and scholars of print culture in her *Print Culture and Music in Sixteenth-century Venice* (Oxford: Oxford University Press, 2001), p. 10.

[22] Angela Nuovo and Chris Coppens, *I Giolito e la stampa nell'Italia del XVI secolo* (Geneva: Droz, 2005).

[23] Kim, *The Traveling Artist*, p. 1.

Italian peninsula, and the 'fifth crown', Birgitte of Sweden, had travelled to Rome in 1349, where she spent the remainder of her life.[24]

Translators and *Intertraffique*

Humanistic internationalism – the mobility of scholars, educators, translators and diplomats – generated 'sites of [cultural] exchange and merchandising'. Here knowledge and skills were offered and received as a commodity that furnished patrons with cultural capital.[25] 'Humanists' were extremely shrewd multilingual communicators. Most translators from Latin, Greek, Arabic and Hebrew were trained in the five key disciplines of the humanities: grammar, poetry, history, rhetoric and moral philosophy. Such training (also called *translatio studii*) gave learners strong communicative skills that could be applied to oratory, diplomacy, governance, literature, philosophy and history.[26] Translation was therefore part and parcel of humanists' background: the study and appreciation of languages such as Greek, Latin and vernaculars was an essential aspect of their career. By their cross-disciplinary skills and versatility, early modern translators were well qualified for positions in international governments and in cultural institutions such as universities, schools, academies.

The number of early modern intellectuals engaging with scribal and printed translation for rulers, patrons and readers is much more extensive than previously entertained. At least ninety vernacular translators are documented as active in Quattrocento Italy before the development of the print industry.[27] A study of the Torrentino press in Florence for the years 1547–63 shows that one quarter of the total output was comprised of translations.[28] The data show the scale of sustained collaboration between translators, editors, printers and

---

[24] On the five crowns, see Wallace, *Europe*, I, pp. xxxiii–xxxv.

[25] Jacques Lezra, '*Nationum Origo*', in *Nation, Language, and the Ethics of Translation*, ed. by Sandra Berman and Michael Wood (Princeton: Princeton University Press, 2005), pp. 203–28. On cultural capital and humanism, see Christopher S. Celenza, 'From Center to Periphery in the Florentine Intellectual Field: Orthodoxy Reconsidered', in *Artistic Exchange and Cultural Translation in the Italian Renaissance City*, ed. by Stephen J. Campbell and Stephen Milner (Cambridge: Cambridge University Press, 2004), pp. 273–92.

[26] See Douglas Biow, *Doctors, Ambassadors, Secretaries: Humanism and Profession in Renaissance Italy* (Chicago: University of Chicago Press, 2002).

[27] Rizzi, *Vernacular*.

[28] Dario Brancato, 'L'epistola dedicatoria della "Consolazione della filosofia" di Benedetto Varchi (1551) fra retorica e politica culturale', *Studi Rinascimentali*, 1 (2003), 83–91 (pp. 84–85).

patrons in the production of translations. In the printing business, translators worked closely with editors and printers, to the extent that it is not always possible to discern a clear division of labour between them.

How did these translators contribute to the Renaissance transnational 'intellectual community' – that is, to the flourishing of an autonomous group with a 'shared set of interests informed by common material for reflection'?[29] Understanding why certain texts were translated instead of others, for whom translations were produced, and by whom, illuminates the literary history of *intertraffique* – whether with reference to the sometimes peripatetic lives of translators, the entrepreneurship of master printers or the dissemination of knowledge. Such understanding can be gleaned by studying the first-person prefatory statements that translators included in their publications. These nearly always underscore the wish of their elite patrons and readers to find literary context for the state's geopolitical territory, historical memories and traditions.

This demand for cultural capital stirred strong competition between nations and city states. For instance, in the 1460s and 1470s the cultural relationship between Florence and Ferrara was driven by rivalry, emulation and a strong concern for cultural difference.[30] Despite the political allegiance between the two city states, Ferrara-based orators, authors and translators underscored the political contrasts between their own ruler and Lorenzo de' Medici in Florence, depicting the latter as a *parvenu* and the Florentine court as lacking a real princely leader. A passage from Ludovico Carbone's account of the state visit, in 1473, of members of the Este court of Ferrara to Naples and Florence sheds light on the perceived dissimilarity between the two powers:

> I believe you [Federico da Montefeltro, Duke of Urbino] have heard about how earnestly they maintain the new University of Pisa, so that they lure the most famous masters of learning from all over Italy with large sums of money. What more can I say? If my lord Ercole ruled over Florence, there is no other place I would live.[31]

Through irony, Carbone exposes the intense competition for cultural excellence that saw Lorenzo de' Medici actively poach a number of professors and

---

[29] Celenza, 'From Center to Periphery', p. 276.

[30] Stephen J. Campbell, 'Our Eagles Always Held Fast to your Lilies', in *Artistic Exchange and Cultural Translation in the Italian Renaissance City*, ed. by Stephen J. Campbell and Stephen Milner (Cambridge: Cambridge University Press, 2004), pp. 138–60 (p. 147).

[31] Campbell, 'Our Eagles', p. 149.

intellectuals from Ferrara and other Renaissance centres. This exemplifies one of the many ways in which cultural-political competition called for skilled professionals from neighbouring states, and, as a consequence, simultaneously broke down and exploited political and economic boundaries. In Ferrara during the same period, exiled Florentine families experienced a privileged condition that allowed them the status of respected citizens in the host state while also retaining strong connections with their city and ruler of origin. Hence, in the 1460s, the Lanfredini family of Florentine merchant bankers ran a banking business in Ferrara and Lendinara. While living and working in Ferrara, they became diplomatic agents for Lorenzo de' Medici.[32]

Their direct appeals for patronage often show translators working rhetorically with the same impulse to exceed and exploit geopolitical and other boundaries. An extreme example is that of Cola de Jennaro, who dedicated his Neapolitan version of the pseudo-Aristotelian *Secretum de Secretis* to King Ferrante of Naples (r. 1458–94). De Jennaro took on the task while he was a prisoner of the King of Tunis. He decided to recast a Catalan version of the treatise into Neapolitan to garner support for his release from captivity; on the third folio of the manuscript, he drew himself kneeling before the Aragonese coat of arms while shackled and pleading for rescue. The painted image of abjection is complemented by the translator's written account of himself on the same folio. He notes that the coarseness of his prison clothes and his low social status match his unsteady translative praxis and ill-refined lexical and syntactical choices.[33] Yet in the preface de Jennaro also emphasizes his work ethic, explaining how, as soon as he learned of the existence of the Catalan text, 'appi iudicio del tinore de quisto lo quale con bona deligencia et ingegnu procuray averlo' [I assessed the quality of this work and used good diligence and effort to obtain it].[34] In this dramatic instance, rather than competitively seeking employment or intellectual recognition, the translator hoped to exchange his work for physical freedom.

King Ferrante of Naples was among several sixteenth-century rulers who increasingly cultivated interest in vernacular texts and culture. In the prefaces to his vernacular translations, Bartolomeo Fonzio (1446–1513) discusses a related literary struggle, which was shared by several other Renaissance translators. He fashions his translation as a challenge to trade the elegance of the ancients for the Tuscan vernacular. Fonzio's career led him to seek work in several European centres, from Florence to Rome, Ferrara and Buda. This forced him to try to make his translations especially appealing to various

---

[32] Campbell, 'Our Eagles', p. 152.
[33] Paris, Bibliothèque Nationale de France, MS Ital. 447, fol. 3v.
[34] Ms. Ital. 447, fol. 5r.

prospective readers or employers. In 1467–68, Fonzio translated the second-century BCE letter of Aristeas from Leonardo Bruni's Latin rendition (*Aristea de lxxii interpreti*), dedicating his work to Borso d'Este Marquis of Ferrara. Introducing the translation, Fonzio states that he does not wish his work to appear as a rough and inelegant exercise in which the source is translated literally. Nevertheless, he insists, he tried as hard as he could ('con summo studio') to translate accurately, while retaining the elegance of the source text. The 'elegance' to which Fonzio refers encompasses two key elements needed for vernacular translation to be positioned within a cultural trade that still favoured the linguistic and cultural Latin model: the textual virtue of elegance combined correctness and clarity with readability – making knowledge useful. Whether they attributed this model to ancient Roman authors or early fifteenth-century humanists such as Leon Battista Alberti, vernacular translators gave context to their achievements by invoking the much-vaunted elegance of Latin. Even when pronouncing such elegance difficult or impossible to attain (because of the instability or lack of prestige of a vernacular language), translators professed great concern about conveying this quality from texts by the ancients, and by their humanist counterparts.

In the sixteenth century, Antonio Brucioli took a flexible stance on vernacular. He dedicated his vernacular translation of Solomon's proverbs (1533) to Alfonso, Marquis of Vasto, governor of Milan. Addressing the marquis, Brucioli reveals that he had translated the work from Hebrew into 'nostro vulgare Italiano'.[35] In 1529, Brucioli had been banished from his native city of Florence. Since then, he had acquired considerable experience as translator and editor. The reference to 'our [...] Italian' in his translation is an indication of the progressive establishment of a more standard literary Italian language that could be accessed across the Italian peninsula and beyond. In other words, Italian was gaining recognition as a language capable of facilitating the 'intertraffique of the minde' described by Daniel in his preface to Florio's translation of Montaigne. Even so, five years later, in his edition of Boccaccio's *Decameron*, Brucioli took a different approach: he produced notes at the end of each story, together with an index of the terms he had annotated. Evidently assuming that no reader would understand Boccaccio's idiom, he

---

[35] Antonio Brucioli, *Annotationi sopra i Proverbii di Salomo. Tradotti dalla ebraica verità in lingua toscana* (Venice: Aurelio Pincio [Antonio Brucioli], 1533), USTC 802633 – quotation at iia. On Brucioli, see Eva Del Soldato, *'Illa litteris Graecis abdita*: Bessarion, Plato, and the Western World', in *Translatio Studiorum. Ancient Medieval and Modern Bearers of Intellectual History*, ed. by Marco Sgarbi (Leiden and Boston: Brill, 2012), pp. 109–22 and Simona Brambilla, 'Antonio Brucioli curatore e traduttore di Plinio', *Archives Internationales d'Histoire des Sciences*, 61 (2011), pp. 163–74.

felt compelled to explain terms such as *zio* or *lavandaia* for Veneto and Lombard readers unfamiliar with Tuscan literary language. As a Florentine, this was an effective means for Brucioli to assert his indispensable role in the dissemination of literature at a transnational scale. He fashioned himself as translator and editor either addressing transnational patrons and readers or catering for local readers who needed guidance to understand the newly established *lingua franca* of Italian culture.[36]

Pietro Lauro of Modena (Modena 1510–*c.* 1568) was likewise a prolific translator whose texts enact comparable strategies to promote his services and role as intercultural mediator. As with Brucioli, Lauro was attracted to Venice for the city's thriving printing business. Venice was also a reasonably safe haven for Lutherans, and it seems that Lauro belonged to this group.[37] His first two translations are dedicated to influential patrons working in Venice: the ambassador to the emperor Charles V in Venice, Diego Hurtado de Mendoz and Pietro Orio (deputy *podestà* of Vicenza in 1543).[38] Lauro underscores his cultural programme to produce translations for a transnational readership: the Latin or Spanish texts he agreed to translate were not yet known to 'Italy' ('non fusse all'Italia ancora manifesta') and deserved to be bestowed upon the Italian language ('donarlo alla lengua Italiana').[39]

At times, Renaissance translators declared their state of displacement and uncertainty. In his published letters Lauro confesses to fearing the dangers of being away from his motherland, and feeling 'suspended and doubtful' ('sospesi et dubbiosi').[40] In his 1554 translation and improvement ('adornati') of Boccaccio's *De genealogia*, Giuseppe Betussi (1512–*c.* 1573) mentions a trip to England that kept him from fulfilling his patron's wish to carry out the

---

[36] Giovanni Boccaccio, *Il Decamerone nuouamente stampato et ricorretto per Antonio Brucioli* [...] (Venice: B. Zanetti, ad instantia di G. Giolitto, 1538), USTC 814809. See Paolo Trovato, *Con ogni diligenza corretto* (Bologna: Il Mulino, 1991), p. 237 n. 33. See also Richardson, *Print Culture*, pp. 98–100.

[37] See Gabriele Dini, 'Lauro, Pietro', in *Dizionario Biografico degli Italiani*, vol. 64 (Rome: Istituto dell'Enciclopedia Italiana, 2005), available at: http://www.treccani. it/enciclopedia/ricerca/pietro-lauro/. In 1545, Lauro translated Erasmus's *Colloquii famigliari* and dedicated his work to Renée of France, Duchess of Ferrara, who was known for supporting heretics until her husband and the French Inquisition forced her to desist in 1554.

[38] On Pietro Orio see Luigi Forti, *Notizie statistiche della provincia di Vicenza per l'anno 1823* (Padua: Tipografia della Minerva, 1823), p. 36.

[39] Constantino Cesare, *De' notevoli et vtilissimi ammaestramenti dell'agricoltura, di Greco in volgare novamente tradotto*, trans. by Pietro Lauro (Venice: Gabriel Giolito, 1542), USTC 802993, p. iib.

[40] *De le lettere di m. Pietro modonese. Il primo libro* (Tramezzino, 1552), p. 2.

translation.[41] The material texts of translations could also suffer precarious fortunes. Annibal Caro (1507–*c.* 1566) translated Virgil's *Aeneid* from Latin into vernacular; his expressive rendition of the poem was published posthumously in 1581 and reveals the hazardous journey to publication of a work destined straightaway for transnational circulation and literary influence.[42] Caro spent the last years of his life in Rome, and completed his *Eneide* just before his death. In 1581, a nephew, Lepido, dedicated the edition published by Bernardo Giunti and brothers in Venice to Cardinal Alessandro Farnese. Lepido apologizes for having been unable to produce the book sooner – plague in Venice and several family losses and incumbencies ('travagli') delayed the printing of his uncle's translation.

Transnational translations often needed to be repackaged to suit new patrons, networks and readerships. Published in Florence, the mid-sixteenth-century translation of Boethius's *De consolatione philosophiae* made by Lodovico Domenichi (1515–64) ensued from a literal and busy 'traffic' of translations within the Italian peninsula and to the court of Holy Roman Emperor Charles V in Brussels. Domenichi was born in Piacenza, but worked in Venice and Florence. In 1550, he presented to the Cardinal of Ferrara his translation of Boethius's treatise, published by Lorenzo Torrentino in Florence with the title *De' conforti filosofici*. In the preface, Domenichi recounts that, following a request from Charles V, the same translation had been dedicated to Cosimo de' Medici, Duke of Florence. Upon receiving the request from the Hapsburg emperor, both Domenichi and Benedetto Varchi were asked by the Florentine ruler to translate Boethius's work.[43] In effect, the latter mediated the Holy Roman Emperor's patronage of the translation. Meanwhile, independently, Cosimo Bartoli (1503–72) was translating the same text. Bartoli was the first to complete the task, but Domenichi's version was the first to reach the emperor in Brussels. Unfortunately, it arrived in poor condition, to the extent that another copy had to be sent. To make things worse, Domenichi could not find the manuscript of his first translation. By necessity Cosimo de' Medici decided to send Bartoli's version as soon as it became available, while Domenichi began compiling a second version. It is this version that was eventually printed in

---

[41] Betussi's patron in this case was Count Collatino di Collalto. I used here *Geneologia de gli dei. I quindici libri di m. Giouanni Boccaccio sopra la origine, et discendenza di tutti gli dei de' gentili* [...] (Venice: Comin da Trino, 1554).

[42] See Diego Poli, Laura Melosi and Angela Bianchi, eds, *Annibal Caro a cinquecento anni dalla nascita. Atti del convegno di studi. Macerata, 16–17 giugno 2007* (Macerata: Eum, 2009).

[43] Dario Brancato, 'Il *Boezio* (1550) di Lodovico Domenichi, le "traduttioni de' begli ingegni" e il "lordo nome" del Doni', *Bollettino Storico Piacentino*, 110 (2015), 38–55.

1550, and dedicated to both the Cardinal of Ferrara and Cosimo de' Medici. Domenichi's preface emphasizes the importance of the Tuscan language as a key medium for the dissemination of knowledge ('sapienza') across the Italian peninsula and beyond. The emperor was therefore able to read this text in a language shared by all of Italy ('mosse la Maestà di tanto Imperatore a voler leggere questo libro in lingua commune a tutta Italia').

Conclusion

Inevitably, the translators' prefaces discussed above can only suggest partial insight into the intricate transnational and collaborative work of translators writing in the Italian vernaculars. Nevertheless, they offer an indication of the strategies, the self-aware agency and collaboration enacted by translators in their *intertraffique* of texts and knowledge. As discussed above, Renaissance translators crossed political and linguistic borders (sometimes many), and their printed texts straddled other kinds of boundaries.

Returning to the methodological question mentioned at the beginning of this chapter, the complex political, cultural and linguistic factors underpinning the mobility of translators and the transnational trade of translations require a 'new inclusivity' in Renaissance studies and literary history. By this I mean an interdisciplinary approach to the social, cultural, political, linguistic and material study of intellectual communities and their cultural trade. As Peter C. Herman remarked almost twenty years ago, 'just as the borders between theoretical approaches and disciplines have started to erode, so have the borders between the study of national literatures'.[44] Collaboration facilitates the erosion of borders and allows disciplines to situate themselves both locally and globally. As this volume and other recent projects in Italian studies attest, a fresh dialogue is a good way to begin.[45]

Certainly, the study of Renaissance translators offers a deep perspective on transnational cultural exchange. In particular, Renaissance translators' versatility and self-avowed diligence seem to have been part of an ethos informed as much by rigorous respect for the salutary powers of linguistic precision as by the more 'mercantile' ideals expressed by Daniel by means of 'intertraffique'.

---

[44] Peter C. Herman, ed., *Opening the Borders: Inclusivity in Early Modern Studies: Essays in Honor of James V. Mirollo* (Newark and London: University of Delaware Press, 1999), p. 16.

[45] See, for example, Sergio Luzzato and Gabriele Pedullà, eds, *Atlante della letteratura italiana*, 3 vols (Turin: Einaudi, 2010). At a smaller scale, see Wallace, *Europe*; McLean and Barker, *International Exchange*; Andrea Rizzi, ed., *Trust and Proof. Translators in Renaissance Print Culture* (Leiden and Boston: Brill, 2018).

3

Linguistic Landscapes of Urban Italy

Perspectives on Transnational Identities

Stefania Tufi

Introduction

This chapter aims to introduce and discuss the linguistic landscape (LL) as a relatively recent development within sociolinguistics (the study of language in society) which puts space and its inscriptions, both verbal and non-verbal, at the centre of scientific enquiry. In a world where visual culture has become increasingly preponderant and where communication technologies have generated new spaces for, and forms of, written communication, urban environments provide multiple opportunities for social actors not just to be at the receiving end of visual messages, but to interact with written signs, and to engender and conjure up spaces of living. This is particularly significant at a time when debates about citizenship, national belonging and mobility are often dominated by institutional discourses of exclusion, which in turn cling to nineteenth-century ideas promoting narrow concepts of legitimacy, entitlement and communal living within national boundaries. These public discourses also tend to emphasize the exceptionalism of multilingualism, which is in fact a normal state of affairs in all corners of the world. Through the prism of LL, therefore, the chapter exemplifies alternative forms of citizenship as they are enacted in everyday living and configured through the LL of transnational urban spaces. The argument is that contemporary Italy is an ideal site for the observation of multilingualism in action, which in turn fosters the performance of a citizenship of the everyday – those forms of belonging and civic engagement that contribute to participatory communal living and extend beyond territorial views of civic agency. Section 2 provides the background for a discussion of Italian studies from the perspective of multilingualism and multiculturalism, while Section 3 sketches the main aspects of LL studies. This preliminary discussion will inform the interpretation of the geographies of citizenship as articulated through LL in the given settings (Section 4) before conclusive remarks are provided in the final part of the chapter (Section 5).

Italian Studies and Neo-Plurilingualism

Italian studies represents a privileged vantage point for the study of multilingualism and multiculturalism. This is due on the one hand to the extremely diverse linguistic make-up that has characterized the Italian peninsula and, on the other, to the peculiarities of the language question in relation to changeable understandings of what constitutes 'Italian'.[1] Students are introduced to issues revolving around the language question early on in their courses and learn to manipulate complex concepts as they refine their linguistic tools. These concepts relate to the interconnectivity and fluidity of linguistic and cultural subjectivities,[2] and to the complexities of linguistic repertoires which underpin multiple and overlapping identities.

Italian studies can be a laboratory for dissecting and putting to the test arguments underpinning language ideology and prejudice. Understanding the impact of historical processes and of enculturation practices leading to the consolidation of *standard* languages is a crucial aspect of language learning. Explicit reflections on the influence that standard languages (and their speakers) exert on power relations are,[3] from a sociolinguistic perspective, part of language education and an indispensable basis from which to relativize the status of language varieties endowed with prestige as socio-historical constructs. All language varieties are viable and effective means of communication because in principle all of them can develop to articulate new meanings, and therefore in linguistic terms there is no hierarchical relationship between

---

[1] The bibliography on these issues is vast. The reader who is not familiar with the main linguistic developments in modern Italy may want to start with Tullio De Mauro, *Storia linguistica dell'Italia unita* (Rome and Bari: Laterza, 1963) and, for a twenty-first-century view, Tullio De Mauro, *Storia linguistica dell'Italia repubblicana: dal 1946 ai nostri giorni* (Rome and Bari: Laterza, 2014). Robert J. Blackwood and Stefania Tufi, *The Linguistic Landscape of the Mediterranean: French and Italian Coastal Cities* (Basingstoke: Palgrave Macmillan, 2015), pp. 18–38, provides an English-language introductory outline.

[2] Rooted in philosophical concepts relating to the formation of the individual, in this chapter 'subjectivity' refers to the configuration of individuality as a result of the interaction with the social world.

[3] See for example Norman Fairclough, *Language and Power*, 3rd edn (London: Routledge, 2015).

standard languages and vernacular, non-codified varieties. It is only because of given historical contexts that some languages are elevated to a higher status than others. In other words, there is nothing inherently superior in standard and official languages.

In the Italian case, early codification of a certain type of literary Italian (we refer to Bembo's *Prose della volgar lingua*, published in 1525)[4] was the result of a careful balancing act which took into account both intellectual positions which valued a classicist tradition and a new canon introduced by the Tuscan writers in the fourteenth century – Petrarch for poetry and Boccaccio for prose (and to a lesser extent Dante, whom Bembo considered too innovative in that he employed words and expressions which were too close to the language of ordinary people).[5]

The features of Italy's developments over the centuries invite us to adopt an approach that looks at Italian *cultures* rather than *culture*, and this is easily underpinned by the study of multilingual and multicultural Italy as an ultra-nation (*ultra-nazione* as defined by La Fauci),[6] due to the plurality of its linguistic and cultural make-up. Different historiographical traditions rooted both in Italy and in the Anglophone world have struggled to pin down the peculiarities of the 'nation' of Italy when constrained within the narrow parameters of nineteenth-century nationalism and of its developments, including an emphasis on linguistic nationalism.[7]

The high degree of linguistic diversity observable in Italy, a reality which is unparalleled within Europe,[8] explains the relevance of the concepts of *language repertoire* and *linguistic continuum*[9] in discussions about language

---

[4] Pietro Bembo, *Prose della volgar lingua. L'editio princeps del 1525 riscontrata con l'autografo Vaticano latino 3210*, critical edition by Claudio Vela (Venezia: CLUEB, 2001).

[5] Again, the bibliography about the 'language question' is vast. For an introduction, see Claudio Marazzini, *Da Dante alla lingua selvaggia. Sette secoli di dibattiti sull'italiano* (Rome: Carocci, 2009).

[6] See Nunzio La Fauci, *L'ultra-nazione* (Pisa: Edizioni ETS, 2010).

[7] For an initial bibliography on these issues see, for example, Riccardo Giumelli, 'Scoprirsi italici. Una riflessione sull'identità italiana in tempi della globalizzazione', *Visioni LatinoAmericane*, 7 (2012), 58–71.

[8] De Mauro, *Storia linguistica dell'Italia unita*, pp. 1–12; De Mauro, *Storia linguistica dell'Italia repubblicana*, pp. 3–18.

[9] *Linguistic repertoire* refers to the set of linguistic resources that speakers draw upon in verbal communication. A linguistic repertoire in contemporary Italy can include, for instance, a local dialect as learned within the family or with peers, a so-called historical minority language (such as the type of Catalan used in the Sardinian city of Alghero), Italian as the language learnt formally and a heritage language such as Amharic, one of the languages in use in Ethiopia. *Linguistic continuum* points to the fluidity of, and

practices that have characterized Italian sociolinguistic studies, a legacy of Italian dialectology as it developed in the nineteenth century.[10] The versatility of this model in turn explains the currency of the above terms within post-structuralist approaches to the study of language in society, such as critical discourse analysis and 'performative' perspectives on language, culture and identity.[11] Non-static, but instead fluid and negotiated views of identity as something that we perform in discourse are reflected in notions of *trans-languaging* (i.e., the simultaneous deployment of different sets of linguistic resources). The use of this term and other related terminology in recent academic work documents a shift from an emphasis on systems to one on language agents. This new focus on language as something we *do* (and not something we *have*) allows us to capture what goes on in verbal communication not just in relation to social indexicality ('I say *x* and therefore I am, or aspire to be, *y*'), but as a practice allowing speakers to contest normative stances by *doing* language.[12] Wei, in particular, discusses translanguaging space as 'a space for the act of translanguaging as well as a space created through translanguaging'.[13] In this space different identities and loyalties do not just coexist. On the contrary, translanguaging allows speakers to create and articulate 'different dimensions of their personal history, experience and

interconnections between, linguistic systems that have traditionally been described as bounded entities. For example, in Italy two towns A and B positioned consecutively along an imaginary line share more linguistic similarities than A and a third town, C, which is further away from A, because of geographical proximity and historical contact. Linguistic boundaries are therefore not abrupt.

[10] Corrado Grassi, Alberto A. Sobrero and Tullio Telmon, *Fondamenti di dialettologia italiana* (Rome and Bari: Laterza, 1997), pp. 161–75; Gaetano Berruto, *Sociolinguistica dell'italiano contemporaneo* (Rome: Carocci, 2012), pp. 13–19.

[11] For a discussion, see Phillip M. Carter, 'Poststructuralist Theory and Sociolinguistics: Mapping the Linguistic Turn in Social Theory', *Language and Linguistics Compass*, 7.11 (2013), 580–96.

[12] See, for example, Adrian Blackledge and Angela Creese, *Multilingualism: A Critical Perspective* (London: Continuum, 2010); Ofelia García, 'Education, Multilingualism and Translanguaging in the 21st Century', in *Multilingual Education for Social Justice: Globalising the Local*, ed. by Ajit K. Mohanty, Minati Panda, Robert Phillipson and Tove Skutnabb-Kangas (New Delhi: Orient BlackSwan, 2009), pp. 140–58; J. Normann Jørgensen, 'Polylingual Languaging around and among Children and Adolescents', *International Journal of Multilingualism*, 5.3 (2008), 161–76; Emi Otsuji and Alastair Pennycook, 'Metrolingualism: Fixity, Fluidity and Language in Flux', *International Journal of Multilingualism*, 7.3 (2010), 240–54.

[13] Li Wei, 'Moment Analysis and Translanguaging Space: Discursive Construction of Identities by Multilingual Chinese Youth in Britain', *Journal of Pragmatics*, 43 (2011), 1222–35 (p. 1222).

environment, their attitude, belief and ideology, their cognitive and physical capacity'.[14] Translanguaging therefore refers to the practice of using different language varieties (which are available within a linguistic repertoire) in an integrated way. In addition, it also refers to the simultaneous creation of spaces of belonging in the act of multilingual communication.

With respect to Italian studies, an LL approach (which investigates written language practices in public space) allows us to employ both theoretical frameworks and methodologies that enhance the understanding of what has been termed *neo-plurilingualism* (and *neo-pluriculturalism*), as will become apparent in the next section. New plurilingual repertoires observable in Italy do not simply include those migrant languages brought by conspicuous groups of mobile people originating from a wide range of geographical locations, which have increasingly diversified familiar patterns of linguistic variety. A mix of languages are often part of migrants' communication practices, either because language use is already complex in their place of origin or because personal stories of multiple moves have led to the development of a complex web of language resources.[15] These resources are in turn deployed and exchanged in the myriad contact situations and language encounters brought about by practical needs. In this context Italian has been termed a *lingua filiale* (*filial* as opposed to *parental*). This refers not just to the fact that children of migrant background often act as linguistic and cultural mediators between their parents and the outside world: *lingua filiale* also refers to the psychological and emotional mechanisms whereby children of migrant backgrounds integrate Italian into the family's linguistic repertoire via the interweaving of the *filial* language with the *mother* language in the enactment of multiple and simultaneous intercultural agency.[16]

If we consider the linguistic history of Italy, however, Italian has always been a filial language. It has been estimated that at the time of unification (1861) as little as 2.5 per cent of the Italian population could use (a form of) Italian.[17] The process of linguistic Italianization was long and complex, and it accelerated as late as in the 1960s, in a climate of profound socio-economic transformation which included mass education and national TV broadcasts. At the time, it was usually children who were exposed to what was generally

[14] Wei, 'Moment Analysis', p. 1223.

[15] See, for example, Mari D'Agostino, 'Immigrati a Palermo. Contatti e/o conflitti linguistici e immagini urbane', in *Città Plurilingui. Lingue e culture a confronto in situazioni urbane*, ed. by Raffaella Bombi and Fabiana Fusco (Udine: Forum, 2004), pp. 191–212.

[16] Graziella Favaro, 'Parole, lingue e alfabeti nella classe multiculturale', *Italiano LinguaDue*, 1 (2012), 251–62.

[17] De Mauro, *Storia linguistica dell'Italia unita*, pp. 12–13.

perceived as a lingua *matrigna* (the wicked stepmother) in school and took it back into their dialectophone families. The legacy of this linguistic history characterized by distance and unrelatedness re-emerges in the spoken mode of Italian-dominant repertoires to this day, in the sense that standard Italian remains an abstraction and, in their oral interactions, speakers use forms of Italian that are always regional to some extent – on a metaphorical level, Italian is like a recalcitrant child who rebels against the constraints of monolingual normativity.

With respect to neo-plurilingualism, Massimo Palermo identifies three main outcomes observable in contemporary Italy.[18] One is the creative use of Italian on the part of writers with different linguistic backgrounds who make a deliberate choice to use Italian as their elected literary language. This phenomenon is not new and in the past authors such as Voltaire, Byron or Joyce made Italian their elected language of writing. What is new in contemporary writers such as Amara Lakhous or Jhumpa Lahiri, however, is that writing in Italian amounts to a process of heteroglossic transmigration which enables them to fulfil a plurilingual and multicultural identity.[19] From this perspective, a linguistic repertoire includes not just linguistic resources which are readily available to speakers but also linguistic resources that speakers would like to be able to employ. This repertoire-in-the-making represents a space of potentiality, a concept which will be further explored over the course of the chapter.[20]

A second outcome of neo-plurilingualism is the fact that Italian has become a lingua franca in the multiple exchanges involving language agents who have settled in Italy (or are passing through the country) – exchanges which are dictated by daily, practical needs. This function of Italian as a contact language has had an important role in scholarly debates concerning the deconstruction of existing interpretive models and frameworks. For example, it has contributed to the development of new perspectives and methodologies both for the analysis of neo-plurilingualism in Italy and for the documentation of the presence of Italian in the world.[21]

---

[18] Massimo Palermo, 'I nuovi italiani e il nuovo italiano', http://www.treccani.it/magazine/lingua_italiana/speciali/domani/Palermo.html [accessed 6 June 2017].

[19] See, for example, Amara Lakhous, *Scontro di civiltà per un ascensore a Piazza Vittorio* (Rome: Edizioni e/o, 2011) and Jumpa Lahiri, *In altre parole* (Parma: Guanda, 2015).

[20] The concept is discussed in Brigitta Busch, '"Without language, everything is chaos and confusion …": Corporal-Emotional Linguistic Experience and the Linguistic Repertoire', in *Emotion in Language: Theory, Research, Application*, ed. by Ulrike M. Lüdtke (Amsterdam and Philadelphia: John Benjamins, 2015), pp. 273–88.

[21] See, for example, Carla Bagna, Monica Barni and Massimo Vedovelli, 'Italiano in contatto con lingue immigrate: nuovi modelli e metodi per il neoplurilinguismo

As a third outcome, Palermo mentions the 'impronta semiotica' (semiotic imprint), that is, visual traces of languages and writing systems that have been populating Italian (primarily) urban spaces and that contribute to the construction of new subjectivities. LL encapsulates this semiotic imprint while creating new spaces of agency and turbulence, where turbulence refers to 'discordant and competing processes out of which events and sites, including semiotic landscapes, emerge and change over time'.[22] An introduction to LL as a field of enquiry is provided in the next section.

Linguistic Landscape Studies

LL investigates the linguistic construction of space and the extent to which writing performs functions that are beyond simply indexing the presence of an individual or a group in a given context. For instance, a sign featuring both Neapolitan and Italian displayed in Naples city centre does not just point to the existence of Neapolitan-speaking people living in or passing through that area, and who are the target readership because they are assumed to be able to decode the verbal message. Figure 3.1[23] reproduces a sign placed under a modern-day 'shrine' to Maradona (see Figure 3.2), the legendary Argentinian footballer who made Napoli football club internationally famous in the 1980s. The shrine is positioned outside a famous coffee bar in the historic centre of Naples and the sign in Figure 3.1 asks 'Have you taken a picture yet? And shouldn't you have a coffee now? WARNING – A word to the wise! If you take a picture and don't have a coffee, you might inadvertently drop your camera (which would be a real shame) ...' . Leaving aside the jokey tone of the message and any references to accidents such as the (non-)fortuitous dropping/damaging of one's camera, all of which can be easily decoded by an Italian audience, the act of employing written Neapolitan (together with Italian) on a sign that is likely to be seen by mostly non-Neapolitan tourists performs several functions. For example, it marks the authenticity of the establishment, validates external perceptions of Neapolitans as being football-obsessed and markets the (supposedly inherent) good quality of Neapolitan

in Italia', in *Minoranze linguistiche. Prospettive, strumenti, territori,* ed. by Carlo Consani and Paola Desideri (Rome: Carocci, 2007), pp. 270–89; Massimo Vedovelli, 'L'italiano degli stranieri, l'italiano fuori d'Italia (dall'Unità)', in *Manuale di linguistica italiana,* ed. by Sergio Lubello (Berlin and Boston: de Gruyter, 2016), pp. 459–83.

[22] See Christopher Stroud, 'Turbulent Linguistic Landscapes and the Semiotics of Citizenship', in *Negotiating and Contesting Identities in the Linguistic Landscape,* ed. by Robert Blackwood, Elizabeth Lanza and Hirut Woldemariam (London: Bloomsbury, 2016), p. 13.

[23] All images in this chapter are my own.

Figure 3.1 – Sign by a coffee bar in central Naples.
Photograph by the author.

espresso coffee by association. The wider semiotic landscape (i.e., the wider universe of signs made available by the sign originator) makes the message universally accessible: the picture of Diego Maradona, who made much of the recent history of Napoli football club 'mythical', dominates the purpose-built 'shrine' above the sign (Figure 3.2 – the altar-like composition is complete with a single framed hair presented as a relic), and is in fact much more salient than the small religious icon positioned to the left. The Neapolitan spelling of 'cafè' (Italian *caffè*) is easily decoded by an international audience and viewers' perceptions are manipulated in the foregrounding of the 'mythical' coffee against just as iconic a background, where white and sky blue, the colours of the football club, are another powerful signifier.

LL represents a relatively recent development within sociolinguistics and has increasingly attracted scholars from different disciplines as a result of what has been termed the 'spatial turn' in the humanities,[24] an outcome of post-structuralist developments in human geography and urban studies. Space, as a result, has been revisited as a dynamic dimension of human experience which is not fixed or absolute (a container or a backdrop), but

---

[24] David Cosgrove, *Mappings* (London: Reaktion Books, 1999), p. 7.

Figure 3.2 – The Diego Maradona 'shrine' above the sign in Figure 3.1.
Photograph by the author.

rather relative and contingent on the specific actions through which it is constructed.

With respect to LL, these developments underpin seminal work by Scollon and Scollon on geosemiotics (i.e., discourses in place),[25] work that has been developed and extended via investigations adopting such perspectives as linguistic anthropology and discursive constructions of space.[26] Scholarly endeavours of this kind have enabled the framing of debates and reflections in manners which are well suited to transnational Italian studies.

The emphasis on the centrality of space for human experience and on spatialization practices for the construction of meaning[27] is of primary concern in LL. As part of relatively swift developments, and after an initial

---

[25] Ron Scollon and Suzie W. Scollon, *Discourses in Place: Language in the Material World* (London: Routledge, 2003).

[26] Asif Agha, *Language and Social Relations* (Cambridge: Cambridge University Press, 2007); Barbara Johnstone, 'Pittsburghese Shirts: Commodification and the Enregisterment of an Urban Dialect', *American Speech*, 84.2 (2009), 157–75.

[27] Michel Foucault, *L'Archéologie du savoir* (Paris: Gallimard, 1969); Henri Lefebvre, *The Production of Space*, trans. by Donald Nicholson-Smith (Oxford: Blackwell, 1991).

emphasis on the documentation of visual communication in urban environments, LL has expanded to encapsulate a more holistic view of spatialities and consider space as a dynamic actor in semiotic processes, rather than simply as a backdrop against which to position writing acts.[28]

Sociolinguistics has traditionally privileged oral communication.[29] Conversely, a renewed attention to writing practices and multimodality in communication can be considered to be a result of late modernity and the unprecedented flows of people and goods facilitated by virtual networks.[30] Simply put, multimodality refers to the different modes that enable communication – aural and visual, but also gestures, postures, etc. Mixed modes of communication have multiplied in recent decades due to technological developments. For example, a webpage does not just require us to read and make sense of a verbal text (when such a text is included) – it requires a reader to decode images, videos and a host of intertextual connections, and to understand a webpage as a hypertext. This awareness is also at the centre

[28] Adam Jaworski and Crispin Thurlow, eds, *Semiotic Landscapes: Language, Image, Space* (London: Continuum, 2010). *Linguistic Landscape: An International Journal* was inaugurated in 2015. The articles published in Volume 1.1–2 take stock of past LL research and discuss possible future developments. Edited volumes have been published regularly in the last ten years or so, as outcomes of both annual Linguistic Landscape Workshops and additional discussions and conferences. See, for example, Elana Shohamy and Durk Gorter, eds, *Linguistic Landscape: Expanding the Scenery* (New York: Routledge, 2009); Elana Shohamy, Eliezer Ben-Rafael and Monica Barni, eds, *Linguistic Landscape in the City* (Bristol: Multilingual Matters, 2011); Durk Gorter, Heiko Marten and Luk van Mensel, eds, *Minority Languages in the Linguistic Landscape* (Basingstoke: Palgrave Macmillan, 2012); Robert Blackwood, Elizabeth Lanza and Hirut Woldemariam, eds., *Negotiating and Contesting Identities in Linguistic Landscapes* (London: Bloomsbury, 2016); David Malinowski and Stefania Tufi, eds, *Questioning Boundaries, Opening Spaces: Reterritorialising Linguistic Landscapes* (London: Bloomsbury, 2020). An ongoing debate about methodological issues relating to modalities of data collection and the identification of (a necessarily finite) set of signs for scholarly investigations has been an integral part of these developments. Data collection techniques have incorporated a wide range of methodologies with varying emphasis on both quantitative and qualitative approaches. There is a consensus that methodologies need to be adapted depending on the object of the enquiry and the research questions, on the condition that the researcher adopts transparency and rigour in the handling of the data. On the methodology employed for the present study, the reader is referred to Blackwood and Tufi, *Linguistic Landscape of the Mediterranean*, pp. 12–15, upon which the discussion in Section 3 draws.

[29] For an overview, see Robert Bayley, Richard Cameron and Ceil Lucas, eds, *The Oxford Handbook of Sociolinguistics* (Oxford: Oxford University Press, 2013).

[30] Gunther Kress and Theo van Leeuwen, *Multimodal Discourse: The Modes and Media of Contemporary Communication* (London: Hodder Arnold Education, 2001).

of current scholarly debates in sociolinguistics, following the critique that the divide between orality and literacy reflects a Western-centric bias. Lillis and McKinney,[31] for instance, advocate the repositioning of writing in sociolinguistics because, amongst other aspects, neglecting written language would prevent us from investigating the new written modes brought about by digital technologies and therefore exclude multimodal frameworks which reassess the role of writing as part of social semiotics (i.e., meaning-making) as a social practice.[32]

LL has emerged as a distinctly interdisciplinary field drawing upon diverse scholarly areas while it endeavours to investigate discourses and ideologies of writing and to reassess writing as an ordinary, everyday social practice where boundaries are blurred and language use is versatile, creative and subversive. LL investigations often uncover ways in which language practices in super-diverse urban environments contradict views of linguistic discreteness (i.e., the idea that languages are bounded entities), critique consolidated language ideologies and articulate counter-discourses of language and identity. These practices are, therefore, endowed with a transformative potential.

For the reasons outlined above, the field of enquiry presented in this chapter is particularly significant for the purposes of the present volume. The focus is on the spatialities of globalization, where *spatialities* stands for (im)material sites where social relations and their repercussions at the global level are bidirectional, and where the interweaving of relational processes amongst individuals and groups challenges any linear and orderly construction of place as territorially fixed.[33] From this perspective, the local and the global cannot be essentialized as two categories with permanent characteristics, and the production of territories is constantly contested. As a result, we witness a proliferation of rescaling processes which are concomitant with varied spatialities (and temporalities), and terms referring to predefined ambits such as the *local*, the *national* and the *global* are used for the sake of convenience

---

[31] Theresa Lillis and Carolyn McKinney, 'The Sociolinguistics of Writing in a Global Context: Objects, Lenses, Consequences', *Journal of Sociolinguistics*, 17.4 (2013), 415–39.

[32] In this respect technology-mediated forms of communication provide the researcher with unprecedented opportunities to observe and analyse individual and group communicative repertoires. Virtual interaction practices, however, present scholars with a host of new challenges. For a discussion of these issues (and their repercussions for sociolinguistics), see for example Alexandra Georgakopoulou and Tereza Spilioti, eds, *The Routledge Handbook of Language and Digital Communication* (London: Routledge, 2016).

[33] Ash Amin, 'Spatialities of Globalisation', *Environment and Planning A: Economy and Space*, 34.3 (2002), 385–99.

and as heuristic devices. This points to an approach where epistemology is necessarily situated[34] – a theoretical stance which posits that what we know and how we know it is influenced by the positioning of the human subject in social relations. This approach is particularly fruitful when observing transnational identities.

In what follows, I will provide LL evidence which exemplifies the arguments developed in this chapter. Due to the limits on this contribution, the discussion is necessarily focused on a selection of signs which inspired reflections along the lines outlined above. The reader should bear in mind, however, that an LL site does not exist in isolation. On the contrary, it is an emplaced nexus of practice,[35] it is embedded in changeable social semiotics, and it needs to be historicized.[36] The same applies to individual tokens, which are part of wider frameworks and where intertextuality facilitates (or hinders) decoding processes. Writing acts displayed in public spaces are generated by different agents for different purposes,[37] and real and symbolic audiences are interpellated in different manners. Decoding processes are dependent on a multitude of factors that vary for individuals and groups,[38] and the materiality of written signs interacts with physical perception and cognitive processes.[39] A note of caution is also needed here to point out that there is no straightforward correlation between language visibility and language use in any given context, yet LL can uncover social dynamics and creative processes which would not emerge should this type of spatial marking not feature in investigations into late modernity.

Observing and engaging with what goes on in LL prompts us to question issues of entitlement, belonging and territoriality, to sound out existing power hierarchies and to rethink linguistic and cultural practices as plural, situated and in the making. These linguistically hybrid spaces of encounter that characterize much of the Italian urban environment can be amongst

---

[34] Nigel Thrift, 'Steps to an Ecology of Place', in *Human Geography Today*, ed. by Doreen B. Massey, John Allen and Philip Sarre (Cambridge: Polity, 1999), pp. 295–322.

[35] Scollon and Scollon, *Discourses*, pp. 197–207.

[36] Jan Blommaert, *Ethnography, Superdiversity and Linguistic Landscapes: Chronicles of Complexity* (Bristol: Multilingual Matters, 2013), pp. 23–37.

[37] David Malinowski, 'Authorship in the Linguistic Landscape: A Multimodal-Performative View', in *Linguistic Landscape: Expanding the Scenery*, ed. by Elana Shohamy and Durk Gorter (New York: Routledge, 2009), pp. 107–25.

[38] Stefania Tufi and Robert J. Blackwood, 'Trademarks in the Linguistic Landscape: Methodological and Theoretical Challenges in Qualifying Brand Names in the Public Space', *International Journal of Multilingualism*, 7.3 (2010), 197–210.

[39] Keith Rayner, 'Eye Movements and Attention in Reading, Scene Perception, and Visual Search', *Quarterly Journal of Experimental Psychology*, 62.8 (2009), 1457–506.

the factors engendering *interlinguality* (i.e., 'a construct that includes inter-culturality, criticality and a commitment to creative and flexible use of other languages in shared, pluralistic spaces').[40] Lamb mentions, amongst other aspects, the importance of public celebratory events and grass-roots-level localities in creating multidimensional spaces engendering interlinguality.[41] LL data discussed in the next section will provide examples of these spati-alities as the sites in which multidimensional subjectivities shape, and are shaped by, the city.

The Citizenship of the Everyday[42]

As mentioned in the Introduction, the focus of this chapter is on the *citizenship of the everyday*[43] as it is enacted by city subjectivities in transnational and transcultural spaces of urban Italy via written acts of translanguaging and trans-semioticization (the latter term pointing to LL shifts between script and other means of visual representation). It will become apparent that inter-secting dimensions of belonging and participation coexist in the dynamic geographies of citizenship in urban Italy, and that a range of linguistic reper-toires articulate spaces of potentiality and of agency.

Traditional conceptions of citizenship see the individual as an active participant in the public affairs of the *polis*. These ideas are rooted in antiquity and challenged by liberal constructions of the citizen as a passive recipient of rights.[44] The main developments of the twentieth century concurred to mark a separation between *formal* citizenship, that is membership of a nation state, and *substantive* citizenship with an emphasis on sets of civil, political and social rights.[45] In this view, the granting of rights is a consequence of territorialized visions of citizenship, which is in turn performed within the

---

[40] Terry Lamb, 'Towards a Plurilingual Habitus: Engendering Interlinguality in Urban Spaces', *International Journal of Pedagogies and Learning*, 10.2 (2015), 151–65.

[41] Lamb, 'Towards a Plurilingual Habitus', pp. 160–61.

[42] The discussion in this section develops material presented in Blackwood and Tufi, *Linguistic Landscape of the Mediterranean*, pp. 66–71. The data were gathered via fieldwork trips including Genoa, Palermo and Rome within the period 2008–15.

[43] Jen Dickinson, Max J. Andrucki, Emma Rawlins, Daniel Hale and Victoria Cook, 'Introduction: Geographies of Everyday Citizenship', *ACME: An International E-Journal for Critical Geography*, 7.2 (2008), 100–12.

[44] See Thomas H. Marshall, *Citizenship and Social Class, and Other Essays* (Cambridge: Cambridge University Press, 1950), for a theorization of liberal views of citizenship.

[45] Tom Bottomore, 'Citizenship', in *The Blackwell Dictionary of Modern Social Thought*, ed. by William Outhwaite (Oxford: Blackwell, 2002), pp. 76–77.

bounded entity of the nation state. The increasingly diversified and mobile societies that have characterized (at least parts of) the world since the late twentieth century have enacted new forms of citizenship which operate at the sub-, supra- and transnational levels. Although 'This process has in many cases deepened unequal and geographically uneven access to political, civil and social rights',[46] transversal forms of engagement and participation have changed the geography of citizenship so that new spaces and discourses of citizenship are being articulated, at times as forms of contestation in response to exclusionary practices.

The citizenship of the everyday emphasizes the social and relational aspects of participation and engagement with the urban dimension and, therefore, it provides us with a particularly suitable framework in the identification of dimensions of citizenship as enacted by new city subjectivities and diasporic groups. As for existing city subjectivities (those who enjoy the rights granted by structured institutions), we shall see that place can be constructed as a constitutive aspect of a mobile and transformative citizenship and not merely as an exclusive feature of identity articulated in national terms. Evidence suggests that the mismatch of formal and substantive citizenship accounts for denationalizing discursive practices and fosters multiple outcomes which challenge the human rights system and the permanence of stable identities.

The signs that have been identified for this chapter contribute to the construction of transnational spaces in urban Italy, where the citizenship of the everyday affords groups and individuals the opportunity to employ different degrees of agency, therefore allowing them to reappropriate an active role in the life that the urban dimension affords its dwellers. It is particularly relevant for our purposes that the mix of languages involved in the formulation of invitations to events is in itself a metadiscursive device disanchoring citizenship from particular national contexts. In addition, the simultaneous deployment of diverse linguistic repertoires directly critiques existing ideologies of monolingualism (and related monoculturalism).

Zena Zuena ('young Genoa' in Genoese) featured on a poster (Figure 3.3) advertising a charity event appealing to connected, globalized and engaged youngsters.

The multilingual sign features Genoese in the title (with a primarily connotative function), Italian in its informative content (the where, what and how of the event) and English in music-related vocabulary ('concerti live and dj set'), in the phrase 'drink and food', in the website and related proper name 'redhouse', and in the 'music for peace' logo. Words such as 'festival' and 'cabaret' are established borrowings, but they contribute to the generally

---

[46] Dickinson et al., *Introduction*, p. 102.

Figure 3.3 – Poster about a charity event (Genoa).
Photograph by the author.

multicultural feel of the event, where, in addition to being entertained, it will be possible to participate in debates and film showings and taste multi-ethnic cuisine. Tickets are not bought conventionally. Rather, in an anti-capitalist stance, participants will be allowed onto the festival grounds upon the donation of *prima necessità* items (basic necessities), staple foods such as flour and rice or objects such as blankets and soap.[47]

The sign constructs a composite form of citizenship which highlights traits of agency such as pacifist, engaged, mobile, multi-ethnic, multilingual, alternative and so on. These traits are not to be understood in binary and mutually exclusive terms and therefore the suggestion of global citizenship is not in opposition to the reference to a locality (i.e., Zena/Genoa). On the contrary, the use of the dialect alongside Italian and English, together with the employment of globally recognized markers such as the rainbow in the top left-hand corner of the poster (a symbol of peace), point to an identification with a translocal identity which is both situated and connected.[48]

---

[47] Details were provided in the *Quotidiano Ligure* (n.d.), https://quotidianoligure. wordpress.com/2008/05/26/genova-presentato-zena-zuena-2008/ [accessed 19 June 2017].

[48] The term 'translocality' is used here in the sense of 'a simultaneous situatedness across different locales'. See Katherine Brickell and Ayona Datta, eds, *Translocal Geographies: Spaces, Places, Connections* (Farnham: Ashgate, 2011), p. 4.

Figure 3.4 – Church poster (Palermo). Photograph by the author.

Figure 3.4 is a sign which was displayed on a church noticeboard positioned on a main road in central Palermo. The poster is about a charity initiative to raise funds for access to clean water in Kenya. The dialectal slogan *VIVI E LASSA VIVIRI* (emphasis in the original) dominates the verbal message of the sign and is intentionally used in its double meaning. On the one hand, it is a Sicilianized version of the Italian *vivi e lascia vivere* [live and let live]; on the other hand, in dialectal Sicilian the phrase means 'drink and let drink'. Therefore the poster is directly appealing to a local audience who will decode both semantic contents of the homograph and establish the link between water and life. This link is also made at the verbal-visual level through the repeated use of bold type for the word *VIVI* (in yellow in the image). In order to capture the powerful underlying message, 'No clean water means no life', non-dialect speakers will be aided by the explanatory subtitle in Italian 'Music and cabaret to guarantee the right to water in Kenya' and by the image of the child drinking water from a bottle. The use of the local dialect in this context reinforces community ties via a call for solidarity, therefore speaking a language that is closer to their emotional and affective sphere. In addition, the universalistic message of the poster expressed in the local language challenges notions of national citizenship and assigns dialectal speakers a dynamic and transformative role, whilst constructing a metageographical space of agency which upsets common understandings of distance and proximity.

The sign reproduced in Figure 3.5 was issued by a self-defined 'anarchist' library in Rome (Biblioteca L'Idea) located in the Pigneto, once a working-class area which has been partly gentrified in recent times and has become a hub of cultural and artistic activities.[49]

The language employed in the notice about a forthcoming raffle is meant to appeal to the mixed make-up of the area, hence the use of both Roman dialect and Italian. The Roman dialect is also a means to anchor the event in local understandings of place that do not contradict the intellectual and political aspirations of the library, and which are likely to match those of a sophisticated clientele. The deliberate mix of different language varieties includes Italian, Roman dialect and English borrowings within the same sentence (*Giocate affondo perduto e spaccio dell'urtimi bijetti co' un monte de premi della distro; Merenda e cena vegan, cicchetti, vino e quello che nun vòi fa' mancà ... portalo!*), whilst other semiotic features, such as the utopian atmosphere conveyed by iconic magic and fantasy details, contribute to the construction of discourses which are critical of late modernity and official culture, and provide a platform for the performance of alternative forms of citizenship. It is noteworthy that the typographic mix constitutes a visual metalanguage which anchors the sign in worlds that are 'other', via

[49] See information in the related website of the Biblioteca L'Idea (n.d.) http://www. inventati.org/biblidea/ [accessed 16 June 2017].

Figure 3.5 – Invitation to a raffle (Rome). Photograph by the author.

letterforms and non-colours (black and white) that are reminiscent of typed material created and duplicated with old-fashioned means and which mimic cuttings from different sources to preserve anonymity – a strategy traditionally employed by anarchist and revolutionary groups in the production of political leaflets before word processing became widely available. The vaguely esoteric flavour of the image is enhanced by the use of dripping font lettering, often found in graffiti. On the whole, the semiotic features contribute to the construction of discourses which are critical of late modernity and official culture, and provide a platform for the performance of alternative forms of citizenship.

In Figures 3.3–3.5 the everyday lived as participation in a localized event is central to the construction of a new geography of citizenship which can be transformative and potentially subversive, in so far as it is in opposition to institutional understandings of rights and obligations. Complementary dimensions of group membership are exemplified by Figures 3.6–3.8, which reproduce signs displayed in the same urban settings. The citizenship of the everyday here is enacted in transnational and transcultural LLs, where the quotidian is experienced in multifaceted forms in the constant re-elaboration

Figure 3.6 – Latin-American and Arab restaurant (Genoa).
Photograph by the author.

of social relations. The use of different languages itself is integral to the discourses of contestation that they convey.

The shop sign in Figure 3.6 was found in an area of central Genoa which is characterized by high migrant presence. The establishment offers an interesting combination of Latino and Arab cuisine. The semiotics of the sign indicates a deliberate expression of a wider diasporic identity that encapsulates Latin-American and Arab identities (including a concession for Italy), and groups together different national 'signatures' represented by the individual flags (from the left, these are the Moroccan, Ecuadorian, Italian, Tunisian, Colombian and Peruvian flags). The verbal message is a creative mix of resources which draws upon Italian (*Gusto Latino E Arabo*), Spanish (*Restaurante*) and French or English (*Carthage*, although the presence of the Moroccan and Tunisian flags would suggest French as would the ancient city of Carthage, located near modern Tunis, where French is widely used). The Roman *biga* (two-horse chariot), which stands out as a bas-relief on both sides of the sign, could be interpreted as a reference to a wider Latin heritage and influence, and in this vein the background of the sign reminds us of the geometric pattern of a Roman mosaic. This would establish a link with local heritage as part of a discourse of inclusiveness. The exclusion of Arabic script would therefore point to a desire to be transparent to an Italophone audience.

The sign in Figure 3.7 was painted above a shop providing services for the Ghanaian community of Palermo. The language in this sign is Twi, one of the main (group of) languages in use in Ghana. The religious expression *Yesu ka wo ho* [Jesus loves you] is widely used in Gospel lyrics (performances are available on YouTube). The reference to religious practices is not casual. The windows of the establishment in fact displayed a variety of signs ranging from an electoral announcement to an advert about courier services and film

Figure 3.7 – Shop providing services for the Ghanaian community
(Palermo). Photograph by the author.

posters, all entirely in English, the official language of Ghana. The main sign
above the entrance signals the presence of the given group in the area and
identifies it as the main local hub of activities: people meet there, they use it
for private and public announcements and it is part of a network of hubs in
a very eventful and lively area, the market, which is frequented by all sorts
of people every day. The intertextuality and the multimediality of the signs
in the shop window construct the community via the representation of their
meaning-making practices. Socio-religious practices, such as a 'naming and
child dedication' (Figure 3.8) for a newborn baby announced by a notice
posted in the shop window, are an integral part of this process and point to
institutions (the Pentecostal Christ Apostolic Church and the Catholic Santa
Chiara) which are infrastructures of superdiversity.[50]

The 'naming and child dedication' represents a traditional rite-of-passage
event whereby the newborn's introduction into the community marks their
becoming an actual person. Rooted cultural practices will subsequently be
enacted in a space that has been transformed into a place of worship, the
Christ Apostolic Church, where the ceremony is celebrated. The party will
eventually take place at Santa Chiara, a Catholic church in the Albergheria
area that has carried out activities in support of migrant communities,
regardless of their particular faiths, since the 1980s. The given LL and its

---

[50] Blommaert, *Ethnography*, pp. 85–86.

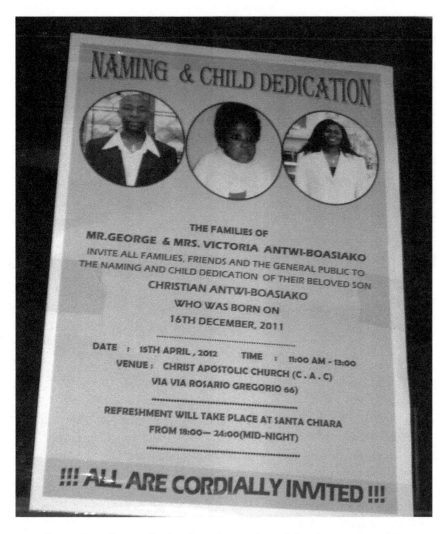

Figure 3.8 – Poster displayed on the window of the shop portrayed in
Figure 3.7. Photograph by the author.

explicit intertextuality contribute to the construction of a semiotics of participation and belonging for diasporic groups. Transcultural practices such as
introducing a newborn into the local community enable these groups to enact
citizenship as a component of the quotidian.

The signs in Figure 3.9 below were displayed in an area in the outskirts of
Rome (Tor Pignattara) with a high density of migrants. They featured Bengali,
Arabic, Italian, Spanish, English and French. The English version of the text is
reproduced here for clarity:

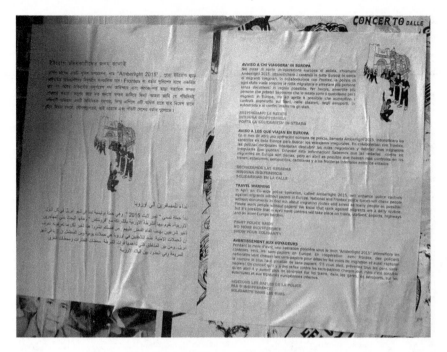

Figure 3.9 – Notice about Amberlight 2015 (Rome).
Photograph by the author.

TRAVEL WARNING
In April an EU-wide police operation, called Amberlight 2015, will enhance police controls against migrants without papers in Europe. National and Frontex [the European Border and Coast Guard Agency] police forces will chase people without documents to find out about migration routes and arrest as many people as possible. Please warn people without papers! We know that raids against migrants are a daily routine, but it's possible that in April more controls will take place on trains, stations, airports, highways and on inner-Europe borders.

FIGHT POLICE RAIDS
NO MORE INDIFFERENCE
SHOW YOUR SOLIDARITY

The text refers to the latest of several EU initiatives to curb irregular migration, called Amberlight 2015. This consisted of joint police operations targeting specific areas such as airports and internal borders in order to identify 'overstayers', that is migrants with expired visas. The text is both a

Figure 3.10 – Detail of notice about Amberlight 2015. Photograph by the author.

warning for those who are potentially at risk of being caught and a call for solidarity against this type of action.

Although the two signs display European and non-European languages separately, possibly for reasons of space, they can be considered to be part of the same 'frame' in Backhaus's terms:[51] the message is identical, the initiators and the technological source are the same (as typographical details suggest) and they address different groups and individuals who engage with similar perceptions of institutional abuse, with an emphasis on rights. In this respect, the image included in both signs sums up both the verbal text and the values it promotes (Figure 3.10).

People displaying different ethnic characteristics are standing in a human chain (representing solidarity) outside a gated city – the gate to the city resembles a tower and represents Fortress Europe. The police are walking out of the city in order to carry out checks, whilst a man who

---

[51] Peter Backhaus, *Linguistic Landscapes: A Comparative Study of Urban Multilingualism in Tokyo* (Clevedon: Multilingual Matters, 2007), p. 66.

seems to be using a mobile phone is pointing to them, probably in the act of spreading the word about checks taking place. The image is a representation of exclusionary practices as enforced by institutions and of embodied forms of resistance and contestation (or acts of turbulence) on the part of new city subjectivities.

Conclusion

Figures 3.3–3.10 exemplify a denationalizing process of meaning-making through language and other semiotic devices in the Italian LL. Emplaced local languages such as dialects characterize place as a function of citizenship experienced within movable identity borders and, on a metalinguistic level, critique monolingual normativity and enhance translanguaging, a space where identity is multiple and in the making. Transnational LLs construct dynamic spaces of agency where the politics of national belonging and self-representation as a result of structured, top-down models coexists with forms of citizenship of the everyday.[52] The LL of urban Italy also affords othered groups who experience social and spatial marginalization[53] the opportunity to create spaces of citizenship where ethnic, cultural, religious and other identities are promoted by diasporic groups and where the production of everyday reality is situated at the intersection of the transient and the familiar. Transcultural and transnational LLs therefore articulate forms of multilayered citizenship in the process of a continuous rescaling of degrees of participation from the supranational to the subnational. As such, and by continually enabling and disabling the mechanisms inherent in regimes of citizenship, LL creates spaces of contestation and empowerment in which to situate the citizenship of the everyday. These spaces challenge formally established boundaries erected by formal institutions. From this perspective, the citizenship of the everyday allows (formal) citizens to renegotiate and (re)place the obligations of citizenship, and enables non-citizens to self-enact as new political, social and civic subjects.

The deployment of linguistic repertoires as spaces of potentiality is particularly fruitful as a lens through which Italian culture(s) can be observed. Vernacular forms of verbal language which were deemed to be likely to disappear[54] are being disinvented and reconstituted (as Makoni and Pennycook

---

[52] Dickinson et al., *Introduction*, pp. 100–22.

[53] Luke Desforges, Rhys Jones and Mike Woods, 'New Geographies of Citizenship', *Citizenship Studies*, 9.5 (2005), 439–51.

[54] Gaetano Berruto, 'Quale dialetto per l'Italia del Duemila? Aspetti dell'italianizzazione e risorgenze dialettali in Piemonte (e altrove)', in *Lingua e*

put it),[55] as well as displayed in writing acts which engender spatialities of involvement.[56] These material sites of engagement provide an ideal terrain for questioning institutionalized assumptions about rights and obligations, and for rethinking notions of entitlement, belonging and participation. LL is therefore a process investing social relations rather than a display of identity based on commonality of ethnic characteristics, and it contributes to the performance of citizenship via the quotidian, experienced in its multifaceted forms and multiple encounters. Language is, therefore, a significant means of empowerment and, as summarized by Valentine, Sporton and Bang Nielsen, 'Space might shape hegemonic communicative practices, but language can also (re)order space'.[57] It is important to stress that language does not merely reflect cultural content; rather, it constructs meaning by turning the ineffable and the impossible into the realizable. Language is therefore central to a view of transnationalism as a social space inhabited by diverse actors and where alternative dimensions of citizenship are enacted in the creation and re-creation of multiple spaces of potentiality.

dialetto nell'Italia del Duemila, ed. by Alberto A. Sobrero and Annarita Miglietta (Galatina: Congedo, 2006), pp. 101–27.

[55] Sinfree Makoni and Alistair Pennycook, eds, *Disinventing and Reconstituting Languages* (Clevedon: Multilingual Matters, 2007), pp. 1–41.

[56] Amin, *Spatialities*, p. 397.

[57] Gill Valentine, Deborah Sporton and Katrine Bang Nielsen, 'Language Use on the Move: Sites of Encounter, Identities and Belonging', *Transactions of the Institute of British Geographers*, 33 (2008), 376–87 (p. 385).

4

Transnational Flows
and Translanguaging Repertoires

Exploring Multilingualism and Migration in Contemporary Italy*

Naomi Wells

Introduction

Multilingualism and migration are not new phenomena and, as illustrated across the series of which this volume is part, remain a constant in human history. Nevertheless, studying these subjects in the contemporary context of intensified cultural flows and new patterns of human mobility requires distinct methodological and theoretical approaches. It also relates directly to the context in which we live, research and study, requiring us to maintain a heightened awareness of our own subjectivity and position in relation to those with whom we research.

Following an introduction to terms that illustrate the complexity of contemporary migration patterns and multilingual repertoires, this chapter explores what can be gained by exploring multilingualism and migration in a specific place and time. Drawing on ethnographically oriented fieldwork with migrant communities in the city of Bologna, I focus on the teaching

* The research conducted in Bologna reported here would not have been possible without the insight offered by the individuals and associations who generously gave their time to talk to me and also welcomed me into their community spaces. I am also grateful for the invaluable help and support of the staff of the Centro Zonarelli who hosted me during my fieldwork. The research was made possible by the funding of the AHRC as part of the Translating Cultures large grant 'Transnationalizing Modern Language: Mobility, Identity and Translation in Modern Italian Cultures', as well as the support and advice of the wider project team, and particularly my mentor on the project, Jennifer Burns. I would also like to acknowledge the insights offered by the undergraduate students at the University of Warwick, who illustrated in practice how such research could be adapted to form part of their own modern languages degrees.

of community language to younger generations and more specifically on the motivations of parents and those involved in organizing these courses. The chapter concludes by addressing how similar engagements with students' multilingual environments can be integrated into undergraduate programmes of study in order to further students' understandings of their own and others' multilingual subjectivities.

New Lenses and Theories: Superdiversity, Translanguaging and Transnationalism

In recent years, new terms have arisen which offer new ways of under-standing the contemporary context of migratory flows and related language practices. The term 'superdiversity', for example, is intended to emphasize the greater diversity in the countries of origins of migrants, particularly in European urban contexts.[1] While previous migration patterns tended to be more permanent and involved large numbers originating from a limited set of countries and settling in the same location, newer patterns of migration tend to be more mobile, with less of a tendency for single groups to dominate. Critics of superdiversity have questioned whether such diversity is an entirely 'new' phenomenon, but it would appear to be a useful term for understanding new migratory patterns and the diversity in countries of origin among migrants to contemporary Italy. In particular, superdi-versity emphasizes the unpredictability of migrants' origins and profiles, which broad 'national' or 'ethnic' descriptions fail to capture. In relation to language, for example, it is much harder to make assumptions about profi-ciency and the types of languages known by individuals when migration trajectories involve movement across multiple cities, regions and states.[2] This can lead to the development of extremely complex multilingual reper-toires, which consist of varying levels of fluency and literacy in a number of languages and varieties.

A focus on linguistic repertoires made up of 'bits' of various languages, rather than an emphasis on fluency or 'native' proficiency in one or two specific languages, brings us to the 'translanguaging' orientation. Just as superdiversity questions the usefulness of focusing on single 'ethnic' or 'national' categories, translanguaging highlights how treating languages as clearly separate named entities (e.g., Italian, English, French, etc.) fails to adequately reflect how

---

[1] Fran Meissner and Steven Vertovec, 'Comparing Super-Diversity', *Ethnic and Racial Studies*, 38.4 (2015), 541–55.

[2] Jan Blommaert and Ben Rampton, 'Language and Superdiversity', *Superdiversities*, 13 (2011), 1–22.

people use language.[3] Translanguaging emphasizes that, in practice, multi-lingual speakers will often draw upon their wider range of linguistic resources to communicate and produce meaning, selecting resources which may traditionally have been defined as belonging to discrete and separate languages.[4] Furthermore, a translanguaging perspective highlights that even so-called 'native speakers' never possess the entirety of their supposed 'native' language. No English speaker, for example, can ever know all of the vocabulary of every register and variety of English; instead, what each speaker possesses are 'bits' of language which together make up their individual repertoire.

While certain elements of one's repertoire may overlap with others, each individual's repertoire is personal and unique, and is tied to their biography and, in some cases, their migration trajectory. The ways in which people maintain transnational connections across multiple locations also affect the make-up of individual linguistic repertoires. Technological developments and the greater ease with which people are able to travel and communicate across geographically dispersed communities provide new opportunities for individuals and groups to maintain connections which stretch to multiple sites and people across the globe.[5] In sum, both this (super)diversification of societies and the ways in which individuals sustain transnational ties have inevitable consequences for how linguistic resources are transmitted, picked up, used and perceived. Given the distinct and complex migration trajectories and linguistic repertoires of each individual, however, it is impossible to make generalizations about precisely what these consequences may be.

Beyond Methodological Nationalism

This leads us to ask how we can investigate the complexity of this contemporary context. Even when we take a single state context, such as Italy, as our focus of study, we are still faced with challenges in attempting to provide generic descriptions which apply across hugely diverse migration contexts. The make-up of the migrant populations in each city or town differs significantly across Italy, each individual bringing with them distinct linguistic and

---

[3] Ofelia García and Li Wei, *Translanguaging: Language, Bilingualism and Education* (Basingstoke and New York: Palgrave Macmillan, 2014); Ricardo Otheguy, Ofelia García and Wallis Reid, 'Clarifying Translanguaging and Deconstructing Named Languages: A Perspective from Linguistics', *Applied Linguistics Review*, 6.3 (2015), 281–307.

[4] Angela Creese and Adrian Blackledge, 'Translanguaging and Identity in Educational Settings', *Annual Review of Applied Linguistics*, 35 (2015), 20–35.

[5] Steven Vertovec, *Transnationalism* (London and New York: Routledge, 2009).

cultural repertoires.[6] Equally, the existing local population with whom they enter into contact and live alongside will also have distinct repertoires, for example with the so-called Italian 'dialects' or regional languages still widely used in some areas and almost invisible in others.[7]

As a result, we must begin by acknowledging that our understanding of this complex linguistic context will only ever be partial and that we can never make claims to being complete or exhaustive. Once we abandon claims to generalizability or comprehensiveness, however, we start to see paths of inquiry opening up, by focusing not on a whole national context but on specific sites and the situated linguistic and cultural practices which occur within them. This is not to say that the wider national context or national identities are ignored, but the focus is instead on how these are negotiated or enter into play in specific contexts, alongside the local, the transnational and the global.[8]

It is here that research methods influenced by an ethnographic perspective can provide a grounded approach to making sense of the situated practices of individuals and groups. Ethnographic approaches typically involve research methods such as observation, participation and interviews,[9] and most importantly require the researcher to focus closely on a specific time and place. It may appear contradictory to focus on a specific place when studying mobility and migration, but a focus on place reminds us that these movements and the related patterns of multilingual language use still take place in concrete spaces, where people live and interact. When people move and migrate, they do not do so through 'empty' or 'neutral' spaces, but through spaces which have their own norms, expectations and judgements. Or, as Blommaert and Jie explain, 'what works well in one place can backfire elsewhere'.[10] Students

---

[6] Marina Chini, 'New Linguistic Minorities: Repertoires, Language Maintenance and Shift', *International Journal of the Sociology of Language*, 210 (2011), https://doi.org/10.1515/ijsl.2011.030.

[7] Istat, *L'uso della lingua italiana, dei dialetti e di altre lingue in Italia (anno 2012)*, 2014 http://www.istat.it/it/files/2014/10/Lingua-italiana-e-dialetti_PC.pdf?title=Lingua+italiana%2C+dialetti+e+altre+lingue+-+27%2Fott%2F2014+-+Testo+integrale.pdf [accessed 29 August 2017].

[8] Anna Amelina et al., eds, *Beyond Methodological Nationalism: Research Methodologies for Cross-Border Studies* (New York and London: Routledge, 2014).

[9] Jan Blommaert and Jie Dong, *Ethnographic Fieldwork: A Beginner's Guide* (Bristol: Multilingual Matters, 2010); Celia Roberts et al., *Language Learners as Ethnographers* (Clevedon: Multilingual Matters, 2001).

[10] Jan Blommaert and Jie Dong, 'Language and Movement in Space', in *The Handbook of Language and Globalization*, ed. by Nikolas Coupland (Oxford: Wiley-Blackwell, 2010), pp. 366–85 (p. 381).

who at home use a different language to the dominant language of formal education, for example, are often aware of implicit, and in many cases explicit, expectations that they not use their home language in the classroom.

An ethnographic orientation can also help us to value the voices and experiences of individuals who are themselves embedded within wider social structures. The aim of ethnographic research is not to seek out 'typical' cases which can be used to generalize about whole 'national' or 'ethnic' communities; instead, the aim is to produce what Rampton and others describe as 'theoretically "telling" cases'.[11] At the same time, by focusing on the specific context in which specific individuals are located, we are able to see how their singular experiences fit into wider patterns and structures.

The Teaching of the 'Mother Language' in Bologna

While migration to Italy has been a focus of attention in recent decades, the discussion has been dominated by an 'emergency' or 'crisis' discourse of migration. Often neglected are the longer-term practices of linguistic and cultural adaptation among those who migrate and the local residents alongside whom they live. In order to explore and understand these more 'everyday' practices, my own research focused on the city of Bologna and, more specifically, on the Centro Interculturale Massimo Zonarelli used by a large number of migrant and intercultural associations in the city. The city of Bologna has seen migration from a range of countries, with Eastern Europe the primary area of origin in recent years, and earlier periods with significant migration from Italy's former colonies of Eritrea and Somalia starting from the 1970s, and from the Maghreb and particularly Morocco from the 1980s. Other large populations in the city include those originating from China, the Philippines, Senegal, Nigeria, Bangladesh and Peru.[12] Most notable, however,

[11] Ben Rampton, Janet Maybin and Celia Roberts, 'Theory and Method in Linguistic Ethnography', in *Linguistic Ethnography: Interdisciplinary Explorations*, ed. by Julia Snell, Sara Shaw and Fiona Copland (Basingstoke: Palgrave Macmillan, 2015), pp. 14–50 (p. 16).

[12] Asher Colombo, Debora Mantovani and Valerio Vanelli, *Cittadini stranieri in Provincia di Bologna: Caratteristiche e tendenze* (Bologna: Osservatorio delle Immigrazioni della Provincia di Bologna and Fondazione di ricerca Istituto Carlo Cattaneo, 2014), https://www.cittametropolitana.bo.it/sanitasociale/Engine/RAServeFile.php/f/Documenti/Cittadini_stranieri_in_provincia_di_Bologna_caratteristiche_e_tendenze.pdf [accessed 20 June 2018]; Comune di Bologna, *Cittadini Stranieri a Bologna. Le tendenze 2014* (Bologna: Settore Statistico, 2015), http://www.comune.bologna.it/iperbole/piancont/Stranieri/StudiStranieri/Stranieri_aBo/2015/Stranieri_2014_12.pdf [accessed 20 June 2018].

is the diversity in countries of origin and, consequently, it would seem appropriate to describe the city as a superdiverse urban environment.

As a site of daily encounters and everyday cultural exchanges between multiple migrant communities and local residents, the Centro Zonarelli offered rich, if inevitably partial, insights into broader processes affecting contemporary Italy, namely recent migratory flows and new forms of societal multilingualism. Here it is not possible to give a full account of the Centro and its many users; however, to give a brief overview, the Centro is owned by Bologna's City Council and its primary function is to offer a space free of charge to cultural associations with an 'intercultural' focus. In practice, this means associations run either by or for migrant communities who, with very little intervention, determine what takes place in the various spaces of the Centro. As a result, a huge range of activities take place, such as theatre workshops, cookery classes, dance courses and more. Some of these activities involve participants of both Italian and migrant origin, while others are run by single-nationality associations and are directed primarily at members of that community.

One of the primary activities that many single-nationality associations lead at the Centro are the 'Scuole di Lingue Madri' [Mother Language Schools], which in other locations are often termed community language or complementary schools. These courses are run almost entirely on a voluntary basis and represent a significant investment of time, typically at weekends, for those involved. The languages taught by a range of associations include Arabic, Spanish, Tamil, Tigrinya and Amharic. Classes are primarily aimed at younger members of these communities born and educated in Italy or who arrived in Italy at a young age, who are often termed the 'second generation'. Although only representing one aspect of the Centro's activities, this example illustrates the insights gained by taking a closer look at what the teaching of these languages in this specific place and time means to those involved in these courses. While there are studies of language use and attitudes within specific migrant communities in different cities and towns in Italy,[13] as well as more quantitative investigations of language maintenance,[14] the role of

---

[13] See, for example, Federica Guerini, *Language Alternation Strategies in Multilingual Settings: A Case Study: Ghanaian Immigrants in Northern Italy*, European University Studies (Bern and New York: Peter Lang, 2006); Gerardo Mazzaferro, 'Language Maintenance within New Linguistic Minorities in Italy: A Translanguaging Perspective', in *Translanguaging as Everyday Practice*, ed. by Gerardo Mazzaferro (Cham: Springer, 2018), pp. 87–106; Maya Smith, 'Multilingual Practices of Senegalese Immigrants in Rome: Construction of Identities and Negotiation of Boundaries', *Italian Culture*, 33.2 (2015), 126–46.

[14] See, for example, Marina Chini, ed., *Plurilinguismo e immigrazione in Italia:*

courses like these in the Italian context, and more specifically the motivations of parents and those who organize them, remain largely unexplored.

The respondents included here belonged to two of the most prominent and long-standing associations based at the Centro. Mohamed Rafia Boukhbiza and Antonella Selva lead the Moroccan-Italian Sopra i Ponti Association, which was involved in organizing some of the first Arabic courses at the Centro Zonarelli. Their own children attended these courses and they have played a prominent role in supporting the wider network of Scuole di Lingue Madri through the association's political and cultural activism. Hend Ahmed, of Egyptian origin, and Hajiba Radouane, originally from Morocco, draw primarily on their own parenting experiences. They were also attached to a mixed women's association, Annassim, of which Hend was president, and which was extremely active in political and cultural activism across the city.

As the most widely taught language in the city, the following examples focus primarily on the teaching of Arabic, but the research also involved observing classes and talking to teachers and parents who spoke and/ or taught other languages, such as Tigrinya and Spanish. Interviews were carried out towards the end of fieldwork, with my own questions and prompts informed by earlier observations and oriented towards topics which had attracted my attention. This approach allowed me to draw connections between reported and observed practices, with the interviews understood as one element of a broader engagement with the context which informs the following analysis.

Negotiating Intergenerational Differences
Particularly with their designation as mother language schools, these courses may initially appear to be a fairly straightforward attempt to maintain a community's identity and cultural heritage through the transmission of the community's primary language. Closer attention through observation of classes and a series of interviews reveals, however, the more complex and multiple motivations of those involved. The undeniably emotive but potentially misleading term 'mother language',[15] for example, suggests that the language being taught is already well-known to these pupils, and that there

---

Un'indagine sociolinguistica a Pavia e Torino (Milan: F. Angeli, 2004); Francesco Goglia and Veronica Fincati, 'Immigrant Languages and the Veneto Dialect in the Linguistic Repertoires of Secondary School Pupils of Immigrant Origin in the Veneto Region', *Studi Italiani di Linguistica Teorica ed Applicata*, XLV (2017), 497–517.

[15] Yasemin Yildiz, *Beyond the Mother Tongue: The Postmonolingual Condition* (New York: Fordham University Press, 2012).

is a continuity between parents of migrant origin and their children in terms of sharing the same linguistic and cultural repertoires. However, the reality for children living and educated in Italy is that there are what Vertovec has described as 'distinct transnational orientations' between parents and children.[16] These can be the cause of tension as parents and children attempt to reconcile their distinct linguistic practices and resources, which are the result of their experiences of early socialization and education in very different linguistic environments.

In many cases, while students may have some familiarity with oral varieties of the 'mother language' used in the home, receiving their formal education in Italian means students are likely to have a more limited familiarity with standard written varieties. This illustrates the reality of repertoires made up not of 'whole' languages but of varying levels of fluency and literacy in different language varieties and modes. This was particularly salient in Arabic classes, where the language spoken at home by the family was typically a very distinct national or regional variety of Arabic, while previous contact with standard or classical Arabic, which is taught as the theoretical 'mother language', is rarer. As explained in a booklet describing some of the early experiences of one of these schools: 'Non si trattava quindi di motivare il non abbandono di una lingua materna poco praticata, ma di affrontare a tutti gli effetti una lingua 2, anche se con qualche conoscenza di base' [It was not a case of encouraging the maintenance of a rarely practiced maternal language, then, but of confronting what was in all respects a second language, albeit with some basic knowledge].[17] Furthermore, teachers face challenges in finding appropriate teaching resources, particularly for less widely spoken languages not supported by existing resources for teaching the language outside of the countries of origin. For example, the Tigrinya school had to rely on copies of teaching materials from Eritrea which were designed for pupils who would have more daily contact with the language than those living in Italy.

On this subject, it is important to note that the teachers and parents interviewed were acutely aware of these challenges and clearly did not position these classes as an attempt to recreate or transpose the classroom in the country of origin. This is reflected most clearly in comments from Mohamed Rafia, the president of a Moroccan-Italian association who repeatedly emphasized the importance of responding to the specific lived experiences of children raised in Italy:

[16] Vertovec, *Transnationalism*, p. 63.

[17] Sopra i Ponti, *La costruzione della doppia appartenenza nei bambini arabi-italiani. Un'esperienza di attività laboratoriale extrascuola alla ludoteca del Centro Zonarelli di Bologna* (Bologna, 2004), p. 5.

Extract 1[18]

Mohamed Rafia: È questo il caso, insomma no, di insegnare l'arabo, che viene un insegnante dal Marocco, dal Marocco, che non conosce la- la realtà italiana. E viene inserito in un ambiente dove deve insegnare l'arabo, al bambino nato in Italia. E chi è sradicato in questo caso? È sradicato in questo caso è l'insegnante, che non ha- li manca una metà delle cose, li manca- li manca la cultura di quel bambino, che non è marocchino. Lui è nato qua e parte qua, quindi non è preparato.

[This is the case, well, you know, of teaching Arabic, that a teacher from Morocco comes, from Morocco, who doesn't know the– the Italian reality. And he's inserted into an environment where he has to teach Arabic, to the child born in Italy. And who is uprooted in this case? It's the teacher who is uprooted in this case, that doesn't have– who lacks half of things, he lacks– he lacks the culture of that child, who isn't Moroccan. He is born here and starts from here, and so (the teacher) is not prepared]

Rafia emphasizes the importance of responding to the specific needs of children educated in Italy, with Arabic teachers needing to understand the children's distinct and hybrid cultural and linguistic repertoires developed as a result of early socialization across multiple cultural fields,[19] rather than attempting to recreate an idealized model of the 'native' speaker as in the country of origin.

In practice, the teachers observed were often community members who themselves were bringing up their own children in Italy, this overlapping role meaning they were able to draw on their experiences as parents in responding to students' multilingual repertoires. This was evident in observations of some of the classes, where not just pupils but also teachers would move between Italian and the 'mother language' for instructions and discussions, illustrating the translanguaging practices common in such environments where speakers draw from across their repertoires to communicate and produce meaning. Further 'bits' of language varieties were also sometimes used, such as different varieties of Arabic, with the differences between the Tunisian and Moroccan varieties a cause of discussion initiated by the teacher in one class. In this

[18] All extracts are transcribed to reflect the spoken language of the informal interview setting, as is common practice in linguistics research. Translations are mine.

[19] Vertovec, *Transnationalism*, p. 7.

sense, the teacher was drawing attention to the differences between individual students' repertoires and highlighting the existing linguistic resources that students brought to the classroom. As has been noted in relation to community language schools in the UK, these classrooms are often spaces of regular and relatively fluid movements across languages, what we might describe as 'translanguaging spaces' in which multilingual language users can draw and also reflect on their full range of linguistic resources.[20] While also dependent, as Rafia highlights, on the approach of individual teachers, such social spaces have the potential to provide students with opportunities to translate and negotiate across their hybrid linguistic and cultural repertoires.

On a related note, parents' desire to ensure that their children also have some knowledge of these languages in their written form as part of their repertoires was often connected to the transnational ties to family in the country of origin and, where political and family circumstances allowed, to extended visits back to that country:

Extract 2

Hajiba: Noi, quello dialetto si parla a casa, per forza. E poi quando erano piccoli io stavo a casa, vado giù in ferie dai miei. Sto il più lungo possibile. Facevo il lavoro che mi permetteva di stare tutto l'estate. Così li lasciavo con la famiglia e con i cugini, e parlano là, il dialetto lo parlano benissimo. Ma vogliamo anche che lo scrivono. Se andiamo a un ristorante, leggono il menu, se l'autostrada ci sono i cartelli in arabo, tante cose per loro.

[Us, that dialect is spoken at home, absolutely. And then when they were small I was at home and I go down in the holidays to stay with my family. I stay as long as possible. I did work that allowed me to stay there all summer. That way I'd leave them with the family and with their cousins, and they speak it there, they speak the dialect really well. But we also want them to write it. If we go to a restaurant, they read the menu, if on the motorway there are signs in Arabic, so many things for them]

---

[20] Li Wei, 'Moment Analysis and Translanguaging Space: Discursive Construction of Identities by Multilingual Chinese Youth in Britain', *Journal of Pragmatics*, 43.5 (2011), 1222–35.

Extract 3

Hend [discussing why it is important for children to learn to read and write Arabic when visiting their parents' country of origin]: Così vanno in giro da soli, riescono. E nessuno li prende in giro perché se ti dà un foglio tu dici, io capisco cos'è. E non sai mai se stai qua per tutta la vita o vai giù di nuovo.

[This way they go around on their own, they manage to. And nobody makes fun of them because if someone gives you a piece of paper you say, I understand what it is. And you never know if you're here all your life or if you go south again]

The similar motivations given in these separate interviews highlight how the transnational ties and bonds which many individuals and communities maintain across national borders, as well as more mobile and potentially temporary patterns of migration, can contribute to both the motivations and opportunities for continuing to learn and use these languages. In attempting to ensure a greater alignment between their own and their children's linguistic repertoires, these parents actively sought to maintain their children's transnational ties and connections to their own country of origin. At the same time, the transmission of these languages was not concerned merely with maintaining a connection to the past but also to the present and, given the unpredictability of the migratory trajectory highlighted by Hend, to possible futures where these languages may again become more salient in their children's lives.

Strategies and Spaces of Resistance
Parents highlighted the challenges of living transnationally and of finding ways to negotiate these intergenerational differences, particularly in a context where their own linguistic and cultural expertise are rarely valued in their own workplaces and in their children's formal school environments. As a result, the motivations of parents, teachers and organizers go beyond questions of linguistic proficiency and correspond also to the histories and experiences of marginalization faced by migrant communities. Experiences of marginalization differ across both communities and individuals, but the exclusion of migrant citizens from positions of authority, as well as being documented in various studies,[21] was a notable structural feature visible in

---

[21] Colombo, Mantovani and Vanelli, *Cittadini stranieri*; Ministero del Lavoro e delle Politiche Sociali, *Quarto rapporto annuale: Gli immigrati nel mercato del lavoro in Italia* (Rome: Direzione Generale dell'Immigrazione e delle Politiche di

my own observations and also discussed across interviews and conversations during fieldwork. One of the main points that emerged in interviews and class observations was the importance of these schools in placing members of the migrant community in positions of knowledge and authority from which they are often absent within the Italian context. This was emphasized by Antonella, who played an active role in coordinating some of the first Arabic courses at the Centro Zonarelli. She also made reference to my own British context to highlight what she perceived as the more heightened inequalities in Italy:

Extract 4

Antonella: Penso che da voi sia più avanzata la situazione, cioè da voi esistono già probabilmente insegnanti di provenienza immigrata. Mentre qua è- al momento è ancora quasi impossibile e quindi un bambino non incontra mai una persona della origine della sua famiglia in una posizione autorevole.

[I think that where you're from the situation is more advanced, that is to say where you're from there are probably already teachers from immigrant backgrounds. While here it's– at the moment it's still almost impossible and so a child never meets a person from the same background as their family in a position of authority]

Antonella refers primarily here to the role of the teacher, but Hajiba also mentioned the importance of parents and other family members being able to help with homework from these courses as a rare opportunity to see their own expertise valued in the eyes of their children. This illustrates how economic and political marginalization is closely interwoven with cultural and linguistic concerns.

On a related note, Hajiba positioned these courses more explicitly as a response to the restrictive political context for migrant communities, thinking particularly of the lack of citizenship rights for those born in Italy. In Italy, citizenship laws have infamously primarily followed the principle of *jus sanguinis*, meaning citizenship by blood, rather than that of *jus soli*, citizenship by place of birth.[22] This has meant children born in Italy to parents

Integrazione, 2014), https://www.anpalservizi.it/documents/20181/73483/IV_Rapporto_annuale_MdL_immigrati_2014.pdf/c9d1d9a6-4db3-46a1-9c46-1d72e4ba631c [accessed 20 June 2018].

[22] Georgia E. Bianchi, 'Italiani Nuovi o Nuova Italia? Citizenship and Attitudes

who are not Italian citizens are legally treated as 'foreign' residents until they are able to apply for citizenship at the age of 18. After detailing the restrictions placed on both migrants and their children, Hajiba explained how these language courses respond to this exclusionary, and inevitably racialized, context in which children risk 'feeling marginal in both places':[23]

Extract 5

Hajiba: Questo ha creato nei nostri figli il senso di non appartenere da nessuna parte perché a casa nostra sono stranieri perché sono nati qua, sono cresciuti qua. Lì non conoscono niente, non sanno niente, a parte la famiglia, non-. E qua vengono così trattati e rifiutati in certo modo. Non lo so, per me non va bene.

Me: No no no, capisco esattamente che è molto difficile. Mi sembrano importanti questi corsi di arabo anche per avere uno spazio per la comunità di incontrar- incontrarsi?

Hajiba: No, ma anche ricuperare un po' d'iden- identità, dare al bimbo quell'identità che- che questo paese non le dà. Intanto si sente- lo fanno sentire straniero, lo fanno sentire-. Allora noi cerchiamo di farlo comunque avere una cultura nostra, avere una lingua nostra. Tu non sei perso, anche questo è l'origine. Tu almeno credi chi sei da questo albero, e poi vediamo nel futuro cosa offre questa terra.

[Hajiba: This has created in our children a sense of not belonging anywhere because where we're from they're foreigners because they were born here, they grew up here. There they don't know about anything, they don't know anything, apart from the family, they don't–. And here they are treated like this and in a certain way rejected. I don't know, for me this isn't right.

Me: No no no, I understand completely that it's very difficult. These Arabic courses seem important to me, too, for the community to have a chance to mee– meet up?

towards the Second Generation in Contemporary Italy', *Journal of Modern Italian Studies*, 16.3 (2011), 321–33.

[23] Marjorie Faulstich Orellana et al., 'Transnational Childhoods: The Participation of Children in Processes of Family Migration', *Social Problems*, 48.4 (2001), 572–79 (p. 583).

Hajiba: No, but also to recover some sense of iden– identity, to give the child that identity that– that this country won't give them. For now they feel– they make them feel foreign, they make them feel–. So we try to make them have in any case a culture of our own, to have a language of our own. You are not lost, this is also your origin. You at least believe that you're from this tree, and then we'll see in the future what this land offers]

Hajiba highlights the contradictions faced by children born to parents of migrant origin in Italy, educated and living in a context which 'assigns to [them] a single language while prohibiting [them] from appropriating it'.[24]

Furthermore, we see here how discussions about language are never 'just' about language. Discourses surrounding language are connected to highly politicized and racialized questions of citizenship, identity and national belonging. Hajiba's comments illustrate the dialogic and intertextual nature of language in context, or what is often referred to as 'discourse'. As Blackledge establishes, 'a text is always aware of, responding to, and anticipating other texts'.[25] The extract from Hajiba's interview, with the interview understood as a form of text, illustrates this point. The motivations for ensuring that her own children learn Arabic are framed as a direct response to restrictive citizenship and migration laws, as well as associated media, political and societal discourses of discrimination which the unspecified subject in the phrase 'lo fanno sentire straniero' appears to reference.

This positioning of these language schools within a broader social and political context of marginalization was further emphasized at an event in February 2015, organized jointly by the wider network of cultural associations involved in the teaching of these languages to celebrate UNESCO's International Mother Language Day. The event was titled 'Lingue Madri: Pratiche di Cittadinanza Attiva' [Mother Languages: Practices of Active Citizenship], which highlights its clear political purpose in attempting to 'talk back'[26] to dominant political and media discourses that have repeatedly positioned Italian as the sole language of citizenship in Italy.[27] Paying attention

---

[24] Jacques Derrida, *The Monolingualism of the Other: The Prosthesis of Origin*, trans. by Patrick Mensah (Stanford: Stanford University Press, 1998), p. 27.

[25] Adrian Blackledge, 'Critical Discourse Analysis', in *The Blackwell Guide to Research Methods in Bilingualism and Multilingualism*, ed. by Li Wei and Melissa G. Moyer (Oxford: Blackwell, 2009), pp. 296–310 (p. 304).

[26] Graziella Parati, *Migration Italy: The Art of Talking Back in a Destination Culture* (Toronto: University of Toronto Press, 2005).

[27] Stephanie V. Love, 'Language Testing, "Integration" and Subtractive Multilingualism

to the local context, the politically engaged culture of the city of Bologna also appears to facilitate these strategies of 'talking back', as illustrated by the fact that the Mother Language Day event was hosted by the city's central public library. Equally, migrant-led associations are supported by the existence of the city-run Centro, which provides a space in which migrant communities can both gather and build networks of solidarity across communities, which in turn are particularly important in contexts of superdiversity where smaller migrant communities may find it more challenging to sustain such efforts and, in particular, be heard.

In this sense, we see the agency of individual actors in initiating and sustaining these activities in the face of restrictive policies and exclusionary discourses. While our attention is often drawn to dominant media and political discourses, the ethnographic approach allows us to understand how these are actually experienced and responded to within a specific set of circumstances. We see, for example, that a focus on the local and the transnational does not mean ignoring the effects of wider national discourses and policies, which are particularly salient for those of migrant origin whose residency and/or citizenship status is dependent on the regulating power of the state. We also see how these individuals find unique ways to respond to highly discriminatory and restrictive contexts of migration, carving out opportunities to create their own spaces and strategies of resistance, which here include the teaching and transmission of languages other than Italian. Equally, in continuing to use and transmit these languages alongside Italian, we see how parents are 'obliged to come to terms with and to make something new of the cultures they inhabit, without simply assimilating to them'.[28]

Exploring Multilingual Subjectivities

Before drawing to a close, it is important to highlight that ethnographic approaches involve an active reflection on the researcher's own positioning and experiences. All research requires reflexivity on how one's inevitably subjective engagement shapes the research, but this is particularly heightened in the emplaced and embodied experience of fieldwork and ethnographic encounters. For, as Puri notes, 'When a researcher reads in a library, nobody is reading her back. When one reads in the field, one is constantly being scripted, being made the object of a counter-gaze, and is thereby forced to

in Italy: Challenges for Adult Immigrant Second Language and Literacy Education', *Current Issues in Language Planning*, 16.1–2 (2015), 26–42.

[28] Stuart Hall, 'Culture, Community, Nation', *Cultural Studies*, 7.3 (1993), 349–63 (p. 362).

confront not only one's geographical but also one's historical location'.[29] Fieldwork is thus a necessarily reflexive experience, with one's own role as observer, participant and interviewer inevitably and unavoidably contributing to how those contexts and encounters are shaped and develop. The interview, for example, is not a neutral context, but a site in which certain kinds of identities are presented and a certain type of discourse is co-constructed by interviewer and interviewee.[30]

To return to the interviews above, in Extract 4 we see in the comment 'penso che da voi ...' a clear reference to my positioning as an 'outsider' to this specific context. At the same time, this extract highlights how being an 'outsider' can be useful for eliciting longer explanations and clarifications which are rich with detail and insight. In Extract 5, my own interjection and prompt question also highlights my active role in the interview. While potentially interpreted as 'leading', such prompts are common in less-structured interviews, and Hajiba's response illustrates the potential for interviewees to contradict the interviewer's interpretation rather than passively agreeing.[31] The forcefulness of Hajiba's response further highlights her efforts to explain to me the contexts of marginalization in which she and her children were operating, and which were very clearly distant from my own lived experiences. Focusing specifically on the subject of these 'mother language' classrooms heightened my awareness of the very distinct experience of having English, both the language of my formal education and an unavoidably global language, as my own home language, as well as being an unchallenged 'native' speaker of that language – an experience which is inarguably connected to a privileged racial positioning.[32]

Ethnographically oriented research thus provides not just insight into the lives of others but also space to reflect on one's own biography in interaction with those with whom we research. Particularly when conducting language-related research and doing so across multiple languages, it can offer insight into one's own subjectivity as a language learner who lives, studies and works

[29] Shalini Puri, 'Finding the Field: Notes on Caribbean Cultural Criticism, Area Studies, and the Forms of Engagement', in *Theorizing Fieldwork in the Humanities*, ed. by Debra A. Castillo and Shalini Puri (New York: Palgrave Macmillan, 2016), pp. 29–50 (p. 40).

[30] Anna De Fina, 'Researcher and Informant Roles in Narrative Interactions: Constructions of Belonging and Foreign-Ness', *Language in Society*, 40.1 (2011), 27–38 (p. 30).

[31] Fiona Copland and Angela Creese, *Linguistic Ethnography: Collecting, Analysing and Presenting Data* (Los Angeles: SAGE, 2015), p. 33.

[32] Alastair Pennycook, *Unexpected Places: Language and Mobility* (Bristol: Multilingual Matters, 2012), p. 94.

in multilingual environments. Such reflexivity is rarely addressed among those of us who study and research on Italy from the UK, a position which requires us to adopt a hybrid stance as both insider and outsider through a level of immersion in the Italian language and culture.[33] An awareness of the transnational nature of the Italian language and culture, which in no place or time has existed in isolation from other languages and cultures, also requires us to confront the limitations of our own cultural and linguistic repertoires. While it is inevitable when working in multilingual contexts that the researcher is unlikely to speak all of the languages of potential interviewees, it is nevertheless undeniable that my own positioning and the type of information I gathered would have differed had I been able to conduct interviews in Arabic, for example. Accounting for the partial nature of the information we gather is central to the ethnographic process of knowledge gathering and can be a critical learning experience which encourages a greater receptiveness in relation to the knowledge of those with whom we engage and research.

Conducting extended ethnographic fieldwork is unlikely to be viable at the level of undergraduate study. Nevertheless, a modern languages degree does offer opportunities to implement aspects of the intersubjective experience of ethnographic research, such as during the year abroad. Roberts and others have demonstrated how the curriculum and year abroad can be shaped to include more formal ethnographic projects, which have been incorporated into some modern languages programmes in the UK.[34] However, students do not need to travel abroad to undertake such research, with opportunities to draw instead upon the wider multilingual environment in which they live and study, as well as their own transnational connections. Both the university campus and the towns or cities in which we live offer opportunities to meet Italian and multilingual speakers, and consequently potential interviewees who may be willing to reflect on their own language practices, repertoires and attitudes. Technological affordances can also provide the opportunity to conduct online interviews, for example with friends met during one's year abroad.

In addition to encouraging a greater engagement with our surrounding multilingual environments, and the role of Italian within these transnational contexts, conducting an ethnographically oriented interview offers an ideal, and practical, opportunity to explore how our own role and positioning

---

[33] Beverley Mullings, 'Insider or Outsider, Both or Neither: Some Dilemmas of Interviewing in a Cross-Cultural Setting', *Geoforum*, 30.4 (1999), 337–50.

[34] Roberts et al., *Language Learners as Ethnographers*; University of Southampton, *Ethnographic Encounters Project: Cultural Knowledge for Language Learners*, https://generic.wordpress.soton.ac.uk/ethnographicencounters/ [accessed 27 August 2017].

contributes to shaping the context and discourse produced within them. While evidently on a smaller scale and not allowing for the same contextual knowledge as more in-depth and extended ethnographic study, reflecting on the limitations of such research can also be approached as a critical learning experience. Interview data, particularly where it is not possible to combine such data with participant observation, must be analysed with an awareness that people's self-presentation and practices reported in interviews may differ to their more spontaneous actions observed in practice. Equally, a single interview should not be treated as representative of a whole community and culture, but instead should encourage critical reflection on individual experiences and repertoires, and can reveal what broader attempts to define a whole 'national' culture or community may neglect or obscure.

Conclusion

This chapter has offered an overview of theoretical and methodological approaches to studying contemporary migration flows and related multilingual practices and repertoires in Italy, by emphasizing the value of focusing on the situated practices and discourses of individuals within a specific context. While not representative of the whole national context, my research in Bologna offered insight into lived experiences of migration and the role language can play in relation to how families negotiate their distinct transnational orientations, as well as how language intersects with political and media discourses concerning questions of citizenship, identity and belonging. In this sense, we see how questions of language are inextricably bound up with wider political, social and cultural issues, as well as how individuals respond agentively to dominant discourses and restrictive migratory contexts.

Thus, while large-scale language surveys may be able to give us a broader picture of the languages spoken across Italy, they tell us little about the complex motivations for why such languages continue to be used and transmitted. Adopting an ethnographic orientation illustrates the complexity of everyday activities and discourses related to language, and how these situated cultural and linguistic practices are embedded within wider national and transnational social structures. Ethnographic approaches also offer a uniquely experiential learning experience, which can be creatively adapted for modern languages programmes to develop critical reflexivity and to tie together our language learning experiences with the multiple and diverse cultural, social and political contexts in which such languages are used.

Part Two

Spatiality

5

Transnationalism and the Epic Tradition in Baroque Italian Travel Literature

Nathalie Hester

In an essay advocating for what she terms 'imperium studies', Barbara Fuchs addresses the advantages and limits of the transnational turn in early modern studies. While applying the notion of the transnational to contexts predating the nation-state may evoke skepticism, Fuchs writes, a 'focus on the transnational foregrounds a political purchase on early modernity, replacing source or transmission studies with a more explicitly politicized approach'.[1] Indeed, while studies of early modernity have long addressed movement across boundaries and network creation – from the exchange of ideas in the *res publica literaria* to the circulation of human beings and objects across land and sea – transnational approaches make the important intervention of highlighting the power dynamics and ideological implications of such circulations. Fuchs's formulation, which underscores the need to address the emergence of proto-nations as deeply connected to European expansion, offers compelling ways to examine travel culture and its related textual production in seventeenth-century Italy. Although Fuchs addresses primarily English and Spanish colonial contexts, her notion is relevant for considering the specificity of the Italian peninsula in relation to questions of proto-nationalism and imperium. Italians were participants in European colonial endeavors as navigators, missionaries, bankers, merchants, secretaries, diplomats and scholars, for example, but their home city (*patria*) or the courts where they served were principal reference points, since Italy did not exist as a geopolitical entity. Furthermore, much of the Italian peninsula

---

[1] Barbara Fuchs, 'Another Turn for Transnationalism: Empire, Nation, and Imperium in Early Modern Studies', *PMLA*, 130.2 (2015), 412–18 (p. 412).

was under Spanish control, and imperial powers, from the Habsburgs to the Ottoman Turks, were a fundamental concern.[2]

In representations of travel from Italy during this period, from first-person accounts to fictional retellings in poetic form, questions of *imperium*, of political entities having dominion over large swaths of territory, are central.[3] Attending to connections between local and imperial powers helps shed light both on aesthetic choices in these works and the expression of Italian political concerns in specific city-states as well as on the global stage. This essay considers briefly two representations of seventeenth-century Italian travel, one Roman and one Florentine, to the East and to the West, in order to elucidate how the aesthetic and the political play out in transnational and imperial contexts. Specifically, in these examples, the epic tradition is the thematic and formal anchor for establishing Italy's role in European political, religious and economic expansion. For writers of lengthy travels, heroic tales of navigation and conquest were key reference points.[4] Italian authors in particular saw themselves as heirs to an illustrious Latin-Italian tradition of epic poetry that included Virgil, Dante, Petrarch, Ariosto and Tasso. Furthermore, as David Quint writes in his foundational study, *Epic and Empire*, 'the equation of power and the very possibility of narrative is a

---

[2] Fuchs argues that 'if a transnational approach is not balanced with an attention to empire, it returns our fields relentlessly to a European metropole, negating even the cautious embrace of postcolonialism by early modern studies, or the more capacious horizons of world or connected histories' ('Another Turn', p. 415). While Fuchs is concerned here with European imperialism, its connection to other major non-European powers is relevant.

[3] The first edition of the dictionary of the Accademia della Crusca (1612) defines *imperium* (*imperio*) as 'Supremo dominio, e signoria' [Ultimate dominion, and sovereignty]. 'Imperio', *Lessicografia della Crusca in Rete*, 3rd ed., http://www.lessicografia.it/Controller?lemma=IMPERIO_ed1 [accessed 28 July 2018]. For the purposes of this essay, I consider 'empire' to be defined as a 'major political unit in which the metropolis, or single sovereign authority, exercises control over territory of great extent or a number of territories or peoples through formal annexations or various forms of informal domination'. See Daniel I. O'Neill, 'Empire', *Encyclopaedia Britannica*, updated July 2016, https://www.britannica.com/topic/empire-political-science [accessed 15 May 2019].

[4] Since Italy did not exist as a proto-nation in the pre-modern era, literary travel writers harnessed the prestige of the classical and Italian letters to express Italian-ness. References to this tradition were not simply reflections of humanist learning and literary tastes of the time but powerful indicators of an imagined Italian identity, one not based in transnational dominion but in cultural renown. For a consideration of the relation between Italian travel writing, the literary canon and Italian identity, see Theodore J. Cachey, Jr., 'An Italian Literary History of Travel', *Annali d'Italianistica*, 14 (1996), 55–64.

defining feature of the [epic] genre'.[5] Epic poetry was imbued with political resonances, whether contemporary to an individual poem's production or part of its historical reception.[6] In addition, and significantly for Italians writing of travel across long distances, epic poetry held narrative possibilities both for acclaiming empire and for critiquing it. In this way, the epic model allowed for the celebration of Italian deeds while also addressing the problematic nature of imperial power.

The *Viaggi* (*Travels*, 1650–63) of Roman patrician Pietro della Valle and *L'America* (1650) by Florentine academic Girolamo Bartolomei Smeducci present compelling responses to imperial expansion, both geopolitical and religious, and Italy's role in that expansion. These texts, while different, both turn to the epic genre to represent an Italian presence and influence in transnational contexts in the East and West. Della Valle's text comprises 54 of his original letters, sent to a scholar friend, Mario Schipano, during a trip in the Mediterranean, the Middle East and India between 1614 and 1626. Bartolomei's *L'America* is an allegorical heroic epic poem celebrating Amerigo Vespucci's navigations, real and invented. In both texts, however, the epic tradition, tied to a vision of Catholic evangelism, is a model for framing and asserting Italian participation in imperial forays. In della Valle's initial letters from his six-year stay in Persia, he refers regularly to the *Aeneid* and the *Gerusalemme liberata*, for instance, and represents himself as the skilled Roman protagonist discussing world politics with Shah 'Abbas I, the ruler of the Safavid empire. Della Valle envisions aiding the Persians in their continuing territorial conflicts with the Turks, and even muses about establishing a new city of Rome in Persia. His letters stage a captivating encounter with imperial power and construct an Italian contribution to Mediterranean and Middle Eastern politics through the keen eye of a cosmopolitan representative of the *caput mundi*, seat of the Catholic Church and of the ancient Roman empire. Bartolomei's *L'America*, modeled after the *Odyssey*, acclaims the global travels of a contemplative Amerigo Vespucci, an ideal Medici subject who brings the example of Christian piety from Europe to Africa and the Americas. In this epic poem, exploration of the New World – both the voyage itself and its recounting in the Tuscan literary vernacular – is a distinctly Florentine creation. Both della Valle's and Bartolomei's texts, reflective of

---

[5] David Quint, *Epic and Empire: Politics and Generic Form from Virgil to Milton* (Princeton: Princeton University Press, 1993), p. 15.

[6] 'Although they can be returned to their original political occasion, these narratives also acquire a life of their own, especially as they draw on and, in turn, become part of a literary tradition whose very continuity seems to constitute another second-order master narrative, a kind of second nature'. Quint, *Epic and Empire*, p. 15.

local belonging and identity (papal Rome for della Valle, Medicean Florence for Bartolomei), create a methodology for recounting Italian travel that heeds the baroque literary expectations of academic circles, affirms the high status of the classical and Italian textual traditions, and ultimately serves to make a claim for Italy's central role in global affairs. Despite their differences, the two works offer a literary antidote, grounded in the epic tradition, to the Italian peninsula's subservience to the Habsburg empire and vulnerability to Ottoman power; an antidote that promotes alternative narratives of imperial power dynamics.

When Pietro della Valle, dressed in pilgrim's garb and fleeing unrequited love, set out on his travels to the East, he already had it in mind to publish an account of his travels.[7] A rare independent traveler on such a lengthy journey, he planned to send letters to Mario Schipano, a professor of medicine at the University of Naples, who was to fashion them into a prose narrative. Della Valle, whose missives follow the popular *familiar letter* genre, envisioned a new form of writing, a kind of prose epic that would lend a high discursive register to contemporary international travel.[8] Della Valle's geographical ambitions went hand in hand with his literary ones, and his epistolary writing possesses deliberately performative qualities. In his extraordinarily rich travel account, della Valle is self-conscious of his role as the protagonist of his travels and views his encounters with a multitude of different cultural contexts as material for a dramatic narrative. The planned literary adaptation never came to fruition, and della Valle's letters to Schipano instead came out in four volumes between 1650 and 1663.[9]

In his letters anticipating a visit to the Persian court, della Valle often refers to epic tradition. The traveler urges his correspondent to develop a narrative style that will convey the significance and heroism of the upcoming encounter with the Safavid empire and della Valle's pledge to help fight

[7] Pietro della Valle (1586–1652) was a member of the Accademia degli Umoristi [Academy of Wits], one of the most prominent Roman literary academies, and was active in literary and musical circles. He spent several years in Naples, where he befriended Schipano. Recent studies consider his scientific interests in non-Western contexts. See Avner Ben-Zaken, 'From Naples to Goa and Back: A Secretive Galileian Messenger and a Radical Hermeneutist', *History of Science*, 47 (2009), 147–74; Sonja Brentjes and Volkmar Schüller, 'Pietro Della Valle's Latin Geography of Safavid Iran (1624–1628): Introduction', *Journal of Early Modern History*, 10.3 (2006), 169–219.

[8] Schipano was known for his collection of texts from the Levant and was a member of several Neapolitan academies.

[9] The first volume, *La Turchia* [Turkey], was published in 1650 by Mascardi in Rome. Following della Valle's death, his sons published two volumes of his letters from Persia in 1958 and a third on India in 1663.

the Turks. This was a golden narrative opportunity, since Shah 'Abbas regularly received Europeans at his court.[10] With histrionic flourish, della Valle instructs Schipano that his entry into the Shah's court chamber should be recounted in a high stylistic register associated with epic poetry:

> E dopo che io sarò co'l re, si potrebbe, e forse molto a proposito, cominciare un'altra seconda parte di relationi più gravi; alla quale spero che non mancherà materiale, degna, per avventura, di più alto stile. Perché, per l'avvenire, nelle lettere, che sin ch'io viva non cesserò mai di scriverle, non le darò più avvisi di semplici viaggi o di ordinarie curiosità osservate nei camini; ma, piacendo a Dio, la ragguaglierò di hospitii, e ricevimenti regii, di grandezze di corti, di negotii di principi, di guerre, di trasmigrationi di popoli, di fondationi di città, di ambascerie straniere, e di altri avvenimenti heroici e grandi, che io stesso con gli occhi proprii havrò veduto, e de' quali, forse, con la gratia di Dio, sarò *pars magna*.[11]

> [And once I will be with the king, one could, perhaps most aptly, begin another, second part of the account, and a weightier one which, I hope,

---

[10] Shah 'Abbas I 'The Great' ruled the Safavid empire from 1588 to 1629. He instituted numerous administrative, military and political reforms and brought the court to Isfahan, which prospered under his rule. Isfahan was a host city to merchants from the East and West, ambassadors from Europe and members of Catholic monastic orders. Eager to establish anti-Ottoman alliances and to maintain commercial and political rapports with the West, 'Abbas was tolerant of non-Muslim religions. See Roger Savory, *Iran under the Safavids* (Cambridge: Cambridge University Press, 1980), pp. 76–103.

[11] Della Valle to Schipano, Isfahan, 18 December 1617, in Franco Gaeta and Laurence Lockhart, eds, *I viaggi di Pietro della Valle: Lettere dalla Persia* (Rome: Istituto poligrafico dello Stato, 1972), p. 99. I have modernized the capitalization in quotations from the text. All translations of della Valle's letters are mine. Quotations of della Valle's Persia letters are taken from Gaeta and Lockhart's edition of the pre-publication manuscript held at the Società Geografica Italiana in Rome. Some portions of this manuscript (on the subject of Church policy and foreign relations) were censored or modified before publication. See Gaeta and Lockhart, *Viaggi*, pp. xix–xxi. Della Valle uses a similarly dramatic tone in a later letter from Persia: 'Hora, ripigliando dove già lasciai, seguiterò gl'interrotti ragguagli, e solcando il mare con maggiori vele, racconterò diverse attioni eroiche, per dir così' [And now, taking up again where I left off, I will continue my interrupted account and, riding the ocean with larger sails, will tell of several heroic actions, so to speak]. Della Valle to Schipano, Isfahan, 22 April and 8 May 1619, in Gaeta and Lockhart, *Viaggi*, p. 297. In adding 'per dir così', della Valle signals a certain ironic distance and understanding that his experience may not match the heroic deeds of the epic tradition.

will not lack subject matter worthy, with luck, of a more elevated style. Because in the future, in my letters, as long as I live, I will never stop writing to you, and I will not give you just news of simple travels or ordinary curiosities observed on the road, but, if it pleases God, I will inform you of regal hospitality and receptions, of the greatness of courts, of the commerce of princes, of wars, of the migrations of peoples, of the founding of cities, of foreign embassies, and of other great and heroic events that I myself will have seen with my own eyes and of which perhaps, by the grace of God, I will be a large part]

Della Valle anticipates that war-making and heroic events – in which he, a Roman, will partake – warrant an appropriate stylistic change.[12] His own stylistic and lexical choices in this letter are meant to serve as prompts for Schipano. On several occasions the traveler makes more explicit comparisons between his intended deeds and those of epic heroes. After discussing his political aims at the Persian court, for example, he announces:

[I]ntende adesso, con quanto fervore, per quel poco che posso, io non cesso mai di far guerra a i turchi per diverse strade, usando hora le armi di Aiace, hora quelle di Ulisse, secondo che il tempo ricerca e le occasioni che di giorno in giorno mi si presentano.[13]

[You (Mario Schipano) now understand with what fervor, in the little that I can do, I never cease to wage war against the Turks along various paths, now using the weapons of Ajax, now those of Ulysses,

---

[12] Della Valle, defending himself against anticipated critiques of a travel account written by someone, Schipano, who did not travel himself, compares his project with Schipano to Homer's. Again, della Valle's comments reveal a vision of the narrative as evocative of epic adventures, with della Valle in the role of a modern Ulysses: 'Una [difficoltà è] che non essendosi ella trovata presente al viaggio, non ha garbo che scriva di cose non vedute in materia che ricerca tanto l'operatione della vista. Rispondo [...] che Homero non si sdegnò di scrivere e di comporre sopra i viaggi di Ulisse, che le relationi de' viaggi sono spetie d'historie per tali stimate' [One difficulty is that, since you were not present during the trip, you might be unwilling to write of things that you have not seen on a topic that assuredly requires visual appraisal. I will respond (...) that Homer did not disdain writing and composing the travels of Ulysses, because travel accounts are a kind of history, esteemed as such]. Della Valle to Schipano, Isfahan, 19 March 1617, in Gaeta and Lockhart, *Viaggi*, p. 56.

[13] Della Valle to Schipano, Ferhabad and Qazvin, 25 July 1618, in Gaeta and Lockhart, *Viaggi*, p. 284.

according to what circumstances bring and the opportunities that present themselves day by day]

His account is peppered with quotations from and references to classical and modern epic poems, in particular when discussing war, conflict and politics.[14]

As he characterizes the good and bad empires, the Persian and the Turkish, respectively, della Valle quotes from classical epic poetry to establish Shah 'Abbas as a worthy political partner. Della Valle links Shah 'Abbas's savvy as a leader to the wisdom of Anchises's dictum to Aeneas in the *Aeneid*, praising the leader's ability to acquire the goodwill of conquered enemies:

> [V]iene anco a mettere in esecutione molto bene quel bel precetto politico, che fa dar Virgilio dall'Anima di Anchise ad Enea, e che è restato poi hereditario a noi altri Romani, cioè: *Parcere subiectis, et debellare superbos*.[15]

> [He (Shah 'Abbas) also puts into practice very well that great political precept, which Virgil has Anchises's soul pronounce to Aeneas, and which then became tradition to us Romans, that is, *to spare defeated peoples, tame the proud*]

With this reference to the *Aeneid*, della Valle accomplishes several tasks: first, he appeals to his readers by making textual references. Then, he continues to shape the narrative for Schipano in grand, adventurous and compelling terms. In addition, the traveler makes Shah 'Abbas sympathetic

---

[14] For instance, he refers to the *Gerusalemme liberata* when describing the Persian army: 'Militano però tutti a cavallo, et i cavalli son piccoli; e per quello che vidi, si può dir di loro molto bene quel che disse de' Greci il nostro Tasso. *Asciutti hanno i cavalli, al corso usati,/A la fatica invitti, al cibo parchi*' [They all fight on horseback, and the horses are small, and from what I saw, one can say of them that which our Tasso said so well of the Greeks: '*Their horses well inured to chase and ride, in diet spare, untired with labor long; ready to charge, and to retire at will*']. Della Valle to Schipano, Isfahan, 17 March 1617, in Gaeta and Lockhart, *Viaggi*, pp. 9–10. See also Tasso, *Jerusalem Delivered*, 1.50, translated by Edward Fairfax (London, 1600), http://mcllibrary.org/Tasso/ [accessed 12 January 2019]. This allusion is a typical strategy in della Valle's missives, one that helps make a distant context more familiar and reinforces the heroic dimension of his travels.

[15] Della Valle to Schipano, Isfahan, 22 April and 8 May 1619, in Gaeta and Lockhart, *Viaggi*, p. 318; Virgil, *Aeneid*, 6.850. English translations of the *Aeneid* are from *The Aeneid of Virgil*, trans. by Allen Mandelbaum (New York: Bantam, 1971).

by attributing to him the positive traits of the leaders of imperial Rome, and by logical extension connecting Catholic, missionary, contemporary Rome to its imperial past: 'noi altri romani'. Finally, by invoking a collective Roman heritage, della Valle is able to place himself in a heroic position and close to Shah 'Abbas.[16] Despite being an imperial Muslim sovereign, the Persian ruler can become a worthy ally in the fight against the Turks – a controversial notion for Counter-Reformation Rome but one in line with della Valle's cosmopolitan vision.[17]

Within this framing of imperial encounters as reminiscent of the epic tradition, della Valle takes on the role of the Roman protagonist and well-placed interlocutor. However, while the letter establishes the possibility of a Roman-Persian friendship, the courtly conversation also reveals the vulnerabilities of

---

[16]   Della Valle also refers to the *Aeneid* in expressing admiration for Shah 'Abbas's ability to dissimulate his melancholic nature, which della Valle attributes in part to 'Abbas's having put his own son to death: 'Solo adunque accennerò che il re, in secreto, sta malinconico assai, per le cose già dette, e per altri pensieri gravi e molesti, e della guerra e di altro; e benché in publico mostri tutto il contrario, e saggiamente si finga allegrissimo, perché così conviene, tuttavia *premit altum corde dolorem,* e alle volte non può finger tanto che non se ne vedano fuori evidentissimi segni' [I will therefore only mention that the king, in private, is quite melancholy, because of the previously mentioned things, and because of other grave and upsetting concerns, and war, and other matters. And although in public he shows wholly the opposite, and wisely feigns being very joyful, because that is appropriate, nevertheless *his pain is held within, hidden* and sometimes he cannot feign so well that very evident signs cannot be seen]. Della Valle to Schipano, Ferhabad and Qazvin, 25 July 1618, in Gaeta and Lockhart, *Viaggi,* p. 257. The Latin quote is from Virgil, *Aeneid,* 1.209. Concerning 'Abbas's remorse over ordering the assassination of his son, see Savory, *Iran under the Safavids,* p. 95.

[17]   Della Valle describes his first meeting with Shah 'Abbas as a courtly and ludic event, and one that he greatly enjoyed. He expresses similar pleasure in his published treatise on Shah 'Abbas and his court: 'E io, come ospite, ch'era del re, essendomi più volte in tali congressi trovato presente, vi aveva gusto infinito, e stimandoli per una grandissima scuola di prudenza, per sentir trattar di cose grandi, quanto comporta la macchina di quello grande imperio, da un re di grandissimo valore' [And I, as the guest of the king, and having found myself in such conversations on several occasions, took infinite delight in it and, esteeming them a very great school of prudence, since I could hear considerations of great things, and of what comprise the workings of that great empire, led by a king of very great valor]. Pietro della Valle, *Delle conditioni di Abbàs rè di Persia* (Venice: Francesco Baba, 1628), p. 29. This work was put on the Vatican's Index of Forbidden Books, a clear indication that certain positive characterizations of a Muslim ruler were deemed unacceptable by the Church. See Gaeta and Lockhart, *Viaggi,* p. xxi.

European geopolitics.[18] The territorial structure of empire is at the forefront of their discussion. Of particular concern is the fact that the Habsburg empire does not have the geographical contiguity of the Ottoman or the Safavid empire. Della Valle uses both indirect and direct discourse in recounting the conversation and, when the Shah asks della Valle why Spain does not attack the Turks, the Roman traveler must concede Europe's disadvantage:

> Risposi io che in Persia si poteva far questo perché il paese era unito e tutto insieme, se standoci il re dentro, e in mezzo, con esercito potente, poteva agevolmente rivolgersi ove gli piaceva [...] ma che non poteva far così il re di Spagna ne' suoi stati; perché, come haveva detto, erano tutti disuniti e lontani, e non si poteva andare, o condur le forze, da uno all'altro, senza passar per terre di nimici o di poco confidenti.[19]

> [I responded that in Persia, this was possible (to mobilize large forces to fight the Turks) because the country was united and all conjoined, and the king was in the center and in the middle, with a powerful army, and could easily go where he pleased, but that the king (of Spain) could not do the same in his states because, as I had said, they were all disunited and distant, and one could not go or lead forces from one to the next without passing through the land of enemies or those untrustworthy]

Della Valle's account of the discussion makes evident Europe's political disunity and, by consequence, its inability to defeat the Ottoman empire. Significantly, the passage also highlights the religious fractures in Europe and the limited powers of the pope in matters of international politics. Della Valle comments on the state of Italy, one of fragmentation long lamented by literary and political figures:

> Soggiunse ['Abbas] per tanto, e conchiuse, che, se i principi christiani non obbedivano al papa in questo, non amavano la loro religione [...]

[18] Della Valle makes a generic distinction when discussing Shah 'Abbas's personal matters, and writes that his king's woes are 'degne in vero di esser compatite e celebrate in versi' [worthy of being pitied and celebrated in verse]. He also underscores the importance of keeping his account enjoyable: 'non ho gusto d'imbrattare i miei scritti allegri infin' adesso con cose lugubri e tale sorte' [I have no wish to tarnish my writings, which have been merry until now, with lugubrious things of the sort]. Della Valle to Schipano, Ferhabad and Qazvin, 25 July 1618, in Gaeta and Lockhart, *Viaggi*, p. 257.

[19] Della Valle to Schipano, Ferhabad and Qazvin, 25 July 1618, in Gaeta and Lockhart, *Viaggi*, p. 244.

Vergogna, per certo, del christianesimo, che così da gli estranei ci sia rimproverata la nostra negligenza: e che, per due palmi di terra in Italia, pensiamo più a mangiarci con invidia l'un altro, senza rispetto di amicitia, né di sangue, né delle stesse cose sacre che a mover l'armi contro gl'infedeli, per acquistar con giustissimo titolo e con immensa gloria ampissimi regni.[20]

[He ('Abbas) then added and concluded that, if the Christian princes did not obey the pope in this (fighting the Turks), they did not love their religion. Shame on Christianity, for sure, if our negligence is reproached thus by foreigners; and that, for two lengths of land in Italy, we think more about devouring one another with envy – without respect or friendship, either for kinship or for similar sacred things – than about waging war against the infidels, to obtain very extensive reigns very rightfully and with immeasurable glory]

Although della Valle positions himself as the hero of a new form of Italian epic narrative and a protagonist able to engage in sophisticated conversations with the Shah, their discussion leads della Valle to address the political vulnerability of the Italian peninsula. The Roman-Persian dialogue ultimately results in della Valle's deploring the continued conflicts among Italian city-states, conflicts that remain a formidable obstacle to the 'immensa gloria' that would warrant an epic retelling.

At about the same time that Pietro della Valle was establishing himself as an intrepid hero-chronicler, courtly observer and literary raconteur of multicultural encounters with the East, several Italian writers took up in epic poetry the subject of westward navigation to the Americas. Between 1596 and 1650, 11 such poems were published, in partial or complete form, each hailing either Columbus or Vespucci as an infallible protagonist and evangelic hero.[21] Nevertheless, at a time when many Italian courts were subject to Hapsburg

[20] Della Valle to Schipano, Ferhabad and Qazvin, 25 July 1618, in Gaeta and Lockhart, *Viaggi*, p. 240. Della Valle notes that Persia mostly defends its current territories rather than attacking the Turks: 'Ma queste cose le tacqui, perché non volsi dargli disgusto, mentre mi usava cortesie; e senza che io le dicessi, era sicuro che molto ben le sapeva, benché non volesse confessarle' [But I kept quiet about these things, because I did not want to offend him, while he was bestowing me such courtesies. And, without having to say it, I was certain that he knew it quite well, even if he did not wish to admit it]. Della Valle to Schipano, Ferhabad and Qazvin, 25 July 1618, in Gaeta and Lockhart, *Viaggi*, p. 249.

[21] For an extensive although inexhaustive list of new epic poems published in this

dominion, recounting Columbus's and Vespucci's expeditions on behalf of the Spanish or Portuguese crowns could be problematic. These New World poems were the products of literary debates over heroic epic poetry and about the representation of colonial and imperial contexts in Counter-Reformation Italy. Girolamo Bartolomei's *L'America* (1650) is a telling example of how these elements play out in Medicean Florence, which had, beginning in the sixteenth century, cultivated representations of imperial connections to the Americas.[22] *L'America*, like della Valle's early letters from Persia, relies on the epic tradition as a model for representing Italian participation in global travel and European expansion. Here again, the notion of *imperium studies* provides a lens through which to connect representations of Italian travel to pressing political concerns about Italian autonomy and, in this example, Habsburg power.

Bartolomei, a member of the Accademia della Crusca and the Accademia Fiorentina, dedicates his poem to Louis XIV and, in his version of Vespucci's travels, poetic invention eclipses historical accuracy.[23] The 40-canto epic poem recounts Vespucci's navigations to the Americas, Africa and Europe, then back to Brazil, where, in the last canto, with Virgilian echoes, he founds the city of San Salvador de Bahia, where its indigenous inhabitants joyfully convert to Catholicism.[24] The poem unfolds around a series of encounters, at sea and on land, with peoples and creatures of several continents. Vespucci meets with Amazons and Patagonian giants and stays with the King of Ethiopia, where, in one canto, the Florentine game of *calcio* is played. He also meets members of other European expeditions, a narrative device that allows for the recounting of Columbus's and Vasco de Gama's navigations, among others. The narrative also incorporates Dantean elements, as when Vespucci converses with damned

period, see Antonio Belloni, *Gli epigoni della* Gerusalemme liberata (Padua: Angelo Draghi, 1893).

[22] Among the most notable epic poems were Tommaso Stigliani's *Mondo nuovo* (1617, 1628) and Alessandro Tassoni's unfinished *Oceano* (1622), which was in part a response to Stigliani's work.

[23] In the preface to the poem, Bartolomei declares that the *Odyssey* is the best model for representing Vespucci's travels, an explicit response to critiques of epic poems about Columbus that portray him as a protagonist waging war against indigenous Americans. Bartolomei sides with Tassoni, who saw Columbus as praiseworthy for his navigational and not military skills. Girolamo Bartolomei già Smeducci, *L'America* (Rome: Lodovico Grignani, 1650), 'Al benigno e saggio lettore', a verso–a2. For Tassoni, if Columbus is to be praised as a hero in an epic poem, it can only be as a navigator and explorer, and the appropriate poetic model is the *Odyssey*, not the *Iliad*. See Alessandro Tassoni, *La secchia rapita, l'Oceano e le rime*, ed. by Giorgio Rossi (Bari: Laterza, 1930), p. 263.

[24] The city was founded by the Portuguese in 1549.

souls in a volcano in the Americas, in a manner reminiscent of the *Inferno*.[25] At the end of each canto, a section entitled 'allegoria' explains the Christian symbols and meanings of the various episodes.

Vespucci's fictional, pluricontinental navigations in *L'America* emerge from the context of the Medicis' desire, never fulfilled, to participate concretely in global economic expansion alongside Spain and Portugal, among others. For example, the attention accorded to navigation around Africa and the Americas evokes the legacy of Grand Duke Ferdinand I, Cosimo II's father, who attempted to establish colonies on both continents. Ferdinand sent an expedition to Brazil in 1608 with the intention of exploiting resources there, including cane sugar, for which he hoped to build a sugar refinery in the port of Livorno.[26] The same year the expedition returned to Florence, 1609, Ferdinand sought to purchase the settlement grant of Sierra Leone owned by a Portuguese nobleman.[27] Although the Spanish crown, unsurprisingly, did not allow the Medici family to establish colonies in Brazil or Sierra Leone, Ferdinand's plans demonstrated grand ducal imperial ambitions that permeated the Florentine reception of the Americas and response to European global expansion.[28]

The poem's focus on Vespucci as a Florentine captain, rather than a member of an Iberian expedition, reflects his salience in the Medici narrative of participation in the American conquest and the underlying anxiety about Habsburg domination both on the Italian peninsula and in the Americas. Lia Markey, in her study of the reception of the Americas in Medici Florence, writes of the Medicis' 'vicarious conquest' in light of its subordination to Spain and the

[25] Sergio Zatti emphasizes the complex layers of intertextuality and citation in Italian epic poetry of the sixteenth and seventeenth centuries in *L'ombra del Tasso: Epica e romanzo nel Cinquecento* (Milan: Mondadori, 1996), pp. 148–50.

[26] The so-called Thornton Expedition was led by Englishmen in Ferdinand I's service. The ship, the *Santa Lucia Buonaventura*, returned to Livorno carrying several indigenous Americans in July 1609. See Brian Brege, 'Renaissance Florentines in the Tropics: Brazil, the Grand Duchy of Tuscany, and the Limits of Empire', in *The New World in Early Modern Italy, 1492–1750*, ed. by Elizabeth Horodowich and Lia Markey (Cambridge: Cambridge University Press, 2017), pp. 206–22.

[27] Portuguese nobleman Pedro Alvares Pereira had relinquished the settlement grant after running into legal trouble. See P. E. H. Hair and Jonathan D. Davies, 'Sierra Leone and the Grand Duke of Tuscany', *History in Africa*, 20 (1993), 61–69.

[28] The Medicis sought to develop global networks, and Ferdinand I exchanged letters with Shah 'Abbas about political and economic alliances, in part to address Ottoman Turkish power. Livorno, according to laws passed in 1593, specifically allowed for trade with Persians and Armenians. Mahnaz Yousefzadeh, 'Sea of Oman: Ferdinand I, G. B. Vecchietti and the Armour of Shah Abbas I', *Rivista degli Studi Orientali*, 90.1–4 (2017), 51–74.

Holy Roman empire: 'To compete with or at least to respond to the colonization of these growing European powers, the Medici grand dukes of Tuscany
promoted their relations with and knowledge of the New World via artistic
production and collection'.[29] The Medici's response to European expansion
in the Americas, then, was to have a role in the collection and reception of
international knowledge and, in a related manner, to celebrate the contributions of Florence's great navigator, Vespucci. In 1608, the wedding celebrations
of Cosimo II to Maria Magdalena of Austria, for example, included noblemen
dressed as indigenous Americans. The opera performed at the Pitti Palace on
that occasion, *The Judgment of Paris*, included one *intermedio* about Vespucci
in the New World, the only historical (and non-mythological) element in the
spectacle.[30] Furthermore, as Markey notes, none of the New World elements
included allusions to the Holy Roman Empire or to Spain.[31]

L'America not only builds upon the narrative of Florentine 'vicarious
conquest', it also incorporates an implied denunciation of Spanish colonial
practices.[32] Certainly the dedication to Louis XIV and the poem's opening
encomium of the French monarch are part of an impulse to downplay Spanish
expansion:

> Già che canto sarai fra dotte carte / saggio in pace, o Luigi, e' n guerre
> forte, / t'accenda a quelle altri dal canto; io l'arte / spieghi d'Ulisse, e'
> giochi della sorte. / Qui legger puoi fra l'altre quella parte, / che della
> Francia tuo il nome parte, / fra gl'Indi Esperi, là 've più s'attenda, / che
> 'l tuo chiaro valor l'impero stenda.[33]

> [Since I sing, you will figure on erudite pages, wise in peacetime, oh
> Louis, and strong in wartime, and may others, from my song, inspire

---

[29] Lia Markey, *Imagining the Americas in Medici Florence* (University Park: The
Pennsylvania State University Press, 2016), p. 161.

[30] Markey, *Imagining the Americas*, pp. 152–55.

[31] Markey, *Imagining the Americas*, p. 157. Markey continues, 'Rather, the Vespucci
intermedio [...] boasted of Florence's participation in the discovery, and the natives in
the *gioco* displayed their allegiance firmly to Florence'.

[32] Florentine heroic poems celebrating Vespucci, in line with representations that
downplayed his Spanish and Portuguese patrons, tended to cast him as a navigator
working independently of Spain and Portugal. These include Strozzi the Younger's
(1551–1634) single manuscript canto and Raffaello Gualterotti's *L'America* (1611), a
single published canto. See Franco Fido, *L'America: Primo canto di un poema inedito
di Giovan Battista Strozzi Il Giovane* (Florence: Leo S. Olschki, 1982).

[33] Bartolomei, *L'America*, canto 1, octave 5, p. 2. I have modernized the capitalization in quotations from the text. The translations from this text are mine.

you to them (wars). May I unfurl the art of Ulysses and the games of fortune. Here you read, among others, of that land that France shares with your name, in the West Indies, there where all await your clear valor to broaden your empire]

In this version of the European presence in the Americas, France has the privileged imperial position, and the poetic 'I' promises to evoke French triumphs and conquests, thus proposing a different vision of European expansion in the New World.

After this declaration, the narrative turns to Vespucci and his men, whose initial forays into the Americas reveal the cruelties of empire-making. The principal narrative threads of cantos 4 through 7 illustrate the brutality of the Spaniards in the New World at the time of Columbus's expeditions. The repeated descriptions of violence, destruction, exploitation, torture and rape reinforce the contrast between the Spaniards' endeavors and Louis XIV's – and also with Vespucci's relatively benign navigations.[34] Canto 4 includes the firsthand account of Spanish cruelty by a Taino cacique, Guacanagari. In the canto, Vespucci and his men arrive at an island with an active volcano, which Vespucci enters at night. There he witnesses the fighting armies of damned souls. He listens to Guacanagari's retelling of the fate of the La Navidad settlement on Hispaniola between Columbus's first and second voyages, when Spaniards exploited and slaughtered Tainos, who then killed all the Spaniards, only to face terrible retaliation upon Columbus's return. The account focuses on the particular cruelty of the local governor, Françisco Roldán (Roldano in the poem), towards the Tainos. Guacanagari recounts his torture at the hands of Roldano with baroque élan:

Fra l'ampla sala alla mia regia mensa, / S'affide l'empio, e beve il vin col ghiaccio; / Mentr'io meschino sovra brace accensa / arrostisco le carni, e mi disfaccio: / Egli ride, e sgavazza, e più non pensa / al duro letto, ov'io disteso giaccio. / Io raccolgo perciò doppio tormento, / dal proprio duolo, e dal beffar ch'io sento.[35]

---

[34] In his study, 'Materia del mondo nuovo', Lorenzo Geri notes the correspondences between Bartolomei's critique of Spanish colonial rule and De las Casas's *De la destrucción de las Indias* (1552). Geri also notes intertextual connections to Giambattista Marino's *Adone* (1623). Lorenzo Geri, 'La "materia del mondo nuovo" nella poesia epica italiana. Da Lorenzo Gambara a Girolamo Bartolomei (1581–1650)', in *Epica e oceano*, ed. by Roberto Gigliucci. Studi e (testi) italiani 34 (Rome: Bulzoni, 2014), pp. 19–61.

[35] Bartolomei, *L'America*, canto 4, octave 103, p. 48.

[In the ample hall, at my royal table, sits the impious one, and drinks wine with ice, while I, miserable, am lit over the brazier. My flesh burns, and I am undone. He laughs and guffaws, and thinks no more of the hard bed where I lie. I suffer doubly from his laughter: from the pain, and from the mocking]

In this ventriloquism of an indigenous voice, Guacanagari, although a pagan, is a fair and decent king whose rank and person are violated by a sadistic Spaniard.

The story of Guacanagari and the destruction of the La Navidad settlement is retold in cantos 6 and 7, when Vespucci and his men rescue a shipwrecked Spaniard, Oristano, who repents for having aided Roldano in his plan to destroy the indigenous peoples. As part of his penitence, Oristano confesses in detail the atrocities ordered by Roldano, acts in which Oristano himself participated. Thus, these two cantos serve as an echo or reinforcement of the words of Guacanagari, whom Oristano characterizes as noble and innocent. Dozens of octaves include a repetition, with some variation, of a series of offenses, emphasizing through metaphor the innocence of the indigenous peoples and the heartlessness of the Spanish. The contrast inevitably underlines the failure of the Spanish project. Oristano confesses:

Io preparo tragedia, che riserba
doppo un lieto principio atroce fine,
cui scena fur d'isola mena i lidi,
suggetto gl'indi, che straziar io vidi.[36]

[I prepare the tragedy that holds an abominable end after a happy beginning, which had the shores of a beautiful island as its scene and, as its subject, the Indians, whom I saw torn asunder]

Although the Spanish crown remains free of direct blame, there is a clear criticism of poor leadership, including the Spanish policy of sending *personae non gratae* to the colonies:

Mestier fu d'inviar feccia di genti,
che pien di vili affetti il cor serbaro;
anzi a molti fu d'uopo, che sia dato
il navigar in pena del peccato.[37]

---

[36] Bartolomei, *L'America*, canto 6, octave 8, p. 63.
[37] Bartolomei, *L'America*, canto 6, octave 13, p. 63.

[The plan was to send the dregs of humanity, who kept their hearts full of vile intentions. In fact, many were forced to sail, as punishment for their sins]

In Oristano's retelling, Columbus is equally at fault, having left Roldano in charge:

> Ad huom crudel raccomandò la pace,
> e con quegl'indi un dolce portamento,
> ne mirò, che fidava ad un rapace
> lupo l'agnelle, ed al leon l'armento.[38]

[He appointed a cruel man to keep the peace, and in leaving him with the Indians of a gentle disposition, did not see he was entrusting lambs to a rapacious wolf and the herd (of lambs) to the lion]

Significantly, Columbus's responsibility figures in the explanation of the allegorical meaning of the canto:

> Prudente in vari modi s'appalesò quell'eroe gloria della Liguria, ma fra tali eccellenze trascorse in un errore umano che, gravissimo si rese dall'evento, mentre n'elesse nella sua partenza dall'Indie disco-perte suo successore, e viceregente Roldano, che riuscì sentina d'ogni ribalderia, fulmine fatale destruttore d'un nuovo mondo.[39]

[This hero, the glory of Liguria, proved himself prudent in various ways but, among these excellent ways, he fell into human error, and in this event fell into very grave error when, upon leaving the Indies, he chose as his successor and vice-regent Roldano, who was the den of every vice, the fatal thunderbolt and destroyer of a new world]

These words, with characteristically dramatic metaphors, present a forceful moral indictment of Columbus's actions. The powerful narrative of imperial failure and colonial violence allows Vespucci, by contrast, to become the peaceful agent of Catholic expansion. The Florentine navigator, shocked and moved by the tale of Spanish cruelty, can represent a different, ostensibly benign colonial evangelism, as demonstrated by his prayer, recited after Oristano's confession:

---

[38] Bartolomei, *L'America*, canto 6, octave 101, p. 72.
[39] Bartolomei, *L'America*, p. 74.

O se tal grazia a me conceda Dio,
che con destro camin solcando l'onde
salvo io giunga, complendo il mio desio
a destinate occidentali sponde:
quant'altri fu crudel, cotanto pio
mostrarmi intendo, e far, che 'l zelo abbonde,
salutar guerra io moverò, soldato
più di virtude, che di ferro armato.[40]

[And should God grant me such grace, that I, riding the waves on a straight path, may accomplish my desire and arrive safely to destined western shores; as cruel as others have been, let me show myself equally pious, and full of zeal. I will wage a war of salvation, a soldier armed more with virtue than with a sword]

Vespucci embodies the ideal, Florentine antidote to Spanish misdeeds. He is also – conveniently for the time – only intent on Christian evangelization. While his motives are seemingly peaceful, the language ('war', 'soldier') is nevertheless that of a crusade and evocative of the Spanish Reconquista. As with della Valle, but more forcefully, a tale of Italian travel allows for the development of a substitute narrative of Italian might. At the end of the poem, Vespucci arrives in Brazil and, Aeneas-like, founds a city, in this case, San Salvador de Bahia. The Portuguese colonization of Brazil is written over, as a Medici subject provides the remedy to the ills of European expansion.[41] Vespucci is the expression of a Florentine invention of the New World, the symbolic naming – and therefore possessing – of a territory to be known as America.[42]

Both della Valle's letters from Persia and Bartolomei's *L'America* put in place narrative frameworks that take and adapt from the epic tradition in order to connect local points of departure with transnational and imperial contexts. In these texts, cosmopolitan Catholicism, with an Italian as its

[40] Bartolomei, *L'America*, canto 8, octave 10, p. 91.

[41] The final verses read: 'dal nome d'immortal gloria erede / si meritò dar nome a Novo Mondo, / da prudenza, valor, pietade e zelo / reso famoso in terra e grato al cielo' [Heir, by his name, of immortal glory, he deserved to give his name to a New World, and because of his prudence, valor, piety, and zeal, became famous on Earth and pleasing to Heaven]. Bartolomei, *L'America*, canto 40, octave 114, p. 562.

[42] German cartographer Martin Waldseemüller's 1507 map, *Universalis Cosmographia*, is the first known map to name the continent after Vespucci. The only surviving complete map is held at the Library of Congress. See https://www.loc.gov/rr/geogmap/waldexh.html [accessed 1 October 2019].

privileged, heroic exporter, allows for the imagining of alternative geopolitical empires that support fruitful Italian alliances and limited powers for the Ottoman Turks and the Spanish Habsburgs. For Pietro della Valle, the savvy, cultivated, tolerant Persians are desirable allies against the Turks and friends of Rome. In Bartolomei's *L'America*, the recounting of Vespucci's voyage replaces Portuguese colonial history, so that Brazil can become the privileged site of peaceful, colonial-evangelical success, made possible by a Florentine and told in literary Tuscan. However, the Florentine Italian conquest of the Americas, just like Rome's defeat of the Ottoman Turks through an alliance with the Persians, remains a projection of Italian transnational desire.

6

La fuga dei cervelli, the Grand Tour and the Circulation of Knowledge

Transnational Italian Culture in the Long Eighteenth Century

Clorinda Donato

Introduction

Franco Venturi's seven-volume compendium of eighteenth-century Italy, *Settecento riformatore*, constituted a watershed in the historiography of the eighteenth century for its sheer stamina in addressing Italy's long eighteenth century as a whole for the first time.[1] Through the prism of reform, Venturi had found a *fil rouge* that united Italy's polycentric *secolo dei lumi*. And while the impetus for renewal and reform certainly characterized much of eighteenth-century Italy's intellectual output, Venturi's masterwork unwittingly also provided the blueprint for analysis of its thriving transnational activity, for he mapped the interplay of Italian reformists who engaged with the Austrians, French and Spaniards who ruled in Lombardy, Tuscany, Parma and Naples. Reform in Italy was transnational by definition, as Venturi's volumes amply demonstrate. The phenomenon constituted by the prodigious quantity of reformist literature in every field flowing from the pens of scores of individuals in Italy's transnational eighteenth century has been largely ignored, however, by a tradition of erudition that has valorized a few great men and built its reputation on them. To be sure, France had Voltaire, Diderot and Montesquieu, but how are we to evaluate the collective work

---

[1] Franco Venturi, *Settecento riformatore*, I: *Da Muratori a Beccaria* (Turin: Einaudi, 1969), *Settecento riformatore*, II: *La chiesa e la repubblica entro i loro limiti (1758–1774)* (Turin: Einaudi, 1976), *Settecento riformatore*, III: *La prima crisi dell'Antico Regime (1768–1776)* (Turin: Einaudi, 1979), *Settecento riformatore*, IV: *La caduta dell'Antico Regime (1776–1789)*, 2 vols (Turin: Einaudi, 1984) and *Settecento riformatore*, V: *L'Italia dei lumi (1764–1790)*, 2 vols (Turin: Einaudi, 1987–90).

of any number of highly eloquent Italian eighteenth-century figures, often considered derogatorily as 'minor', whose collective output from sites both inside and outside Italy has so far received short shrift?

Transnational Italian studies offers, for the first time, a set of critical tools that restores to eighteenth-century studies the place of intercultural prestige and renown that Italy held as *the* site for transnational exchange where new categories of players, akin to modern-day 'influencers', interacted with every stripe of notable and socially mobile figures who crossed boundaries carrying with them not a transgressional stigma, but a solid belief in the lifestyles they espoused. These beliefs and lifestyles created new, transnational communities, and while much has been made of the Republic of Letters, such a designation today seems static, limiting and somewhat 'ivory tower', especially when applied to those individuals who gathered in multiple configurations. These gatherings were flexible, fluid and defined by the very movement that continually enabled reconfigurations.

As a locus of widespread, bidirectional movement, Italy became a crossroads for extensive exchange and experimentation which established new paradigms for lifestyles, culture, class and sociability. From a transnational perspective, that movement and circulation of knowledge can be discussed through the related phenomena of the 'fuga dei cervelli' [intellectual flight] and the Grand Tour tradition, with movement across national boundaries of every kind constituting a new paradigm of knowledge formation that we may rightly call transnational. Far from being a recent phenomenon, 'the fuga dei cervelli' – i.e., the need to relocate in the interest of seeking financial support for cultural work and the international fame its purveyors believed they deserved, coupled with the ability to relocate as a function of possessing a highly desirable skill set and the right connections, consolidated through participation in one or several transnational networks – certainly fueled a good deal of eighteenth-century Italian mobility. That phenomenon constitutes a blueprint for the flight of Italian experts today, who, like their eighteenth-century counterparts, seek opportunities abroad as an escape from fraught political, religious and economic realities at home, but also as a means of improving Italy from the outside.

Avid for Italian expertise and the storehouse of knowledge acquired over centuries of brilliance in painting, music, medicine, architecture, physics, theology, geography, literature and printing, European nations and the fledgling United States sought out and welcomed Italian travelers and exiles into their academies, publishing houses and universities. Indeed, geographic and social mobility became the very tenets of cosmopolitanism, the new form of *sprezzatura*, honed by these itinerant courtiers and spread by Grand Tour practices and networks that were rooted in the Italian peninsula. Members of those networks performed wit, erudition, sociability, sexualities and *conversazione* across cultures, identities and classes.[2] Indeed, there is arguably no other period of Italian culture in which individuals underwent such powerful transformations, thanks to the new conditions afforded by mobility and the erosion of *ancien régime* mentalities, now replaced by mentalities of reform (to reiterate the insight that guided Venturi's project), which encouraged actual reform of every kind in lifestyles, behaviors and personal practices.[3] This chapter, therefore, examines how the processes of cultural, linguistic and scientific transfer in the long eighteenth century were carried out by a number of consummate experts whose knowledge and creativity established bridges between other nations and localities within the Italian peninsula, while fostering new sites of exchange, knowledge transfer and dissemination of Italian culture. Their influence on lifestyles and perspectives is evident in the prolific writings of men and women who came through Italy, absorbing its social *modus operandi* in cultural centers that dotted the peninsula and its islands.

Thus the ability to reinvent oneself and one's identity constitutes a hallmark of eighteenth-century Italian culture. Such reinvention was made possible by the unprecedented exchange of people, taste, goods, views and knowledge of which Italy was the nexus of activity, with people coming and going from and through all of the points that make up Italy's polycentric eighteenth century. This, indeed, is the other story that emerges from Venturi's compendium. Published over a 20-year period (1969–84), Venturi's opus dazzles for the sheer number of people, places and projects that percolated throughout the peninsula and its islands, documenting reformist thinking and activity in Italy's long eighteenth century. As we take up the transnational turn of Italy's eighteenth century, we hew closely to Venturi's conviction that this (still) neglected period requires a concrete lens, grounded in the circulation of political and social ideals, the evolution of new mentalities and public opinion – all honed by concrete people who forged the relationships between ideas and real needs that undergird the formation of culture. Venturi saw the eighteenth century not as a monolithic block of sterile ideas, but rather as the contribution of each single center in the peninsula to a shared world of lights: a history of the

---

[2] The term *sprezzatura* was invented by Baldassare Castiglione in *Il libro del cortegiano* (1528) to describe the appearance of ease, or nonchalance, masking the effort and skill invested by the courtier in achieving his seamless outcome. I am likening it to cosmopolitanism in the eighteenth century, where ease of movement, this time as a citizen of the world rather than a member of court, was a sought-after attribute.

[3] Venturi, *Settecento riformatore*, I, pp. 3–5.

Italian Enlightenment whose point of departure resides in the diversity of its many realities.[4]

Great Groups as Opposed to Great Men

The life stories of all of the figures populating Venturi's *Settecento riformatore* read like fiction: banishments, reinventions and new identities, both for native inhabitants and foreigners taking up residence on Italian soil, either in the form of extended Grand Tour visits, such as those of English notable Horace Walpole and noblewoman Lady Mary Wortley Montagu, or semi-permanent and permanent residencies, such as those of Prussian art and antiquities purveyor Philipp von Stosch and his countryman, art historian Johann Joachim Winckelmann, or the Englishman Horace Mann and Frenchmen like Cardinal Melchior de Polignac and astronomer Joseph Jérôme de Lalande. Fictionalized versions of these transnational figures populate the works of many writers and playwrights, including Venetian Carlo Goldoni, whose plays, such as *La locandiera* [The Mistress of the Inn] (1752) and *La vedova scaltra* [The Cunning Widow] (1748), feature traveling foreigners in Venice vying for the hand of the working-class Mirandolina or the widowed noble-woman Rosaura. And while the port cities of Genoa, Naples and Venice had always been points of exchange, along with the universities of Padua and Bologna, or Renaissance Florence and Papal Rome, smaller towns and cities and their residents rose to prominence on the Grand Tour as well.

The focus of recent scholarship on eighteenth-century networks as vibrant means for the horizontal promotion of ideas, intellectuals, culture and trade (in contrast with the vertical, hierarchical and more circumscribed loci of cultural transmission represented by the various courts throughout Italy and Europe) has shed light on the nature of these networks and the new perspective from which they must be viewed. Digital humanities projects have contributed quantitative grist and order to the massive amount of documentation that eighteenth-century scholars have been trying to digest in some sort of cohesive fashion, so as to better distinguish a century in Italian scholarship that has been understudied and 'skipped over', lodged as it is between the Renaissance and the Risorgimento.[5] The vast proliferation of correspond-

---

[4] Venturi expressed this vision of the Italian Enlightenment in the 1953 paper he delivered at the History of the Italian Risorgimento Congress, 'La circolazione delle idee', published in *Rapporto al XXXII Congresso del Risorgimento, Firenze, 9–12 settembre 1953* (Rome: Istituto Poligrafico dello Stato, 1954), pp. 203–22.

[5] Paula Findlen, 'Introduction: Gender and Culture in Eighteenth-Century Italy', in *Italy's Eighteenth Century: Gender and Culture in the Age of the Grand Tour*, ed. by

ences, journals, encyclopedias, voyages and biographies examined through digital humanities methods informs Chloe Edmonson and Daniel Edelstein's provocative characterization of the Enlightenment as a period of history in which 'great groups' excelled, in contrast to the prominence of 'great men' in previous periods.[6] This view is highly pertinent to the study of the Italian transnational Enlightenment that is the focus of this chapter, for it valorizes the numbers of Italian eighteenth-century figures who populate Venturi's volumes as a fully engaged, highly productive group, rather than a collection of 'minor' figures, devoid of 'great men'.

Masonic Networks and Masonic Spaces on the Grand Tour

Networks abounded in eighteenth-century Europe and Italy, but none was more powerful as a tool of intellectual and social promotion than that of Freemasonry, whose members espoused a form of speculative fraternalism that replaced the concrete building tools of operative masonry (established in England in the 1550s as an underground trade union) with ideas. As Margaret Jacob has shown, the new Freemasons that emerged at the cusp of the eighteenth century were inspired by ancient as well as new knowledge, by the sharing and circulation of knowledge, and by religious tolerance.[7] Europeans admired the fraternal ideals of Freemasonry, which appeared to flourish unperturbed in England, in a political environment where the strictures on knowledge production and transfer that burdened intellectuals in other parts of Europe had been eliminated. Freemasons were stalwart supporters of Newtonian ideas, and throughout Europe Newtonianism and Freemasonry became powerful means of expanding social networks among like-minded scientists. Members espoused guiding tenets such as religious and political tolerance, cosmopolitanism and equality across social classes. Freemasons relished the opportunity to encounter new brothers, whom they identified and received thanks to letters of recommendation from other Masons. This form of fraternal sociability served the multiple interests of scientific exchange and transnational friendship, built along the networks of Masonic travel. Scientists of every stripe were practicing Freemasons, including 45 percent

Paula Findlen, Wendy Wassyng Roworth and Catherine M. Sama (Stanford: Stanford University Press, 2009), pp. 1–32 (p. 14).

 [6] Chloe Edmonson and Dan Edelstein, eds, *Networks of Enlightenment: Digital Approaches to the Republic of Letters*, Oxford University Studies in the Enlightenment (Liverpool: University of Liverpool Press, 2019), p. 6.

 [7] Margaret C. Jacob, *Living the Enlightenment: Freemasonry and Politics in Eighteenth-Century Europe* (Oxford and New York: Oxford University Press, 1991), p. 38.

of the members of Britain's Royal Society in the 1720s and 1730s. Founded in 1662 in London, the Society was home to the first scientific journal, *The Philosophical Transactions*, in which Newtonian science figured prominently.[8] It is not surprising to find the Italian Francesco Algarotti admitted to the Society's ranks, considering his work of divulgation on Newtonian science, *Il Newtonianismo per le dame*.[9] Newtonianism became the lynchpin of Freemasonry in Italy, launching English-language nodes of science and fraternalism in the two most important sites for Italian Freemasonry on the peninsula, Florence (1731) and Naples (1746). And while repression, fomented by the Jesuits, would result in an official ban on Freemasonry in Italy, its underground networks continued to flourish and support Italians in their pursuit of social mobility and connections throughout Europe. Indeed, almost every individual discussed in this chapter profited from Masonic connections, as will become evident in our ongoing discussion, with Masonic travel being a salient feature of the period. As Charles Withers has discussed in *Placing the Enlightenment*, the movement of enlightened ideas (including Freemasonry, which itself constituted an important form of enlightened thinking in the eighteenth century), their local reshaping, resignifying, revision and subsequent dissemination through other networks to other Enlightenment/Masonic centers, offers a methodological framework for the study of the movement of people and ideas.[10] Withers also stresses the strong connection between trade and learning when encountering the world empirically, through the prism of empire. That connection goes hand in hand with the exchange of knowledge systems,[11] which figured prominently in Masonic travel, where shared goals about the purpose of fraternal mobility prevailed, uniting members across space and time.

Yves-Pierre Beaurepaire wrote about Masonic travel and sociability among like-minded men and women across cultural and linguistic boundaries in *L'Europe des francs-maçons*. The book's third chapter, 'Un Espace de circulation en réseau', describes the kind of Masonic travel and sociability enjoyed by grand tourists Wilhelmine, Margravine of Bayreuth, and her husband the Margrave when they visited Raimondo Di Sangro, the Prince of San Severo, who had been the grand master of the Masonic lodges in Naples before the

---

[8] Margaret C. Jacob, *Strangers Nowhere in the World: The Rise of Cosmopolitanism in Early Modern Europe* (Philadelphia: University of Pennsylvania Press, 2006), p. 8.

[9] Francesco Algarotti, *Il Newtonianesimo per le dame ovvero dialoghi sopra la luce e i colori* (Naples [Venice]: n.p., 1737).

[10] Charles Withers, *Placing the Enlightenment: Thinking Geographically about the Age of Reason* (Chicago: University of Chicago Press, 2007), pp. 6–7.

[11] Withers, *Placing the Enlightenment*, p. 87.

Church shuttered Freemasonry in the city in 1751. Di Sangro went underground with his Masonic ideals, remaining an active practitioner of Masonic virtues, especially the sharing of knowledge and science, which he performed through frequent transnational encounters.[12] Freemasons on the Grand Tour in Italy sought out other Masons, whose insights into antiquities and sites of artistic, cultural and scientific significance were as much a motivating factor in undertaking the voyage as visiting the sites themselves. The numerous visits to the Prince of San Severo by grand tourists were no exception and the connections between the prince, Wilhelmine von Bayreuth and her brother, Frederick the Great, offer a concrete example of this kind of network in action.[13]

Di Sangro was a key figure in such networks. He embodied the salon model of sociability in his daily life in Naples, and his home became a primary locus for the exchange of ideas at a time when the reform of Neapolitan institutions animated discussions. His lodge drew from the ranks of his friends and followers, and by 1749 Di Sangro had succeeded in recruiting an impressive cross-section of Neapolitan nobility, clergy, artisans and merchants into the burgeoning ranks of the Italian Freemasons. Many of these individuals make up the entourage that the Margrave and Margravine von Bayreuth met in their three documented visits to the Prince and Princess of San Severo during their Neapolitan sojourn. From the 1740s on, enlightened nobles in Rome and Naples who cultivated antiquarian interests entered into ever greater contact with a wide range of travelers. Di Sangro rightly aspired to European-wide recognition for his dramatic work as an inventor and alchemist. He sought, in particular, to pinpoint the secret of the life force by experimenting with San Gennaro's blood and its liquefaction – an episode that had already acquired some form of notoriety, stimulating curiosity, replication or even parody. The margravine shared with the prince a passion for chemistry, alchemy and anatomy. She admired his alchemically created lapis lazuli but also, and in even greater measure, his experimentation with blood. He was known throughout Europe for his debunking of the 'miracle' of San Gennaro's blood, which liquefied in response to intense prayer, at regular intervals, in the phial where it was kept in a Neapolitan

---

[12] Pierre-Yves Beaurepaire, *L'Europe des francs-maçons XVIIIe–XXIe siècle* (Paris: Belin, 2018), p. 123.

[13] For a discussion of their close bonds and the documents that elucidate their relationship, see my 'Masonic Friendships and Shared Visions: Wilhelmine von Bayreuth and Raimondo di Sangro, the Prince of San Severo', in *Markgräfin Wilhelmine von Bayreuth und die Erlanger Universität: Künste und Wissenschaften im Dialog*, ed. by Christina Strunck (Petersberg: Michael Imhof Verlag, 2019), pp. 288–304.

church. For Neapolitans, it was and still is a portent of good times if the blood runs, while bad times await if it fails to flow.

The saint's blood and Di Sangro's performance were legendary.[14] Paolo de Ceglia's research on the miracle of San Gennaro has revealed its popularity among grand tourists, particularly those from the German-speaking lands, where reenactments regularly took place. Though such events were often presented as a Protestant parody of a Catholic miracle and meant to prove that chemical substances could achieve the same results, they nonetheless shared a probable Masonic meaning as well, reflecting to a large degree the thinking of Di Sangro himself.[15] There is no better example of how the transnational Enlightenment in Italy functioned than the participation in and recounting of Raimondo di Sangro's 'parlor game' (as de Ceglia calls it) of offering grand tourists demonstrations of how the blood, or the chemical mix that looked like blood, actually liquefied. French traveler, scientist and geographer Charles Marie de La Condamine described the experience of the 'miracle' as follows:

Being gone one evening to pay my court to her royal highness the margravine of Bareith, a phial was brought to that princess set in a circle of brass or silver gilt, and mounted on a pedestal very richly ornamented, which was surmounted again with a caduceus, in order to distinguish the mounting of this from the phial kept in the cathedral. All this apparatus was put in the hands of the princess, from whence it passed into those of the margrave, and several other persons, as well as into mine; and the following is a true account of what we all saw. The phial appeared to be half filled with a gray-coloured fixed mass or paste, and its sides tarnished with dust. On inclining it alternately several ways, and shaking it for about half a minute, more or less, the paste became liquid, and melted, sometimes only partially; at other times it grew fixed again, and on shaking it anew it was either a shorter or longer time in liquefying. All this was done before our eyes.[16]

---

[14] Francesco Paolo de Ceglia, 'Playing God: Testing, Modeling, and Imitating Blood Miracles in Eighteenth-Century Europe', *Bulletin of the History of Medicine*, Johns Hopkins University Press, 91.2 (Summer 2017), pp. 391–419.

[15] See Yasmine Marcil, 'Entre voyage savant et campagne médicale: le séjour en Italie de La Condamine (1755–1756)', *Diciottesimo Secolo*, III (2018), pp. 23–46; Charles-Marie de La Condamine, *Journal of a Tour to Italy* (London: T. Lewis and G. Kearsly, 1763), pp. xix–xx.

[16] La Condamine, *Journal of a Tour*, p. 146. This English translation appeared one year after La Condamine's French travel narrative was published, 'Extrait d'un journal de Voyage en Italie', in *Histoire de l'Académie Royale des Sciences avec les Mémoires de*

Despite the excruciating detail with which La Condamine relates the experiment itself, he does not mention where the experiment took place, nor does he explicitly name the person who provided the participants with the phial and the apparatus holding it. However, thanks to Lalande's *Voyage en Italie*, we know that it was the prince himself who supplied the travelers with the materials for witnessing the liquefaction of the blood.

La Condamine's write-up of the story reverberated beyond his work. He viewed the scientific explanation of the purported miracle as part of his mission during his Italian travels, even though he had stated at the outset that he was undertaking the trip solely to improve his health. And while the members of the Académie des Sciences were disappointed in the lack of anecdote in his *Voyage*, La Condamine's English translator and editors found his scientific discussions the high point of the work – especially his debunking of the 'Papist' myth of the liquefaction of San Gennaro's blood.[17] The discussion of the saint's blood and the prince's multiple achievements were also disseminated in articles in the *Encyclopédie* d'Yverdon, a compilation that was the brainchild of the Prince of San Severo with his protégé, Fortunato Bartolomeo De Felice, in the early 1750s.[18]

A number of other published Italian *voyages* also document this kind of thriving cultural exchange. The most famous is astronomer and Freemason Jérôme-Joseph de Lalande's *Voyage d'un François en Italie fait dans les années 1765 et 1766*.[19] With its eight volumes, Lalande's *Voyage en Italie* is, in the author's own words, a 'grande encyclopédie rationaliste de l'Italie'. The artistic and cultural debates of the century inform his descriptions of Italy's monuments and antiquities, many of which had been overlooked or misunderstood by previous travelers. Animated by meetings with the most illustrious proponents of science and culture in Italy, the pages of Lalande's *Voyage* exude transnational dynamism. And the *Voyage*, published in multiple editions and translations well into the nineteenth century, replaced the perfunctory descriptions of bland guidebooks with the verve of transnational encounter and exchange.[20]

---

mathématique et de physique tirés des registres de cette Académie, année 1757 (Paris: Imprimerie royale, 1762), pp. 336–410.

[17] See Marcil, 'Entre voyage savant et campagne médicale'.

[18] See, in particular, Fortunato Bartolomeo De Felice, 'Severo, Raimond de Sangro, prince de San-Naples', in *Encyclopédie d'Yverdon* (Yverdon: Fortunato Bartolomeo De Felice), 38:482–486, 1774.

[19] Joseph J. L. F. de Lalande, *Voyage d'un François en Italie, fait dans les années 1765 & 1766: contenant l'histoire & les anecdotes les plus singulieres de l'italie*, 8 vols (Yverdon: n.p., 1769–70).

[20] See Imma Cecere, *Il Voyage en Italie di Joseph-Jérôme de Lalande* (Naples:

Italian antiquities, Renaissance and Baroque architecture, and natural history inspired grand tourists to travel to Rimini to see the patrimony of the Malatesta on the Adriatic Coast, or Spoleto and Terni in Umbria, for Spoleto's imposing Baroque façades and Terni's spectacular Marmore Falls.[21] However, it was also the intelligent conversation and erudite camaraderie offered by the academies dotting virtually every Italian town worthy of the designation which brought grand tourists back repeatedly. The many branches of the Arcadia Academy, in particular, were held in great esteem for their cultivation of the poetic improvisation that Madame de Staël immortalized in her 1804 novel *Corinne, ou l'Italie.*

'Cervelli in fuga': Intellectual Transit and Cultural Production

The twenty-first-century rediscovery of Giacomo Casanova as a figure worthy of serious consideration operates as a bellwether for the growing recognition of Italy's transnational eighteenth century. Maligned and reviled in Federico Fellini's 1976 film *Casanova*, alternately dismissed by generations of Italian scholars for writing in French and by French scholars for being Italian, he now may take a deep bow as the quintessential persona of the Italian transnational eighteenth century (and the proliferation of Casanova scholarship over the past 25 years is an indication of this rehabilitation). For Fellini, Casanova was merely a 'Latin lover' of whom he was simultaneously jealous, dismissive and curious. Far from understanding the horizontal movement and networking that makes Casanova's *Histoire de ma vie* (penned over a ten-year period, 1788–98) a breathtaking read, Fellini could only fathom repetitive and stylized sexual vignettes to portray him. Yet the Casanova that emerges from the pages of the *Histoire de ma vie* is a consummate cosmopolitan who exudes a new form of Italian eighteenth-century *sprezzatura*, as cultivated, constructed, sought after, and imitated as Castiglione's Renaissance courtier had been.

The thousand-plus pages of Casanova's memoir read as an encyclopedia of how the Enlightenment worked, in particular the transnational Italian

---

Luciano, 'Monumenta Documenta', 2013) for an analysis the *Voyage*, its editions and translations.

[21] See Nicola Moorby, *'Cascata delle Marmore, from the Belvedere Inferiore* 1819 by Joseph Mallord William Turner', catalogue entry, November 2008, in David Blayney Brown, ed., *J. M. W. Turner: Sketchbooks, Drawings and Watercolours*, Tate Research Publication, December 2012, https://www.tate.org.uk/art/research-publications/jmw-turner/joseph-mallord-william-turner-cascata-delle-marmore-from-the-belvedere-inferiore-r1138923 [accessed 8 December 2019].

Enlightenment. The book features big cities, but also smaller venues of cosmopolitan sociability, like Rimini and Siena, not to mention the venues outside of Italy where Casanova travelled – Paris, Switzerland, England, the German States and finally Dux, in Bohemia, where he was Count von Waldstein's librarian and wrote his expansive memoir. In it, he reveals his resolute ability to self-promote and reinvent himself with the finely honed toolset of erudite sociability. He unabashedly shares himself in the *Histoire de ma vie*, a conduct manual for new lives. His accentless French, achieved thanks to thrice weekly tutoring sessions with playwright and poet Crébillon the Elder in Paris, became an advantageous tool in his peregrinations. Impressed by the young Venetian's translation and recitation of one of his tragedies in Italian, Crébillon had offered to tutor Casanova, thereby ushering him into a powerful network of French literati who respected, imitated and studied the Italian tradition and language.[22] The French admired witty repartee and currency in culture, dress and erudite news. Casanova comments on the need to update his wardrobe, plagued by an excess of ruffles, but he amply made up for his fashion *faux pas* with brilliant conversation and erudition. Thus his social *savoir faire* gained him *entrée* to coveted venues, where his basic needs were taken care of: food, drink, lodging and, of course, sex, including the entire spectrum of heterosexual and homosexual encounters, which he either viewed or entertained without judgment. The freedom he felt in expressing his constantly evolving experiences in the *Histoire* commands our attention and the book, replete now with recently discovered rewritten chapters, deserves to be seen as a monument of the Enlightenment comparable to the *Encyclopédie*.[23]

Previously cast in a derogatory light, Casanova's libertine sociability emerges as a transnational Enlightenment practice. Albrecht von Haller, an austere Bernese giant of anatomy and poetry, recognized in Giacomo an able and erudite interlocutor rather than the rascal we erroneously snicker about today. Casanova moved seamlessly through encounters with every social and political class in theaters, *conversazioni*, Masonic lodges and private homes. And why not recognize his gender-balanced representations, too, for as many women fill his pages as men, women whose qualities and virtues he steadfastly extols as statements of fact. Casanova is singularly capable

---

[22] See Françoise Waquet, *Le modèle français et l'Italie savante: conscience de soi et perception de l'autre dans la République des Lettres (1660–1750)* (Rome: École française de Rome, Palais Farnèse, 1989).

[23] All versions of Casanova's rewrites of particular sections are included in Casanova, *Histoire de ma vie*, ed. by Gérard Lahouati and Marie-Françoise Luna, 3 vols (Paris: Gallimard, 'Bibliothèque de la Pléiade', 2013–15).

of communicating the essence, goodness and qualities of the people he encountered, offering a cornucopia of eighteenth-century interactions and exchanges that memorialize how the lifestyle of an itinerant member of the Republic of Letters unfolded. When he encounters the beautifully dressed Bernese woman, Madame de Saone, whose face, due to an illness she had contracted after the birth of her first child, was nothing but a blackened scab, he nonetheless notes her fiery eyes and perfect teeth – albeit in a mouth that could barely move from the pain caused by the tightness of the skin. Casanova recounts that he found himself intrigued by her conversation and company. He admires her zest for life and how she overcame the adversity of her disfigurement. As charmed as Casanova was by physical beauty, he was nonetheless attracted by diversity, which he celebrated in his minute descriptions of people whose physical features differed from the norm, and whose qualities (often unexpected attributes) rapidly became the basis for discovering the richness of their personality. His forays into the *conversazioni* of Siena are yet another example of Casanova's interest in the variety of humanity. The *conversazioni* were Italian salons where gossip, intermingled with intellectual musings, was accompanied by music and performance. In Siena he met a physically unattractive woman whose abilities as an *improvisatrice*, however, immediately transformed her into the greatest of beauties. It was the imprint of an ethereal, performative beauty that he extolled in the *Histoire.*

Ettore Scola's aged Casanova, performed by Marcello Mastroianni in the 1982 French-Italian co-production *La nuit de Varenne*, moves through Europe, albeit slowly, as an icon of the Enlightenment – indeed, of the transnational Italian Enlightenment. His character is delineated with a far greater insight by Scola than Fellini. Travelling through France in an elegant, single-seat white carriage, he meets Restif de la Bretonne on the road to Metz. Restif – author of *Les Nuits révolutionnaires*, the chronicles of his nightly rounds of Paris during the tense years following the storming of the Bastille, 1789–93 – senses subterfuge. When, in 1791, Louis XVI and Marie-Antoinette attempt to end their humiliating captivity at the hands of the revolutionaries by escaping to Metz, where a gathering of European nobles await them, Restif is on their trail. He is travelling in a carriage with Thomas Paine, Marie-Antoinette's lady in waiting incognito, an Italian opera singer, a wealthy couple from the countryside and Casanova, who, following the breakdown of his own carriage, is now seated in the more capacious vehicle. There, he entertains his companions in the kind of genteel, lascivious philosophical dialogue that fills the pages of the *Histoire*. Though apocryphal in its imagined meeting of Paine, Restif and Casanova, the film brilliantly succeeds in capturing the end of the Enlightenment, as well as the ever-restless

Casanova, thoroughly at ease in his cosmopolitan, transnational wanderings. Women and men alike revere him in Scola's telling. They admire and idealize his lifestyle, his freedom and his measured outlook. Even Thomas Paine pays homage to Casanova and his ability to command the conversation, while his occasional lapses, brought on by senility, never provoke laughter among his fellow travelers, only polite respect for the dignity of his person. Scola understood perfectly the Casanova of the *Histoire de ma vie* – never hierarchical, always admiring of his fellow travelers, dinner companions, women, musicians, artists and anyone whose path he crossed. He admired the art of their existence, and they, his.

In his travels he also sought out birds of a feather, in flight, like him, but also entrusted with responsible positions in the making of culture and connections. One of these fellow Italian cultural refugees was Fortunato Bartolomeo De Felice, whom Casanova met in Berne, in the literary café that De Felice, coming from Naples, had been recruited to spearhead. De Felice hailed from the circle of Antonio Genovesi, where he enjoyed the protection and mentorship of Raimondo di Sangro, the Prince of San Severo.

De Felice, the brilliant young son of a shoemaker, had been sponsored to attend the Jesuit college in Rome, where Celestino Galiani discovered him, bringing him back to Naples to help renew the university curriculum. De Felice had shown himself to be particularly gifted in Newtonian physics and had participated in the rich ferment of activity in Rome, the first Italian city where Newtonian science was studied, thanks to the circulation of Newton's *Opticks* and *Principia* in the first decade of the eighteenth century. However, Rome was also a dangerous place for Newton's disciples, due to the proximity of the Vatican. This remained true despite the confirmation, in 1740, of Cardinal Prospero Lambertini as Pope Benedict XIV, who was a proponent of erudition from abroad and of university reform. In Naples, Galiani entrusted De Felice with the task of translating the most salient works of recent scholarship into Italian, for university students. He produced the *Scelta de' migliori opuscoli*, writing in his preface that translation, compilation and the dissemination of scientific work could only be performed by experts who understood what they were translating, not by hacks.[24] De Felice had begun to make a name for himself in the field of erudite translation with his Latin version of Scottish physicist John Arbuthnot's 1733 *An Essay*

---

[24] Fortunato Bartolomeo De Felice, *Scelta de' migliori opuscoli tanto di quelli che vanno volanti quanto di quelli che inseriti ritrovansi negli atti delle principali accademie d'Europa, concernenti le scienze e le arti che la vita umana interessano: tradotti in italiana favella, commentati, illustrati, accresciuti* (Naples: Giuseppe Raimondi, 1755).

Concerning the Effect of Air on Human Bodies.[25] The Bernese contact with De Felice (believed to have been a Mason) was made through Di Sangro's connections with Vincenz von Tscharner, a likely Masonic sympathizer and friend of Baron von Tschoudy. The latter was a Swiss military officer residing in Naples who belonged to Di Sangro's lodge. In a 1756 letter that reads like a Masonic letter of introduction, Di Sangro praises De Felice's many talents and outlines how they can be put to good use in the Bernese-ruled territory, which included the French-speaking Pays de Vaud. Bernese anatomist Albrecht von Haller favored De Felice's arrival, having cited his translation of Arbuthnot extensively in his magnum opus, *Elements of Physiology*, published in Latin. Wrongly characterized as an *abbé galant* by Voltaire, De Felice had been obliged to leave for Switzerland undercover due to a scandal involving a passionate affair with Countess Agnese Arcuato Panzutti. De Felice helped her escape from the convent where her husband had locked her away due to marital strife. They then traveled in Germany and Switzerland, until their limited means forced them to return to Italy. She had no choice but to return to the convent, while he was mildly reprimanded by the ecclesiastical authorities 'over a cup of hot chocolate', according to Giuseppe Gorani.[26] Unhappy with the strictures of the Catholic Church regarding celibacy, the increasingly repressive environment following the death of the enlightened pope Benedict XIV and the unequal treatment of women, De Felice, prompted by his mentor Raimondo Di Sangro, the Prince of San Severo, decided to leave Italy for Switzerland, where he would undertake the encyclopedic project conceived with Di Sangro, the *Encyclopédie* d'Yverdon (1770–80). He arrived in Switzerland in 1757 and immediately set to work, opening a literary café and establishing two periodicals under the guidance of the Bernese patrician class, who aspired to attract visitors to their city, hoping to turn it into a site of sociability for those who visited Switzerland's mountains and valleys. De Felice launched his literary career in Switzerland as the editor of two periodicals, the Italian-language *Estratto della letteratura europea* and the Latin *Excerptum totius Italicae nec non Helveticae literaturae*, each launched in 1758. The periodicals received high praise, their

---

[25] John Arbuthnot, *Clarissimi viri Johannis Arbuthnot [...] Specimen edfectuum aëris in humano corpore. Quod primum ex anglico idiomate interpretatus est gallico Clar. Boyerus [...] Mox vero latine reddidit, atque additionibus, auctariisque illustravit, ornavit, auxit P. F. Fortunatus de Felici* (Naples: Raymundi, 1753), p. 335.

[26] For a thorough discussion of De Felice's affair and his views on celibacy as contrary to natural law and human rights, see Alessandra Doria, '"Un oggetto considerabile di mondana politica". Celibato del clero e critica illuminista in Europa nel XVIII secolo' (unpublished doctoral thesis, Milan, Università degli Studi, 2013), pp. 93–100.

Bernese imprint giving the city the cachet it was seeking. In reality, however, they were not published in Berne at all, but rather in Milan, by Giuseppe Galeazzi, in collaboration with Pietro Verri and Cesare Beccaria, for whom they became a precursor to *Il Caffé*, the most important eighteenth-century Italian-language periodical.

Transnational Projects and Their Purveyors

The transnational nature of Italian eighteenth-century periodicals has been alluded to above and deserves a more in-depth treatment than I can offer here. Often understood as a singular stroke of Milanese Enlightenment genius, *Il Caffé* was instead one of a cluster – the most well-known to be sure – of Italian-Swiss eighteenth-century periodicals that emerged in the shared conceptual Swiss-Lombardian space, where De Felice and Beccaria, the Verris and the rest of the members of the Accademia dei pugni [Academy of Fisticuffs] realized a set of transnational periodical projects. The little-known *Estratto della letteratura europea* was published in three different venues during the second half of the eighteenth century: Berne, 1758–62; Yverdon-les-Bains (Switzerland), 1762–66; and Milan, 1767–71. When its first issue was published in 1758, editor-in-chief De Felice reflected on the glut of newspapers in Europe, commenting that the public might think that creating yet another paper would be 'Like bringing clay pots to Samos, owls to Athens or crocodiles to Egypt'.[27] However, his periodical was going to be different. It was designed to bring news about European publications in all genres to an Italian-reading public, with the term 'literature' covering both scientific and creative writing. The *Estratto* became an important point of reference for the dissemination of knowledge in Italy in the second half of the eighteenth century and, though hardly known today, it also represented a joint venture with the Milanese Enlightenment periodical *Il Caffè* (1764–66), which overlapped with the *Estratto* not only in terms of dates, but also in themes, politics and journalists. The connection between the two periodicals is best shown through the mention of the *Estratto* in the introduction to the very first volume of *Il Caffè*. In answer to the rhetorical question, 'Why are you calling this paper *Il Caffè*?', the narrator replies that a Greek from Citera had traveled to the island of Mocha, where he traded in coffee, and then brought a large supply to Italy, where he had decided

---

[27] 'Portar, come si dice, a Samo vasi, Nottole a Atene, e Coccodrilli a Egitto'. This often-cited quote from Canto XL of Ariosto's Orlando furioso is used here to set up imagined public reaction to the publishing of yet another journal, and then to answer with all of the attributes that this new journal possesses over others. *Estratto della letteratura* III (1758), p. xii.

to settle. Moving through Livorno, he finally settled in Milan, where he began serving coffee in a *bottega*, also known as *Il Caffè*. There people would come and drink the best coffee:

> In essa bottega primieramente si beve un caffè che merita il nome veramente di caffè; caffè vero verissimo di Levante, e profumato col legno d'aloe, che chiunque lo prova, quand'anche fosse l'uomo il più grave, l'uomo il più plombeo della terra bisogna che per necessità si risvegli, e almeno per una mezz'ora diventi uomo ragionevole. In essa bottega vi sono comodi sedili, vi si respira un'aria sempre tepida e profumata che consola; la notte è illuminata, cosicché brilla in ogni parte l'iride negli specchi e ne' cristalli sospesi intorno le pareti e in mezzo alla bottega; in essa bottega chi vuol leggere trova sempre i fogli di novelle politiche, e quei di Colonia, e quei di Sciaffusa, e quei di Lugano, e vari altri; in essa bottega chi vuol leggere trova per suo uso e il *Giornale enciclopedico*, e l'*Estratto della letteratura europea*, e simili buone raccolte di novelle interessanti, le quali fanno che gli uomini che in prima erano Romani, Fiorentini, Genovesi o Lombardi, ora sieno tutti presso a poco Europei.[28]

> [In this shop, one mainly drinks coffee that is worthy of the name coffee, true coffee, the truest of coffees from the Levant, enhanced with aloe wood, and whoever tries it, whether he be the most serious of men, or the most leaden of those who ever walked the earth, is forced to wake up and become a reasonable man for at least half an hour. In this *bottega* there are comfortable chairs and you breathe in the warm, sweet-smelling air that consoles us; the night is lit and everything sparkles in the crystal sconces that line the *bottega* walls and in the chandeliers that hang from above. In this *bottega* those who wish to read will always find papers on political news from Cologne, Schaffhausen, Lugano and many others; in this *bottega* those who wish to read will find available for their use the *Giornale enciclopedico* and the *Estratto della letteratura europea* and similar, good collections of interesting news made by men who start out as Romans, Florentines, Genoese or Lombards, but all end up more or less Europeans]

The last lines of the passage express the excitement that spaces of public exchange could generate when periodicals offered cultural and political grist

---

[28] 'Introduzione', *Il Caffé*, 1, http://illuminismolombardo.it/testo/il-caffe-tomo-i/ [accessed 10 December 2019]. The translation of the passage is mine.

for discussion, all lubricated with a strong cup of coffee. The *Estratto*, together with other periodicals, was conceived of by these journalists as a tool that could transform the provincial views of the various regions of Italy (not yet part of a nation), fostering the transnational thinking that those in transit saw as critical to existing in the eighteenth century. Since the *Estratto* brought to the Italian-reading public translated excerpts from foreign works, together with reviews of books the editors believed Italians should know, its role in the dissemination of new knowledge in transnational perspective becomes central.

Even more transnational, though, is Italian encyclopedism, which has received little attention for some of the same reasons that Casanova's memoir was until recently largely denied as the masterpiece of transnational, cosmopolitan living that it is. These reasons include the French language flowing from the pens of Italian encyclopedists (in this case, Fortunato Bartolomeo De Felice), resulting in the 58-volume *Encyclopédie* d'Yverdon that he produced with an international group of encyclopedists in Switzerland (following the Masonic desire of his mentor, Di Sangro, to promote knowledge production and dissemination).[29] The Yverdon encyclopedia had European ambitions and sought to overcome the Paris *Encyclopédie*'s French hegemonic perspective. De Felice made geographical articles one of the focal points of his work, with cultural, economic, human and political geography offering content that was lacking in Diderot and D'Alembert's work. Diderot himself admitted that geography had been overlooked in his compilation. De Felice's sources were also far more diverse than those employed by the French encyclopedists, many of them being translations of Italian works that he commissioned and published at his Yverdon presses. Editions of Cesare Beccaria's *Dei delitti e delle pene* and Pietro Verri's *Meditazioni sulla felicià* are only two of the many translations he produced.

Yet another encyclopedic compilation warrants mention: the *Encyclopédie méthodique de Padoue*, published at the presses of the Seminario di Padova.

---

[29] Fortunato Bartolomeo De Felice, ed., *Encyclopédie, ou Dictionnaire universel raisonné des connoissances humaines*, 58 vols (Yverdon-les-Bains: n.p., 1770–80). On the Masonic *Encyclopédie* d'Yverdon, see my 'Fortunato Bartolomeo De Felice e l'*Encyclopédie* d'Yverdon: reti massoniche e cosmopolite nel transfer di conoscenza e cultura enciclopedica nel secolo dei lumi', in *Fortunato Bartolomeo De Felice (1723–1789): Un intellettuale cosmopolita nell'Europa dei lumi*, ed. by Stefano Ferrari (Milan: FrancoAngeli, 2017), pp. 103–40; on the transnational dimensions of the work, see my 'Reconceptualizing Enlightened Networks and their Mediators: Fortunato Bartolomeo De Felice and the Transmission of Knowledge across Eighteenth-Century Europe', *The Internationalization of Intellectual Exchange in a Globalizing Europe, 1636–1780*, ed. by Robert Mankin (Lewisburg: Bucknell University Press, 2017), pp. 163–95.

The editor of this revised edition of Charles-Joseph Panckoucke's 248-volume *Encyclopédie méthodique*, Giovanni Coi, engaged the services of Este librarian Girolamo Tiraboschi, author of the *Storia della letteratura italiana* which measured Italian letters against Spanish writing, in the interest of settling the Bouhours' controversy over taste. Tiraboschi revised the volumes on geography and history, which he found to be too French-leaning in their treatment and also in need of a thorough overhaul, particularly with respect to Italian content that had either been overlooked or purposefully left out. And while the decision of whether to publish in French or Italian was hotly debated by the editors and backers of the enterprise, the Seminario ultimately opted to publish in French. This was seen as a means of reaching a larger reading public, but also as a transnational challenge to prove that the Seminario was capable of being a viable French-language publisher for the world, with more reliable global content. These Italian publishers sought to delineate a less hegemonic, more egalitarian transnational perspective in a generic French language, akin to todays 'Globish', whether operating from across the Alps or within the Republic of Venice.[30]

Conclusion

Concluding this chapter about Italy's transnational eighteenth century feels like an arbitrary exercise, for there are so many reflections that have been barely articulated – the most obvious being perhaps those on gender and sexuality. Did women have a transnational Italian Enlightenment? What about queer Italian transnationalities? Where are the treatments of Lady Mary Wortley Montague and Joachim Winckelmann, whose sexuality as lived on Italian soil was as much a part of their transnational renown as were their writings? Not to mention the grand tourists, who practiced a version of sexual tourism in eighteenth-century Italy, with suggestive portraits captured by the sly brush of Pompeo Battoni, the highly sought after portrait artist of British grand tourists. As outlined in George Haggerty's seminal work *Men in Love: Masculinity and Sexuality in the Eighteenth Century* (New York: Columbia University Press, 1999), Italy was a site where homoerotic desire

---

[30] On the *Encyclopédie méthodique de Padoue*, see Giuseppe Bellini, *Storia della tipografia del Seminario di Padova* (Padua: Gregoriana editrice, 1938); Pietro Gnan, ed., *Un affare di dinaro, di diligenza, di scienza: L'edizione padovana dell'Encyclopédie méthodique, 1774–1817* (Padua: Biblioteca Universitaria, 2005); Clorinda Donato, 'Writing the Italian Nation in French: Cultural Politics in the *Encyclopédie méthodique de Padoue*', *New Perspectives on the Eighteenth Century*, 8 (Spring 2013), 12–27.

Figure 6.1 – Conversation in Zoffany's Study, attributed to Joseph McPherson (Florence 1726–82), courtesy of The Gallery of Modern Art, Pitti Palace, Florence.

was more easily practiced and expressed across national boundaries. We could also have easily devoted the entire chapter to Francesco Algarotti, transnational figure *par excellence*, whose queer relationships with Frederick the Great and Lord Hervey have been discussed in Giovanni dell'Orto's 'Socrate veneziano: Francesco Algarotti 1712–1764'.[31] The institution of *cicisbeismo*, which granted women the right to have sexual partners who were younger than the ones they had married for reasons of class and the protection of the family patrimony, constitutes another important aspect of lifestyle fashioning, this time overseen by women. And the Countess Panzutti – though only mentioned briefly here as De Felice's lover, liberated from the convent to pursue her sexual life with him as they traveled through Europe – defied the limits imposed by the husband who had locked her up. The sexual pursuits of the many women of every class with whom Casanova

---

[31] http://www.giovannidallorto.com/biografie/algarotti/algarotti.html [accessed 10 December 2019].

interacts in the *Histoire de ma vie* and the reasoned way he describes their right to pleasure and respect as a group remind us that his rational libertine beliefs contributed to new images and models of womanhood. Transnational Italian sexualities inform the anatomical research of anatomist Giovanni Bianchi, who wrote a medical novella about the transgendered Catterina Vizzani/Giovanni Bordoni, following his view that sexual preference is not determined by one's genitalia, and that all beliefs about anatomical sexuality are to be debunked. Bianchi also wrote about the actress Antonia Cavalucci and her right to be recognized for her craft, as were actresses in England. And while Bianchi's 1754 *In Lode dell'arte comica* earned him a listing on the Index, the impetus to write about what had heretofore been an obscure life offers us a view of a transnational Italian woman who, though vilified by some, was nonetheless able to capitalize on her agency along networks of sociability that advanced her career, and ultimately, her ability to craft her own life. We can read in the desire for sexual freedom a corollary to the intellectual freedom that so many sought in their transnational pursuits. Ultimately, lifestyle choices and experimentation with new relationships and family configurations were as much a part of the transnational Italian Enlightenment as were erudition and mobility. We are reminded here of the 'great groups' as a hallmark of the transnational Enlightenment discussed earlier, and it is the desire to emancipate all of humankind from limitations that perhaps best distinguishes Enlightenment transnationalism from its Renaissance counterpart. Indeed, it is the multiplicity of these lives and their capacity to unlock heretofore unimagined possibilities for the making of new forms of sociability, for themselves and their counterparts, that makes the eighteenth-century Italian transnational moment the most akin to our twenty-first-century life.

7

Italians in Hollywood

Giuliana Muscio

Transnational accounts overcome the limits of national historiographies and favor more interactive interpretative models, especially in the field of cinema, a truly international art and industry. In (Italian) film history this approach allows the discovery of hitherto ignored interactions, showing, for instance, how Italian silent cinema served as a model for the early American film industry; it also leads to an understanding of the complex professional, personal and political relations between American and Italian film practices. A transnational study escapes the trap whereby national film histories erase the experience of the Italian immigrant stage (present in many American cities with a diasporic community, where Italian companies of immigrant actors performed) from both Italian theater and American cinema and ignore the at times contradictory interactions of Italian silent cinema and Italian performers with the American film industry both in the US and in Italy.[1] Between 1880 and the early 1900s, the Italian immigrant stage was indeed a crucial cultural institution for the migrant communities in the US and above all in New York, where southern Italians were most numerous. Immigrant performers represented one of the most cohesive forces within the community from both the linguistic and cultural points of view, enacting and embodying *italianità* for American audiences, who

[1] Anita Loos, titlist of D. W. Griffith's *Intolerance*, recognized the impact of the literary intertitles written by D'Annunzio for *Cabiria* (Giovanni Pastrone, 1914) on her own work in 'Photoplay Writing', *Photoplay* (April 1918), 88–89, 121. See Giuliana Muscio, *Napoli/New York/Hollywood: Film between Italy and the United States* (New York: Fordham University Press, 2019) and Giuliana Muscio, 'Italiani a Hollywood', in *Italia a Hollywood*, ed. by Stefania Ricci (Milan: Skira, 2018), pp. 116–81.

did not disdain their shows. Music, too, played a key role: having 'always been central to Italian self-representations in the United States and their diasporic nation-making. Between 1899 and 1910, musicians represented by far the largest segment of the "skilled and professional" category of Italian immigrants in New York'.[2]

The silencing of this experience in both American and Italian historiography arguably constitutes a tremendous cultural loss in terms of diversity, for which a transnational approach may well provide a remedy. This historical analysis, based on archive research, aims to examine the role of immigrant performers in American media, while ignoring the complex vicissitudes of the production of at least a dozen silent American films in Italy[3] and the impact of the coming of sound, not only in relation to the issue of the *questione della lingua*, but because of the production of a number of Italian American films in the early 1930s, made mostly on the East Coast.[4] Before my book *Napoli/New York/Hollywood*, none of these aspects had received due attention, with the exception of work on sound, often limited to issues of dubbing, translation and multiple language versions. Recently, scholarly research has demonstrated that the first film spoken in Italian, *Sei tu l'amore?* (Alfredo Sabato, 1930), was made in Hollywood by migrant performers Guido Trento, Alberto Rabagliati, Luisa Caselotti and Henry Armetta, and that it actually premiered in Italy *before* what is conventionally considered the first Italian sound film, *Canzone dell'amore* (Gennaro Righelli, 1930).[5]

Italian film history has never investigated the presence of Italian performers and film professionals in American cinema before World War II, nor has it claimed any kind of 'Italian imprinting' on filmmakers such as Frank Capra and Robert Vignola, both born in Italy, and Italian Americans Gregory La Cava and Frank Borzage.[6]

Unlike other European film experiences in the US, only a minuscule number of Italian performers active in silent American cinema came

---

[2] Emelise Aleandri, *The Italian-American Immigrant Theatre of New York City* (Charleston: Arcadia, 1999).

[3] See Chapter 3, 'A Filmic Grand Tour', in Muscio, *Napoli/New York/Hollywood*, pp. 100–56.

[4] See Giuliana Muscio, 'Italian Americans and Cinema', in *The Routledge History of Italian Americans*, ed. by William Connell and Stanislao Pugliese (New York: Routledge, 2018), pp. 433–50.

[5] Denis Lotti, 'Babilonia e ritorno', in Alberto Rabagliati, *Quattro anni fra le 'Stelle'*, ed. by Denis Lotti (Cuneo: Nerosubianco, 2017), pp. 189–206.

[6] Jonathan J. Cavallero addresses the issue, but with scarce attention for the silent period, in *Hollywood's Italian American Filmmakers: Capra, Scorsese, Savoca, Coppola, and Tarantino* (Urbana: University of Illinois Press, 2011).

from Italian silent cinema; most of them were first- or second-generation immigrants performing on the immigrant stage. However, this key diasporic cultural institution does not appear at all in the histories of Italian theater, confirming the scarcity of engagement with the study of the Italian diaspora and its cultural manifestations in Italian history textbooks. The silence surrounding these figures cannot be explained but through their status as emigrants, since they were quite successful in their careers, with hundreds of titles in their filmographies; they also maintained their last names ending in a vowel and were thus recognizable as Italians in Hollywood; and they were regularly appreciated and positively reviewed by the American press. In Italy, however, only very specialized sources recorded their existence (e.g., the encyclopedia *Filmlexicon*); additionally, two articles discussed their work after fascism started claiming emigrants as 'Italians abroad'.[7]

The first step must therefore be to investigate the historical context able to explain this silence, namely national histories of emigration-immigration, in order to recognize the multidirectionality and circularity of the Italian diaspora and denounce Italian 'negationism' in relation to emigration and issues of 'race' – understood in the sense in which the concept was used during the time in question.[8] A transatlantic and transcultural approach can highlight the peculiarities of the history of Italian emigration to the Americas, the flow of exchange characterizing these phenomena, the symbolic impact of the concept of race on the construction of the Italian stereotype (by American media) at the time of the Great Immigration, and also how migration is not only a phenomenon of the past.[9] Furthermore, a

---

[7] The definition of 'Italians abroad' refers to the acute historical analysis by Mark Choate in *Emigrant Nation: The Making of Italy Abroad* (Cambridge, MA: Harvard University Press, 2008). The two articles are Gianni Puccini, 'Italiani nel mondo del cinema', *Cinema*, 20, 25 April 1937, pp. 329–31 and Mantica Barzini, 'Hollywood e gli Italiani', *Comoedia*, 12.5 (15 May–15 June 1930), 35–37.

[8] See Donna Gabaccia, 'Is Everywhere Nowhere? Nomads, Nations, and the Immigrant Paradigm of United States History', *Journal of American History*, 86.3 (December 1999), 1115–34 (p. 1120). See also Piero Bevilacqua, Andreina De Clementi and Emilio Franzina, *Storia dell'emigrazione italiana*, Vol. 2 (Rome: Donzelli, 2001); Stefano Luconi and Matteo Pretelli, *L'immigrazione negli Stati Uniti* (Bologna: il Mulino, 2008); Donna R. Gabaccia, *Italy's Many Diasporas* (London: University College London Press, 2000); Nancy Carnevale, *A New Language, A New World* (Urbana: University of Illinois Press, 2009).

[9] Italian migration to the US continued in the interwar years, when four million people left Italy, and after World War II, when eight million Italians left home to move also within Europe and to Australia and Canada. See Laura Ruberto and Joseph Sciorra, eds, *New Italian Migrations to the U.S.* (Urbana: University of Illinois Press, 2017).

transnational approach demonstrates how the US was certainly not the only destination of the Italian diaspora, although it was, in numerical terms, the main one. The numbers of Italian migrants to the US and Latin America were roughly equivalent, amounting to approximately five million each. However, the two flows differ both with regard to the points of departure and arrival, as well as having different time frames.[10] These differences had relevant cultural and racial implications: while Italian immigrants to South America integrated within Hispanic colonial societies, the Italian diaspora, like other 'new immigrants' from southern and eastern Europe, were not similarly welcomed in the US, and not entirely recognized as white.[11] 'Approximately 80 percent of [them] came from the poor, backward southern portion of Italy known as the *Mezzogiorno* – "the land that time forgot"', as Cosco defines it.[12] This description of Italian migration to the US highlights the implications of the Southern Question at the point of arrival, as well as its putative racial ramifications in WASP culture at the time, but it ignores the remaining 20 percent of Italian emigration and the fragmentation of Italian regional culture and social differences, rarely addressing, among other things, the diverse pattern of 'integration' of Italians in California.[13]

In addition to the regional and fragmented composition and the multi-directionality of the Italian diaspora, it is necessary to take into account its circularity, with a significant number of returns: from the US 58.6 percent

[10] The majority of northern Italian emigrants moved to South America before unification in 1861, while southern Italians emigrated later, as a result of the economic and social failure of unification, and settled in the urban industrial areas on the East coast of the US.

[11] John Higham, *Strangers in the Land: Patterns of American Nativism, 1895–1925* (New Brunswick: Rutgers University Press, 2002). On racialization see David Roediger, *Working Toward Whiteness* (New York: Perseus Book Group, 2005); Jennifer Guglielmo and Salvatore Salerno, *Gli italiani sono bianchi?* (Milan: Il saggiatore, 2003); and David Richards, *Italian American: The Racialization of an Ethnic Identity* (New York: New York University Press, 1999).

[12] Joseph Cosco, *Imagining Italians: The Clash of Romance and Race in American Perceptions 1880–1910* (Albany: State University of New York Press, 2003), pp. 3–4. See also John Dickie, *Darkest Italy: The Nation and Stereotypes of the Mezzogiorno 1860–1900* (New York: St. Martin's Press, 1999) and Nelson Moe, *The View from Vesuvius: Italian Culture and the Southern Question* (Berkeley: University of California Press, 2002).

[13] Gloria Ricci Lathrop, ed., *Fulfilling the Promise of California: An Anthology of Essays on the Italian American Experience in California* (Spokane: California Italian American Task Force, 2000) and Andrew Rolle, *Westward the Immigrants: Italian Adventures and Colonists in an Expanding America* (Niwot: University Press of Colorado, 1999).

Italians returned home, and from Latin America 44.5 percent.[14] These statistics suggest a radical revision in the analysis of the cultural strategies of the diasporic community. If in many – or most – cases returning home was a pre-established plan, it encouraged resistance to assimilation, shown by a scarce interest in learning English, for instance, and reinforced attachment to traditions. 'No other people emigrated in so many different directions, reaching numbers so elevated both in relative and absolute terms, and few others showed an attachment so visceral to the region of origin or returned in such a large percentage'.[15] Usually considered a regressive attitude, a form of nostalgia, the desire and intent to return home and maintain the roots of one's culture actually stimulated industriousness among Italian immigrants. It encouraged them to utilize modern modes of production in order to preserve their culture, such as producing food and entertainment according to tradition, both in New York and California. And within this process they interacted with other ethnic communities too: they did not simply come up against 'American culture'.[16]

Therefore, a cosmopolitan[17] and transnational perspective must focus on the historical specificity of both the transcultural traits of the American experience of Italian migrants and the Italian *cultura dello spettacolo*, where *spettacolo* includes all performing arts, from dance to opera, theater and even the circus. This approach embraces exchanges, interactions and commonalities, rather than establishing a primacy of Italian-ness or American-ness, thus favoring 'in-betweenness',[18] which in turn avoids freezing the complex Italian cultural identity into a fixed model.

---

[14] Francesco P. Cerase, 'L'onda di ritorno: i rimpatri', in *Storia dell'emigrazione italiana*, v.1, pp. 113–25 (p. 116). According to William Uricchio, the figure reached 73 percent between 1907 and 1911; see 'L'Italia Americana, l'America di Valentino', in *Valentino*, ed. by Paola Cristalli (Ancona: Cinegrafie, 1996), pp. 93–98 (p. 94).

[15] Donna Gabaccia, *Emigranti* (Turin: Einaudi, 2003), p. 73; my translation.

[16] See Simone Cinotto, *Making Italian America: Consumer Culture and the Production of Ethnic Identities* (New York: Fordham University Press, 2014), p. 2.

[17] Cosmopolitanism is 'a mode of critical thinking that is committed to struggling with the paradoxes and contradictions of cultural identity and discourse', and provides a useful model to escape the 'unproductive double binds of multiculturalism and an unreflective hegemonic universalism', going 'beyond cultural pluralism by thinking, at one and the same time, about difference *and* a democratic common ground and cultural field of mutual influence and growth'. Tania Friedel, *Racial Discourse and Cosmopolitanism in Twentieth-Century African American Writing* (New York: Routledge, 2008), p. 7.

[18] Roediger, *Working Toward Whiteness*, Part II, 'Inbetweenness', pp. 57–132.

Italian Performers in Silent American Film

It could easily be argued that performers are inherently cosmopolitan but this seems especially true in the instance of Italian immigrant actors, since they often traveled to Europe, the colonies and Latin America before reaching American shores; they inherited the traditions of the ancient Italian *cultura dello spettacolo*, often handed down through families of traveling players, and contributed to creating an international Hollywood and transnational media. An examination of the careers of a number of Italian immigrant actors in the US provides a key to identifying the artistic qualities appreciated by American audiences, showing how these artists learned new skills from Americans and from other immigrant performers in a reciprocal exchange. It also shows that the casting of Italian immigrants draws attention to the issue of American nativism (the anti-emigrationist prejudice characterizing WASP culture in connection with the Great Wave of emigration).

Interestingly enough, the international popularity of Italian cinema and culture coincided with the Great Wave of Italian emigration, but it interacted with the life and career of the Italian performers abroad in particularly complex ways in the United States. Contradictory as it may seem, at the very moment when Italomania reached its peak in the tastes of the Americans of the Golden Age, the Great Wave of immigration instigated strong anti-Italian prejudice and, as Russo writes, quickly turned Italophilia into Italophobia.[19] This profound contradiction clearly surfaces at times in this analysis.

Sicilian Antonio Maiori was an immigrant Shakespearean actor described by the American press as the 'Salvini of the Bowery' who appeared in *Poor Little Peppina* (Sidney Olcott, 1916) alongside silent star Mary Pickford. Cesare Gravina was an operetta conductor from Sorrento who became Eric von Stroheim's favorite player. Frank Puglia was a baritone who worked on the immigrant stage; he was discovered by D. W. Griffith, who offered him his debut in *Orphans of the Storm* (1921), with the Gish sisters. Tina Modotti, from Friuli, performed on the immigrant stage in San Francisco with the same company as Puglia, before starring in at least three films in Hollywood and going on to become one of the leading photographers of her time and an active communist militant. William Ricciardi, from Campania, started out on the immigrant stage with Maiori but separated from his company and moved to Broadway, appearing on screen in more or less minor roles, including

---

[19] John Paul Russo, 'From Italophilia to Italophobia: Representations of Italian Americans in the Early Gilded Age', *Differentia*, 6–7 (1994), 45–46. On this contradictory attitude see also Richard H. Broadhead, 'Strangers on a Train: The Double Dream of Italy in the American Gilded Age', *Modernism/Modernity*, 1.2 (1994), 1–19.

alongside Greta Garbo in the American film adaptation of Pirandello's *As You Desire Me* (George Fitzmaurice, 1932). Paul Porcasi launched the figure of the gangster-musical impresario with a pinstripe suit and a cigar, starting with a major success in *Broadway* (Paul Fejos, 1929). Henry Armetta left Palermo for Boston as a clandestine; he became a very popular character actor with a substantial film career, the only one to play a range of Italian characters on screen. Guido Trento, invited to Hollywood by director Gordon Edwards, left a promising film career in Italy as one of the leading men in Neapolitan and Italian silent cinema after working on the location shooting of *Nero* and *The Shepherd King* in Rome. In the US he, too, acted on the Italian immigrant stage and on Italian radio in San Francisco; he was responsible for the adventurous *Sei tu l'amore?* project. Being a star of nationalist Italian radio, he was interned at the start of World War II in a concentration camp in Missoula, Montana.[20] Neapolitan Fred Malatesta was a traveling player working in Europe, Latin America and American silent cinema, playing significant roles in *Little Lord Fauntleroy* (Alfred Green, 1921) alongside Mary Pickford, and as the French ambassador who courts Czarina Pola Negri in Lubitsch's *Forbidden Paradise* (1924). Monty Banks, alias Mario Bianchi from Cesena, was one of the main performers and directors of a particular type of sophisticated acrobatic and gracious variant of slapstick comedy. Mimì Aguglia, an international stage star very popular in Latin America, was offered the same contract as Eleonora Duse to tour the US. However, she would only obtain important film roles after the advent of sound.[21]

As with Italian migrants, the trajectory of these careers was multidirectional, not only transatlantic but circular, including surprisingly high numbers of returns home. Indeed, the expression used to describe the protagonists of the circularity of diasporic travels, 'birds of passage', applies particularly well to Italian performers, who at times returned to Italy to stay in touch with the professional scene, whether it be musical or stage.[22] But most of all, they 'returned' regularly to their culture, remaining loyal to traditional forms as well as innovating them. In fact, these performers were Italian

[20] Giuliana Muscio, 'Guido Trento: From the "Neapolitan Synecdoche" to *Italian American-ness*', in Anthony Tamburri, Carla Francellini and Sabrina Vellucci, eds, *Re-Mapping Italian America* (New York: Bordighera Press, 2018), pp. 229–46. On internment see Lawrence DiStasi, ed., *Una Storia Segreta: The Secret History of Italian American Evacuation and Internment during World War II* (Berkeley: Heyday Books, 2001).

[21] See Argentina Brunetti, *In Sicilian Company* (Boalsburg: Bear Manor Media, 2005).

[22] See Simona Frasca, *Italian Birds of Passage: The Diaspora of Neapolitan Musicians in New York* (New York: Palgrave MacMillan, 2014).

not only by birth, but because their very theatrical culture was Italian. Indeed, Italian performers could count on long-standing traditions of *spettacolo* such as *Commedia dell'Arte* (improvised representation), *melodrama* (opera), and *opera buffa* (comic opera, inaugurated by Pergolesi with *La serva padrona*, 1733, and continued by Mozart, Donizetti and Rossini). These forms implied naturalism and improvisation, embraced high and low art, tragedy and comedy, music, dance and, at times, acrobatics, within an articulate use of the body, facial expressions and gestures. Furthermore, the very programming of Italian companies, changing show every night and adding musical and comic intervals, implied and nurtured their uncommon versatility. In a sense, the art of these performers bridged the very contradiction onto which the love-hate relation with Italy was founded in the US: nature vs. culture. American silent cinema appreciated their qualities: a naturalism well suited to a narrative cinema that often focused on action, less mannered than in the American stage tradition; and a versatility that allowed the use of their professional services in the (fast) productions of different genres.

On stage in the US, these actors performed Shakespeare and the classics in Italian also for American audiences,[23] thus evoking the image of the great tradition of Italian *spettacolo*, an image of Italy associated with art, emotions and naturalism. The 'Grande Attore Italiano' of the nineteenth century, as studied by Stanislavsky,[24] was particularly appreciated by the same American upper classes who enjoyed the Grand Tour, Italian opera and coeval Italian theatre, from Sem Benelli's *The Jest* (translation of *La cena delle beffe*, the *pièce de resistance* of the Barrymores) to Pirandello and D'Annunzio.[25]

In the figure of the Italian diasporic performer, two different cultural layers always coexisted, actually forming one complex entity: the popular southern tradition, embodied by the Neapolitan *cultura dello spettacolo*, typical of the East Coast immigrant stage with its *sceneggiate* and *macchiette* – a tradition that still runs strongly in Italian American culture – and an upper-class *italianità*, made of opera and the classics, well represented by the 'Teatro italiano' constituted by Mimì Aguglia in San Francisco in the 1930s.[26] Just like puff pastry, there is simply no way of separating these layers, which

---

[23] Lawrence Levine, *Highbrow/Lowbrow: The Emergence of Cultural Hierarchy in America* (Cambridge, MA: Harvard University Press, 1988), pp. 86–87.

[24] Konstantin Stanislavsky, *An Actor's Work: A Student Diary* [1938] (London: Routledge, 2008).

[25] 'Known as "The Jest" in English it was later performed by the Barrymore family in 1919'. Lawrence Estavan, *The Italian Theatre in San Francisco* (San Bernardino: Borgo Press, 1991), p. 85. On the popularity of D'Annunzio in the US see Luca Scarlini, *D'Annunzio a Little Italy* (Rome: Donzelli, 2008).

[26] See Estavan, *The Italian Theatre in San Francisco*, p. 96.

create an articulate image of the Italian performer as holding together high and low, tragic and comic, naturalism and irony. This dual nature of Italian *cultura dello spettacolo*, both popular and 'Southernist'[27] and upscale classical, is inextricable and explains the contradictions and oscillations between fame, glory and prejudice that emerge in its story and lasting success.

Mostly born in southern Italy, these performers could count on the fertile popular theatrical culture of that area, thus (re)creating the Neapolitan cultural *koinè*, the common southern language/culture. As noted in the still-relevant work of Giuseppe Galasso, Naples meant not only the city itself, but 'a synthesis, also in ethnic and social terms, of the entire south of Italy', a regional metropolis with a significant 'continuity between the city and the countryside', rooted in ancient folk/popular traditions and a long history of interaction.[28] Cross-class and long-lasting cultural forms in the musical field, such as *opera buffa* and *canzone napoletana*, help explain why the *cultura dello spettacolo* of this cosmopolitan metropolis came to represent Italian popular culture *tout court*, both in Italy and worldwide. Furthermore, an extensive use of the concept of the Neapolitan metropolis allows one to consider southern Italian performers as part of the hegemonic Neapolitan *cultura dello spettacolo*, emphasizing how this *koinè* became the foundation on which Italian American culture would be built and the backbone of the Italian American stereotype. An interesting phenomenon, given that these performers were rarely called upon to interpret Italian characters.

As an implicit rule that can be detected from filmographies, American silent cinema avoided casting Italian actors and actresses, especially those coming from the immigrant stage, as Italian characters, in order not to combine the ethnicity of the actor (problematic in itself at the time of the Great Emigration) with that of the character. In fact, anti-Italian prejudice reveals itself in American silent cinema both in terms of casting and characterization. In reference to national identity, at a time in which accents were of no importance, Italians played mostly a vague Continental European identity or else Latin Americans and light-colored people. With regard to characters, there is a passive/active alternative on a fixed axis of emotionality, with Italians being

---

[27] 'Attuned to the cosmopolitan and intermedial fascination with the picturesque, a Southernist aesthetic traveled', as Bertellini argues, 'like its dialectically opposed *Romanitas*, across geographical borders and media forms [...] It eventually found the most fertile terrain of re-actualization in the small-time vaudeville houses and movie theatres of the Lower East Side, where it matched American nativist prejudices with performances of vernacular authenticity'. Giorgio Bertellini, *Italy in Early American Cinema* (Bloomington: Indiana University Press, 2010), p. 50.

[28] On Naples and the South see Giuseppe Galasso's *Il Mezzogiorno nella storia d'Italia* (Florence: Le Monnier, 1977) and *Napoli* (Bari: Laterza, 1987).

either pathetic or violent. The casts and plots of American silent films indicate that Italian performers often interpreted aristocrats or circus and musical artists, whereas the Italian characters were equally divided between criminals and musicians. There was indeed a perverse dialectic by which Italian actors were appreciated and engaged to play any type of nationality and class, while Italian characters were definitely polarized as negative (criminal) types or sentimental and ineffectual figures. Keeping in mind this complex relationship between actor and character, it is possible to reconstruct a more complex discourse about Italian identity and Italian culture in American media, emphasizing the divergence between the rigidity of the Italian stereotype and the versatility of the performers. The stereotype being constructed was associated with sentimentality, the family, food, music and weapons and holds even today in American media. And yet it was the versatility of these actors that contributed to the construction of film genres related to music or sophisticated continental high life, with their Italian last names on the credits meant to sanction a convincing representation. Therefore, Hollywood made good use of these performers, and they repaid this by functioning well in its system.

The geographical origins of the artists so far discussed are quite relevant to this dynamic, but they are certainly not the sole or best way to group these performers. Class and gender constitute another important grid, keeping in mind that 'class' also has to do with the branch of the performing arts practiced by the individual artist: for audiences and producers, a stage actor or an opera singer belonged on a higher plane than a comedian performing on the immigrant stage.

Indeed, a small segment of the Italian performers in American silent films was constituted by personalities of true (or, at least, not contested) aristocratic origins like Albert Conti and Tullio Carminati, from Trieste and Dalmatia, respectively, or Neapolitans Mario Carillo (Caracciolo) and Eugenio De Liguoro. Rudolph Valentino was not aristocratic, but production companies played on this mythology, easily associated with his elegant personality. The *ballerine* Maria Gambarelli and Francesca Biaggiotti were also part of the upper echelon of this crowd, together with the few actors, such as Agostino Borgato and Lido Manetti, who left the agonizing Italian film industry for Hollywood. While performers from the immigrant stage worked mostly as character actors, aristocratic personalities or actors from Italian cinema enjoyed greater chances of playing leading or important roles in American silent films. Had Manetti not died in a mysterious accident,[29] he might even have become a star.

---

[29] In an interview, Sergio Leone stated that his father, Roberto Roberti, who had directed Manetti in his Italian career, suggested that the actor's death was not accidental. Diego Gabutti, *C'era una volta in America* (Milan: Rizzoli, 1984).

The profession of highest standing in the performing arts at this time was that of the opera singer: American silent cinema immediately seized the opportunity to cast worldwide celebrities such as Lina Cavalieri and Enrico Caruso in fiction films, even though their voices could not be heard.[30] In fact, Famous Players-Lasky 'hired' Cavalieri and Caruso as celebrities – as the very name of the company suggests – and as representatives of a high-status cultural form that could bestow its legitimation on American silent film, still in search of a definitive international affirmation. The films Cavalieri and Caruso made constitute a sort of exemplary unit: they were produced in the same period (1917–19), mostly directed by the same filmmaker (Edward José) and written by the same screenwriter (Margaret Turnbull), but they were not particularly successful.

Lina Cavalieri[31] had had an early start in film in the US, appearing in *Manon Lescaut*, a prestigious six-reel picture made in 1914, a year before soprano Geraldine Farrar's much-discussed film debut in Cecil B. DeMille's *Carmen*. She made four films for Famous Players-Lasky: *The Eternal Temptress* (Emile Chautard, 1917), *Love's Conquest* (Edward José, 1918), *A Woman of Impulse* (José, 1918) and *The Two Brides* (José, 1919). The plots of Cavalieri's American pictures evoke melodramatic Italian *diva films*, in that she comes across as a seductress, almost a vamp – the symbolic expression of eugenic fears.[32] As in the case of Caruso's films, the film characters that Cavalieri interprets share some traits with her true person, including nationality (they are Italian), and have to do with culture, music and seduction. Since her fame preceded her on screen, the narratives exploited it in order to reinforce her roles (though to no avail in terms of commercial success). However, Cavalieri was the only Italian actress cast in protagonist roles as an Italian in American silent cinema – a particularly interesting detail as regards gender. From what is known so far, there were no other Italian actresses on the American silent screens, apart from Tina Modotti, who moved over from the immigrant stage and interpreted Mexican characters in minor productions. In fact, the immigrant stage did not develop strong female performers, with the exception of Gilda Mignonette in the world of popular music. Mimì Aguglia, the leading light

[30] Paul Fryer, *The Opera Singer and the Silent Film* (Jefferson, NC: McFarland & Co., 2006).

[31] See Elena Mosconi, 'Lina Cavalieri sullo schermo', in *Italia a Hollywood*, ed. by Stefania Ricci (Milan: Skira, 2018), pp. 210–29.

[32] As Bram Dijkstra argues in *Evil Sisters*, in American popular culture the vamp expressed both the fear of and the fascination with foreign women and with the aggressive sensuality of the modern woman. Bram Dijkstra, *Evil Sisters: The Threat of Female Sexuality and the Cult of Manhood* (New York: Henry Holt, 1996).

of 'teatro italiano' in the US, refused film roles and played only an uncredited cameo in *The Last Man on Earth* (John Blystone, 1924).

This discussion on the casting of female roles cannot fail to underline, however, that most of the greatest American stars interpreted at least one Italian character on the silent screen, either as a poor orphan girl (Lillian Gish, Mary Pickford) or a dangerous vamp (Theda Bara, Greta Garbo). This duality is not surprising, given the way anti-Italian prejudice worked in relation to feminine characters in Victorian times in the US, mostly presenting them either as victims or destructive women in early films.

Enrico Caruso escaped the stigma of his national (and southern) identity only in part.[33] In his American film career he acted in two silent films: *My Cousin* (1918) and *The Splendid Romance* (1919, now lost), both by Edward José. Aside from this, his presence in silent pictures includes numerous appearances in newsreels documenting his career, his extensive travels and his daily life, with his Italian sons, American wife Dorothy and their daughter, Gloria. He also participated in early experimentations with synchronized sound, although no actual footage exists. Given his passion for mechanics and media technology, he shot some comic home movies, too.

In the summer of 1918, Caruso accepted Famous Players-Lasky's exceptional offer of $200,000 for two films (*My Cousin* and *The Splendid Romance*) to be shot in New York at the Artcraft studios.[34] Set in Little Italy, *My Cousin* proposes the tenor in a double role, as Tommasso [*sic*], an Italian immigrant *figurinaio*, that is, a sculptor of sorts, and as his famous cousin, the great singer Caroli. Unexpected as it might have appeared to anyone unfamiliar with Caruso's identification with the Italian diaspora, the most important role in the film is that of the poor immigrant, while 'the tenor' is seen in a few sequences documenting his success, including a scene on the stage of the Metropolitan, where he is singing his most famous aria, *Vesti la giubba* – the first record in the history of music to sell one million copies. Compared with the performance style typical not only of opera but also of silent cinema, Caruso's naturalistic interpretation, in line with the *verismo* school he represented, is incredibly modern. He gives the two figures different characterizations, based on different

---

[33] For instance, in January 1906, *The New York Evening Telegram* published this item: 'Everyone is wondering now if Signor Caruso eats garlic. Because if he does eat garlic then everybody thinks that there shouldn't be another performance of *Tosca* at the Metropolitan Opera House this winter [...] neither Emma Eames or Lillian Nordica should have their delicate sensibilities over-taxed by the smell of garlic on the breath of their leading man'. Fryer, *The Opera Singer*, p. 19.

[34] On this experience, I curated the exhibit 'Starring Enrico Caruso' for the Cineteca of Bologna in June 2010.

aspects of his personality: the *figurinaio* is shy but warm and humorous, the tenor authoritative, almost arrogant, but self-ironic. And yet, for complex reasons, having to do mostly with the fact that his singing could not be heard and that he was on screen as an immigrant more than as an opera star, the film was a commercial flop, and his second film, *The Splendid Romance*, was not even distributed in the US. Indeed, Caruso's film experience is rarely mentioned, even though *My Cousin* is no minor picture, and, furthermore, it allows us to perceive the superior and modern quality of his performing style.

Newspaper coverage of the making of the films documents the presence of immigrant actor Cesare Gravina on the set as a 'personal film trainer' for Caruso.[35] Together with the role played by William Ricciardi as a restaurant owner in *My Cousin*, Gravina's presence on the set indicates an unexpected osmosis within the performers' community of the Italian diaspora: musicians and actors, the opera star and the local celebrities of Little Italy group together, assisting each other and interacting with different media.

The ability of the performers of the diaspora to move from stage to screen and soon also to radio – from music and ballet to drama – essentially operating among different media, is a trait of this culture that maintained its national character, all the while being able to capture the interest of an increasingly wide public. In music it absorbed and exchanged experiences with Afro-American and Latin counterparts, whereas on the stage it was close to the Yiddish theatre, the American vaudeville or Broadway.

The work of Italian performers was also a force for innovation. It can be argued that Caruso was the first modern media star:[36] he had used the new recording technology before reaching the US and utilized media skillfully, controlling his own photographic image, populating newspapers with the caricatures he drew himself and being a testimonial for anything from musical instruments to food and even tobacco. He introduced *verismo* into opera performances and, by combining *bel canto* with popular Neapolitan songs, formed a new cross-class audience.

Valentino was a sensual romantic star, able to combine erotic seduction with emotional fragility and spiritual affect, becoming the first actor to be the object of cult-like fandom. Southern Italian performers could count on the cultural power of Italian stage traditions and on their individual artistry to resist nativist and racialized prejudice. Indeed, in the 1920s, at the peak of

---

[35] Undated clipping, 'Gatti's Star Tenor Invading Domain of Movies Playing Double Role in "My Cousin Caruso"' (Caruso Collection, Peabody Institute).

[36] Giuliana Muscio, 'Caruso First Modern Media Star' in *Divinità canore. La canzone napoletana e lo spettacolo popolare*, ed. by Enrico Careri and Anna Masecchia. Quaderno del Centro Studi Canzone Napoletana (forthcoming).

anti-Italianism, the worldwide popularity of Neapolitan Enrico Caruso and of Rudolph Valentino from Puglia coincided, in the US, with the imposition of restrictive quotas on Italian immigration and with the Sacco and Vanzetti case.[37]

Italian performers in American cinema participated – unwillingly and/or unconsciously – in the construction of the American imaginary that brought about the 'irresistible empire'.[38] They functioned well within the strategy of ethnic flexibility adopted by the American film industry, that is, within the Hollywood 'melting pot' that distributed nationalities and ethnicities in an (apparently?) cosmopolitan geography. However, Italian performers partly challenged this social construction of Americanization because their strong stage traditions maintained a mark of national distinction in their performances, confirmed in the credits by their last names ending in a vowel.

The Italian *cultura dello spettacolo* penetrated American media from the very beginning and it continues to assert its presence, linking Antonio Maiori (the 'Salvini of the Bowery') to Al Pacino in the interpretation of Shakespeare; connecting Caruso to Frank Sinatra and Lady Gaga as singers transformed into actors; and associating Martin Scorsese and Francis Coppola with the traditions of *sceneggiata*.[39] Italian-American artists are also staking a claim to a share in continuity through the recuperation of this patrimony, either materially, like Scorsese, who sponsored the restoration of two of the Italian American films produced in New York in the early 1930s: *The Movie Actor* with the *macchiettista* Farfariello (Eduardo Migliaccio) and the *sceneggiata Santa Lucia Luntana*; or culturally, as in the case of John Turturro, with his film *Illuminata*, in which he re-enacted the colorful experience of a company on the immigrant stage; or genetically, in the case of Francis Coppola, grandson of Neapolitan Francesco Pennino, writer of Italian-American *sceneggiate* composed in the US. This cultural heritage is not yet recorded in books, but it has left an undeniable mark on the cultural production of contemporary Italian American filmmakers.[40]

[37] Bartolomeo Vanzetti and Nicola Sacco were two Italian anarchists accused of homicide and robbery. Having been tried and sentenced to death, although there was massive international pressure in their defense, they were executed in 1927.

[38] Victoria de Grazia, *Irresistible Empire: America's Advance through 20th-Century Europe* (Cambridge, MA: The Belknap Press, 2005).

[39] Aaron Baker, ed., *A Companion to Martin Scorsese* (Oxford: Wiley Blackwell, 2016).

[40] See Giuliana Muscio, Joseph Sciorra, Giovanni Spagnoletti and Anthony Tamburri, eds, *Mediated Ethnicity: New Italian-American Cinema* (New York: John D. Calandra Italian American Institute, 2010), a publication related to the film festival devoted to Italian American Contemporary Cinema held in Pesaro, in 2007.

A transatlantic and transcultural approach reveals the major cultural role of immigrant performers in the history of Italian emigration to the Americas, showing the importance of the flow of exchanges while, at the same time, pointing to a view of 'race' with its roots in the Italian southern question and to its impact on the construction of the Italian stereotype by American media.

8

Italy and Italian Studies in the Transnational Space of Migration and Colonial Routes

Teresa Fiore

Introduction: The Aporia of Italy and Italian Studies

The current challenges faced by the arts and humanities and foreign languages in the education system, but in particular in higher education, have prompted the need, as well as the desire, to rethink the scope of these disciplines and better serve the needs of the students of the third millennium. To show their relevance, or even usefulness, such disciplines have found themselves undergoing some radical changes in terms of content, methods and goals in order to expose students to topical questions. The consideration of critical contemporary issues in a globalized world has functioned as a major driver in this direction (the protection of the environment, the impact of technology, the ethical implications of scientific experimentation). At the same time, the fields of foreign, modern and world languages, which in countries such as the US are terms used quite interchangeably to label departments of languages, have increasingly, although not uniformly, embraced historical and social phenomena able to transcend the borders of the nation-state. Departments sensitive to this approach have in fact proposed a porous perception and understanding of cultures within a transnational framework embracing various forms of mobility from colonial to postcolonial and migrant, with which twenty-first-century, often multilingual, students with multifarious family and life backgrounds are increasingly in tune.

This chapter looks at the shift from a national to a transnational model in the field of Italian, in particular, as part of a recognition of the intrinsic history and culture of mobility of the country. In providing the context and reasons for this shift at this point in time, the chapter illustrates specific pedagogical routes and teaching materials, as well as opportunities and challenges within the classroom, especially at the linguistic level. Due to the country's long and complex process of unification and identity formation as well as its deep concern with internal regional diversity, Italian programs and departments have tended to cling on to the idea of the nation in more tenacious ways, in part to find full acknowledgment in the academic establishment abroad, at least in the US. Historically, majors and minors in Italian at US institutions have been asked to engage with Italy's complex identity as a diverse country but in the direction of a binding canon designed to ground the culture in a geographically contained tradition. Even the critiques advanced against the canon in the past 20 years,[1] when attention has shifted, for instance, towards other genres (cinema, the graphic novel), have left the national space largely unchallenged. Despite the expanded vision of the European Union, students have been asked to continue to explore an essentially enclosed national space, often perceived as relatively small and homogeneous in US academia (especially *vis-à-vis* French and Spanish with their global breadth), except when the country's regionalism reveals variety and porosity, and its 'areas of excellence' (cultural niches, Made in Italy, UNESCO sites) place it in an internationally recognized position.

One of the critical moves in the rupturing of this national/ist drive has been the introduction, in both the research agendas and the curricula of roughly the past two decades, of the analysis of migrations from and to Italy and their layered imbrications with past colonial enterprises and postcolonial legacies.[2] Interestingly, in order to look forward, the discipline has had to look back, and in the process has foregrounded the dynamics of intercultural encounters and conflicts that by definition blur the national boundaries and define a space in which Italy abroad and the abroad in Italy interact closely.

---

[1] Among the US-related interventions, see Maria Marotti, ed., *Italian Women Writers from the Renaissance to the Present: Revising the Canon* (University Park: Penn State University Press, 1996); Millicent Marcus, 'A Coming-of-Age-Story: Some Thoughts on the Rise of Italian Film Studies in the United States', *Italian Studies*, 63.2 (2008), 266–69; Graziella Parati's two-volume edited collection *New Perspectives in Italian Cultural Studies* (Lanham: Rowman & Littlefield, 2012) and her co-edited volume *Italian Cultural Studies* with Ben Lawton (Berkeley: Small Press Distribution, 2001). A British article that focuses on new routes for the discipline is Florian Mussgnug, Giuliana Pieri and Clodagh Brook, 'Italian Studies: An Interdisciplinary Perspective', *Italian Studies*, 72.4 (2017), 380–92.

[2] A quick look at the Modern Language Association list of open positions from 2005 to the present shows an increasing inclusion of terms such as 'migration' and 'diaspora' in job descriptions, while the most recent ones openly refer to transnational studies (University of California, Santa Barbara, November 2019). See https://recruit.ap.ucsb.edu/JPF01601 [accessed 15 May 2020].

What stories can Italy's millions of emigrants since the unification of the country tell us that function as a mirror to the experience of millions of migrants who have arrived in Italy over decades? Can academic institutions still define Italy in national terms *vis-à-vis* these long-term transnational movements in multiple directions (departure, arrival, return, transit), which have changed the demographic and cultural outlook of both Italy and the countries that Italians have moved to? The preoccupation of the discipline with its future[3] has turned for many into the realization that Italy as a cultural and political space can be better and more dynamically explored by looking at those spaces pre-occupied by the cultures and politics of past mobility, and at the impact they have (had) on the present.[4] Through this approach, the country's outbound and inbound migrations as well as its colonial and imperial experience constitute fulcra rather than epiphenomena of the country's national formation. A veritable spatial aporia, national Italy cannot fully exist without the vast transnational Italy.

This essay will offer an overview of these transnational forms of mobility. While the awareness of these movements is widespread, interestingly, specific knowledge of dates, locations, statistics, etc. is often lacking as part of a shared repertoire of information, even among Italians and people of Italian descent abroad. The essay will also address the pivotal role of cultural texts, by which I mean works of literature, music, film, etc. reflecting stories of mobility, and in particular in a correlated way (i.e., by dynamically linking experiences of outbound and inbound migration as well as colonialism). The final section of the chapter includes the close analysis of a text that connects these routes in powerful ways. The 2011 play *Italianesi*, written and performed by Saverio La Ruina, weaves tales of Italian departures and returns prompted by colonial expansion, international politics and the lure of Italy that productively 'confuse' the notion of Italian-ness *vis-à-vis* an Albanian identity. In the conclusion, I offer new prospects for Italian studies via the as-yet-unexplored possibility of a multi-migration, and perhaps multi-language, learning space for migrations from/to Italy.

---

[3] A number of targeted conferences in the past few years, along with special panels at conventions, have focused on the so-called 'crisis' of the field and on the strategies and innovation to be embraced in order to rethink Italian departments and programs. See Georgetown University's annual conference in October for the Settimana della Lingua Italiana nel mondo, and the regular American Association of Italian Studies (AAIS), Italian Association of Italian Teachers (AATI) and MLA conferences.

[4] The concepts of preoccupation and pre-occupation are central to Teresa Fiore, *Pre-Occupied Spaces: Remapping Italy's Transnational Migrations and Colonial Legacies* (New York: Fordham University Press, 2017). With the publisher's permission, this essay is in small part adapted from the 'Introduction', pp. 1–20.

In this chapter, Italy clearly emerges as an intrinsically migratory country whose vast patrimony of mobility ironically continues to foster the production of (partial) amnesia and invisibility, or excessive stories of success and failure prompted by mythicization or demonization of migrants of all times. As I claim, the careful observation of these experiences of pluridirectional migrations, especially as reflected in cultural texts, instead sheds light on the nonlinear, often contradictory, and for that reason fascinating, nature of the migratory experience. In summary, Italy offers a trove of these complex stories that have the potential to revolutionize our understanding of the country.

Italy Abroad, Abroad in Italy: The Intricate Overlapping of Italian Migration and Colonial Routes

I will start this section with an anecdote. The hairdressing studio that I – an Italian who moved to the US over 20 years ago – go to in New York is a veritable melting pot: founded by an Italian immigrant in partnership with a Jew, it rests mostly on the work of employees from Eastern Europe and Latin America. Yet it is a subtext of this melting pot that is particularly striking. The young Italian American woman at the reception counter, Rosa, addresses me in Italian and shares stories of her regular vacations in Sicily with her parents to visit *la famiglia*, while Vera, from Albania, also speaks Italian as she tends to my hair and shares stories of Italians in Albania during the brief colonial period, as well as of Albanians in Italy today. However, as my conversations with them have revealed, both these subjects and storytellers of Italy's transnational mobility have only a partial awareness of the historical circumstances underlying their shared knowledge of Italian.

The anecdote contains all the elements of the mobility paradigm – circular and/or overlapping routes of emigration, colonialism and immigration – that are at the core of a transnational reading of Italy. In this section, I illustrate these routes of mobility from a historical and sociological perspective in order to provide a stratified and interlinked backdrop to Italian stories of movement. The complicated genesis of the country resulting from the stitching together over decades (from the first half of the 1800s all the way to World War I) of territories that belonged to foreign powers or the Church coexists with what can also be viewed as a foundational tale (i.e., the powerful story that unraveled outside the national borders, even when they were still newly formed). From 1876 to 1976, approximately 27 million Italians left the country and emigrated to practically all continents,[5] a 'flow' that is probably

---

[5] Emilio Franzina, *Gli Italiani al Nuovo Mondo: L'emigrazione italiana in America 1492–1942* (Milan: Mondadori, 1995), p. 145.

more accurately described as a hemorrhage, and that constitutes the largest emigration from any country,[6] with peaks in the period 1880–1920 and after World War II. Italians emigrated virtually everywhere, giving priority to different continents and countries at different times due to specific economic and political reasons. As a result of their strong regional affiliations (north vs. south), they were treated differently in different places, but overall integration was never easy, not even in places where the Italian community, or 'colony' as it was called back then, was large and mixed. Primary destinations initially included Argentina and Brazil (starting in the 1870s), especially from the northern regions of Italy, while with the mass emigration of 1880–1920, the US became a major receiving country for Italian immigrants, especially from the south. While Italian emigration is strongly linked to 'America' in the common perception, in reality, Italians emigrated predominantly to Europe (Germany, France, Belgium) in the course of the century under discussion and added Canada, Australia and Venezuela to their routes mainly after World War II. The strong impact of the Italian presence abroad is oddly unequal to the faint trace it has left in Italy's collective imaginary, due perhaps to a preponderance of either family-focused stories or academic studies over public educational projects.[7] Yet the space of the Italian diaspora is integral to that of Italy in economic terms (revenues from emigrants, creation of markets for Italian products) and cultural terms (diffusion of the language, music, arts, literature, social practices, intellectual thought, political ideas).

Shortly after the official unification in 1861 and coterminous with the diaspora described above, Italy embarked on the colonial enterprise: over the decades, this economic and military process created an offshore empire, known as the Empire of Oriental Africa in the mid-1930s, comprising the African Horn, Libya, the Dodecanese Islands and Albania. The majority of these colonies were lost during and after World War II.[8] Italian colonialism

---

[6] Rudolph Vecoli, 'The Italian Diaspora, 1876–1976', in *The Cambridge Survey of World Migration*, ed. by Robin Cohen (Cambridge: Cambridge University Press, 1995), pp. 114–22 (p. 114).

[7] Among the canonical studies, see the two-volume *Storia dell'emigrazione italiana: Partenze* and *Storia dell'emigrazione italiana: Arrivi*, ed. by Piero Bevilacqua, Andreina De Clementi and Emilio Franzina (Rome: Donzelli, 2001–02); *Migrazioni italiane: Storia e storie dall'Ancien régime a oggi*, ed. by Patrizia Audenino and Maddalena Tirabassi (Milan: Mondadori, 2008); Donna Gabaccia, *Italy's Many Diasporas* (Seattle: University of Washington Press, 2000).

[8] For an overview of Italian colonialism, see Ruth Ben-Ghiat, 'Italy and Its Colonies', in *A Historical Companion to Postcolonial Literatures – Continental Europe and Its Empires*, ed. by Lars Jensen, Prem Poddar and Rajeev Patke (Edinburgh: Edinburgh University Press, 2008), pp. 262–312; Nicola Labanca, *Oltremare: Storia dell'espansione*

is a complex mosaic of both brief and extended forms of control of territories, which due to its fragmentation has often been dismissed as secondary or harmless. Fraught with contradictions and misinterpretations that the country has too slowly uncovered, Italy's colonialism/imperialism overlapped with emigration. Together, the two projects contributed fundamentally to the atypical formation of national identity outside the country, marked as both these initiatives were by demographic relocations towards what were called *colonie* in both cases.[9] The apparently small percentage of Italians who moved to the territorial colonies between the end of the nineteenth century and the first half of the twentieth – 2 percent of the total of Italian emigrants in the world[10] – indicates a multidirectional demographic flow that along with emigration shaped the modern nation of Italy away from its centuries-long fragmentation into small states and regions. The nationalist propaganda accompanying both emigration and the colonial/imperial enterprise functioned as cultural connective tissue for Italy and also for Italians outside the country, while forming a model of a nation in motion variously characterized by brief seasonal and definitive long-term relocations of people for economic, military and political reasons. In other words, the space of transnational Italy has been strategically used to strengthen the national rhetoric at specific points in time, thus corroborating the argument that the two spaces are complementary.

In an interesting reversal, since the mid-1970s Italy has become a country of destination, virtually as soon as it stopped sending emigrants abroad in large quantities. After the first arrivals of domestic helpers from Catholic countries such as the Philippines in the 1970s, the 1980s mark the more numerically visible presence of immigrants from Africa: yet it is in the following decade that the phenomenon becomes even more tangible, variegated and rooted. In Italy today, so-called regular immigrants represent roughly 8 percent of the

coloniale italiana (Bologna: il Mulino, 2007); Angelo Del Boca, *Gli italiani in Africa orientale*, 4 vols (Milan: Mondadori, 1992); Angelo Del Boca, *Gli italiani in Libia*, 2 vols (Milan: Mondadori, 1993–94); Jaqueline Andall and Derek Duncan, eds, *Italian Colonialism: Legacy and Memory* (New York: Peter Lang, 2005).

[9] On liberal and fascist Italy's demographic colonialism (human labor-intensive rather than financial capital-intensive) in the Italian colonies, see Nicola Labanca, 'Nelle colonie', in *Storie dell'emigrazione italiana*, Vol. 2: *Arrivi*, ed. by P. Bevilacqua, A. De Clementi and E. Franzina (Rome: Donnizelli, 2001), pp. 193–204. On the double meaning of *colonia*, see Mark Choate, *Emigrant Nation: The Making of Italy Abroad* (Cambridge, MA: Harvard University Press, 2008).

[10] Nicola Labanca, 'History and Memory of Italian Colonialism Today', *Italian Colonialism: Legacy and Memory*, ed. by Jaqueline Andall and Derek Duncan (New York: Peter Lang, 2005), pp. 29–46 (p. 31).

entire population, a percentage in line with other major European countries with a long history of postcolonial immigration. They are generally younger than the existing population of citizens, thus more active in the economy, and have higher birth rates. Scattered throughout Italy in both urban and rural areas, with greater population densities in certain regions, immigrants come from a wide range of countries, which has created a cultural, religious and linguistic variety of an unprecedented nature in Europe for the fast pace at which this 'superdiversity' has taken shape.[11] Immigrants' countries of origin practically span the entire globe, including, albeit in small part, former Italian colonies in the African Horn and the Mediterranean basin. Indeed, immigration in Italy is characterized by what I call 'indirect postcoloniality', since today's immigrants in Italy come for the most part from colonies that once belonged to other countries. Primary areas of provenance include Eastern Europe – especially Romania (an EU country), Albania, Ukraine, Moldavia; Africa (particularly Morocco, Egypt, and Tunisia); and Asia (mostly China, the Philippines, India, and Bangladesh).[12] Mixed marriages with Italians have been steadily growing and the population of Italian-born children of immigrants, both from mixed and non-mixed marriages, now constitutes a solid group of 'new Italians' whose presence is openly challenging enclosed perceptions of Italian-ness. Indeed, as demographic and sociological studies have demonstrated for years, immigration to Italy is not a temporary or circumstantial phenomenon but an intrinsic fact in the current and future development of the country for the tangible contribution that immigrants make to the country's demographic growth, economic and fiscal structure, cultural vitality and international exchanges.[13] This increasingly established role makes the representation of immigrants as 'others' particularly untenable and, consequently, renders Italy's *ius sanguinis*-based citizenship law questionable from a practical and philosophical point of view. (Specifically, why exclude 'new Italians' born and/or living in the country, while recognizing descendants of Italians who may have never set foot in the country?)

This representation also clashes with the current exodus of Italians looking for better life opportunities abroad, who are also interestingly referred to as

---

[11] On this concept coined by Steven Vertovec, see Wells in this volume.

[12] 'Scheda di sintesi', *Dossier Statistico Immigrazione 2019* (Rome: Edizioni Idos, 2019), p. 8, https://immigrazione.it/docs/2019/scheda-dossier-idos-2019.pdf [accessed 15 May 2020].

[13] For an overview of immigration in Italy, see Fabio Amato, ed., *Atlante dell'immigrazione in Italia* (Rome: Società Geografica Italiana, 2008). For immigration culture in Italy, see the publications of Graziella Parati and the key volume co-edited by Cristina Lombardi-Diop and Caterina Romeo, *Postcolonial Italy: The Colonial Past in Contemporary Italy* (New York: Palgrave, 2012).

'new Italians': ISTAT data indicate that the annual outbound flow embraces over 110,000 people, a number that has been increasing steadily and has once again made Italy a country of departure as of 2012.[14] Italians have been migrants abroad in the past, and continue to be so, albeit in different conditions. They still embody the desire to go beyond national borders to find alternatives abroad often in the space of a transnational Italy formerly built by emigration and colonialism. The intricate overlapping of Italian e/immigration and (post)colonial routes draws a fascinating map of transnational mobility across time and space, which poses fruitful questions about belonging and shows the potential in store for a country that is so diverse internally and so diversely present around the world.

This condition is captivatingly encapsulated in some data that are somewhat self-explanatory of the transnational condition of national Italy – the aporia mentioned above. Today, Italy is home to a large and growing foreign population of 5 million people, a number strikingly close to the slightly over 5 million Italian citizens registered in the list of Italians abroad (AIRE, 2018) – people who have moved to a new country and retained Italian citizenship, as well as descendants of Italians who have recently acquired citizenship through the 1992 law. This parallel is also tellingly identifiable in the realm of emigration: Italy's demographic dispersion has over time produced a population of an estimated 60 million descendants scattered around the globe, a number curiously close to that of the residents of Italy in 2014 (almost 60 million).[15] These coincidental numerical correspondences are mentioned here not just for anecdotal purposes nor to fall prey to an empty numerology but to actually expose the unfounded nature of practices and policies identifiable in the current national landscape, from invasion myths to anti-immigrant sentiments and the resistance to even the soft or cultural versions of the *ius soli* citizenship law, based on the length of the immigrant parents' residence in Italy or their children's number of years in school. As a country occupied by a multilayered history of migrations, today's Italy appears to be preoccupied with safeguarding a national uniformity that in reality openly clashes with its pride in regionalism, its cultural role in the Mediterranean, uninterrupted north- and Rome-bound internal migratory

---

[14] 'ISTAT Bilancio demografico nazionale Anno 2018', p. 2, https://www.istat.it/it/files//2019/07/Statistica-report-Bilancio-demografico-2018.pdf [accessed 15 May 2020].

[15] The data on descendants can be found in 'Sintesi', *Rapporto Italiani nel mondo 2012*, Fondazione Migrantes/TAU Edizioni, p. 2, https://www.museoemigrazioneitaliana.org/assets/Uploads/Rapporto-Italiani-nel-Mondo-2012-scheda-di-sintesi.pdf, while for the population data access see 'Tavola' at http://demo.istat.it/pop2019/index.html [accessed 15 May 2020].

flows since unification, the unresolved economic distance between north and south, the country's dramatically low birth rate,[16] the connecting forces of the controversial EU project, the current exodus of Italians for economic and political reasons despite Italy's designation as a G7 country, and the mechanisms of financial and informational globalization affecting Italy and the entire world. This set of complex dynamics shapes a multifaceted scenario within which Italian language and culture travel and are negotiated across space and time. Charles Burdett's invitation 'to combine the study of the national with the study of the transnational and, in the process, to demonstrate how inquiry into linguistic and cultural translation is at the basis of our branch of study' accurately describes the type of rethinking the discipline of Italian studies ought to structurally engage in, 'in a world of ever increasing mobility and global interaction'.[17] The following section addresses this specific aspect of the discussion and proposes the reading of a text that illustrates the national and transnational dynamics described so far.

The Cultural Text as a Transnational Space

At the center of this remapping lies the cultural text, because of its simultaneous powers of documentation, evocation and imagination at the crossroads of the local, the national and the transnational. Fiction, non-fiction, films, music, etc. are spaces that provide opportunities to learn more about mobility from historical and socioeconomic points of view, but also essentially transcend this function by zooming in on the individual to extrapolate a collective story and by representing both the challenges and possibilities linked to intercultural exchanges. While the widespread perception is that this lens tends 'to draw attention to the non-canonical and to more marginal texts, voices, and genres, which resist conventional "national" categorization',[18] canonical works and authors of the twentieth century have been investigated by scholars and taught in order to shed light on these phenomena of mobility from/to Italy: Ennio Flaiano's *Tempo di uccidere* for colonialism and Luigi

---

[16] In 2018, the average birth rate was 1.29 children per woman (see the ISTAT site, https://www.istat.it/it/archivio/235964 [accessed 15 May 2020], which recently placed Italy as number 215 in a list of 226 countries in the world, according to the CIA World Factbook, https://www.cia.gov/library/publications/the-world-factbook/rankorder/2054rank.html [accessed 15 May 2020].

[17] Charles Burdett, 'Moving from a National to a Transnational Curriculum: The Case of Italian Studies', *Languages, Society and Policy*, 10 July 2018, http://www.meits.org/policy-papers/paper/moving-from-a-national-to-a-transnational-curriculum-the-case-of-italian-st [accessed 15 May 2020].

[18] See Kay in this volume.

Capuana's *Gli Americani di Rabbato* along with Carlo Levi's *Cristo si è fermato a Eboli* for emigration are just a few examples. At the same time, contemporary authors such as Melania Mazzucco, Laura Pariani and Luigi Meneghello have been studied for their focus on past and more recent emigration to the Americas and Europe; Igiaba Scego and Giuseppe Catozzella are read for their attention to immigrant and postcolonial themes; Andrea Segre's cinema continues to denounce abuse against migrants; and, interestingly, writers such as John Fante have become cult figures for their works on the experience of Italian descendants in the US, films by Mazzacurati and Crialese have repeatedly addressed topics linked to migration while, in the realm of music, Almamegretta's dub tracks have continued to challenge the ethnic 'purity' of Italians. The non-fiction work of Gian Antonio Stella (*L'orda* and *Odissee*) has provided a much-needed exploration of the forms of exclusion and suffering experienced by Italian emigrants. Of course, this overall area of study has also been keen on giving visibility to lesser-known texts and authors in the attempt to challenge and expand the canon, but mostly to redesign the notion of the 'national'. Examples include: Ubah Cristina Ali Farah's novels on Somalia and its own diaspora, Dagmawi Yimer's films about the migrant space of the Mediterranean, and Amir Aissa's recent rap songs questioning forms of belonging to Italian society for the G2.

Yet I think it is crucial to highlight the richness of texts that connect the various strands of transnational Italy, or, even more relevant, that belong to the entire production of authors intent on building and showing these connections as an intrinsic trait of their artistic and political vision. The list has grown in size and interest over the decades, and the following names are just representatives of a much larger group: Amara Lakhous's and Carmine Abate's novels regularly interweave tales of mobility across spaces and times as a source of tension and enrichment; Gianni Amelio's film *Lamerica* and Vincenzo Marra's *Tornando a casa* overlay geographical and chronological planes to show the overlapping of identities; Gabriella Ghermandi's literary, musical and theatrical work interrogates the colonial past to understand the postcolonial present; and Agostino Ferrente's docufilm *Orchestra of Piazza Vittorio* (and obviously the orchestra itself) intersects stories of circular movements from/to Italy with the rhythm of music that connects beyond differences. It is in the agile linkage of these experiences that the national acquires and loses meaning in the transnational and vice versa.[19]

---

[19] For works that connect outbound and inbound migrations, and in some cases (post)colonialism, see for instance Enrico Pugliese, *L'Italia tra migrazioni internazionali e migrazioni interne* (Bologna: il Mulino, 2002); *Quelli di fuori: Dall'emigrazione all'immigrazione, il caso italiano*, ed. by Luigi Di Comite and Anna

A Displaced Notion of National Belonging: La Ruina's *Italianesi*

So, I returned to my hometown as well. A town where I'd been a prisoner for forty years because I was Italian, then in Italy I was treated as a foreigner for twenty years because I was Albanian, and then when I returned to Albania, my Albanian friends said: 'Hey, look, the Italian's back'.[20]

A work that effectively offers a transnational Italian story is *Italianesi* (2011), a play that pivots on the tension produced by relocation and displacement and sheds interesting light on issues of cultural hybridity. Written and performed by Saverio La Ruina, the co-founder and artistic co-director of the Calabria-based company Scena Verticale, *Italianesi* was nominated for Best Italian Script in the prestigious Ubu competition, and won an Ubu for La Ruina's exquisite performance. The play delicately unmasks the little-known history of Italians in Albania during the communist regime, and creates meaningful echoes with the presence of Albanians in contemporary Italy (among immigrant groups, the Albanian community is the second largest today). Unlike the media coverage and political rhetoric that for decades have predicated the distance and difference between Italy and Albania, starting from the 'invasion' of poor immigrants on overloaded boats in the early 1990s all the way up to the criminalization of the *albanese* in Italian society, the play's goal is to create links between the Albanian and Italian realities and ultimately fuse them. *Italianesi* recounts the story of those Italians who remained in Albania when the borders of the country were sealed by the hyper-controlling communist dictator Hoxha. They had originally moved there as part of the colonial and war enterprise between the very end of the 1930s and the early 1940s, when Albania was briefly annexed to the colonial empire by Mussolini. After the war, the majority of them repatriated, except for those who stayed behind to work in the infrastructure development

Paterno (Milan: Franco Angeli, 2002); Adam Ledgeway and Anna Laura Lepschy, eds, *In and Out of Italy: Lingua e cultura della migrazione italiana* (Perugia: Guerra Edizioni, 2010); Jennifer Burns and Loredana Polezzi, eds, *Borderlines: Migrazioni e identità nel Novecento* (Isernia: Iannone, 2003); Graziella Parati and Anthony Tamburri, eds, *The Cultures of Italian Migration* (Madison, NJ: Fairleigh Dickinson University Press, 2011); and the seminal work by Pasquale Verdicchio, *Bound by Distance: Rethinking Nationalism through the Italian Diaspora*, 2nd edn (New York: Bordighera Press, 2016). A more recent volume also includes the mobility prompted by tourism, but leaves out emigration: Ruth Ben-Ghiat and Stephanie Malia Hom, eds, *Italian Mobilities* (*Changing Mobilities*) (New York: Routledge, 2015).

[20] This and other translations from the play are mine.

business or those who had built families. Perceived as enemies of the regime (they were variously depicted as Vatican spies, capitalist US supporters and fascists), these Italians were subject to monitoring, and in some cases sentenced to prison or isolated in concentration camps, despite the international agreement between the two countries that purportedly safeguarded them and that Hoxha ignored (even consulate employees in Tirana were barred from making contact with them). The protagonist and only character of *Italianesi*, the gentle Tonino Cantisani, is the most dramatic embodiment of this experience, as he was born in a camp to an Italian woman whose husband was repatriated while she stayed behind.

An example of the established tradition of 'teatro di narrazione' in Italy, with its long monologues, first-person narrator and extremely sparse stage (one chair in this case), *Italianesi* is based on a real account and unfolds an individual rather than collective story, although it gives voice to an entire group, effectively constituting a postcolonial enclave outside of Italy. Tonino is a recorder of this acute form of repression and, at the same time, an inveterate dreamer. Notwithstanding the forced labor, torture, full subjection to prison guards for even basic functions, crowded living spaces, no contact with the outside world and no information about his family in Italy, Tonino endures the camp by playing soccer, working as a skillful tailor, learning how to speak Italian and forming a family (he gets married and has children in the camp). Tonino considers himself 'taliano', as he claims in his unique accent, which drops or distorts the vowel 'i'. He dreams of Italy as a better world for four decades based on his mother's aggrandizing stories, in turn heard through her husband. The refrain of the story captures the clichéd image of a postcard-like Italy but with a melancholic undertone that anticipates the crumbling of the dream: 'Italy is the most beautiful place in the world; the most beautiful cities in the world are in Italy; in Italy we are all painters, musicians, singers'. Indeed, the gilded icon of the Bel Paese, resting on its artistic patrimony and humanistic legacy, is almost immediately tarnished when Tonino returns to Italy with his own family. A reunion with his father, of whom he had lost all trace until the thawing of relationships between the Italian and Albanian governments, is imbued with disappointment, as Tonino is treated coldly. Despite this painful experience of the metaphorical death of the father, Tonino decides to move with his family to Italy, still driven by the fairy tale-ish stories heard about the country's beauty. To do so, he takes advantage of 'Cora Operation', a real-life repatriation program of 300 Italian camp prisoners in 1990–91. While most of the press hailed them as 'true' Italians, the status and identity of these captives was much more layered and required a careful reading, which is both La Ruina's ethical and artistic goal with *Italianesi*. The fact that their return coincided with the arrival of tens of thousands of Albanians finally able to escape a repressive country after the fall of the communist regime made Italy's reaction particularly complicated and revealed the alleys of repressed history (Italy's colonialism in Albania, the Cold War balancing act between the Soviet bloc and the NATO, and the erasure of the historical immigration of Albanians fleeing as refugees from the fifteenth through the eighteenth centuries and creating established enclaves in the south). As Tonino bluntly puts it in the play: 'When we actually got to Italy, I expected an orchestra at the Rome station. Yet no playing and no singing. At the police station they examined us: "Look at these Albanians", the officers told us repeatedly over a five-day interrogation'.

The national perception of Albanians crossing the Adriatic to reach Italy as soon as the borders finally opened up in the early 1990s is so filled with preoc-cupation about the 'other' that Italians are not able to read into their history fairly or to comprehend the existence of multiple transnational identities shaped by uncomfortable histories. Tonino is seen as an Albanian in the factory, in part because of his unique way of speaking Italian; his wife is seen as Albanian in the store, as are his children at school. Hence Tonino's powerful question: 'If I am not like them, what am I?' It is in this space of disorientation that Tonino uncon-ventionally decides to go back to Albania: he realizes that he belongs to the camp as much as to a long-desired yet disappointing Italy. His multiple identities, or rather absences,[21] are then the result of experience as well as external perception, as eloquently summarized in the epigraph to this section. This return is surpris-ingly, or perhaps not too surprisingly, cast as the return home of the emigrants. Tonino feels the urge to visit the camp, and yet understands it is an unusual choice: 'I thought "I have to go back to Albania", and indeed I came back exactly like the uncles from America went back to Italy. "Why do you go back?" "Because we always go back to the village where we were born". The same for me'. It's not clear whether Tonino will move back to Albania permanently nor whether he returns to Italy since the closing scene of his flight to Cagliari is wrapped in a dream-like atmosphere. With a creative double or triple twist, the space of colonialism hosts that of emigration: Tonino is returning to a postcolonial condition that, from the perspective of Italy, becomes an emigrant condition, or perhaps he is returning to Italy as a previous emigrant in what is for him an increasingly complex cycle of shifting identities.[22]

---

[21] Algerian sociologist Abdelmalek Sayad has written eloquently about the pain implicit in the erasure of the self experienced by migrants in his powerfully titled book *Double Absence*, which in the English translation has retained only a section of the subtitle: *The Suffering of the Immigrant* (Cambridge: Polity, 2004).

[22] See Daniele Comberiati and Federica Martucci, 'Non l'avevo mai vista, ma conoscevo tutto dell'Italia: Identità ibride nel monologo *Italianesi* di Saverio La Ruina',

The in-between condition of the disoriented protagonist in whose heart and mind the two coasts of the Adriatic are not clearly distinguishable is brilliantly captured by the title of the play, *Italianesi*, which melds the Italian root and Albanian ending of nationality adjectives into one made-up word: despite its novelty, its meaning is immediately decipherable. Tonino's displacement – ultimately, he lives in the missing vowel 'i' of his being 'taliano' – speaks to the power and yet impalpability of labels. Each country he is affiliated with sees him as belonging to the other in a game of reversals that explodes the meaning of national belonging.[23] Besides being a fine piece of theatrical bravura with its agile alternation of flashbacks and flashforwards, La Ruina's play constitutes an antidote against amnesia as it reactivates the relationships with repressed aspects of national and international history, which indirectly shed light on other past and present conditions.

Conclusions: The Unexplored Space of Transnational Italian Studies

Italianesi is an ideal example of how a text can trigger a whole array of historical and cultural explorations in unexpected, if not unlikely, directions. A similar vision of transnational Italy can be found in Carmine Abate's short story 'Prima la vita' (2010), or other novels by him about cyclical movements such as *Il mosaico del tempo grande* (1991) and *Il ballo tondo* (2006). Yet these texts, like many others mentioned in this essay, are mainly available in Italian. Despite the growing availability of some of these texts in translation, the current reality is that of a cultural transnationality that remains bound by the 'national' quality of the language in which they were produced. This situation has in part been responsible for the limitations experienced by the field of Italian (post)colonialism and migrations, which continues to be somehow isolated both in the academic and general discourse, compared to the more established fields of English, Spanish and French postcolonialism, in part because of the extension, duration and capillary nature of these countries' colonial enterprises and the broader use of their national languages. While French studies more automatically includes the concept of *francophonie*, and Spanish studies incorporates Latin America, Italian studies has to cross several linguistic borders in order to embrace transnational Italy. Translation should and will continue to serve as a mechanism of increased accessibility: in

---

Ecritures, 8: Entre Charybde et Scylla. Art, mythes et société au pays des monstres oubliés, ed. by Christine and Stéphane Reche (2016), 311–15 (p. 317).

[23] On the slippages of the very category of the 'nation', see Homi Bhabha's *The Location of Culture* (New York: Routledge, 1994), and in particular the chapter 'DissemiNation: Time, Narrative and the Margins of the Modern Nation' (pp. 139–70).

this sense, texts can also be analyzed as they transition from one language to another, including in the realm of audiovisual translation (subtitles for films and surtitles for the performing arts) in order to identify practices of erasure and misunderstanding, or even untranslatability, when we look at cultural products that cross or live on borders. This is until the day when a truly transnational and thus translingual approach is adopted to include texts written in French and Spanish as well. François Cavanna's linguistically explosive *Les Ritals* (1978) or Mempo Giardinelli's *Santo Oficio de la Memoria* (1993) could open up a space of discovery of Italian experiences in places that are not automatically associated with Italian immigration, like France – or in places that are easily associated with Italian immigration like Argentina, but not necessarily studied within Italian studies. Actually, many of these texts offer a model of trans-Italian, a language that transits through other languages as part of the code-switching, melding and fusion of different languages so characteristic of experiences of mobility.

Within this kinetic vision, even learning Italian at the beginning and intermediate level can be part of a translingual and transcultural experience. As a matter of fact, this is already a reality on campuses where Italian language is taught to Spanish-, French- and Portuguese-speakers in multicompetence classes. This learning environment transcends the classic second language acquisition method and adopts a Euro-Mediterranean framework that interestingly presupposes mobility of people and texts over the centuries for these Latin-derived languages.[24] By the same token, established literary figures like Dante, Machiavelli and Foscolo, and political colossuses like Mazzini and Garibaldi, are presented as exiles, in a move that recanvasses the literary and political canon in dynamic ways. Indeed, if movement and displacement are both central themes of contemporary societies, it should not be as disorienting to see dislocation as the locus of Italian culture at large. It is then possible to expand gender and cultural studies beyond the national borders, for instance, by looking at women whose Italian-ness was always defined from abroad due to colonialism and migration, from Fausta Cialente to Helen Barolini. By the same token, even one of the 'trendiest' aspects of Italian culture abroad today (i.e., Made in Italy), has the potential to explode national traits by revealing the fundamentally transnational dimension of the circulation of Italian products in markets created by old and new migrations to a huge degree.

Ultimately, this transnational dimension defines a much more porous and inclusive Italian geography, where the central question is: What does it mean to be 'Italian' in a culture defined by boundary crossing, movements,

---

[24] For more information on interlinguistic competence approaches see: http://www.eurom5.com [accessed 15 May 2020].

displacements and differences in the past and in the present? And, by extension, what specific knowledge can Italian studies offer? In a globalized world, oddly veering towards a nationalist resurgence, Italy presents itself as a unique laboratory of thought and practices related to mobility that are able to provide interesting lessons about cultural coexistence and mutual enrichment. At a time of retrenching into a fabricated pure Italian-ness that clashes with its own inevitable and necessary inbound and outbound migratory movements, Italian studies can much better serve Italy itself, including if not primarily from abroad, by transnationalizing it.

9

Mobile Homes

Transnational Subjects and the (Re)Creation of Home Spaces

Jennifer Burns

Spaces identified as 'home' in transnational cultures commonly connect different geographical locations in order to form a space which serves at once as a stable reference point and an expression of mobile national, cultural and linguistic belongings. This chapter analyses the objects, structures and practices which find their place in spaces constructed as 'home' by migrants or minority communities, and the ways in which these spaces are narrated as 'home'. The connections between 'here' and 'elsewhere' actively made and remade in the living environment of the transnational home create an experience of space which transcends conventional understandings of home as fixed point of origin. Articulated instead is a notion of home built upon the affects (negative and positive) generated by family, community, territory, heritage and tradition, but predicated also upon the capacity of these bonds to stretch and turn according to changing material conditions and experiences of detachment. Narratives of the home as physical, domestic space will be analysed alongside those of shared or public spaces constructed as 'home', including the virtual spaces of digital community. The discussion will expose the sense of being at once settled and unsettled that is articulated when homes become mobile.

My emphasis here, responding to the practices emerging from the sites studied, will be less on discrete homes than on homing as a process of building relations and creating a sense of belonging in one space or between one immediate space and others more distant. Homing involves work: an extended emotional and social labour to create a sense of functional and rewarding emplacement in a particular environment. Paolo Boccagni notes as an opening premise of his work on migration and homing, that 'Migration in itself is a source of de-naturalization of the home, as it reveals how its familiarity and obviousness has been culturally constructed and is ultimately fictitious'.[1] This radical removal of what was likely understood as a given – the foundational importance of home – leaves a migrating subject inhabiting a condition between, on one hand, critical consciousness of the instability of the home left behind as well as a likely emotional attachment to it, and on the other, the need to find the means to create a home in the destination environment, for material and economic as well as emotional and social reasons. That this condition of unsettlement in turn generates a desire to become (re)settled, to recreate home in some way, is questionable. Whether the subject has left home because of forced migration, personal choice or motivations lying along a spectrum in between, it is important not to assume that migrants long for home, old or new. Any subject leaving home may have distinctly ambivalent feelings about the losses and the opportunities of moving away and of establishing presence somewhere new. It is for this reason that a focus on what migrant subjects and communities *do* in any one instance both to make present some elements of home and to distance themselves from others is revealing of what home might mean when apprehended through the lens of the transnational.

The practice of homing also invites a negotiation of the features or qualities of a home according to national or cultural paradigms, which themselves are clearly a significant example of how, as Boccagni notes, the home is 'culturally constructed'. What, for example, does an 'Italian' home look or feel like, and what changes, if anything, when it is (re)constructed outside the national borders of Italy? To explore this process, I will look firstly at a fictional narrative of a transnational subject's homes, in order to trace the emotional negotiations involved in homing and the revealing outcomes of imagining new and old homes. I will then turn to different forms of empirical evidence of homing practices amongst transnational communities and individuals in the UK, to bring to the surface the shared concerns, aspirations and values which fuel the establishment of a sense of collective belonging and 'ownership' of social space in a new environment.

Fictional stories of migration into Italy published since the 1990s are often constructed around a powerful gaze towards the site of departure and communicate a sense of nostalgia towards a place left behind: the title of Shirin Ramzanali Fazel's first work, *Far from Mogadishu*, captures this position.[2]

---

[1] Paolo Boccagni, *Migration and the Search for Home: Mapping Domestic Space in Migrants' Everyday Lives* (New York: Palgrave Macmillan, 2017), p. xxiii.

[2] Shirin Ramzanali Fazel, *Far from Mogadishu*, ed. by Simone Brioni (CreateSpace Independent Publishing Platform, 2016). Originally published in Italian: *Lontano da Mogadiscio* (Rome: Datanews, 1994).

The distant place represented as home may be figured as a specific domestic environment, a village or city, or a particular kind of landscape and climate. Constructions across diverse narratives related to different countries and cultures of departure and different identities of the migrating subject-narrator tend to articulate a comparable draw towards a location and its people as a profound and permanent reference point for the mobile individual, repro-duced in the text with vivid reference to the five human senses and with an immediacy sharpened by loss.[3] As Michel de Certeau describes it, 'the implicit givens of life as it is lived appear with a strange lucidity that often rejoins – in many facets – the foreign perspicacity of the ethnologist'.[4] This reproduction or reinvention of home spaces through the medium of the distantiated recol-lection of past images and sensations focuses often on the cultural practices of a family group or small community. Against the model of an individual or sharply nuclear family inhabiting a defined property is set the image of a more porous and flexible form of kinship, in which extended family and neighbours inhabit a shared physical area described in terms of the relations which create and connect it. In a sense, this is already a home in movement, a space made mobile by multiple comings and goings and particularly by intergenerational living: more sedentary elderly relations create a focal point to and from which other generations gravitate and depart. Home is, in other words, defined less by the material space and architecture of a house than by a collection of practices and movements around a loosely defined area, and by the affects which it provokes as the distant subject recollects it. These affects are then interpreted and defined as distinct emotions through the process of creating a narrative of home.[5]

Gabriella Ghermandi's novel *Queen of Flowers and Pearls* offers a striking example of home as a condition of being at once deeply settled but always potentially unsettled.[6] The novel tells the story (in the first person) of Mahlet,

[3] Examples include Amor Dekhis, *I lupi della notte* [Wolves of the Night] (Naples: L'ancora, 2008) and Younis Tawfik, *La straniera* [The Foreign Woman] (Milan: Bompiani, 1999). For critical discussion of these figurations of home, see 'Home', in Jennifer Burns, *Migrant Imaginaries: Figures in Italian Migration Literature* (Oxford: Peter Lang, 2013), pp. 101–30.

[4] Michel de Certeau, *The Capture of Speech and Other Political Writings*, ed. by Luce Giard, trans. and afterword by Tom Conley (Minneapolis: University of Minnesota Press, 1997), p. 171.

[5] On affective response and how it is articulated, see David Conradson and Deirdre McKay, 'Translocal Subjectivities: Mobility, Connection, Emotion', *Mobilities*, 2.2 (2007), 167–74.

[6] Gabriella Ghermandi, *Queen of Flowers and Pearls, A Novel*, trans. by Giovanna Bellesia-Contuzzi and Victoria Offredi Poletto (Bloomington: Indiana University

a young Ethiopian woman who challenges the hostility to the Italian nation of her parents' generation in order to study at university in Italy, and in so doing to perform the task entrusted to her by an elderly male relative of telling the story of Ethiopia – including its colonial suppression – within the site of the colonizers. The violence that this complex colonial and postcolonial history carries is expressed in part through a disrupted sense of home experienced even before Mahlet's departure to Italy, and through a focus on different houses and the different ways in which the extended family is able or forced to inhabit them. Though these are family homes, their histories of habitation bespeak an uncomfortable impermanence.

A short chapter in the second part of the novel establishes the fulcrum of the family in a specific house in Arada Sefer, part of Addis Ababa. A detailed description of the layout and architectural and decorative forms of the house is combined with comments on how the family used the space, establishing the material structure and the behaviours it harbours as 'home'. The rear courtyard is described as the hub of the household, used for washing laundry, preparing foodstuffs, rearing chickens and growing plants and fruit, and as the space in which the family members gather to exchange news and experiences. The narrator notes that the placentas of all newborn babies in the family were buried under the oldest tree in the courtyard, fortifying the sense of this space within the home as the site and archive of a visceral genealogical memory which fuses the human life of the location with the non-human ecology of its very soil. Interestingly, though, it is an unsettled home from the outset, as the opening paragraph of the chapter (entitled 'Arada Sefer') indicates: 'Our house in Addis Ababa was a big old house in the Indian style, built at the beginning of the twentieth century when Menelik had transferred the capital from Ankober to Addis Ababa and my great-grandfather had moved himself and his whole family to follow Negus Negest'.[7] The apparent rootedness of the large, long-established home is undermined by the mobilities produced by political change, demonstrating how the public impinges on the domestic, or even – as suggested here – manoeuvres it. This is confirmed within the short chapter when Mahlet tells of the 'nationalization' of the house at Arada Sefer when the new Soviet-inspired government takes over following the coup of 1974. Her immediate family having already moved, because of her father's work, to a new home shared with her uncle at Debre Zeit, possession of the empty house is taken by the regime. This abrupt severance of ancestral ties, along with Mahlet's own blunt observation that, 'I had never lived in our

Press, 2015). Originally published in Italian: *Regina di fiori e di perle* (Rome: Donzelli, 2007).

[7] Ghermandi, *Queen of Flowers and Pearls*, p. 102 (*Regina di fiori e di perle*, p. 114).

house in Arada Sefer', articulates an apparent annulment of the family home's emotional and mnemonic value.[8]

Arada Sefer is restored as home after Mahlet's absence in Italy when she returns to Ethiopia for a visit, arriving just after the death of the elderly relative, Yacob, with whom she was particularly close. Interestingly, it is only on the journey from the airport with her parents that Mahlet discovers, when the car fails to take the road towards Debre Zeit, that home has moved, and that they will, at Yacob's request, move temporarily back to the house at Arada Sefer to honour his memory, with Mahlet herself even sleeping in the room in which Yacob had once slept. In this sense, the bond with the past that the family home seems to materialize is restored, realizing Yacob's judgement that Mahlet, uniquely amongst her generation, 'felt the ties to the past'.[9] However, this is not only an unexpected return for Mahlet to the historical home, but also a temporary one for the family, who will reside there just for the 80 days of mourning claimed by Yacob. For Mahlet, in particular, it is a return to a reference point (in a section entitled 'The Return'), but one predicated upon her departure again for Italy. Home is thus represented in the novel as providing a cypher of a deep and resonant emotional matrix and a shared history, but it is never stable, always mobile, both in the material terms influenced by political and social events and in the intimate, emotional terms influenced by individual and familial decisions and desires.

In Ghermandi's postcolonial historical novel, then, the notion of home, materialized in houses, takes on a critical form of the symbolic and social capital that conventionally accrues to homes in the nineteenth-century European novel. In narratives of migration to Italy and of homing practices of migrant and postcolonial subjects within Italy, home generally has a value as a place to live rather than a vehicle for investment (albeit possibly critical) in a set of values and in a memory of past kinship connections to be remodelled for the future. Homes tend to appear as radically impermanent, contingent and instrumental, as suggested in the title of Igiaba Scego's novel, *La mia casa è dove sono* [Home Is Where I Am].[10] Often shared spaces sparsely populated with individual possessions or decorations, homes in the destination country are surprisingly immaterial and unindividuated in narratives of transnational subjects living in Italy, even where residence is relatively permanent.[11] Homes

---

[8] Ghermandi, *Queen of Flowers and Pearls*, p. 103 (*Regina di fiori e di perle*, p. 115).

[9] Ghermandi, *Queen of Flowers and Pearls*, p. 127 (*Regina di fiori e di perle*, p. 141).

[10] Igiaba Scego, *La mia casa è dove sono* [Home is Where I Am] (Milan: Rizzoli, 2010).

[11] Further examples include Amara Lakhous's novels, *Clash of Civilizations over an Elevator in Piazza Vittorio*, trans. by Ann Goldstein (New York: Europa Editions,

left behind in the locality of departure are often constructed more vividly through memory – with the 'strange lucidity' described by de Certeau – but the migrant's impetus noted by sociologists such as Boccagni to recreate home spaces in the destination culture, and the ambition to build 'remittance houses' in the place of departure in order really or symbolically to establish ground for a future return, are more or less absent.[12] This absence points to a displacement of homing activity from the individual house or space of dwelling to an experience and feeling of home constructed transnationally by means of shared practices and the values and memories which inform them. Moreover, these shared practices may be partaken in by individuals whose ties to one another are incidental, generated and sustained by presence in a particular locality, time and set of circumstances, such as the kind of shared apartment mentioned above, an apartment block, area of a town or city, social group or event, or language class.[13] What, then, does home or homing mean in these kinds of transient contexts? Are individuals or communities constituted by homelessness as much as by 'home'?

Transient objects offer one insight into processes of homing in a destination culture that are not invested in the wholesale recreation of a home left behind, or even of a localized modification of it, but rather function metonymically to afford presence to a home experience in a distant place. Loretta Baldassar, engaging with Italian migrants living in Australia and their parents in Italy, observes that:

> A sense of place can be achieved indirectly through objects and people whose physical or virtual presence embodies the spirit of the longed-for people or place. Each of the five senses can be utilized to construct this form of presence (the person or object can be touched, heard, seen, etc.); the physical manifestation of this (proxy) presence in the form of, for example, photos and mementos serves as the abstraction of an imagined presence [...] There is no limit to what can serve as a memento for place, but common items include iconic examples of Italian material culture such as traditional handcrafts (bedcovers, crocheted doilies, lace), cookware (pots that hang over

---

2008) and *Divorce Islamic Style*, trans. by Ann Goldstein (New York: Europa Editions, 2012). In Italian, respectively: *Scontro di civiltà per un ascensore a piazza Vittorio* (Rome: e/o, 2006) and *Divorzio all'islamica a viale Marconi* (Rome: e/o, 2010).

[12] Boccagni, *Migration and the Search for Home*, p. 50.

[13] Lakhous's novel, *Clash of Civilizations* (see n. 11) is a good example of the transfer of a sense of home from an individual dwelling to a heterogeneous, shared living space.

open fireplaces, coffeemakers), and even pebbles from homeland courtyards. Interestingly these items signify connections both to family and to place; they are 'things from home' or 'signs of home'.[14]

Baldassar's observations were materialized in creative writing workshops with multilingual adults which were organized within the 'Transnationalizing Modern Languages' project.[15] Taking place in Birmingham and bringing together a range of languages and cultures indicative of the city's cultural diversity, the meetings brought to the surface the ways in which the languages and cultures of countries of departure were mediated and made 'present' – both spatially and temporally – in the relatively unmarked space of a bare meeting room in the Ikon Gallery in central Birmingham, and at a distance of generally ten or more years from the moment of migration for each participant. In a workshop dedicated to the theme of 'home', participants brought relevant objects, and not only the objects themselves, but the ways in which the participants presented and handled them, exposed powerfully the capacity of the objects to materialize connections and, at substantial distance, to signify immediately as 'things from home'.

Diasporic Somali writer Shirin Ramzanali Fazel showed a decorated leather purse which had belonged to her mother and which sustained her relationship with her deceased parent as well as with the culture that she embodied. Ramzanali Fazel drew attention to the signs of wear on the surface of the leather, made smooth and shiny by regular use (in the past), and so drew attention to her own sense, facilitated by the purse, of her mother's living, haptic presence. The capacity to share her lost mother's touch by means of the almost prosthetic extension of person, place and time was enabled by the object. Nigerian writer Olufemi Abidogun brought the textbook used in his school to teach African literature: an early edition of *A Selection of African Poetry*. The collection, 'introduced and annotated' in this edition by K. E. Senanu and T. Vincent, is written in English and became a 'classic' construction of the poetry of a range of African countries, cultures and

---

[14] Loretta Baldassar, 'Obligation to People and Place: The National in Cultures of Caregiving', in *Intimacy and Italian Migration: Gender and Domestic Lives in a Mobile World*, ed. by Loretta Baldassar and Donna R. Gabaccia (New York: Fordham, 2011), pp. 170–87 (p. 183).

[15] 'Transnationalizing Modern Languages: Mobility, Identity and Translation in Modern Italian Cultures', 2014–17, funded by the Arts and Humanities Research Council (AHRC) under its 'Translating Cultures' theme. The series of creative writing workshops, co-organized by myself and Dr Naomi Wells, took place at Sandwell Arts Centre, Sandwell, in May–October 2015 and at the Ikon Gallery, Birmingham, in February–June 2016.

languages.[16] As a translingual poet himself, living and writing now in the UK, this object articulated in a complex critical sense what both poetry itself and African cultural heritage had meant to Abidogun at different junctures in his adolescence and adulthood and in different locations, and how that process of making meaning out of lived experience through reading and writing continued. He also noted that the book was his elder brother's copy, handed down to him when he moved into the relevant school year. In this respect, the object interestingly enabled familial as well as pedagogical, private as well as public, genealogies to be brought into the 'present' of the workshop and to be discussed. That Abidogun had kept and travelled with the book, and also viewed its pedagogical purpose critically, articulated vividly the point made at the outset of this discussion about the tensions which may animate the relationship between a transnational subject and 'home'.

The capacity of 'things from home' to disrupt nostalgic connections with home was illustrated differently by the object introduced by French writer Pascale Presumey. This was a small china ornament, a figure of what would have been constructed at the time of manufacture (probably 1970s) as an 'Oriental' man. What was meaningful about her choice to bring it, both from France to the UK in the early 1980s and to the workshop on 'Home', was its apparent meaninglessness: she knew nothing of its origin or how it had come into her possession in her adolescence and young adulthood in France. As a man of apparently East Asian origin, the figure represented her early life at home and her experience in no obvious way. It had travelled with her and remained with her over decades of residence in different homes in the UK because its place in her life was unexplained even as it continued to maintain that place, and because it provoked, and continued to provoke, her curiosity. In this respect, the peculiarity and inherently 'out-of-place' quality of the object seemed to bespeak her own somewhat unplanned and serendipitous migration and residence elsewhere, and her feeling of surprise that she had done what she had done and continued to experience new lives in places with which she would never have anticipated forging a connection. The small stranger, out of place, precise origin unknown, portable and always present, emerged as a literal figure of transnational homing.

Objects of these kinds thus enable a materialization of emotional and cultural connections with a place defined as 'home', and facilitate those connections remaining present in a new cultural and domestic environment: the portability of meaningful objects in effect allows departure and destination homes to cohabit. Such objects appear frequently in the homes of

---

[16] K. E. Senanu and T. Vincent, eds, *A Selection of African Poetry* (London: Longman, 1976).

migrants and transnational subjects, as work by sociologists and ethnographers on homing practices (such as Baldassar's) demonstrates.[17] Interesting for my discussion here, however, is the way in which such personalized detail seems to give way, in wider expressions of a transnational community's connections with its place of heritage, to somewhat de-individuated patterns of portability and reconstruction of 'things from home'. Here, practices of homing in new places seem rather to privilege shared experiences and signs which own the capacity to spark recognition and affective resonance across a wide spectrum of forms and times of migration, of generations, genders and classes, and of patterns of settlement, ongoing mobility or return. Not only do these shared elements create community in one context, but they thrive also on durability and flexibility – or, indeed, on their capacity to continue to mean something to a particular community as the size, form, location and characteristics of that community change over time.

Italian communities in London provide a telling object of inquiry into these processes. The histories of these communities since the late nineteenth century (and earlier) are dense and have been documented to a good degree in historiography and cultural studies.[18] My interest here is in the narratives these communities have constructed of themselves and of their sense of being 'at home' in Italy or the UK or both. I will consider first the retrospective story of London's 'Little Italy' constructed by Olive Besagni in two volumes of biographical accounts, oral histories and photographs published in 2011 and 2017.[19] Second, I will look at the online construction of a present-day Italian community – a 'virtual' one – performed by the *Londra, Italia* website.[20]

---

[17] See also other essays in Baldassar and Gabaccia, *Intimacy and Italian Migration*.

[18] See Piero Bevilacqua, Andreina de Clementi and Emiliano Franzina, eds, *Storia dell'emigrazione italiana*, 2 vols (Rome: Donzelli, 2001); Terri Colpi, *The Italian Factor* (Edinburgh: Mainstream, 1991); Alessandro Forte, *La Londra degli italiani* (Rome: Aliberti, 2012); Anne-Marie Fortier, *Migrant Belongings: Memory, Space, Identity* (Oxford, New York: Berg, 2000); Lucio Sponza, *The Italian Immigrants in Nineteenth-Century Britain: Realities and Images* (Leicester: Leicester University Press, 1988) and *Divided Loyalties: Italians in Britain During the Second World War* (Bern: Peter Lang, 2000); Margherita Sprio, *Migrant Memories: Cultural History, Cinema and the Italian Post-War Diaspora in Britain* (Oxford: Peter Lang, 2013).

[19] Olive Besagni, *A Better Life: A History of London's Italian Immigrant Families in Clerkenwell's Little Italy in the 19th and 20th Centuries* (London: Camden History Society and Olive Besagni, 2011) and *Changing Lives: More Stories from London's Little Italy* (London: Camden History Society and the Estate of Olive Besagni, 2017).

[20] *Londra, Italia*, http://www.londraitalia.com/ [accessed 28 February 2019]. All translations from this site that follow are my own.

Besagni's twin volumes look back at the life of London's 'Little Italy' from a position in the 2010s which acknowledges that 'Little Italy' is now barely visible. In collecting and publishing the photographs, stories and multi-sourced forms of evidence of a community developing over around 150 years, the author/editor memorializes that community and its physical spaces, and acknowledges both implicitly and explicitly that its time has passed. Interestingly, the second volume appeared posthumously, one year after Besagni's death at the age of 91, lending force to the autobiographical element of the publishing project, which becomes a memorial to her as well as to the community as she knew it.[21] Besagni curates a diverse collection of memories and histories recounted by others directly to her and reproduced as such, which sit alongside her own accounts, drawing upon her own experience and information offered by others, as well as the documentary evidence offered by photographs, archival documents and 'domestic' data (addresses, dates of birth, marriage and death, prices and wages, family trees, family numbers). As such, her creative and archival process and its products actively disrupt any distinction between autobiography, biography and historiography, and offer instead a diary of a community. This diary ultimately speaks with the voice of the community itself, articulating perhaps a 'transauthorial' narratorial or curatorial position in which questions of selection, organization and of content itself appear to be the domain of a collective: individuals are insistently named, and yet as moving parts in a coordinated whole.

This sense of shared enterprise informs the vision of homing practices in 'Little Italy' which the two volumes narrate. Specific and personalized information is very commonly offered as the opening to an account, for example, from an oral history provided by Giuseppe Longini Rocco Assirati: 'My father Bartolomeo Assirati was born in Casanova, in the province of Bardi, in 1854. He married my mother, Albina Arborini, in 1875. Two years later they emigrated to England where they found a home at No. 23 Eyre Street Hill'.[22] Such factual specificity in these books rarely, however, leads to a detailed account of a family's home space and the kinds of practices and 'things from home' which might illustrate the production of a transnational Italian home in London. What emerges instead from the details of addresses and, occasionally, domestic layouts, is that everyone shares the same kind of experience of home, both in terms of the physical space they are able to

---

[21] See David Hayes, 'Preface', in Besagni, *Changing Lives: More Stories from London's Little Italy* (London: Camden History Society and the Estate of Olive Besagni, 2017), p. 4, and the unattributed 'Afterword' plus photographs in the same volume, pp. 64–69.

[22] Besagni, *A Better Life*, p. 38.

occupy and of how they use that space. In other words, 'No. 23 Eyre Street Hill' is not a significant element of this individual's story because he was born and raised in a distinct domestic environment there, but rather because it places him within the common experience of a community: 'Eyre Street Hill consisted of a lot of tumbledown dwellings, choked with humans of the poverty-stricken, peasant class, from all parts of Italy [...] In a small room at No. 23 dwelt five human beings, comprising husband, wife and children'.[23] The reader/listener is invited to imagine that the same setting was reproduced all along Eyre Street Hill, and, by extension, along all of the streets demarcating 'Little Italy'. 'Home', then, is the entire, communal space of this small area heavily populated by Italian migrants, identified not by any one family's domestic space but by its streets, tenement blocks, and landmark shops and businesses, named repeatedly throughout the accounts in both volumes.

In turn, homing practices are centred on the shared use of these spaces and the values which these practices bear and promote. A consistent refrain throughout the accounts, bolstered by their retrospective positioning, is the celebration of 'traditional' values understood to be the property of Italian culture. Women are figured and celebrated as cooks, carers, often passionate protectors and promoters of the well-being and success of their children and husbands (partnerships outside marriage are not mentioned). Men are characterized as industrious, entrepreneurial, resilient and often quietly dependent upon female sustenance. Both genders (no non-binary identity is envisaged) and all ages are supportive of their own 'kind' and, in ways construed as appropriate to gender and age, of each other. Most behaviours and practices are framed as being rooted in the topographical as well as spiritual centre of the community, which is St Peter's Italian Church on Clerkenwell Road. In fact, though the range of evidence given in the accounts of an individual's or family's contribution to making Clerkenwell 'home' for Italian migrants is vast, varying from minute anecdotes of specific acts to wide chronologies of services to the community, an almost unerring measure is contribution to the annual Procession for Our Lady of Mount Carmel, taking place every July within the space of 'Little Italy'. This contribution is sometimes described in elaborate and celebratory detail (with photographs), but often recorded quite simply, as a datum of appraisal, for example: 'Salvatore often did repair work or made things for the Church. He took his turn carrying the statue of the Madonna during the annual Procession'.[24] These comments suggest that the substitute in this context for the embellishment of a private dwelling with 'things from home' is the material contribution – through labour, craft,

---

[23] Besagni, *A Better Life*, p. 38.
[24] Besagni, *Changing Lives*, p. 13.

finance or simple presence – to the annual procession, which in turn stands in metonymic relation to the vitality and centrality of St Peter's Church.[25] Being present at the procession and playing a part in it – literally, often, a performance – is interpreted as a key and visible indicator of an individual's commitment to creating an Italian 'home' in 'Little Italy' and, as such, a performative practice of homing. It is also part of a collective performance of Italian presence in London, seizing ownership of the urban space in an ostentatious as well as solemn way which may be provisional (confined in time to one day per year, and in space to the physical footprint of the procession) but asserts that Italian diasporic citizens have made this space their home.

At the level of the everyday practices and the microhistories that Besagni's volumes narrate, the London-Italy connection is actively sustained through reference to the foodways, family structures, professions and crafts, physical and somatic characteristics which are constructed in the accounts as 'Italian'. Perhaps most striking is that almost every account begins with or at some point has recourse to a specific origin in Italy: the quotation above from the account of the Assirati family is an example. In this way, the homing activity of the community in London, across decades and generations, is insistently mapped back to the national territory of Italy, confirming the nation as origin and source of this transnational reproduction of the nation, known as 'Little Italy'. As a community initiated in the eighteenth century, but consolidated in the late nineteenth, it is predicated upon the politics of the construction of the unified Italian nation and, more broadly, on the politics of the nation state in the 'West' in that period. In the current era of globalization, what relations to a 'home nation' in Italy do Italians in London collectively imagine and perform?

The *Londra, Italia* website articulates an axis of connection in its very title, but how it operates to activate and articulate practices of Italian 'homing' in London in the present day is, as one would expect, very different from the customs narrated and performed in Besagni's books. A curatorial and journalistic site, selecting and offering news and commentary pieces, *Londra, Italia* is orientated towards the present and future, articulating through the events and issues that it highlights the aspirations of a young, mobile, professional and/or educated population of transnational workers and travellers for whom London offers enhanced opportunity. Written in Italian, it explicitly addresses a native Italian-speaking or bilingual audience, but also uses terms in English fluidly, articulating an expectation that readers are familiar with and probably resident in the UK.[26] News and feature items focus on the issues

---

[25] See Fortier, *Migrant Belongings* on the significance to the community of St Peter's Italian Church.

[26] Articles on the site routinely mix culture-specific terms in English into the text in

which will immediately affect the working and social lives of this imagined community of transnational workers: at the time of writing, Brexit and its possible impacts on travel and working conditions for EU citizens in the UK are constantly prominent, with an interesting emphasis not on the political or cultural hinterland of the negotiations but on practical information about what Italian citizens living and/or working in the UK might need to plan for and act upon. This emphasis on doing rather than discussing suggests that the site envisages its role as enabling the successful transnational mobility of its users, in turn indicating a narrative of Italian community in London which imagines shared values and goals of professional enhancement, social, economic and cultural mobility, and personal resilience and agility.

Dispersed from the identifiable 'Italian' locations in London of the past – primarily, Clerkenwell and Soho – and dematerialized by the medium of digital communication, what concept of 'home' or of 'homing' does the community outlined by *Londra, Italia* sustain, and to what extent is it attached to London and/or Italy? In stark contrast with the names, addresses and dates of birth and migration which populate Besagni's books, a user of the *Londra, Italia* site cannot be individually identified or know what kinds of other users and how many are accessing the same material. The sense of community created resides, then, in the assumption that the site exists because there is a collective of Italians in London who share common concerns, aspirations and experience. 'Belonging' or feeling 'at home' in this collective is expressed – and performed – by subscribing to the set of values and activities that it profiles. The reference to the country and culture of departure is maintained emphatically in the site's content, most obviously through language choice. A promotion of an idea or ideal of Italian-ness – of the specific capital that might accrue to Italian mobile subjects in a competitive transnational context – emerges from reports and features. For example, Techitalia:Lab, an initiative to support new technology start-ups in the UK of specifically Italian provenance, is strongly promoted in an issue from December 2017: 'With Techitalia:Lab, being Italian for once becomes a means of coming together in mutual support, a linguistic and cultural bond which can make a decisive difference in a competitive international marketplace such as London'.[27] The

Italian. One example is an article on a survey of Italians' attitudes to the UK since the Brexit vote, which uses 'nel Regno Unito', 'nell'UK' and the more anglicized 'in UK' to refer to events there. See Antonio Piemontese, 'Nonostante la Brexit, il Regno Unito continua a piacere agli italiani' [Despite Brexit, Italians Still Like the UK], *Londra, Italia*, 22 January 2019, http://www.londraitalia.com/cronaca/uk-italia-sondaggio-brexit/ [accessed 28 February 2019].

[27] Francesco Ragni, 'TechItalia, dalla community nasce a Londra l'acceleratore per

opportunity to capitalize on the skills and innovational creativity of Italian mobile workers and, by association, the reputation that Italians own in this respect in London, is here promoted as distinctive and enabling professional and economic capital. Interestingly, this 'added value' from being Italian is indicated here to be a scarcity ('for once'), suggesting a disaggregation of any form of Italian 'community' in London and a challenging environment of competition amongst transnational workers.

The site constructs also a more 'home-like' narrative of Italians' lives in London, activating a sense of shared preferences and practices. Articles on air quality, housing, health, crime and London transport seek to make the city navigable and liveable for new and/or temporary residents, and these pieces are not simply imported and translated from 'local' sources in the British media but are written or rewritten by Italian journalists and contributors, thus implicitly looking at these issues from an 'Italian' perspective with which a user of the site might identify. Cultural events of Italian provenance are routinely listed and promoted (film screenings and festivals, concerts, exhibitions, artists' visits to London) and Italian restaurant and retailer reviews and news feature prominently, sustaining a connection which enables pastimes and experiences coded as 'Italian' to be individually enjoyed and notionally shared with other users of the site in such a way as to resonate 'home' whilst also maintaining the fluidity of transnational cultural and personal experience.[28] In a very immediate way, a permanent advertisement for Italian energy suppliers in London offers to bring a continuity with domestic experience in Italy directly into the functional space of the home in London.[29]

In certain instances, Italian-ness is asserted more specifically and even defensively. For example, an article from March 2018 responds to a piece in the UK *Sunday Times* about an investigation into the alleged stalking of a

startup italiane' [Techitalia: Out of the [Italian] Community in London Emerges the Booster for Italian Start-ups], *Londra, Italia*, 1 December 2017, http://www.londraitalia. com/cronaca/techitalia-community-londra-acceleratore-startup-italiane-20171201/ [accessed 28 February 2019]. See also the organization's website: http://www.techitalialab.com/ [accessed 28 February 2019].

[28] Baldassar notes the importance of virtual sharing of this kind: 'Watching the same TV programs and sharing music via the Internet appear to be particularly important to recent migrants, who dedicate time to regular virtual communication with family members, keeping up to date with various everyday events and happenings [...] It is in these moments of shared virtual co-presence that people may imagine they are in the same place' ('Obligation to People and Place', p. 185).

[29] The pop-up advertisement is for Green Network Energy, https://greennetworkenergy.co.uk/it/, presented as 'The First Italian Energy Supplier in UK' [accessed 28 March 2019].

successful Italian producer and retailer, Livia Giuggioli, resident in London and wife of the British actor Colin Firth. The author of the *Sunday Times* article had been mockingly critical of the capacity of the Italian authorities to pursue the case to prosecution effectively. The response in the *Londra, Italia* article offers a robust rebuttal:

> We leave to Firth and Giuggioli the task of defending themselves against these vulgar insults, but we do not wish the defamatory lies about our police forces to go uncommented. There may have been an error in the conduct of the case, but this does not permit anyone to denigrate our institutions.
>
> We trust that our Government and our Embassy will intervene in order to return these accusations to their sender and to defend the honour of the Police and Carabinieri as well as of our judicial system.[30]

In the context of the more fluid transnational sense of belonging articulated by most of the site's material and commentary, this unequivocal recourse to the institutions of the home nation and its representatives abroad is striking. Underscored by the repeated use of the possessive adjective 'our', it asserts a national identity and a national pride called into question by the comments of a foreign journalist, and so instates a stark border within the *Londra, Italia* connection by which the site identifies itself.

The narratives of home constructed through different means in this essay together indicate three principal insights. The first is that home matters, and continues to matter for both individual subjects and communities even where transnational mobility introduces a physical departure from a familiar home towards a condition in which home is an object of question: can a new home be established elsewhere, and if so, how, if at all, will it relate to the home left behind? What might be lost and gained in rehoming in a different location? It emerges from the different stories and practices of homing discussed here that the notion of a home – whether as house, locality, culture, language, family, community or nation – persists for transnational subjects as a reference point bearing a significant emotional value. This value may be magnified or minimized in particular moments of the mobile life of an individual or community, and it is the object of the impulses of distantiation

---

[30] Francesco Ragni, 'Il Sunday Times offende Carabinieri e Polizia italiana: "incapaci e parrucchieri"' [The *Sunday Times* Offends the Italian Carabinieri and Police, Calling them 'Ineffectual Hairdressers'], *Londra, Italia*, 12 March 2018, http://www.londraitalia.com/cronaca/giuggioli-firth-polizia-times-stalking-20180312/ [accessed 28 February 2019].

and proximity which may differently regulate the emotional experience of a transnational subject, but those very processes of detachment, attachment and reattachment themselves corroborate the obstinate importance of a sense of home.

That space matters is the second finding which emerges from the examples explored in this discussion. The notion of home – even where identified, as I have here, as practices of homing – is anchored in a physical and material location of some sort. This may be deeply literal and local, as in the case of the fabric of the house and the very soil in which it sits in Ghermandi's novel, or it may be the broader topographical locality of London's 'Little Italy' constructed through the accounts in Besagni's books. It may be the heterogeneous space of contemporary London which is never definitively demarcated in the narrative of London life which the *Londra, Italia* site constructs, but is nevertheless present as the presumed location to which its information, commentary and recommendations refer. My focus on narrative and imaginative constructions of a notion of home might imply a dematerialization of home as physical space, but the evidence from all of the examples is that home has distinct materiality in transnational experience. The haptic realness of the objects brought to the creative writing workshop in Birmingham – the 'things from home' – accentuates this recourse to the material.

That space matters leads to the third conclusion I draw here, which is that home or homing is political. The very importance of the material and spatial dimensions indicates that what is at stake in expressing and disseminating a sense of being at home at both personal and community levels is agency within a particular social context or *polis*.[31] The narratives and accounts of homing practices explored demonstrate the desire for presence, visibility and a sense of belonging in a given location even where the contingency of presence, in terms of either having departed or being a 'migrant' there, is tacitly or explicitly acknowledged. Whether through reviving family, cultural and national memory in the case of Ghermandi's novel, mediating the postcolonial construction of cultures in the case of Abidogun's textbook carried from Nigeria, or insistently asserting the vitality of the annual Clerkenwell procession in the case of Besagni's books, the claim to ownership of a particular space, culture and history, and the demand for recognition of that ownership, are a powerful underlying principle of the homing practices and stories of home discussed in this essay. Homing matters to transnational identity.

---

[31] Boccagni writes: 'Migrants' relations with receiving countries and with countries of origin are highly revealing of the political significance of home, as a stake of inclusion or exclusion' (*Migration and the Search for Home*, p. 88).

Part Three

Temporality

10

Making Pre-Modern Time

Guittone, Dante and Petrarch

David Bowe

Introduction

When we consider pre-modern temporalities from a transnational perspective, the task this chapter is attempting, we are faced with two fairly hefty topics: time and space. To take these in reverse order, the first thing we need to remember about Italy is that before 1861, it did not exist. Indeed, most current European nations did not meaningfully exist in the period increasingly called pre-modern. This period, then, is less transnational than pre-national. This is not to stymie the notion of the transnational as a valuable key in which to read pre-modern texts. While nations may not yet have formed, local and regional identities and delineated communities, which could be either reinforced or transcended, did exist. Writers and texts from this context have also been employed for multiple and sometimes conflicting nationalist and fascist ends.[1] Reminding ourselves of the short-lived and historically porous nature of today's borders allows us to challenge nationalistic, teleological narratives of continuous national cultures.

With this in mind, we are left with another question, 'What shape is time?' We might instinctively imagine a clock face, its hands ticking inexorably

---

[1] Anne O'Connor, 'Dante Alighieri – from Absence to Stony Presence: Building Memories in Nineteenth-Century Florence', *Italian Studies*, 67.3 (2012), 307–35; Luigi Scorrano, 'Il Dante "fascista"', *Deutsches Dante-Jahrbuch*, 75.1 (2000), 85–124; Benjamin Martin, 'Celebrating the Nation's Poets: Petrarch, Leopardi, and the Appropriation of Cultural Symbols in Fascist Italy', in *Donatello among the Blackshirts: History and Modernity in the Visual Culture of Fascist Italy*, ed. by Roger Crum and Claudia Lazzaro (Ithaca: Cornell University Press, 2005), pp. 187–202.

around. Or a digital display on a computer screen, or phone (still sometimes bearing pleasingly skeuomorphic hands and numbers). The oldest surviving mechanical clocks in the world both date to 1386. One is in Salisbury Cathedral, in south-west England, the other in the Torre di Sant'Andrea in Chioggia, in north-east Italy. The first reference to such a clock in literature comes in Dante's *Commedia* (written between c. 1307 and 1321) in a delicate simile describing a whirling circle of blessed souls in heaven.[2] Dante describes how 'one cog pulls one wheel and drives another / chiming "ding-ding" with such a sweet tone'.[3] For Dante, the technological marvel of the clock best illustrates the almost indescribable beauty of Paradise. Dante turns mechanical movement into beautiful, propulsive verse, through his use of *terza rima*, a rhyme scheme that keeps ticking ineluctably forward like the hands of the clock.

Dante's simile provides a space in which to reflect on the intimate relationship between poetry and time, literature and history. Poetry necessarily exists in time; it is measured in time through its metre and its relationship with both song and dance, it is performed and expressed in time. Indeed, according to Dante's *Convivio*, the defining features of poetry are 'rhyme and time and a regulated number of syllables [i.e., metre]'.[4] Poetry may also express the experience of time, an experience that is shifting, subjective, mediated by language and the mechanisms of measurement. In the *Commedia*, Dante's journey through the afterlife takes place as time passes. Dante's poem is also a historical record of sorts, documenting technological inventions and their role in society (here, the mechanical clock which calls the faithful to prayer). This is a microcosmic, concrete example of the ways in which literature provides a window on culture, both communicating social and cultural history and renewing our own cultural outlooks by drawing us across time and difference into the experience of another time, another life in ways authors may have hoped for, but never fully foreseen. Texts like Dante's and texts quite unlike Dante's – love poems, religious poems, debate poems, prose narratives, letters – provide their own pleasures of reading, as well as their own windows: on histories of learning, linguistic developments, political rivalries, transnational cultural exchanges, religious beliefs and cultural assumptions in a different age. Understanding the diversity of a cultural past that exists beyond the borders of modern nations and the boundaries of modern categories is ever more urgent, and

[2] Dante, *Paradiso* X.139–45; John A. Scott, *Understanding Dante* (Notre Dame: Notre Dame University Press, 2004), p. 297.

[3] Dante, *Paradiso* X.142–43. All translations mine unless otherwise noted.

[4] Dante Alighieri, *Convivio*, ed. by Giorgio Inglese (Milan: Rizzoli, 1993), I, x, 12.

literature offers us a particularly direct mode of engagement with this historical plurality.[5]

In short, one could argue that the study of texts from the past allows us to bring their worlds and words a little more into the present, to collapse some of the distance that lies between us as readers and them as writers, to make 'then' more 'now'.

When/Where?

Beyond the *Commedia*, a number of texts within the networks of thirteenth- and fourteenth-century lyric poetry in Italy were deeply concerned with the nature of time and memory. Dante and two other poets stand out from this context as especially invested in engaging with the temporal nature of their writing and in the temporal nature of subjectivity. Each worked to construct a particular, lyric self across their texts:

> Ora parrà s'eo saverò cantare
> e s'eo varrò quanto valer già soglio
> poiché del tutto Amor fuggo e disvoglio,
> e più che cosa mai forte mi spare!

> [Now we will see if I still know how to sing
> and if I will be as worthy as I was used to being valued before
> now that I fully flee from Love and unwant it,
> and it seems worse to me than any other thing!][6]

> In quella parte del libro de la mia memoria dinanzi a la quale poco si potrebbe leggere, si trova una rubrica la quale dice: *Incipit vita nova.* Sotto la quale rubrica io trovo scritte le parole le quali è mio intendimento d'assemplare in questo libello; e se non tutte, almeno la loro sentenzia.

---

[5] E.g., posts on inthemedievalmiddle.com [accessed 17 September 2019]; *The Public Medievalist Special Essay Series: Race, Racism and the Middle Ages*, https://www. publicmedievalist.com/race-racism-middle-ages-toc/ [accessed 17 January 2018]. For a transnational perspective, see Marianne O'Doherty, 'Where Were the Middle Ages', https://www.publicmedievalist.com/where-middle-ages/ [accessed 17 January 2018].

[6] Guittone d'Arezzo, 'Ora parrà', 1–2, in *Poeti del duecento*, ed. by Gianfranco Contini, 2 vols (Turin: Einaudi, 1979), i. Other poems by Guittone in *Le rime di Guittone d'Arezzo*, ed. by Francesco Egidi (Bari: Laterza, 1940).

[In that part of the book of my memory before which there is little
legible, you find a rubric that says: *Incipit vita nova*. Under this rubric,
I find written the words that I intend to copy down in this little book;
and if not all of them, at least their significance][7]

Voi ch'ascoltate in rime sparse il suono
di quei sospiri ond'io nudriva 'l core
in sul mio primo giovenile errore
quand'era in parte altr'uom da quel ch'i' sono.

[You who listen in scattered rhymes to the sound
of those sighs with which I nourished my heart
in my first youthful error
when I was in part another man than I am][8]

These are the opening lines of famous works by three of the most influential authors writing in the transition between late medieval and early
modern culture in Italy. These poets, of three successive generations, each
claimed to be very different from those who came before, sometimes going
as far as to actively disparage the work of their forebears. Guittone d'Arezzo
(*c.* 1230–94) joined a religious order (the *Frati Gaudenti*) 'in middle age',[9]
and turned to religious poetry, condemning his own past writing as sinful.
Dante (1265–1321) then dismissed Guittone's writing as 'more municipal
than courtly' and his fans as 'devotees of ignorance'.[10] Francesco Petrarca or
Petrarch (1304–74) subsequently refused to acknowledge any debt to Dante's
poetic masterpiece, claiming never to have read the *Commedia* to avoid being
influenced by it.[11] However, these three poets had much in common. All
three were Tuscan by birth, all three were affected by exile or banishment,
all three were engaged with their political milieus and all three articulated
complex relationships with time and its implications for human experience
and writing. To acknowledge these similarities is not to elide the differences
between Guittone, Dante and Petrarch. The different ways in which each of

---

[7] Dante Alighieri, *Vita Nuova; Rime*, ed. by Donato Pirovano and Marco Grimaldi
(Rome: Salerno, 2015), I.1. Henceforth *VN*.

[8] Francesco Petrarca, *Canzoniere*, ed. by Marco Santagata (Milan: Mondadori,
1996), 1, 1–4. I will refer to Petrarch's collection by its abbreviated Latin title *RVF*
(*Rerum vulgarium fragmenta*).

[9] Guittone, 'Ahi, quant'ho che vergogni', 6.

[10] Dante, *De vulgari eloquentia* I.xiii.1, II.vi.8. Henceforth *DVE*.

[11] Petrarch, *Familiares* XXI.15.11.

them handles the past, present and future in their writing will shape this chapter's reflections on expressions and functions of time and temporalities in a pre-modern, transnational, Italian vernacular context.

In exploring these poets' approaches to the fraught question of time, one key point of reference will be the concept of conversion. The process of turning towards God plays a narrative role in the works of all three men and, as with many medieval accounts of conversion, Augustine of Hippo's (354–430) *Confessions* provides an essential backdrop to their writing. Guittone, Dante and Petrarch all read Augustine, whose mobile life and internationally diffuse writings make him a transnational figure *par excellence*. Born in what is now Algeria, he was later baptized in Milan before becoming Bishop of Hippo and his works permeated the thought and theology of Latin Europe. Augustine offered a model of accounting for oneself in a public literary work, a framework for thinking about transitions: from sin to salvation, between life stages and modes of expression (Augustine the gifted secular reader and orator became Augustine the eloquent exegete and theologian). Augustine also proposed a theory of time and temporal experience in book 11 of his *Confessions*, which will underpin this discussion of temporalities at play in the works of Guittone, Dante and Petrarch.

Augustine's pan-Mediterranean biography vividly presents the image of a life lived beyond the borders of what we might define as a nation, but Guittone's, Dante's and Petrarch's movements across the geographical space of what is now Italy and (in Petrarch's case) continental Europe are still helpfully viewed through the transnational lens. Guittone, born in Arezzo in Tuscany, went into self-imposed exile in reaction to the 'bothersome and base people' who 'make me hate my homeland'.[12] Dante, famously banished from Florence in 1302, placed his exile from the 'the lovely sheep pen where I slept as a lamb'[13] at the centre of his political and poetic identity. Petrarch was born to a banished Florentine, raised in Avignon, spent time in the Vaucluse, was invited to be crowned Poet Laureate in both Rome and Paris, and eventually died in Arquà.[14] The geographical boundaries of these poets' movements do

---

[12] Guittone, 'Gente noiosa e villana', 1, 5.

[13] Dante, *Paradiso* XXV.5.

[14] On Dante, see Catherine Keen, 'Florence and Faction in Dante's Lyric Poetry', in *'Se mai continga che il poema sacro...': Exile, Politics and Theology in Dante*, ed. by Claire Honess and Matthew Treherne (Ravenna: Longo, 2013), pp. 63–83. On Petrarch as exile, see Laurence Hooper, 'Exile and Petrarch's Reinvention of Authorship', *Renaissance Quarterly*, 69 (2016), 1217–56. On Florentine writers' mobile, distant relationship with 'their' city see K. P. Clarke, 'Florence', in *Europe: A Literary History*, ed. by David Wallace, 2 vols (Oxford: Oxford University Press, 2016), I, pp. 688–706.

not limit their resonance for a transnational perspective. They exemplify an Italian category of internal mobility, 'peculiarly transnational and transnationally peculiar: historically a space characterized by both internal and external transit and movement',[15] and they allow us to destabilize the very notion of a national literary canon.

As noted above, in a pre-modern context the very notion of 'nation' is anachronistic. Guittone, Dante and Petrarch were writing in the context of city states, communes and kingdoms, moving between neighbouring areas of Italy, each with its own government, in a period of wars between cities now governed by the same regional council.[16] This was also a period of linguistic flux, widespread multilingualism (at least among those with greater access to education) and translation. Dante and Petrarch wrote extensively in Latin (aka *gramatica*), as well as the vernacular (illustrious or otherwise), while writers from across Italy wrote and read a number of vernaculars, including Old French and Occitan.[17] This pre-national, multilingual context offers useful cues for studying other periods, reinforcing our sense of the fragility and contingency of the nation in a long historical view. At the same time, these poets did have a sense of a more expansive identity that roughly corresponded to modern Italy. Both Dante and Petrarch address 'Italia' in their writing: Dante's collective treatment of the vernaculars of the peninsula in the *De vulgari eloquentia* (*DVE*), or his excoriating address to 'slavish Italy',[18] and Petrarch's apostrophe of 'my Italy'.[19] This sense of a larger 'Italy' often harked back to the Roman Empire and, in Dante's case, aspired to the revitalization

---

[15] Emma Bond, 'Towards a Trans-national Turn in Italian Studies?', *Italian Studies*, 69.3 (2014), 415–24 (p. 421).

[16] For more on 'the transnational and the pre-national' see Tristan Kay, 'Dante and the Transnational Turn' in this volume.

[17] Dante identifies three vernacular families, dividing the third into three parts defined by their word for yes, 'oc'/'oïl'/'sì'=Occitan/French/Italian (*DVE* I.viii.3–9). The poet Sordello (encountered by Dante in *Purgatorio* VI), wrote in Occitan. Brunetto Latini, author of the *Trésor* and *Rettorica*, wrote in Italian and French. On vernaculars and Latin in this context, see Giulio Lepschy, 'Mother Tongues in the Middle Ages and Dante', in *Dante's Plurilingualism: Authority, Knowledge, Subjectivity*, ed. by Sara Fortune, Manuele Gragnolati and Jürgen Trabant (Abingdon: Routledge, 2010), pp. 16–23; Mirko Tavoni, 'Volgare e latino nella storia di Dante', in *Dante's Plurilingualism*, pp. 52–68. On translation, see Alison Cornish, *Vernacular Translation in Dante's Italy: Illiterate Literature* (Cambridge: Cambridge University Press, 2011). On medieval multilingualism, see also Kay, 'Dante and the Transnational Turn' in this volume.

[18] Dante, *Purgatorio* VI.76.

[19] Petrarch, *RVF* 128.

of the Holy Roman Empire,[20] though these remained nostalgias for trans- or supranational organizations of Italy. From this multiple, 'hyphenated', post-imperial, pre-national landscape emerged a body of (especially Tuscan) vernacular literature that would be produced and circulated through and beyond the boundaries of Florence, Tuscany and Italy, and which would come to define an originary Italian literary and linguistic culture.[21]

Secondly, this circulation of texts went beyond not only spatial but also temporal boundaries. The texts of Dante and Petrarch in particular continue to lead transnational afterlives of adaptation, appropriation, rewriting and translation, becoming part of a globalized literary milieu in a transnation- alization of these authors' works that began very early in their reception.[22] In response to Bond's challenge to consider what a temporally wide-ranging

[20] Dante's *Monarchia*, and *Paradiso* XXX.130–38 illustrate this, though note also the extreme linguistic fragmentation evident in the *DVE*.

[21] The large bodies of work written in other vernaculars did not enjoy the same wide circulation and later canonization as these Tuscan, Florentine examples. The so-called *Tre Corone* [Three Crowns] of Italian literature (Dante, Petrarch and Boccaccio) typify this trend. I have excluded Boccaccio and included Guittone to focus on a particular lyric history and give space to this neglected but significant thirteenth-century author. For similar reasons, this chapter doesn't deal with recently crowned members of the *Cinque Corone*, Catherine of Siena and Brigitte of Sweden, either. There is work to do on temporality in the works of these two authors, especially given the complexities of time in mystical experience (particularly in Brigitte's writings, but also in Catherine's *Dialogo della divina provvidenza*). For the *Cinque Corone*, see David Wallace 'General Introduction', in *Europe: A Literary History*, ed. by David Wallace, 2 vols (Oxford: Oxford University Press, 2016), I, pp. xxxiii–xxxv. On Brigitte and Catherine in Rome, see Pietro Boitani, 'Rome', in *Europe: A Literary History*, pp. 720–31 (esp. pp. 727–29). On Catherine of Siena, see Jane Tylus, *Reclaiming Catherine of Siena: Literature, Literacy, and the Signs of Others* (Chicago: University of Chicago Press, 2008). Within the male-dominated poetic tradition of medieval Italy, one group of sonnets attributed to a woman (the Compiuta Donzella di Firenze) do survive in Vatican Library MS Vaticano Latino 3793. See David Bowe, 'Versions of a Feminine Voice: The Compiuta Donzella di Firenze', *Italian Studies*, 73.1 (2018), 1–13.

[22] Scholarship on Dante's and Petrarch's international receptions includes: Nick Havely, *Dante's British Public: Readers and Texts, from the Fourteenth Century to the Present* (Oxford: Oxford University Press, 2014); Russell Goulbourne, Claire E. Honess and Matthew Treherne, eds, *Dante in France* (Pisa: Fabrizio Serra Editore, 2013); Jennifer Rushworth, *Petrarch and the Literary Culture of Nineteenth-Century France: Translation, Appropriation, Transformation* (Woodbridge: Boydell and Brewer, 2017); and Martin McLaughlin, Letizia Panizza and Peter Hainsworth, eds, *Petrarch in Britain: Interpreters, Imitators, and Translators over 700 years* (Oxford: Oxford University Press for the British Academy, 2007). Guittone has finally been extensively

approach to the transnational might mean for Italian literary studies, this chapter attempts 'a temporal stretching out' of the Italian canon. This stretching out allows us to assert the inherently trans-, because pre-, national nature of this canon and to consider the boundaries that writers crossed then and the transnational afterlives of their works now.[23] Both of these assertions can serve to wrest these texts from nationalist narrative and to remind us of the fragile, imagined nature of nations themselves.

What Time?

If we are to stretch time, we first need to define it, and here we return to Augustine's *Confessions*, in which, having recounted his sinful past and subsequent conversion, he attempts to define what it means to speak about the past, the present and the future. After an extended discourse on the nature of and distinction between divine eternity and earthly time,[24] Augustine sums up his position:[25]

> What is now patently clear is that neither future nor past events exist, and it is incorrect to say, 'there are three times, past, present, and future.' Perhaps it would be appropriate to say, 'There are three times: the present respecting things past, the present respecting things present, and the present respecting things future.' These three things do somehow exist in the soul, and I do not perceive them anywhere else: for the present of things past is memory; the present of things present is paying attention; and the present of things future is expectation.[26]

This understanding of the human experience of time as filtered through a subjective present ('in the soul', not 'anywhere else'), provides a useful structure for a confessional narrative, in which the text becomes the locale

---

translated in *Selected Poems and Prose*, ed. and trans. by Antonello Borra (Toronto: University of Toronto Press, 2017).

[23] Bond, 'Towards a Trans-national Turn', p. 418.

[24] Augustine, *Confessions*, XI.13.15–19.25, in *Augustine: Confessions*, ed. and trans. by Carolyn J. B. Hammond, 2 vols (Cambridge, MA: Harvard University Press, 2014–16).

[25] For commentary on this passage, see Jan Johann Albinn Mooij, 'Saint Augustine: Two Times and Two Creations', in *Time and Mind: The History of a Philosophical Problem* (Leiden: Brill, 2005), pp. 66–75.

[26] Augustine, *Confessions*, XI.20.26.

for this model of temporality. The present of the text of the *Confessions* gives space to an account of the past (of sin), a present in which that account is written (the moment of narration), and an expected future of salvation, which goes hand in hand with the event of conversion.[27]

The experience of all of these times through the present of the text is emphasized at key moments in the narrative, when the historic present crashes into the predominantly past tense narrative. We see this in the pivotal book VIII, first when Augustine questions why he and Alypius are failing to seize heaven,[28] then when he hears the voice singing 'take up and read',[29] and again when he successfully turns his will to God and tells his mother the good news.[30] This collapse of past into present serves to highlight the experience of past time through the subjective, narrative present described three books later, opening the way for a temporal 'stretching out' (*distensio*) of the mind, which creates a '*now* not only spanned by the past and future, but also [...] constituted by them'.[31] This model of time lends itself particularly well to confessional narrative as it allows the convert-narrator to contain the sinful past within the framework of the converted present. This framework comes to the fore in both Guittone's and Dante's poetic self-representations, while Petrarch simultaneously highlights and troubles it in his *Rerum vulgarium fragmenta* (*RVF*). A subjective present through which the events of the present, the past and the future are filtered suggests the structure for this chapter as much as it does for the works used as case studies within it.

Unlike Augustine, however, Guittone, Dante and Petrarch worked in verse, which raises a new set of temporal challenges, highlighted in Jonathan Culler's discussion of the 'lyric present'. Culler contends that lyric texts have a particular relationship with time, which depends on the moment in which

---

[27] Carolyn Dinshaw, *How Soon Is Now? Medieval Texts, Amateur Readers, and the Queerness of Time* (Durham, NC and London: Duke University Press, 2012), pp. 12–16.

[28] Augustine, *Confessions*, VIII.8.19: *invado Alypium: exclamo, 'quid patimur?'* ['I seize Alypius: I cry, "what is wrong with us?"'].

[29] Augustine, *Confessions*, VIII.12.29: *et ecce audio vocem de vicina* ['and then I hear a voice nearby'].

[30] Augustine, *Confessions*, VIII.12.30: *inde ad matrem ingredimur, indicamus: guadet. narramus quemadmodum gestum sit: exultat* et *triumphat* ['Next we go to my mother. We tell her the news. She is delighted. We tell her how it happened. She is jubilant and celebrates'].

[31] Dinshaw, *How Soon Is Now?*, p. 14 (also pp. 105–28, on collapsing temporal distance).

the lyric text is read.[32] This moment gives rise to an 'iterable present', which is neither a simple present tense nor 'timeless'. Instead it is an 'iterable *now* of lyric enunciation, rather than of linear time'.[33] In other words, according to Culler, every time one returns to the lyric text, that text is 'now', its meaning is articulated in the present moment, and cannot be subsumed into the linearity of narrative.

The reactions of Guittone, Dante and Petrarch to the framework of linear human time and the spectre of lyric time, which resists linearity, are the primary focus of the rest of this chapter.

Guittone

To return to the opening lines of Guittone's canzone – 'Ora parrà s'eo saverò cantare / e s'eo varrò quanto valer già soglio' – we see a strictly delineated relationship with the past, from the perspective of the present, and with an eye to the future. Guittone's opening gambit, the deictic 'Ora' [now], sets the tone for his post-conversion poetry – those texts ascribed to 'Frate Guittone d'Arezzo' in manuscript witnesses including the so-called *Canzoniere Vaticano* (MS Vat. Lat. 3793) and MS Laurenziano-Rediano 9. In the second of these, that 'Ora' opens the section dedicated to Guittone's poetry, so a reader making their way sequentially through the manuscript would literally read Guittone's oeuvre through this opening temporal statement. This 'now' declares a new moment, the time of the poet's life in which he has turned to God and cast off his sinful past. As such, Guittone's 'now' does not simply make claims about the present moment, but is situated within an ostensibly linear narrative. Guittone attempts to establish an Augustinian, confessional temporality, filtering the past and looking to the future through a subjective present, only to unwittingly make the case for Culler's 'lyric present' when we read this canzone in relation the rest of his corpus.

The opening lines of the canzone pretend to a linear, autobiographical temporality through their careful unfolding of tenses and temporal indicators, from that opening 'Ora', through a series of future tenses ('parrà' [it will be seen], 'saverò' [I will know], 'varrò' [I will be worth]), to a comparison with the past ('valer già soglio' [I was [lit. am] used to being worth before]). Guittone makes 'now' the pivot on which an account of his self and his writing turns: from a before in which he was esteemed for his writing as a secular love poet,

[32] Jonathan Culler, *Theory of the Lyric* (Cambridge, MA: Harvard University Press, 2015), p. 289.

[33] Culler, *Theory*, pp. 283–85, building on Susan Langer, *Feeling and Form: A Theory of Art Developed from Philosophy in a New Key* (London: Routledge, 1953), pp. 268–69.

a genre that he now flees, to a future – *from this moment on* – in which he hopes to be esteemed for his religious, moral writing and teaching.[34] Every failure, every stumble into the snares of lust ('carnal voglia'),[35] is framed as leading teleologically to this 'now' of conversion and the future to follow. In other words, the 'now' of the conversion poems claims to complete a narrative which begins with the 'before' of the secular poems.[36] The story is more complicated than this, however. Guittone's pre-conversion poetry has more in common with his post-conversion poetry than he cares to admit,[37] and any attempt to flatten the iterable lyric present into linear, narrative time contains the seeds of its own disruption.

Guittone already displays suspicion of secular lyric in his pre-conversion poetry through a crescendo of irony, which undercuts subsequent claims that his literary past was one of sincerely sinful writing.[38] As such, his efforts to frame his past poetry as a work of sin that needs to be recanted are, at best, strained. Returning to earlier poems like his *ars amandi* sonnets, we see Guittone parodying love lyric as a series of linguistic tricks dressed up in pretty words, revealing its ugliness under the ironic guise of a guide for lovers.[39] There is a disconnect between Guittone's linear narrative of sin to redemption and the already critical, ironic pre-conversion poetry as it exists. Here, Culler's lyric present offers a useful vocabulary to explain the ways in which past lyric texts refuse to be subjected to linear narrative. As we read Guittone's pre-conversion lyric texts, they cease to be 'pre-conversion' and become simply lyric; the present of their enunciation overcomes the grand narrative in which they lead inevitably to the confessional now of 'Ora parrà', offering us instead a parodic critique of courtly love lyric.

Guittone cannot keep his texts in order. They continue to lead their own lyric lives, unconstrained by the linear narrative of self that he attempts retrospectively to impose on them.

---

[34] Antonello Borra, *Guittone d'Arezzo e le maschere del poeta: La lirica cortese tra ironia e palinodia* (Ravenna: Longo, 2000), pp. 26–46.

[35] Guittone, 'Ora parrà', 21.

[36] Michelangelo Picone, *Percorsi della lirica duecentesca* (Florence: Cadmo, 2003), pp. 105–22 (p. 109).

[37] Vincent Moleta, *The Early Poetry of Guittone d'Arezzo* (London: MHRA, 1976).

[38] Tristan Kay, *Dante's Lyric Redemption: Eros, Salvation, Vernacular Tradition* (Oxford: Oxford University Press, 2015), pp. 93–154; Dave Bowe, *Poetry in Dialogue in the Duecento and Dante* (Oxford: Oxford University Press, 2020), chapter 1.

[39] Kay, *Dante's Lyric Redemption*, p. 101. See D'Arco Silvio Avalle, *Ai luoghi di delizia pieni. Saggio sulla lirica italiana del XIII secolo* (Milan: R. Ricciardi, 1977), pp. 56–86, on these sonnets (pp. 87–110) as a lover's manual in the style of Ovid's *Ars amatoria* or Andreas Capellanus's *De Amore*.

Dante

In his early work the *Vita nova* Dante attempts a move not unlike Guittone's. He collects a series of lyric texts and embeds them within a prose narrative and commentary. He puts each of these lyric texts in the service of a singular narrative, of his developing love for Beatrice and his poetic reaction to that love, regardless of whether they give any internal indication of it. Dante aims to order and frame lyric texts into linear narrative, presenting the entire project as a memorial, selectively copied from the book of memory into the little book (*libello*) he offers to his readers.

The invocation of memory is polysemous and rhetorically important in shaping the text and the expectations of its readers. The book of memory is a well-established trope in pre-modern Europe,[40] and in the *libello* Dante's memory is filtered through a present of narration that seeks to encapsulate the past and, ultimately, the future; Dante's text begins with the invocation of memory and finishes with the promise of future writing:

> After [writing] this sonnet, a marvellous vision appeared to me, in which I saw things that made me propose to say nothing more of this blessed lady until I could write more worthily about her.[41]

Between beginning and end, memory and expectation, there are 31 lyric texts embedded in the past tense of narrative and ascribed a new, specific, ostensibly fixed meaning by that same narrative.[42] This meaning, however, must remain unstable. While Dante engages in a full-scale authorial performance to actively rewrite the lyrics collected in the *libello*,[43] they remain lyric texts, with their own presents, interrupting Dante's attempted ordering of text and self.

The *libello* is constructed as a present of past things (the 'memory' of the events narrated), a present of present things (the 'attention' of the reader

---

[40] Mary Carruthers, *The Book of Memory: A Study of Memory in Medieval Culture*, 2nd edn (Cambridge: Cambridge University Press, 2008), pp. 274–338 (especially pp. 274–79).

[41] Dante, *VN* XLII.1.

[42] Michelangelo Picone, 'La teoria dell'*Auctoritas* nella *Vita nova*', *Tenzone*, 6 (2005), 173–91 (pp. 177–81).

[43] Manuele Gragnolati, 'Authorship and Performance in Dante's *Vita Nova*', in *Aspects of the Performative in Medieval Culture*, ed. by Manuele Gragnolati and Almut Suerbaum (Berlin and New York: De Gruyter, 2010), pp. 125–41. See also Teodolinda Barolini, *Dante's Poets: Textuality and Truth in the 'Comedy'* (Princeton: Princeton University Press, 1984), p. 15.

to the text at hand), and a present of things to come (the 'expectation' of new writing), but the linearity of this Augustinian model cannot wholly contain the present of enunciation of each lyric text. Hence when Dante's prose claims that 'O voi che per la via d'Amor passate' is about a 'screen lady' who served to disguise his love for Beatrice, readers may still read it as an independent lyric text, and ask whether it contains any of the features he describes. It may still be collected in an edition of Dante's poems without its prose framework, and indeed many of the lyrics of the *Vita nova* were collected in just such a fashion from very early in the history of their circulation.[44] In other words, Dante's attempt to fix those lyrics in aspic were (inevitably) unsuccessful.

Petrarch

Unlike Dante and Guittone, Petrarch's response to the temporal instability of lyric in narratives of self seems to have been one of confrontation, even celebration. In Barolini's words, 'The *Fragmenta*, which thematizes fragmentation or multiplicity in its very title, conjures the existence of the self in time; we are beings subject to constant incremental change and to radical ontological instability'.[45] In the opening quatrain of the first sonnet of the *RVF*, Petrarch establishes a similar model for narrating the self in verse and in time through an address to the reader that encompasses the past of the self, the present of the text and the implications of future reading. In these first lines the tenses unroll out of the present ('Voi ch'ascoltate')[46] into the habitual past of recollection ('ond'io nudriva il core', 'quand'era in parte altr'uom'), before sliding back into the present of the narrating and narrated self ('da quel ch'i'sono').[47] This temporal chiasmus, which shifts the focus from 'you the reader' to 'me the speaker', also implies an iterable present of encounter with the lyric text, which will address itself to any future reader.[48] It also articulates the tensions inherent in narrating a continuous self through fragmented

---

[44] Keen, 'New Lives of Dante's *Vita Nova* Lyrics: Material Translations and Selections', paper given at the Society for Italian Studies Biennial Conference, Oxford, 2015.

[45] Barolini 'The Self in the Labyrinth of Time: *Rerum vulgarium fragmenta*', in *Petrarch: A Critical Guide to the Complete Works*, ed. by Victoria Kirkham and Armando Maggi (Chicago: University of Chicago Press, 2009), pp. 33–62 (p. 33).

[46] Petrarch, *RVF* 1.

[47] Petrarch, *RVF* 2–4.

[48] This sonnet is one of Culler's 'hyper-canonical' examples: for Culler, Petrarch's see-sawing then/now works 'to undermine narrative continuity in the collection as a whole', *Theory*, pp. 285–86.

verse. Petrarch's sonnet shares Guittone's and Dante's desire to account for the past self and past poetry (his 'rime', which nourished his heart when he was, in part, a different man), but it doesn't make the same claims of closure.

Petrarch doesn't claim a clean break with his past self and verse, either. 'Voi ch'ascoltate' doesn't posit a 'now' to which all personal and poetic error is irretrievably prior, as in Guittone's *ora/già* dichotomy; the 'primo giovanile errore'[49] belongs to a time when he was only different 'in parte'. This partial distance is crucial: it allows for the lyric present of texts to erupt into the present of reading. Petrarch's formulation intentionally leaves room for iterability, instead of imposing retrospective linearity. Neither does Petrarch's sonnet try to crystallize his narrative in the same way as the prosimetrum of Dante's *Vita nova*; the poems we hear are defined as 'sparse', scattered, even as they are ostensibly collected into a singular work.[50] Vacillation – the impossibility of straightforward linear narrative in a lyric sequence – comes to the fore in Petrarch's *RVF*. The slipperiness of lyric time within a narrative is only reinforced when we consider the 'anniversary poems', 15 poems that mark anniversaries of Petrarch meeting Laura. While these poems seem to offer a chronology to cling to in the unstable sea of lyric, even these subvert linearity. The poems commemorating 15 and 18 years since Petrarch first laid eyes on Laura are out of chronological order in the lyric sequence.[51]

This disrupted linearity is precisely what undermines any effort to read a comfortable conversion narrative onto Petrarch's shifting texts.[52] Despite the seemingly confessional tone of *RVF* 1, its admission of error and (in line 8) plea for pardon from his readers, and Petrarch's eventual, contingent turn towards the Virgin Mary,[53] this is not a narrative of completion. The *RVF* will always dissolve into the *rime sparse*, a collection that repeats, revisits and cycles melancholically back on itself.[54] Petrarch, unlike Dante and Guittone, embraces the difficulty of lyric time, highlights its incompatibility with Augustinian, confessional temporality.

---

[49] Petrarch, *RVF* 3.

[50] Marco Santagata, *Dal sonetto al canzoniere: ricerche sulla preistoria e la costituzione di un genere* (Padua: Liviana, 1989).

[51] Petrarch, *RVF* 145, 266; Teodolinda Barolini, *Dante and the Origins of Italian Literary Culture* (New York: Fordham University Press, 2006), pp. 202–05.

[52] Christian Moevs, 'Subjectivity and Conversion in Dante and Petrarch', in *Petrarch and Dante: Anti-Dantism, Metaphysics, Tradition* (Notre Dame: University of Notre Dame Press, 2009), pp. 226–58.

[53] Petrarch, *RVF* 366.

[54] Jennifer Rushworth, *Discourses of Mourning in Dante, Petrarch, and Proust* (Oxford: Oxford University Press, 2016), pp. 65–69.

Conclusion: Looking Forward

Thinking about these texts through different, sometimes divergent models of time opens up new possibilities for interpretation and provides useful vocabularies of analysis. The value of temporality as a point of departure lies in this sense of process, of the moving parts of a text or body of work. Identifying these movements – of time, in time, through time – allows us to approach the inner workings of narrative, of self-representation, of historicity and many other aspects of a text. In showing the importance of our understanding of past, present and future to the processes of writing and readership, this chapter provides a glimpse of ways to read pre-modern cultures through a transnational, temporal lens. My focus on texts of the self is no accident; attempts to express who 'I' is play out within and push us to consider the sometimes conflicting cultural and temporal systems in which those writers wrote and we readers read. There are also striking parallels between attempts to build a coherent self through a linear narrative of development and attempts to build a coherent national identity through a teleological approach to cultural history. Thinking transnationally, however, reminds us to read in a more mobile way, to read beyond the boundaries of modern states and recover the political fragmentation and geographical mobility of pre-modern contexts and people. Guittone, Dante and Petrarch were well aware of the potential ephemerality of their self-narratives, of the shifting cultural mediations of time and temporal mediations of culture which could make, remake and unmake their literary identities. I will let Petrarch have the last word, as he seeks to fix his self for future centuries (thus acknowledging its instability) in an address to future readers across time and space:

Fuerit tibi forsan de me aliquid auditum; quanquam et hoc dubium sit: an exiguum et obscurum longe nomen seu locorum seu temporum perventurum sit. Et illud forsitan optabis nosse: quid hominis fuerim aut quis operum exitus meorum.

[Perhaps you will have heard something of me, but even this is doubtful, as such a minor and obscure name will hardly travel so far through time and space. If you do know of me, you might want to know what kind of man I was and the outcome of my efforts][55]

---

[55] Petrarch, *Posteritati*.1, in Petrarca, *Prose*, ed. by Guido Martellotti (Milan: Ricciardi, 1955), pp. 1–19.

11

Italian Renaissance Costume Books

Imagining Nation in an Increasingly Transnational World

Eugenia Paulicelli

But I do not know by what fate it happens that Italy does not
have, as she used to have, a manner of dress recognized to be
Italian: for, although the introduction of these new fashions
makes the former ones seem very crude, still the older were
perhaps a sign of freedom, even as the new ones have proved to
be an augury of servitude, which I think is now most evidently
fulfilled.[1]

At first, it might seem odd to link Venetian costume books, the main topic
of this essay, and one of the most representative books of classicist literature
such as Baldassare Castiglione's *The Book of the Courtier* (1528). Written in
some of the most elegant prose of the Italian literary tradition, Castiglione's
book is a complex text that deals with many important aesthetic, linguistic
and political *questioni* that were affecting the Italian peninsula and court
society in the sixteenth century. One of the most crucial issues debated in
the book was the 'questione della lingua', a question that runs parallel to
other kinds of codifications such as the language of clothing, manners and
behavior. Costume books, which became popular in Europe throughout the
Cinquecento and beyond, can be considered part of visual culture; they are
also a mixed genre using images, costume plates and text, at times relatively
long as in the case of Cesare Vecellio, but also very short as in the case of

---

[1] Baldassare Castiglione, *The Book of the Courtier*, trans. by Charles Singleton, ed.
by Daniel Javitch (New York: Norton, 2002), II, XVI, p. 88. Italian edition: *Il libro del
Cortegiano*, ed. by Walter Barberis (Turin: Einaudi, 1998).

Giacomo Franco. At the same time, another similar genre appeared: namely, illustrated *alba amicorum* and travel albums that circulated throughout Italy and Europe. They depicted how foreign travelers, often European students in Italian universities, perceived and depicted Italians, as in the beautiful example of *Mores Italiae*.[2] These kinds of illustrated publications attest, as historian Giorgio Riello has argued, to the crucial role that 'visual and material culture' had in 'bridging microhistory and global history'[3] – and, in our context, local/national individual life with transnational realities. This leads us back to another question, one of terminology and temporality.

How can words like fashion, city and national identity be used in the context of a by now distant past like the Renaissance when nations as political entities did not exist? Even if nation states as we know them today had not yet been formed, I argue that it was in this crucial period of European history, in the midst of geographical exploration and proto-colonialism, that the idea of nations first emerged. This process intersected with the creation of a 'national' fashion. The language of fashion as documented in print culture, as can be seen in Castiglione's *Book of the Courtier*, was constructed as both local (linked to the formation of vernaculars) and global (seen in the genre of European and Italian costume books). It was through print that the world was translated into images of different 'nations' made recognizable through men's and women's clothing, bringing the faraway and the unknown to Europeans, who were now able to come closer to knowledge of the 'other' via linguistic and visual representation, by way of a two-way process. Costume books 'provide an insight into the ways European contemporaries understood the articulation between locality and global geographies and the ways in which they connected the microscopic dimension of bodies and their dress to wider interpretations of the very shape of the world'.[4] Within the transnational nature of costume books, it is relevant for the scope of this essay to underline the perception of 'Italian-ness' and how it has nourished the evolving narrative of Italian identity and an even much more recent concept such as the 'made in Italy'. As Amedeo Quondam has noted, the courts in Italy during the Renaissance represented a conglomerate of nations. And with them, a distinct

---

[2] Maurizio Rippa Bonati and Valeria Finucci, eds, *Mores Italiae. Costumi e scene di vita del Rinascimento*, bilingual ed. (Cittadella: Biblos, 2007), accompanied by essays by the editors and Margareth F. Rosenthal.

[3] Giorgio Riello, 'The World in a Book: The Creation of the Global in Sixteenth-Century European Costume Books', *Past & Present*, 242 Supplement 14 (2019) 1–37; see also Giulia Calvi, 'Cultures of Space: Costume Books, Maps and Clothing between Europe and Japan (Sixteenth through Nineteenth Centuries)', *I Tatti Studies in Italian Renaissance*, XX.2 (2017), 331–63.

[4] Riello, 'The World in a Book', pp. 1–37.

culture emerges, which in turn has contributed to the composite Italian identity.[5] This dynamic is still relevant today in our globalized world. Indeed, we may ask ourselves why at a time when critics have questioned the nation and the nation-state as obsolete notions, we still have labels such as 'Made in Italy', 'Made in France', 'Made in New York' and even 'Made in Harlem'? These are labels that evoke nation, national identity and localism even in the midst of globalization and deterritorialization. It might seem at first sight paradoxical that labels and geography have gained even stronger currency in the era of technology and globalization. But both paradoxes, one referring to the past and the other to the present, are only apparent.

In so far as we think of everyday gestures and behaviors as part and expression of culture and political values, we may also think of the act of dressing as composed of 'regulated improvisations', as illustrated by Bourdieu's theory of *habitus*. Or we may say that the act of dressing creates in itself the possibility of a negotiation between, on the one hand, 'rule' and 'code' and, on the other, 'improvisation'. Fashion nourishes this process of negotiation materially and symbolically. It is in this in-between space that an embodied narrative is constructed. Fabrics and fashion are intertwined domains that touch on the political and the collective. Fashion has a profound impact on the public self as well as on the most intimate structure of feeling in the construction and perception of identity, always understood as a complex and fluid phenomenon that bears directly on gender, race and class. Abstract concepts such as these would not have been so powerful had they not been materialized in the individual and collective bodies who perform the tempo and the modes of the politics of the national narrative. Fashion, as Walter Benjamin understood it, can be seen as the materialization of historical changes and rhythms. Within Georg Simmel's dualistic paradigm of alternation between uniformity (stasis) and individualism (change), there resides a history and theory of fashion as a rhythm. This 'rhythmanalysis', the title of Henri Lefebvre's seminal work, should ground the study of fashion, and help us to see that 'change' and 'newness' in fashion are linked to rhythmic movements between reuse, return, industrial development in fibers and textiles, techniques, marketing strategies and consumer demands.[6] A rhythmanalysis of fashion can thus pinpoint and understand these variants and

---

[5] Amedeo Quondam, *Questo povero cortigiano. Castiglione, il Libro, la Storia* (Rome: Bulzoni, 2000).

[6] See Philipp Ekardt, *Benjamin on Fashion* (London: Bloomsbury, 2020); Georg Simmel, *Philosophie der Mode* (Berlin: Pan-Verlag, 1905); Henri Lefebvre, *Rhythmanalysis: Space, Time and Everyday Life*, trans. by Stuart Elden and Gerald Moore (London and New York: Continuum, 2013).

their structural changes and technologies. This move has implications for fashion historiography and the debated 'origin' of fashion – and, I would add, for the 'origin' of nation understood in terms of spatiality, borders and location. It is for these reasons that it is productive to investigate further the implications of fashion and cultures in their transnational contexts and inter-relations – and this can be seen very clearly in the case of Italy.

In its broadest context and definition, fashion establishes a set of practices, codes and manners, what we could call 'affective regimes' regulating the rhythms of people's existences, as well as how we communicate with the world and with each other, how we dress and envision our projected desires, and how and what we consume. These sets of practices are far from naturalized. Rather, they are acquired through culture.

It is crucial, then, to go back to the period of the European Renaissance to examine the production of costume books. In particular, I will focus on examples taken from the costume plates of Cesare Vecellio and Giacomo Franco, two pivotal figures in the genre of Italian and more broadly European costume books. First, however, I will contextualize the general framework so as to understand the political and emotional implications of fashion and dress in imagining the nation in an increasingly transnational world.

Already in the early Renaissance and especially in Italy, fashion had been textualized through the discourse on dress and style contained in several works of the conduct book genre as well as in several costume books, such as Vecellio's two editions, published in 1590 and 1598.[7] It was the existence of this discourse that certified the power of fashion as a language and as a cultural and social institution of modernity. As fashion is a system that projects images and identities that offer themselves up for imitation and consumption, it also creates mythologies that are linked, for example, to individual countries and cities and specific genders. The definition of good manners that Baldassare Castiglione gives in his *Book of the Courtier* is built on a set of values and hierarchies that became not only strong images with which to identify but also a paradigmatic and recognizable set of codes for the elite and ruling classes in Italian court society and beyond. Castiglione, a humanist and a diplomat, considers clothing an integral part of both the culture of human beings and the cultures of nations as exemplified in court society. His book elaborates a theory of dress and aesthetics exemplified in one word: *sprezzatura*, the art of

---

[7]   Cesare Vecellio, *De gli habiti antichi et moderni di diverse parti del mondo. Libri due fatti da Cesare Vecellio* (Venice: Zenaro, 1590); *Habiti Antichi et Moderni di tutto il mondo* (Venice: Gio Bernardo Sessa, 1598). See the English edition, translation and introduction by Ann R. Jones and Margaret F. Rosenthal, *Habiti Antichi et Moderni: The Clothing of the Renaissance World* (New York: Thames and Hudson, 2008).

concealing art or in modern terms 'effortless chic'. It is in fact this concept of 'naturalness achieved', as Claudio Scarpati defines it, or the norm of an internalized self-control, that would be a distinctive sign of the gentleman in modern Europe and form a language and an aesthetic pedagogy that would extend to the art of dress and dressing.[8] Castiglione's book has become one of the most popular in world literature and culture and has even been appropriated by contemporary bloggers who discuss menswear.[9] Castiglione did not invent the term *sprezzatura*. Rather, he refashioned it and invested it with a plurality of new meanings. But it is in Castiglione's cultural translation and reuse of the word in a new theoretical and historical framework that his most endurable contribution to literature, the arts, philosophy and fashion resides.[10] As Daniel Roche has observed, in the absence of centralized institutions, as was the case in Castiglione's Italy, 'manners convey history', because they are the only means through which to define the identity of a society, a country, a region.[11]

From the point of view of style and fashion, it is certainly something more than mere speculation to suggest that the notion of *sprezzatura* and the way it has been transmitted through the centuries goes a long way towards explaining the success of twentieth- and twenty-first-century Italian fashion, associated as it is with elegance and ease, the hallmarks of Castiglione's successful courtier. Fashion thus became an institution that went hand in hand with the idea and desire of the nation that came about at the time of the formation of national vernaculars, the technological revolution brought on by the invention of printing, and the geographical explorations and discoveries of new worlds. It is at this moment that a national aspect of fashion emerged. A new awareness of the production and consumption of fashion and dress connected to geography and cultural identity ran parallel to what Benedict Anderson has called 'print capitalism'.[12] If 'print capitalism' fueled the process of imagining nations, 'fashion capitalism' as described by anthropologist Jane

---

[8] Claudio Scarpati, 'Il libro del Cortegiano', in *Studi su Baldassarre Castiglione*, ed. by Claudio Scarpati and Umberto Motta (Milan: Pubblicazioni dell'ISU Università Cattolica, 2002), pp. 17–45.

[9] See Eugenia Paulicelli, *Writing Fashion in Early Modern Italy: From Sprezzatura to Satire* (Aldershot: Ashgate, 2014), pp. 52–53.

[10] Claudio Scarpati, 'Il libro del cortegiano'; Paolo D'Angelo, *Sprezzatura: Concealing the Effort of Art from Aristotle to Duchamp* (New York: Columbia University Press, 2018). D'Angelo does not mention fashion in his investigation of the concept of *sprezzatura*.

[11] Daniel Roche, *La culture des apparences. Une historie du vêtement* (Paris: Fayard, 1989).

[12] Benedict Anderson, *Imagined Communities: Reflections on the Origin and Spread of Nationalism* (New York and London: Verso, 1991).

Schneider and as illustrated in costume books with the circulation of types of people, along with the development of local industries, engendered a culture of fashion linked to particular places and nations.[13]

It is with this background in mind that I consider the early formation of fashion as a system in the making that can be understood in connection with spatiality (geography) and temporality (history). My aim is to examine how crucial this development is, not only for an understanding of the history of Italian fashion and style but also of its processes, which are crucial for exploring in depth the relationship between fashion and nation in a transnational world. The larger systems at play – in the past and in the present – that influence the state of fashion, craft and aesthetics are constantly in development and flux. If there is a pattern, it is that fashion comes to the fore especially in periods of great transformation and of political and economic change. This is the case of the Italian Renaissance.

A further word on method: my focus on what might be called fashion literature does not mean establishing a hierarchy of the verbal over the visual – or divorcing the object from the discourse about it. On the contrary, my intent here is twofold: on the one hand, to see how objects come alive through language in Giacomo Franco's and Cesare Vecellio's texts; and, on the other, to emphasize the key role that literature and language in general played in the Renaissance (a role they still play in our own age of the digital revolution). Words and language share with fashion and clothing a world of materiality and practices that are embedded in a network of relationships between clothing and the body. These relationships take on material form through what is the backbone of fashion: namely, image and text. The genre of costume books is an exemplary illustration of this dynamic between the visual and the verbal. In presenting images of dress and styles alongside the commentary or captions of the images, they materialize a visual side of fashion that became certified in text and discourse where ideology is revealed. In what follows, I consider the images not as a subordinate to or merely an illustration of what is said in the prose accompanying them. Rather, in the case of Franco it is important to consider the images as texts in their own right and in the interplay they establish with the short commentary that the text features. In contrast to Vecellio's costume books, in which the texts are relatively long, in Franco, the texts are often very short. Nevertheless, they reveal a narrative mode. In the imaginary space created by clothing, fashion's affective regimes find form and structure in literature and language materialized in images. Unlike more canonical literary texts, however, costume books are innovative texts in their own right. These texts, accompanied by images, can be compared to the texts

---

[13] Jane Schneider, 'The Anthropology of Cloth', *Annual Review of Anthropology*, 16 (1987), 409–98.

produced by experienced and sophisticated bloggers or instagrammers of our post-digital age. It is not by chance that costume books as a genre came to the fore in the aftermath of the print revolution.

In Vecellio and Franco, Venice takes center stage. Their work leads us to think of the process by which cities are textualized by different media. Cities are shaped via narrative and visual discourses as well as through their literary traditions, including travel writing and costume books, which all create narratives and tropes that define the image of a place for visitors and inhabitants alike. Still today, and perhaps even more so, these mechanisms lie at the core of fashion as an economic and symbolic force and play a huge role in defining the geography of national and global fashion cities.

The links between fashion/geography and the city hold good for several historical periods and identify why and how fashion comes to the fore and contributes to the weaving of the narrative and identity of a given nation or city, adding them to the map of desirable places to be in or dreamt of. If fashion has an impact on spatializing the world, costume books in the age of exploration and scientific advancement had an impact on spatializing the hierarchy of the clothed body. In this way, a new order is presented, or, in Valerie Traub's words, a new epistemology of the body is created, similar to cartography.[14] As Traub writes, the clothed body 'reframes nationality as an implicitly gendered and erotic, as well as incipiently racial phenomenon'.[15] Fashion in costume books can function as an illustration of what Traub identifies as the links between spatializing strategies and historical change very much at the heart of the fashion discourse between the sixteenth and seventeenth centuries.

In particular, using literature and images to uncover what Peter Stallybrass and A. R. Jones have called the 'animatedness of clothing', my hope is to underscore the political meanings that clothing produces – and has always produced – in public space.[16] As fashion is a system that projects images and identities that offer themselves up for imitation (and consumption), it also creates mythologies that are linked, for example, to individual countries. The definition that Castiglione's *Courtier* gives of good manners has the effect of building a set of values and hierarchies that in turn become strong images with which to identify and which form what we might call national identity (a

[14] Valerie Traub, 'Mapping the Global Body: The Making of the Cartographic Body in the Making of Nations', in *Early Modern Visual Culture: Representation, Race and Empire in Renaissance England*, ed. by Peter Erickson and Clark Hulse (Philadelphia: University of Pennsylvania Press, 2000).

[15] Traub, 'Mapping the Global Body', p. 46.

[16] Peter Stallybrass and Ann R. Jones, *Renaissance Clothing and the Material of Memory* (Cambridge: Cambridge University Press, 2000).

more subjective dimension of perception and self-images/a sense of mission, etc.) and national character (an 'objective set of dispositions'), two terms that, according to historian Silvana Patriarca, have different meanings.[17]

In the *Courtier*, for instance, both concepts are presented as discursive. If Italy and Italians are presented as weak entities as compared to more powerful (mainly French and Spanish) others, that weakness is answered, indeed resisted, by the elaboration of a nationally inflected ideal style and politeness that is at the core of what comes to be called *sprezzatura*. In other words, if weakness and fragmentation are the tropes characterizing national identity, *sprezzatura* becomes one of the strongest features of a new identity and desirable character, an attractive and prestigious trope that exists alongside the negative one of weakness and fragmentation. But there is also another reason why I think it important to look at Italian culture at this time. Namely: the understanding of the relationship between fashion and Italian national identity in the context of a long history (when nations were only imagined) allows us to include and compare this political and cultural dynamic in a wider transnational context.

As a manifestation of a pan-European linguistic event, the word 'fashion' gained currency in various languages between the sixteenth and the seventeenth century, and was linked to the social, economic, religious and technological transformations that were then taking place. Arjun Appadurai has noted that 'What we know of Europe allows us to watch a society of sumptuary law slowly changing into a society of fashion. In general, all social organized forms of consumption seem to revolve around some combination of the following three patterns: interdiction, sumptuary law, and fashion'.[18] The 'society of fashion' can only come about after the creation of a language of fashion and the establishment of new codes and ideologies. The two Italian terms *moda* and *moderno* share common etymological roots, both deriving from the Latin *modus* [style, measure, way of doing something]. *Moderno* derives from the Latin *modernus* and refers to what is current, present and contemporaneous; *moda* is the feminine form of the masculine noun *modo* in the Italian language and means manner, norm, tone, rhythm, time. *La moda* shares the same etymological roots as the French term *la mode* and those in other languages such as Spanish, Portuguese and German (*mode*). In Italy the word *moda* has links to change and newness and appears for the first time in the 1640s in Milan in the satirical text *De la carrozza da*

---

[17] Silvana Patriarca, *Italian Vices: Nation and Character from the Risorgimento to the Republic* (Cambridge: Cambridge University Press, 2010).

[18] Arjun Appadurai, 'Consumption, Duration, History', in *Modernity at Large: Cultural Dimensions of Globalization* (Minneapolis: University of Minnesota Press, 1996), pp. 66–85 (p. 71).

nolo by the Benedictine abbot Agostino Lampugnani. Before then, though, words with similar meanings had appeared, such as 'nuove foze' [new styles], 'habiti' [habits], 'la cosa degli habiti' [the matter of clothing] and 'varietà di costumi' [variety of customs]. The English word 'fashion' was adapted from the Old French term *façon*, also derived from the Latin *factio, facere* (hence the verb *fare* in Italian – to make). Fashion linked to change and newness also makes an appearance in Michel de Montaigne's 1580 essays, where he emphasizes that every new way of dressing firmly refuses the old and uses both the term 'façon' and the French neologism 'mode', which he connects to geographical identity. There is then a doubleness inherent in fashion/*moda*: on the one hand, fashion and clothing as a material and empirical basis of the phenomenon; on the other, the inception of the concept of fashion as we know it today, linked to change and newness.

The doubleness of fashion is what makes it difficult to offer a clear-cut definition of the term's ontological and epistemological boundaries. Clothing can be different styles of dress, the empirical, personal and multisensory realms that define the perception of the wearers, viewers and makers; fashion can be understood beyond clothing as part of wider cultural, economic and political systems including manners, behavior, way of life and taste. Or, as Bourdieu would have it, 'habitus'; and in Gramscian terms 'senso comune'.[19] But the tensional relationship that emerges with the convergence of 'la moda' and 'il modo' in early modern Italy creates the conditions for the formation of fashion as a social institution but also as a complex mechanism of desire. It is indeed on this level that fashion cannot be fully understood from the point of view of status and class.

There is, though, another term to be added to the discussion: 'habits'. As we will see, the writings of Vecellio and Franco, both of whose major works contain the term *habiti* in their titles, offer a cartographic rendition of the dressed body in time and space. The term 'habit' derives from Latin. It refers to a way of being and also to external appearance, a mode of clothing oneself. Valerie Traub has noted that 'habit' on maps functions as a static metonym for national character, statute hierarchies, and gender and erotic relations.[20]

As we will see in Vecellio, it is the static dimension of habit that is challenged and transformed. This fixed paradigm will become porous in such a way that it is possible to recognize the features of what Appadurai calls 'the

---

[19] See Pierre Bourdieu, *Distinction: A Social Critique of the Judgment of Taste*, trans. by Peter Nice (Cambridge: Cambridge University Press, 1975) and Antonio Gramsci, 'Philosophy, Common Sense, Language and Folklore', in *The Gramsci Reader: Selected Writings 1916–1935*, ed. by David Forgacs (London: Lawrence and Wishart, 1988), pp. 323–62.

[20] Traub, 'Mapping the Global Body', p. 51.

society of fashion'. Habit, then, contains in itself the tensions and the process of both the ontological and epistemological dimensions of fashion we see in its etymology. In fact, apropos of the concepts of change and newness in *habiti* and clothing, Vecellio and Franco will further articulate the relationship between *moda* and *moderno*, adding the key concept of the spatiotemporal dimension that defines both the one and the other.

The technological revolution in print had a profound impact on the book as it introduced the reproducibility of knowledge in the form of engravings, maps, portraits. This idea and technique were also extended to print textiles and the cheaper versions of sumptuous cloth then made available.[21] As a consequence, time and space were completely transformed. Humanistic culture became a transnational movement that used clothing and fashion as vehicles to translate and transmit the ideology, taste and style with which the European elite forged its various identities and ideals of beauty. Fashion, then, was a powerful medium of cultural translation that had aesthetic, political and economic resonances. It is with these premises in mind that I now turn my attention to Vecellio's and Franco's costume books.

Fashion between Time and Space: Costume Books

Having promised to speak of the diversity of clothing, both ancient and modern, to clarify the present work, I will begin by using everything that can shed light on their description. Human undertakings flow onward like a river and have no permanence or stability: mighty cities have existed in the world, full of people, whose walls or ruins we do not see today, and whose sites we do not even know; and even if we know of and can see some of the most famous, it still seems almost impossible to believe that in past times so many people should have gathered together and lived in them, resplendent with such great nobility [...] From this brief discussion, then, we can understand *the origin of the great variations and diversity of dress that has come into being and still exists, highly susceptible to change.*[22]

Vecellio, a relative of the Venetian painter Titian, published his costume books in two editions: the first in 1590, *Degli habiti*; the second, an expanded

---

[21] Beverly Lemire and Giorgio Riello, 'East and West: Textiles and Fashion in Early Modern Europe', *Journal of Social History*, 41.4 (Summer 2008), 887–916.

[22] Cesare Vecellio, *Habiti antichi et moderni. The Clothing of the Renaissance World*, ed., trans. and intro by Ann R. Jones and Margaret F. Rosenthal (New York: Thames and Hudson, 2008), pp. 1–2, 52–53, emphasis mine.

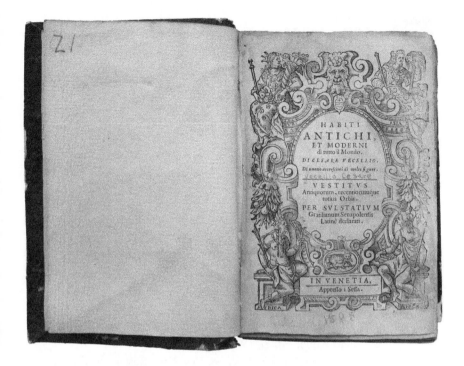

Figure 11.1 – Cesare Vecellio, Frontispiece of
Habiti Antichi et moderni di tutto il mondo, Venice: Sessa, 1598,
Rare books collection, Queens College, The City University of New York,
Rosenthal Library, Courtesy of Queens College.

bilingual version (vernacular and Latin), in 1598 (Figure 11.1). He aimed at an encyclopedic approach that offered through dress a visual and discursive cartography of the world as it was then known. In addition, he gave his readers a picture of the class and gender relationships manifested in a diversified geography of taste, politics of style and production of fashion and textiles. Fashion and the discovery of the New World had a great deal in common, writes Vecellio, as each new discovery brought to the fore new clothes, styles and tastes in dress. Vecellio's ambition, in fact, was to map the diversity of dress, ornaments and customs of the world that was then being discovered under his eyes. Fashion, he tells us, changes fast, according to individual desires and for capricious reasons, and it is on account of this that his project is and can only be an unfinished and provisional one (Figure 11.2).

His encyclopedic approach to dress (he both produced the images and later wrote the text) and the way he sought to represent a codification of taste and behavior link his work to both the genre of conduct literature, books that

Figure 11.2 – Cesare Vecellio, Women from Venice while they dye their
hair blond, *Habiti*, 1598, Rare Books collection,
Queens College, The City University of New York, Rosenthal Library,
Courtesy of Queens College.

gave advice on how to behave, perform, talk and dress in public, epitomized
by Castiglione's *Libro del Cortegiano*, and to the moral geography emerging
with the creations of maps and atlases. Just as the link between fashion and
the New World cannot be denied, neither can the link between the New
World and the publishing industry. Suffice it to say that access to information
about the newly discovered territories and peoples became available to a
larger European audience only through the nascent publishing industry that
produced diaries, travel reportages, maps and so on, representing the new
discoveries in word and image.

Despite Vecellio's curiosity about other cultures and geographical spaces,
his depictions of the 'other' are set against a European model in which Italy,
Rome and Venice play a major role. The sequence of woodcuts of clothes in
the different sections of his books is an attempt to define a sense of 'national
character' for the peoples with whom he deals in his text, such as the Turks,
the Germans, the French and so forth. The study on the discursive nature of
national character by historian Silvana Patriarca referenced above focuses
on the nineteenth century. It would be worthwhile, however, to extend her
argument and widen its reach to include earlier periods in which the Italian

nation, rather than being made, is being imagined. Here we would find that fashion is one of the major vehicles that form and disseminate the discourses, myths and stereotypes that defined Italians, even if in ideal terms. In this context, costume books such as those by Vecellio and Franco are important points of reference for critical analysis and history. For Vecellio, when writing of Italy, variety is the order of the day. In chapter VII of his treatise, for example, he lists 'de popoli diversi, che habitano l'Italia', concluding that such diversity is mainly due to the fact that Italy had been on several occasions 'prey to foreigners and been the crossroads of Fortune. For this reason, it is no wonder that we can see a greater diversity of dress here than in any other major nation or region'. In order to corroborate his point, he refers to *signor* Baldo Antonio Penna, a man of great learning and a renowned professor of the humanities in Venice. Penna wrote that there was once a man who, charged with the task of drawing costumes from several provinces, found himself in a difficult position when it came to drawing Italian clothing. In fact, Vecellio anecdotally reports that the man in Penna's report chose to represent the Italian as a naked man, carrying on his shoulder a piece of cloth ('una pezza di panno su la spalla'). When asked why he chose this unusual representation for Italians, Penna replied that he had not been able to find any single style or item of dress that epitomized a people he describes as being, and wanting to be, different, capricious and changeable in their style of dress. The manner in which Vecellio dresses the naked man is a sign of the individualism, instability and capriciousness of the Italian national character. It is on the shoulders of this individualistic Italian that Vecellio drapes a piece of cloth so that the naked 'national character' can choose for himself which tailor he employs to cut his dress according to his own taste and whim. As some historians have argued, the first formalizations of Italians as irredeemable individualists appear in Burckhardt's *Civilization of Renaissance Italy*, published in 1860. But long before Burkhardt (and proving the connection between, on the one hand, fashion and dress and, on the other, culture and politics), the formulation of the Italian vice of individualism is present in Vecellio's late sixteenth-century costume book. Vecellio's tirade about the individualism of Italians stems from his need, as well as that of many of his contemporaries, to give a semblance of order to the chaos they saw in the emerging and ever-changing world and so establish a paradigmatic structure of moral, aesthetic and political codes with which to rein that chaos in. It is in this context that dress and fashion play a crucial role.

As mentioned earlier, Vecellio published two editions of his costume books. *Habiti* was followed eight years later by a bilingual edition containing costumes from the Americas, consisting of Peru, Mexico, Florida and Virginia. In his commentary, he guides his readers into the folds of dress so that they acquire an awareness of the significance of clothing. This awareness becomes clear in the dialectics between time and space that structures the book as a whole. In fact, Vecellio looks at dress both diachronically and synchronically, recording the several changes that have affected dress from classical antiquity to his present time. Within this time frame, he identifies the impact that different geographical spaces have had on modes of dress and ornament (East/West, southern/northern Europe, Venice/Rome, etc.). The interaction between image and text reveals the 'hybridity' written on the body of the 'other'. Ann Jones has pointed out that in the New World, dress changed constantly as a result of the presence of Europeans. Vecellio includes a particularly striking image of a 'Young man from Mexico' that bears signs of the process of hybridity visible in material culture. Although the title of the picture uses the singular, we see two young men and not one. A dialectic is established between nakedness (the savage body) and the dressed body (the civilized one). The young man in the foreground is covered with fabric but, more importantly, he is carrying flowers in one hand, while in the other he is carrying a mirror, one of the most desirable objects, whose surface is turned towards the viewer. In the text accompanying the picture, Vecellio tells us that mirrors are considered jewels that have been brought by the Spaniards. The young man adopts an effeminate pose that stands in contrast to the other young man in the background, who is uncovered, except for his private parts. The only objects he exhibits are feathers on his head and darts. This picture takes us back once more to the constant interplay between the dressed body and nakedness, the body and its representation that is so central to the discourse on fashion. The mirror is the medium through which one can see the body and, in this case, the mediation between bodies and cultures rests on the object of representation. The mirror both connects and disconnects the vision of the self and other to include viewers and spectatorship. Once again, fashion and dress bring to the fore the process of signification in a time-space framework. More importantly, what this image tells us through the hybrid combination of the 'foreign' body and the European accessory is not so much the reappearance of the object in the new setting and its reuse, as the fact that fashion is a problem of rhythm.[23] Change and the new temporality dictated by fashion and desire (the exotic European object) also affect the New World, something as true during Vecellio's time as it is still today.

Mirrors as well as armor, the latter profusely present in Vecellio, are technologies of bodies and power that recur in Franco's *Habiti* (first published in 1610) and so are geographical maps, produced by Franco, which incorporate

---

[23] Roland Barthes, *Il senso della moda. Forme e significati dell'abbigliamento*, ed. by Gianfranco Marrone (Turin: Einaudi, 2006).

Figure 11.3 – Giacomo Franco, Frontispiece of *Habiti d'huomeni et donne venetiane: con la processione della Serma Signoria et altri particolari cioè trionfi feste et cerimonie pubbliche della nobilissima città di Venetia,* 1609, in Frezzaria all'insegna del Sole, The General Collection, Beinecke Rare Book and Manuscript Library, Yale University, Courtesy of the Beinecke Rare Book and Manuscript Library.

costumes. Franco (1550–1620) was a Venetian engraver, chalcographer, printer and designer ('desegnador'), as he called himself in his will.

If Vecellio aimed at offering an encyclopedic map of costume and dress around the world as it was then known, Franco's focus is on Venice. Around 1610, he published the first edition of *Habiti d'huomeni et donne venetiane*, later to be reprinted along with *La città di Venetia con l'origine e governo di quella* and his third work, *Habiti che già tempo usavano le donne vinetiane* (1614).[24] Already in the frontispiece of *Habiti d'huomeni et donne venetiane*, Venice is presented as a microcosm of the world. Such an idea is at work in the representation of the city in a panoramic view where we can distinguish the globe in which the map of Venice is enclosed as a convex mirror. The globe is a spectacle and Venice is part of it (Figure 11.3). Indeed, to confirm this vision, we might note, above the bird's-eye map of Venice within a globe, another micro-portrait, this time of the Rialto bridge, the hub of commercial activity in Venice.

Dress serves as a map for identity and place. Franco himself had produced some of these maps accompanied by costumes in 1597. The Serenissima is then a microcosm and, in the propagandistic aims of these publications, Venice simply signifies the world.[25] We should not be misled, however, by the fact that Franco's treatment of dress is much less broad in scope than Vecellio's, and its textual part is minimal compared to that of *Habiti*. Franco's treatment of dress and its relationships to gender, high and popular culture, as well as optics and science is fascinating and crucial to understand print culture's contribution to establishing and legitimizing fashion as an institution. Some of his plates and texts can also be seen as a form of proto-journalism documenting and spreading the social life of the city along with its cultural tropes. The trope of Venice as center of the world (*vero ritratto del mondo*) was common to many Venetian writers and authors of costume books. Venice established itself as one of the most important fashion cities in

---

[24] In this chapter I refer to different editions of Franco's costume plates that I have consulted. These editions are held at the Museo Correr in Venice, the library at the Stibbert Museum in Florence and the Beinecke Rare Book and Manuscript library at Yale University. Unless otherwise noted, all translations of the texts accompanying the images are my own. I have also consulted a modern edition of the book *Abiti di uomini e donne veneziane: Venezia ad istanza di Giacomo Franco* (Naples: Liguori, 2004). For a biography of Giacomo Franco see Chiara Stefani's entry in the Treccani bibliographic dictionary, http://www.treccani.it/enciclopedia/giacomo-franco [accessed 20 July 2018]; Carlo Pasero, 'Giacomo Franco, editore, incisore e calcografo nei secoli XVI e XVII', *La Bibliofilia*, 37 (1996), 332–56.

[25] See the detailed study by Bronwen Wilson, *The World in Venice: Print, the City, and Early Modern Identity* (Toronto: Toronto University Press, 2005).

early modern Italy and beyond. The Serenissima was, in fact, characterized by intense commercial activity, public areas, spectacles and festivals that promoted fashion consumption.[26]

The discourse on fashion as a complex system of signification, identity and the city was central in Franco's engravings and intersected with the art of dissimulation that bore on both the personal and the political. It comes as no surprise that 'the sixteenth and seventeenth centuries have been called "the age of dissimulation" in Europe'.[27] The technological reproduction facilitated by the advent of printing as well as by advances in the production of textiles, dyeing and luxury objects, brought to the fore new anxieties concerning the self and its related issues of religion, morality, national identity, class and gender. Dissimulation became a powerful weapon to counteract the anxiety and dangers inherent in a fast-growing and transforming world whose geographical borders and features were being translated into maps, costume books and travel accounts. In this way, it became possible to establish relations between interior and exterior, body and mind, fantasy, desire and emotions. Dissimulation helped to forge and control new emotional regimes that emerged from the cult of civility with its elaborate codes of behavior, dress and appearance, speaking and acting. Dissimulation is, then, essential to pinpoint the dynamics of passions and control in the prismatic aesthetic of the baroque.

Costume books and fashion plates contribute to the construction of the city and its narrative tropes. In their hybridity, costume books epitomize the process of translation and representation that is inherent in fashion. Or, more precisely, we may say the translation of clothing into fashion. But as they do this, costume books also link dress and fashion to geographical spaces, public and private places, as well as to performances of the clothed body within a specific context.

Franco then transforms the story of Venice into an icon of a microcosm of the world, the world in Venice, as Wilson puts it.[28] But Franco goes even further than this. He has us see how crucial fashion and dress are in constructing and projecting the identity of a city that becomes almost tactile, desirable and seductive through the profusion of luxury fabrics and objects. Franco's costume plates call attention to the affective power of fashion, its

---

[26] See Evelyn Welch, *Shopping in the Renaissance* (London and New Haven: Yale University Press, 2005); David Gilbert, 'From Paris to Shanghai: The Changing Geographies of Fashion's World Cities', in *Fashion's World Cities*, ed. by Christopher Breward and David Gilbert (Oxford: Berg, 2005), pp. 3–32.

[27] See Jon R. Snyder, *Dissimulation and the Culture of Secrecy in Early Modern Europe* (Berkeley and London: University of California Press, 2009), p. 5.

[28] Wilson, *The World in Venice.*

emotional charge at a personal and political level through performance and the staging of the clothed self in political, social and private contexts.[29]

What better symbol of the city than the Doge? Franco's strategic choice is to show a portrait of the former Doge Sebastiano Venier in his armor (Figure 11.4). Venier is sitting in a regal pose. In the background of the portrait, his helmet is on a windowsill and features a prominent plume/feathers that lead the eye to an open window onto a scene from the past. A window that looks like a micro-screen, like a film or video, opens on a scene representing the naval battle of Lepanto.

The uniform of a general in wartime creates an impression of great majesty and expresses a truly regal splendor. In the portrait, Venier is depicted in the apparel which he wore when he was appointed General of the Venetian Republic during the last war Venice fought with Selim, the Great Turk. In fact, he was elected Doge after distinguishing himself during that battle. Venier was already 70 when he fought, yet here he is depicted with a powerful body as if he were a young man, a special effect conferred by the armor he wears. In fact, a commentator wrote in 1581 that 'abandoning the toga and with it his old age, [he] dressed with new and strong limbs'.[30] Some corselets, in fact, show the limbs to mimic the natural body and the ideal muscular torso. The same commentator also hints at the different social and political functions of dress and garb and their inscription within a recognizable grammar of power: on the one hand, the civic function of the toga, on the other, physical performance, heroism, muscular masculinity in action and at war.

Interestingly, Venier makes his first appearance in a toga in the 1590 edition of Vecellio's book. The illustration is entitled 'Generale di Venezia' and is included in the section on 'The Clothing of Men and Nobility and Other Ranks in Venice Today', with a commentary explaining the preparations for the battle of Lepanto in great detail, while emphasizing that Venier's courageous performance in battle made him the virile role model for all Venetians and beyond. In concluding the text, Vecellio adds something specific about his sartorial appearance: 'But to speak of his clothing, which is our principal topic, he was dressed entirely in *cremesino* velvet, with the ducal cap on his head and a golden mantle, which we have shown elsewhere was the true Roman *paludamentum*, fastened on the right shoulder with massive gold buttons'.

---

[29] Susan Crane's book *The Performance of Self: Ritual, Clothing and Identity during the Hundred Years War* (Philadelphia: University of Pennsylvania Press, 2002), focuses on late medieval courts and society.

[30] Anna Pallucchini, 'Echi della Battaglia di Lepanto nella pittura veneziana del Cinquecento', in *Il Mediterraneo della seconda meta' del Cinquecento alla luce di Lepanto*, ed. by Giorgio Benzoni (Florence: Olschki, 1974), pp. 279–87.

Figure 11.4 – Giacomo Franco, Sebastiano Venier, *Habiti*, 1609, The General Collection, Beinecke Rare Book and Manuscript Library, Yale University, Courtesy of the Beinecke Rare Book and Manuscript Library.

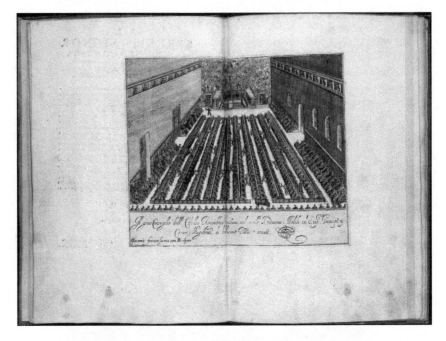

Figure 11.5 – Giacomo Franco, The Gran Consiglio, *Habiti*, 1609, The
General Collection, Beinecke Rare Book and Manuscript Library, Yale
University, Courtesy of the Beinecke Rare Book and Manuscript Library.

In concluding, I would like to comment on how Franco stages political
power in two different Venetian spaces and places, the piazza and the
palazzo. One image depicts the Gran Consiglio, the heart of the Venetian
republic, where the Doge, nobles and magistrates met (Figure 11.5). Here we
see a space and a place that is ordered and geometrized. As opposed to this
straightforward representation of power, in another image (Figure 11.6) we
see the newly elected prince and the *popolo*, scattered in the piazza but still
controlled by state officials. As Lefebvre has argued, the use and production
of space are always politically charged.[31] On the one hand, through the use
of ordered geometry, the controlling power of the government is conveyed;
while on the other, through the less controlled scene, a more open space is
depicted and shorn of the prince's controlling eye. The Doge (Figure 11.6) is in
procession, having pronounced his oration to the people in St. Mark's church.
As recorded by historian Molmenti, this episode, one of the many rites and

[31] Henri Lefebvre, *The Production of Space*, trans. by Donald Nicholson-Smith
(Oxford: Blackwell, 1991).

Figure 11.6 – Giacomo Franco, Il Principe eletto, *Habiti*, 1609,
The General Collection, Beinecke Rare Book and Manuscript Library, Yale
University, Courtesy of the Beinecke Rare Book and Manuscript Library.

celebrations accompanying the election of the new prince, was memorialized by Franco's engraving of the Doge throwing money to the people before entering his palazzo. Here, we can see the juxtaposition of two images of political power: one in the closed space of the Gran Consiglio, where decisions about the state were taken, and one in the open space of the street or St. Mark's square, where the prince fashioned his populist image as a leader by showing prodigality to his subjects, an apparent image of a more open form of state and oligarchic rule. Text here appears only as brief description of the event, in a way reminiscent of today's social media, a combination of Instagram and Twitter, a snapshot of the event in words and image. In this way, Franco becomes an *ante litteram* social media mediator and commentator depicting everyday scenes, from regattas to soccer games, ordinary people and political figures. This is in striking difference with Vecellio, where costumes are mostly (with four exceptions) represented in collective scenes set in the streets of the city, where the action takes place. In Vecellio, the more extensive text is used to contextualize in time and place the individual costume plate.

Let me now return to how, in different modes, Vecellio's and Franco's treatments of dress bring to the fore tensions and trace the relationship between fashion and national/transnational contexts as well as the political and social history hidden in the folds of dress and popular culture, local identity, customs, manners and aesthetics. They both pinpoint how fashion and dress act as a vehicle to uncover the tensions and intersections between the art of dressing the body and spatiality. But they also uncover the complexity of defining cultural identity, as well as identity's links to a diversified geography of gender relations and political representations. Their eye opens up a window on a nonlinear vision of history and an identity (of people and nation) that is multiple, hidden in a kaleidoscopic game of mirrors.

12

Translating People and Places between Sicily and the United States, 1880–1960

Donna R. Gabaccia

In September 1889, the peasant (*contadino*) Audenzio Mangiaracina visited the municipal offices of his Sicilian hometown, Sambuca Zabut, to report the birth of his infant son, Calogero; clerks noted his wife, Angelina Mulè, as a worker (*industriosa*).[1] Twenty years later, the son, Calogero Mangiaracina, failed to report for military service. When clerks inquired about Calogero in the neighborhood, they were told only that the young man was abroad (*all'estero*). By then, port officials in New Orleans in 1907 had already recorded Calogero Mangiaracina arriving by ship, alone, a 'countryman' from 'Sabica Zab'. Two years later Calogero married Rosa Mulè in Centerville, Louisiana; a copy of their marriage certificate found its way to Sambuca's offices as did the birth certificate of their son, Audenzio, named after his paternal grandfather and born in Chicago in 1910. In 1917 'Charles' Mangiaracina, now a 28-year-old foundry laborer, registered with the US military, stating that he lived with his wife and children, including son Audenzio, in Rockford, Illinois. Three years later, American census takers found 30-year-old 'Carl' Mangiaracina still working at a foundry in Rockford where his wife, Rosa, eldest son 'Larry' and three younger Illinois-born children lived with him. Meanwhile, in Sambuca in 1921, his brother in Sicily told municipal clerks conducting Italy's census that Calogero lived in *Roccaforte*; in 1931, he reported to the census surveyors that he was in *America*.

I wish to thank colleagues Natalie Rothman and Jeffrey Pilcher, who read an earlier, longer version of this essay.

[1] All names have been changed; life events were drawn from a database compiling American and Sicilian documentation for the lives of over 3,700 migrants from Sambuca di Sicilia, an agrotown in the southwest Sicilian province of Agrigento.

Calogero returned to Sicily in the mid-1930s, presumably because he was unemployed in Rockford. By 1936, the family appeared in Sambuca's new household registration system with Calogero listed as an *agricoltore* (peasant lessee) and Rosa as devoted to the care of their house (*casalinga*). Six children – Audenzio, Angelina, Maria Audenzia, Calogera, Giovanni and Francesco, all American-born – lived with them.

In the years between 1880 and 1960, millions of international migrants challenged the governments of both the United States and Italy to track their lives through increasingly complex and detailed systems for enumeration and categorization. States have long created knowledge about the people they govern through enumeration and statistical analysis. High rates of mobility have just as often frustrated state efforts to distinguish clearly between residents and non-residents. In the modern era, state bureaucracies began to create and use enumerations more explicitly as a tool of nation-building, distinguishing insiders from outsiders and transforming subjects into loyal citizens.[2] Whether migrants were cast as threats or as boons to nation-building – and both views prevailed at various times in Italy as in the United States[3] – efforts to enumerate and to categorize mobility inevitably forced the two countries to confront little- or unknown languages, posing translation challenges for enumerators and migrants alike. This chapter focuses on American and Sicilian enumeration events that required translation of migrants' residential locations, occupations and names expressed in Italian, Sicilian dialect and English. It treats these translations as clues both to the nation-building projects of the two, relatively new countries and to migrants' resistance or acquiescence to them. The translations revealed different underlying assumptions about who could and could not belong to each nation.

As linguistic encounters, enumeration events do not fit easily within analytical schemes that sharply distinguish interpretation (of verbal communication) from translation (of written materials) and which view even public service translation and interpretation as the work of bilingual professionals

---

[2] Silvana Patriarca, *Numbers and Nationhood: Writing Statistics in Nineteenth-Century Italy* (Cambridge: Cambridge University Press, 1996); Margo Anderson, *The American Census: A Social History*, 2nd edn (New Haven: Yale University Press, 2015); Mariko Asano Tamanoi, 'Knowledge, Power, and Racial Classification: The "Japanese" in 'Manchuria', *Journal of Asian Studies*, 59.2 (May 2000), 248–76.

[3] Aristide Zolberg, *Nation by Design: Immigration Policy in the Fashioning of America* (New York: Russell Sage Foundation Press with Harvard University Press, 2006); Mark Choate, *Emigrant Nation: The Making of Italy Abroad* (Cambridge, MA: Harvard University Press, 2008).

or volunteers.[4] The translations analyzed below more closely resemble the language brokering that linguistic anthropologists study in colonial, postcolonial and medical contexts where verbal statements in one language are translated into written language in another.[5] As relationships of power, these translations implicitly reflected the different nation-building strategies of Italy and the United States, and the agency of migrants who lived in both countries. Biological reproduction and attachment to a particular place of birth defined the Italian nation whereas the American nation tolerated greater individual choice among migrants from Europe.

Nation-Building by Enumeration

We know their numbers because they were enumerated. Between 1870 and 1920 more than 16 million persons left Italy to live abroad; during the same period, more than 4 million entered the United States. Over 3,700 of Italy's migrants began their journey in Sambuca. Sambuca was in most respects a typical Sicilian agrotown of the late nineteenth century. Its large population of peasants walked long distances from their urban homes to distant fields. Sambuca also housed a small number of professionals, notables, barons and rentiers and a sizeable and diverse group of artisans and petty merchants. Its residents all spoke a variation of Sicilian dialect but only the town's elite (and a minority of its artisans) were readers, writers or (less often) speakers of the national language. What made Sambuca somewhat unique in the twentieth century was its vigorous political left.[6]

---

[4] Mustafa Taibi, 'Public Service Translation' (pp. 214–27) and Sandra Hale, 'Public Service Interpreting' (pp. 343–56) in *The Oxford Handbook of Translation Studies*, ed. Kirsten Malmkjaer and Kevin Windle (Oxford: Oxford University Press, 2011). The only study of translation of official documents that I have been able to identify is Asensio R. Mayoral, *Translating Official Documents* (Manchester: St. Jerome, 2003).

[5] Cristiana Giordano, 'Practices of Translation and the Making of Migrant Subjectivities in Contemporary Italy', *American Ethnologist*, 35.4 (November 2008), 588–606; David Winks, 'Forging Post-Colonial Identities through Acts of Translation?', *Journal of African Cultural Studies*, 21.1 (June 2009), 65–74; Jennifer A. Kam and Vanja Vasarevic, 'Communicating for One's Family: An Interdisciplinary Review of Language and Cultural Brokering in Immigrant Families', *Communication Yearbook*, 38 (2014), 3–38.

[6] Jane and Peter Schneider, *Culture and Political Economy in Western Sicily* (New York: Academic Press, 1976); Jane and Peter Schneider, *Festival of the Poor: Fertility Decline and the Ideology of Class in Sicily, 1860–1930* (Tucson: University of Arizona Press, 1996); Donna Gabaccia, *From Sicily to Elizabeth Street: Housing and Social Change among Italian Immigrants, 1880–1930* (Albany: SUNY Press, 1984); Gabaccia, *Militants and Migrants: Rural Sicilians Become American Workers* (New Brunswick:

Sambuca's 3,700 migrants were enumerated often, beginning in their hometown, again as they crossed the Atlantic and even more frequently while living in the United States. This chapter is based on the enumeration of these mobile individuals in documents held in Sambuca's municipal archive and in digitized American local, state and federal documents made accessible through Ancestry.com.

In Sambuca, enumeration events were encounters between elite local clerks, all male, and the peasants and artisans whom the town's middle class found to be fascinating, amusing and colorful but also inferior.[7] Only in 1921 did Sambuca's municipal clerks create the type of household registry (*anagrafe*, with individual enumerations inscribed by hand into preprinted *fogli di famiglia*, or family registers) that Italy first mandated in 1864 and thereafter provided the basis for Italy's decennial censuses. Before that date, Sambuca's clerks had already invented other practices for enumerating migrants – for example, during verbal registrations of births and through queries about draft-age young men listed on a diligently maintained and updated draft list or *lista della leva*). During the censuses of 1921, 1931, 1936 and 1951 they also enumerated the whereabouts of those whose kin reported them as departed.[8] Finally, clerks filed marriage, birth and death certificates sent from the United States by post or delivered by returned migrants.

Beginning around 1883, emigrants from Sambuca began traveling to the United States. (About a third returned.) In the US, Sambucari formed no single transplanted village or 'Little Sambuca'. However, they lived in sizeable clusters around the greater New York area, in Louisiana (where they worked on plantations, as independent truck farmers and in urban petty commerce), in railroad centers such as Kansas City, Missouri, in Midwestern centers of industry such as Chicago and Rockford, and in Illinois mining towns. American enumeration of Sambuca's migrants began before they reached the United States. The United States required ships' captains and their clerks to query migrants verbally in preparation for state or federal inspection in an American port. Once in the United States, a member of migrant households – often it was a bilingual child, translating for an adult parent – responded

Rutgers University Press, 1988). Sambuca's recent political history is recounted in Alfonso di Giovanna, *Inchiostro e trazzere: I venti anni di un giornale di provincia* (Sambuca di Sicilia: Ed. 'La Voce', 1979).

   [7] As evidenced in a novel about local life by Sambuca resident Emanuele Navarro della Miraglia, *La Nana* (Milan: Gaetano Brigola, 1879).

   [8] Robert Foerster, 'A Statistical Survey of Italian Emigration', *The Quarterly Journal of Economics*, 23.1 (1908), 66–103. See also *L'Italia in 150 anni: Sommario di statistiche storiche 1861–2010* (Rome: ISTAT, 2011).

verbally to decennial surveys by English-speaking census enumerators paid by state or federal census bureaucracies to knock on the door of every American home. English-speaking municipal clerks, doctors, hospital clerks and justices of the peace (in lower-level courts) also enumerated Sambuca's migrants as they married, gave birth and died. Male migrants reported to English-speaking military clerks in 1917 and again in 1942. The most consequential enumeration occurred when migrant men applied for and received American citizenship. The applicant brought to federal court supporting documents and witnesses to confirm verbal statements, and he signed a loyalty declaration, often with an 'X his mark'.

From today's standpoint, these enumeration events seem blandly routine and bureaucratic, but all brought together persons of different status, culture and power who could not always understand each other easily. In Sambuca, illiterate peasants may have loathed the requirement of enumeration of births, marriages and deaths (by Catholic priests prior to 1861 and by state officials afterwards). Although they sensed clerks' disdain as their verbal dialect statements were transformed into written, standard Italian, they also generally complied and reported. Encounters with clerks visiting their homes in search of knowledge useful to the military, census or tax bureaucracies were both more fraught and easier to resist through evasion. In the United States differences in language and culture separated enumerators and migrants even more dramatically. Translation accompanied most enumerations and migrants were also sometimes the translators. Still, the power to create and to archive enumeration records rested in the hands of persons far more powerful than the migrants in both countries.

Acts of Translation

It is not possible to know much about the enumerators who translated verbal and written statements and left archival traces in Sambuca or the United States but it is unlikely they knew much of the other country or its language. Until the late twentieth century French was the preferred second language among educated Sicilians. In the United States, knowledge of the Italian language was extremely limited, even among the best educated and most widely traveled. Still, by surveying enumerators' translation of places, occupations and names in American and Sicilian records, the outlines of quite different American and Italian nation-building strategies begin to emerge.

Translating Place
When massive emigration from Sicily to the United States began around 1882, neither enumerators nor migrants possessed firm and detailed imaginaries of

the world beyond their borders. To Sambucari, Italy remained far-off – 'the continent'. Italy was not yet a focus of intense or nationalist identification. Scholars have noted, too, that many in Italy envisioned the world beyond the Mediterranean Sea as a littoral region stretching from Canada to Tierra del Fuego and across the Pacific to Australia and called, simply, 'America'.[9] In the United States, many imagined their country as safely isolated from a corrupt world; even those elite Americans fascinated by European culture rarely traveled south of Rome or Naples.[10] Beginning in 1898, American scientific racists succeeded in introducing categories that distinguished southern from northern Italian 'races' but they marked the boundary between the two regions at the Po River.[11] American enumerators were even less familiar with Italy's geography.

To understand how enumerators in both countries transcribed and translated faraway place names, I examined over 4,000 Sicilian enumerations and roughly 2,000 American enumerations of mobile Sambucari. In both countries, errors in the transcription of place names abounded but were extremely varied and idiosyncratic. However, Sambuca's draft and census records recorded American places in starkly different fashion than its birth records. In the former, vague locational references predominated. For example, in the census and household registration systems, *America* was preferred to United States ('USA' or its Italian equivalent, *SUA or Stati Uniti d'America*) until the late 1930s. Mandates for locating emigrated kin came from the national government during the census years of 1921 and 1931 but were largely ignored. In 1921, three-quarters of clerks' notations to departed kin listed them as living 'in America' and 17 percent as living abroad (*all'estero*): only 8 percent reported a specific American location for emigrated kin. In 1931, Italy's government instead asked local clerks to identify those living abroad permanently as *permanente* or *stabilmente all'estero*. Sambuca's clerks enumerated only 69 households with kin in these mandated categories (over 600 described departed kin in other ways). We cannot know whether it was the clerks or the householders who continued to report kin as living 'in America' or gave a more specific location for them. Draft records were vaguer still. In the 1890s, 40 percent of draft records included a specific American place name; Sicilian clerks who hoped to inform consuls in the United States about the whereabouts of young men could state only that an individual was

---

[9] Richard Bosworth, *Italy and the Wider World* (New York: Routledge, 1996), p. 34.

[10] Donna Gabaccia, *Foreign Relations: Global Perspectives on American Immigration* (Princeton: Princeton University Press, 2011).

[11] Dillingham Commission Reports, *Dictionary of Races* (Washington, DC: Government Printing Office, 1911), p. 81.

espatriato, emigrato or *all'estero*. As the numbers of draft-age male émigrés increased in the 1900s and 1910s, almost half of all draft records included these vague locations. The percentage of more specific locations increased modestly in the 1920s. In a pronounced pattern, peasant men more than artisanal men were enumerated vaguely.

In sharp contrast, 80 to 90 percent of the birth records enumerating migration between 1880 to 1951 listed specific American cities, towns and states, suggesting that householders reporting to municipal clerks at the time of draft and census enumerations almost certainly knew the more precise locations of their sons and kin. Furthermore, every enumeration of Sambucari entering the United States after 1902 listed a specific street address and town and named the relative or friend living at the migrant's destination.

While Sicilian clerks made largely random errors in the transcription of specific American place names (e.g., a 1915 birth record in which Indiana Avenue, Chicago, became 'Avenne, Indiana', or a transcription of Baton Rouge as 'Batin Roog'), several consistent translations of American place names appeared. First, Sambuca's enumerators Italianized many place names in Louisiana. Because of its colonial history, southern Louisiana's town and county names had French origins; clerks in Sambuca felt comfortable translating them into their Italian equivalents. Thus, Louisiana became 'Luisiana' in their enumerations. 'Parish' – the Louisiana term for county – was translated into its Italian equivalent. Louisiana's Terrebonne became 'Terrabuona' and St. Jean Baptiste became 'San Giovanni Battista'. In a related pattern, enumerators also sometimes transformed English-named places into French. Sicilian clerks consistently changed Centerville, Louisiana, into 'Centreville', and one census record from 1931 transformed the Canadian province of Terre-Neuve (Newfoundland) into 'Nuova Terra'. Especially interesting was the consistent transcription of Franklin, Louisiana, as 'Franklyn'. Why? Sambuca's early republicans had been enthusiasts for the American and French revolutions and had named a Sambuca street 'via Franklyn' to honor Benjamin Franklin while adopting the spelling preferred in French publications.[12]

In a final pattern, just two American towns – Rockford, in Illinois, and Brooklyn, in New York – became common, locally used dialect place names as 'Roccaforte' and 'Brookalino'. Brooklyn had appeared regularly in Sambuca's birth, marriage and death records after 1883 while Rockford first appeared around 1910. Sambuca's clerks had consistently transcribed Brooklyn correctly (probably because that city used printed birth certificates from an early date) while the same clerks struggled with the Illinois town, at first transcribing it

---

[12] Assemblée nationale constituante, *Procès-verbal de l'Assemblée nationale* (Paris: Baudouin, imprimeur de l'Assemblée, 1791), pp. 50:28.

variously as 'Rock', 'Rockfort', and even 'Recchfold'. 'Roccaforte' first appeared in a 1918 birth certificate; 'Brookalino' appeared somewhat later, in a 1927 draft record. 'Roccaforte' was of course an existing Italian word ('stronghold'); it was also the name of a local peasant family. The genesis of 'Brookalino' is less clear. Both names became part of local dialect and were still widely used in discussions with anthropologists in the 1970s. Since many other difficult-to-spell-and-to-pronounce American place names (e.g. Kansas City and Chicago) were neither localized nor Italianized, Rockford's and Brooklyn's special reception into dialect still requires explanation.

American enumerators were less interested in migrants' specific birth-places: only men's military and naturalization records and ships' lists (from 1898 until 1921) consistently listed migrants' town of birth or former residence. English-speaking clerks also struggled to record verbalized place names; they made many errors, especially when migrants were illiterate, transforming Sambuca into 'San Buco', 'Sambikka', 'Sabica Zab' and many other forms. 'Sabica Zab' is a reminder that the official name of Sambuca before the fascist era was Sambuca Zabut, Zabut generally being understood to reflect the town's Arab and Muslim origins. When Mussolini's regime changed the town's name to 'Sambuca di Sicilia', the new name appeared immediately in American enumerations. Although misspellings of Sambuca were common in ships' lists, the American military records from 1917 and 1918 were far more accurate, suggesting that both Sicilians' rates of literacy and their English language skills had improved. In a handful of cases, however, military records listed the birthplace of male registrants as 'Sammuca' – an uncannily accurate transcription of Sambuca's local dialect, which tends to drop the 'b' in the town's name.[13]

Translating Occupational Categories

Sicilian enumerators actively resisted the inclusion of both Sicilian dialect occupational and American occupational categories. In the United States, Americans showed little or no interest in migrants' homeland occupation. The gendered enumerations of women's occupations were at first strikingly different in the two countries but they also converged in the 1920s under fascism.

In Sambuca, municipal clerks (like priests before them) had long faced the challenge of translating verbalized dialect occupations into standardized Latin or Italian. They transformed the dialect term for peasant, *viddanu*, into the Italian form, *contadino*. Yet the same clerks also consistently included in

---

[13] For written confirmation of the dialect term, see Giuseppe Pitrè, *Proverbi Siciliani* (Palermo: Ed. 'Il Vespro', 1978; orig. published 1870–1913), III, 163.

their enumerations the dialect term *burgisi* to indicate a landowning peasant. Beginning in 1921 and responding to national census mandates, Sambuca's clerks began introducing new occupational categories for peasants that distinguished *agricoltore* or *mezzadro* (peasant lessee, sharecropper) from the wage-earning proletarian (*bracciante agricolo*); somewhat later, clerks introduced the nationally mandated categories of *coltivatore diretto, conduttore in proprio coltivazione* and other terms that appeared in published census reports. Thus, when a peasant who was absent, working in New York as a barber or machine operator, became a father, his child appeared in Sambuca's birth registry as a *contadino in America*. Only one enumeration contained a possible use of a translated American occupational category: before 1935, there were no automobiles in Sambuca but one returned migrant appeared in his *foglio di famiglia* as an *autista* or driver, presumably describing his work in the United States.

Whether a migrant described himself verbally as *viddanu* or a *contadino* in Sicily probably mattered little to ships' clerks. There simply were no peasants in America. Reporting an occupation to ships' clerks also carried some level of danger. After 1885 (when the US prohibited the entry of contract laborers), migrant men had to demonstrate they would not become public charges (needing charity) without suggesting an American job already awaited them. In the decade between 1895 and 1907, ships' clerks frequently enumerated male Sambucari simply as 'countryman' – an archaic-sounding translation of *contadino* or of *paesano* or *villico* (villager). With no instructions or guidelines from the government, the clerks' choice of 'countryman' remains difficult to explain. In any case, 'countryman' disappeared after 1910, replaced on ships lists by 'laborer' and 'farmer'. Very few of Sicily's artisanal trades received correct shipboard translation – *calzolaio* became 'shoemaker' or 'cobbler' – but American enumerators casually transformed the majority of Sambuca's mobile iron workers, millers and cabinetmakers into either 'laborers' or 'barbers' (a minor trade in Sambuca). Most likely they attributed to new arrivals the occupations migrants were expected to assume once in the United States.

Unlike Sicilian clerks, American enumerators showed no interest in the occupations of Sambuca's female migrants. Between 1880 and 1910, Sambuca's clerks regularly enumerated female occupations in birth, death and marriage records. Yet fewer than one in a hundred women from Sambuca entered the United States with an occupation listed. American immigration officials were more concerned that a woman traveling alone or with children might become a public charge, and almost 10 percent of Sambuca's migrant women were temporarily detained upon arrival. Census takers rarely enumerated married female Sambucari as working for wages, although in cities their teenaged daughters appeared frequently as machine operators or clerks. Sicilians too lost interest in the diversity of women's occupations over time. With the institution of the household registry system in 1921 the *contadina* (female peasant), *industriosa* (female producer by hand of small items), *donna rurale* (woman working in the countryside), *domestica* (servant), *cucitrice* (seamstress), *caffettiera* or *bottegara* (operator of a café or small shop), *sarta* (lady's tailor), *ricamatrice* (embroiderer) and *levatrice* (midwife) disappeared from local enumerations and all women were enumerated as *casalinga* or housewife.

Translating Migrant Names

In assessing the documented changes in migrants' personal names, the biggest challenge is determining what role, if any, migrants played in their translation. Contrary to popular myth in the United States, migrants' names were not changed officially on Ellis Island.[14] By juxtaposing the names of migrants enumerated in Sambuca and the United States, it appears that Sicilian clerks sought to maintain a registry of official names while migrants and American enumerators were both more willing to engage in and to accept informal and variable acts of self-naming. Names given at birth fixed the individual within a Sicilian family; American record keepers were more willing to accept whatever name or nickname a migrant might choose to give himself.

In Sambuca, clerks never enumerated any name other than the one recorded at the time of a migrant's birth. Misspellings of names were exceedingly rare and Sambuca's archive did not reveal any use of Americanized or translated migrant names, not even for returned American-born children, whose American names had appeared repeatedly in census listings in the United States. While it is likely that neighbors and friends colloquially used American names and nicknames for returned migrant *americani* (as the returners and their children were still regularly termed in Sambuca in the 1970s), the consistent use of official birth names in Sambuca's public records held firm through more than eighty years of considerable mobility. Clerks' firm commitments to the practice undoubtedly rested on the long-term exclusions from local registries of local and exceedingly common and commonly used nicknames or *soprannomi*.[15] Even as migrants, Sambucari lived comfortably

---

[14] Vincent J. Cannato, *American Passage: The History of Ellis Island* (New York: Harper, 2009), p. 402.

[15] During my own time in Sambuca, I became *la studentessa* (the female student) while my husband, who wore sandals and a beard (like Capuchin monks), became *il cappuccino con la moglie* (the Capuchin monk with the wife).

with the distinction between official and unofficial names, adding new American names as they moved about.

There is evidence that migrants continued at first to recognize the importance of official names. American ships' lists transcribed Sicilian names with far greater accuracy than Sicilian place names. Given high rates of illiteracy among peasants, the accuracy of these transcriptions suggests that migrants traveled with written documents even before the United States demanded them. (Collections of personal documents from Sambuca, visible in Ancestry. com's genealogy collections, suggest birth certificates were most often carried.) Married women traveling to the United States from Sambuca also universally reported their birth names at the moment of entry, thereby continuing the practice of Sicily's official registries. A comparison of census enumerations, military records and naturalization enumerations for a small group of 50 men from Sambuca also reveals men fairly consistently reverting to official, Sicilian birth names during naturalization and military enumerations.

Once in the United States, the translation, especially of given or first names, began. The most common first names in Sambuca's migrant families (Giuseppe, with over 2,500 appearances in migrants' genealogies, and Maria with almost 2,000) had obvious American equivalents – Joseph, Joe, Marie, Mary. Other common names in Sambuca fell into this category: Rosa (Rose), Antonio/a (Anthony or Antoinette), Francesco/a (Francis, Frances) and Giovanni/a (John, Joanne). Census enumerations of such names revealed very high rates of translation but it is difficult to know whether migrant or enumerator provided the translation for names with obvious cognates.

But other given names could not be so easily translated into English and these provide the best evidence that migrants participated actively in choosing new names, sometimes in surprising ways. Take, for example, the name Calogero (feminine Calogera) which appeared over 1,600 times in Sambuca's migrant genealogies.[16] It is unlikely any American enumerator knew how to translate Calogero; they either had to copy it from a written document or transcribe it from a verbal statement (resulting in census transcriptions such as 'Collagia' or 'Cullujo'). When migrants named Calogera and Calogero reported other names to American enumerators they chose to do so. Men named Calogero usually called themselves Carl or Charles in the United States; occasionally they substituted the Italian cognate for Carl (Carlo). A few more inventive men chose unrelated American names such as Alex or even Edward. Fewer Calogeras changed their name in the United States, becoming Lily or Carlotta. Sambuca's migrants also included

---

[16] Calogero was a hermit saint, patron of the city of Sciacca, a coastal town south of Sambuca.

many people named Audenzio (male) or Audenzia (female) after the town's patron saint, Maria dell'Udienza. In the United States, male Audenzios chose new names – either the Italian Lorenzo or the American Lawrence. Again, Audenzias were less likely to change their names, perhaps because they often carried the double name Maria Audenzia and became simply Maria or Mary.

To interpret name choices simplistically as indicators of migrants' enthusiasm for American individualism would be incorrect, however. The majority of Sambucari living in the United States before 1940 continued to respect the Sicilian custom of naming their first-born son and daughter after the paternal grandparents and their second-born son and daughter after the maternal grandparents. At most, migrant parents and their children used the Americanized versions of the grandparents' names. The Sicilian naming pattern disappeared only as the American-born generation came of age in the United States.

Significantly, American census takers and enumerators of births, deaths and marriages willingly recorded whatever names migrants chose for themselves and their children, regardless of what their parents may have called them at home or on their birth certificate. Almost all of the American-born sons of Sambucari parents registered for the American draft in 1942 with American or Americanized first names. In relationships of nation and state – at least as revealed in enumeration events – the Italian state preserved individual identity as a product of biological reproduction and family social relations while the American state casually accepted far higher levels of individual expression and individual autonomy.

Enumeration, Translation and Nation-Building in Italy and the United States

Both the categories enumerated and patterns of translation point toward a more biological, birth- and birthplace-driven strategy of nation-building in Italy and a more voluntarist, individual and residence-driven strategy of nation-building in the United States. This is scarcely surprising since the United States, along with France, is well known as an exemplar of civic nationalism, based on *ius soli* (residence) while Italy more closely resembles the ethnic nationalism (*ius sanguinis*, based on blood).[17] Still, enumeration provides unique perspectives on how the building of ethnic and civic nations

---

[17] Rogers Brubaker, 'The Manichean Myth: Rethinking the Distinction between "Civic" and "Ethnic" Nationalism', in *Nation and National Identity: The European Experience in Perspective*, ed. Hanspeter Kriesl et al. (Zurich: Verlag Ruegger, 1999), pp. 55–72.

differed. It also identifies elements of nation-building that encouraged similar forms of enumeration and similar patterns of translation in both countries. Finally, it clearly reveals migrants' expressions of ambivalence about and their very selective participation in nation-building projects in the two countries.

As they sought to build new nations, Italy and the United States shared many concerns, reflecting their common location within an Atlantic system of mobility that historical sociologist David Cook has characterized as 'the scramble for citizens'.[18] Which nations would be built and strengthened through population growth, male or female labor, or national loyalty in times of war? In the face of considerable mobility, both countries sought to fix mobile people spatially by repeatedly (as in the case of the United States) or continuously (as in Sambuca after 1921) enumerating individuals' place of residence and employment. Italy's attempt to track and enumerate draft-age men was another continuous form of state-centered nation-building which was duplicated in the United States only intermittently during moments of international warfare. In trying to bureaucratically root individuals spatially, both nations competed to claim the same mobile people. Migrants did not always willingly relinquish information about their location, a sign of their ambivalence if not outright resistance to state control.

The scramble for citizens was also a scramble for labor. This chapter has described the scramble for labor playing out through the categorization of occupations. For most migrants, their labor was their main and sometimes only contribution to nation-building. Just as they were (at this time) denied dual citizenship, migrants also found they could not in any meaningful fashion translate the occupations they held in one country into the occupational categories of the other, revealing the indifference at best and, at worst, the hostility of both countries to transnational transformations of national hierarchies built on control of labor. One could not be a farmer in Sambuca's records and one could not be a *burgisi* in American enumerations, even if the work in both places was largely similar. However, in Sicily, unlike the United States, specific and often skilled forms of female labor were initially acknowledged locally, incorporating Sambuca's women into the nation as workers; only under fascism did Italy make procreation, motherhood and housework the only desired female contributions to the nation.

The Italian state's perception of its own disadvantage in the scramble for citizens expressed itself through largely hopeless efforts to enumerate a distinction between temporary and permanent departures. For many years, Italy anxiously (and incorrectly) tracked overseas departures as a sign of

---

[18] David Cook-Martín, *The Scramble for Citizens: Dual Nationality and State Competition for Immigrants* (Stanford: Stanford University Press, 2013).

expatriation while regarding intra-European moves as temporary. Having resisted the national government's demand for a household registry for 50 years, Sambuca's clerks also either abandoned or refused Italy's request to distinguish in this way among householders' departed kin in the 1931 census. In contrast, the American state faced the scramble for citizens from a position of decided strength – also reflected in its enumeration choices. The United States did not then (and still does not) systematically enumerate those departing its shores permanently; only after 1924, as it built a more restrictive and visa-based immigration system, did the US ask whether foreigners intended to settle as permanent residents. It had long enumerated entries by assuming, wrongly, that all who entered remained. When they noticed the departures of 'immigrants', Americans scorned migrants rather than fearing the loss of their labor or reproductive power, for they had begun to worry that immigrant women produced more children than Americans and that immigrant men were incapable of participating in democratic governance.[19]

American and Italian enumerations also reflected the diverse assumptions of ethnic and civic nation-building. Sicilian clerks remained extremely precise when establishing the exact locations of individual births, whether in Sicily or in the United States; the birth name, birthplace and birth date constituted the most strictly and officially maintained markers of individual identity. In 1912, Italy clarified and expanded its nation by making birth in an Italian town a transportable and reproducible source of nationality, thereby allowing American-born citizens of the United States (and their descendants) to reclaim Italian citizenship if they had Italian-born fathers and returned to Italy. Compared to Italy's careful enumeration of birth, American enumerations of birth were haphazard, uneven and belated. Births outside hospitals and in rural areas were not systematically recorded until well into the twentieth century; American birth records for most children of Sambuca's migrants could not be found in Ancestry.com's collections. American census takers asked about the state (New York, Illinois) or country (Italy) of an individual's birth, not the city. Citizenship and residence, not biological reproduction or kinship ties, mattered in the building of a civic nation. Birth in an American state (not an individual city) defined a birthright claim to citizenship. For those born abroad, ships' clerks recorded their places of prior and next residence; census takers enumerated their national origin (e.g., Italy) and citizenship status (whether alien – e.g., a citizen of a foreign state, Italian – or naturalized as an American citizen). Enumeration of naturalization, not precise place of foreign birth, mattered in American

---

[19] Mark Wyman, *Round Trip to America: The Immigrants Return to Europe, 1880–1930* (Ithaca: Cornell University Press, 1996).

nation-building. Residence and choice of citizenship and nationality through naturalization along with choice of a personal name that differed from the birth name marked American enumerations' role in the creation of a civic, voluntarist and individualist nation.

Migrants navigated these competing national understandings of belonging as they pursued their own life projects. What they thought of either nations or of nation-building can only rarely be known. There was, for example, no evidence in Sicilian enumerations that municipal clerks or migrants objected to Italian nation-building on the basis of birth, blood and reproduction any more than they objected to the overnight change of the town's name to expunge its historical association with Arab rule or Muslim faith. Signs of resistance to nation-building emerged only in unified Italy's demand for taxes, for the enumeration of male labor through military service and for reports on the whereabouts and intentions (to settle in the United States or to return) of Sambuca's inhabitants. In the United States, too, enumeration and translation revealed specific and limited rather than generalized resistance to American nation-building. Sambucari embraced the individualism of choosing and using their self-chosen, American names and nicknames but also remained loyal to Sicilian naming traditions which bound them to intra-generational forms of fictive and 'blood' kinship. Many from Sambuca were simply not counted during the American censuses of 1900 and 1910; the appearance of American census takers in immigrant neighborhoods seems to have sparked such regular avoidance that 'under-enumeration' of foreign-born populations has been a persistent problem of the American census.[20] Men from Sambuca also demonstrated little interest in acquiring American citizenship before World War I. Thereafter, applications and naturalizations of male Sambucari clustered during three periods – 1918–19, 1923–28, and 1935–40. When men newly arrived from Sambuca in the 1920s began to declare an intention to naturalize within mere months of their arrival, they were thinking strategically. With the introduction of discriminatory national origins quotas in 1921 and 1924, American law allowed only those holding American citizenship to continue the circulatory mobility that had characterized so many Sicilians' lives since the 1880s. During the 1930s depression, furthermore, only American citizens could easily claim support, for example from American federal jobs programs for the unemployed. By World War II, when the United States was at war with Italy, the choice to naturalize was far more attractive

---

[20] Office of Population Research, 'Possibility of Under-Enumeration in the Census of Population', *Population Index*, 7.1 (January 1941), 9–11; US Bureau of the Census, *Historical Statistics of the United States, Colonial Times to 1970* (Washington, DC: US Government Printing Office, 1975), part 1, series A, 1.

than the status of male enemy alien. It appears that Sambucari approached naturalization instrumentally rather than emotionally; their national loyalties may have played no role whatsoever in their choices. It is extremely likely, then, that even those voluntarily choosing American citizenship retained significant aspects of Sambucaris' long-standing ambivalence or indifference to nation-building. Unable to escape completely nationalist demands for their loyalty, submission and military service in two countries, migrants silently navigated, resisted and used mobility in whatever way they could to slip through the nation-building nets that ensnared them in the records and bureaucratic categories of Italy and the United States.

13

Addressing the Representation of the Italian Empire and Its Afterlife

Charles Burdett

The endeavour to think of Italy and Italian cultures in transnational perspective brings with it a series of consequences: to begin with, we have to think across a much broader geographical area than we may have imagined; we have to explore the unfolding of economic and social processes, with all their inequalities of power, that motivate and define patterns of mobility; we have to think of cultures not as self-contained or stable but as hybrid, unstable and subject to perpetual change in the way in which they configure reality and the way in which they place the individual within the fabric of practices that they are constantly weaving together. What we tend to define as a specific culture – whether that is a set of identifiably similar practices or a succession of events that are related to a common narrative – is perhaps best seen as a current within the sea of human culture as a whole.[1] Yet, though we may come, more and more, to see the movement and the merging of cultures not only as inevitable but, in many respects, highly desirable since that which is living needs always to be changing and evolving as it comes into contact with new contexts, the appreciation of the manifold benefits that accrue from the mixing of seemingly separate cultures should not blind us to the violence, to the imposition of hierarchies and to the racism that has often accompanied the movement of people and culture. Our understanding of the processes that simultaneously create the present and that will shape (both locally and globally) the future, needs

---

[1] On this subject, see the conversation on the AHRC theme 'Translating Cultures' conducted on 18 July 2019, Barbara Spadaro, Charles Burdett, Angela Creese, Charles Forsdick and Alison Phipps, 'In Conversation: Translating Cultures', *The Translator* (2020), https://doi.org/10.1080/13556509.2019.1735211.

to take account of the colonial past and the extent to which the spectre of colonial attitudes, assumptions and ascriptions continues to haunt the world which we inhabit.[2] It is with this subject that the present chapter is principally concerned.

The relationship between what we now refer to as Italy and colonialism stretches far back into antiquity and is typified by a high degree of complexity: it involves the imperial aspirations of its ruling elites, the ambitions of its neighbours, the lengthy foreign rule of many parts of the peninsula. Within the modern period, the nature of Italy's various attempts at expansionism are, as we might expect, intimately bound up with the development of the nation and with changing discourses of national belonging. In 1889, less than thirty years after unification, Italy seized the opportunity to establish a colonial presence in Eritrea and between 1889 and 1905 it did the same in Somalia. The two colonies were not in themselves enough to satisfy the imperial longings of a relatively small, though powerful elite in Italy, but they did provide a useful springboard for future incursions into the territory of their coveted neighbour, Ethiopia. Italian ambitions in the region were, however, dealt a massive blow at the battle of Adowa in 1896, when the forces of the emperor Menelik annihilated General Baratieri's expeditionary force. It was not until 1911 that Italy again seized an opportunity to extend its overseas territory. Eager to take advantage of the ailing Ottoman Empire and keen not to lose out to French expansion, Italy invaded Libya in September of that year. The Libyan campaign encountered a number of serious obstacles but it was officially concluded in October 1912.[3] The apparently successful conclusion of the campaign did not, however, mark the end of hostilities. The resistance of the Arab-Berber population to the new imperial power far out-stretched anything that the architects of the enterprise had anticipated: the operation to 'reconquer' Libya began in the wake of the First World War and was not concluded until 1932.[4]

---

[2] On this subject, see Walter Mignolo, *The Darker Side of Western Modernity: Global Futures, Decolonial Options* (Durham, NC: Duke University Press, 2011).

[3] For more information on the initial phases of Italian colonialism and on the war in Libya, see Nicola Labanca, *Oltremare: storia dell'espansione coloniale italiana* (Bologna: il Mulino, 2002). Specifically, on the effect of fascism in Libya, see Muhammad T. Jerary, 'Damages Caused by the Italian Fascist Colonization of Libya', in *Italian Colonialism*, ed. by Ruth Ben-Ghiat and Mia Fuller (Basingstoke and New York: Palgrave Macmillan, 2005), pp. 203–09.

[4] On the question of resistance to the imposition of colonial rule, see Ali Abdullatif Ahmida, *Forgotten Voices: Power and Agency in Colonial and Postcolonial Libya* (London: Routledge, 2005). See also David Atkinson, 'Encountering Bare Life in Italian Libya and Colonial Amnesia in Agamben', in *Agamben and Colonialism*, ed. by

The following event in the relatively short history of Italian imperialism was the assault on Ethiopia by Mussolini's fascist regime. The conquest of the country, which began in October 1935, was intended to avenge earlier setbacks and to establish the newly 'reborn' nation as a major power. By the spring of 1936 the ferocious two-pronged attack on Ethiopia had largely succeeded: Addis Ababa had capitulated, Emperor Haile Selassie had gone into exile and Mussolini was able to proclaim the reapparition of the Roman Empire to throngs of ecstatic supporters who gathered in the Italian capital on 9 May 1936 for the declaration of Italy's new role in the world. In the brief life of Italian East Africa, huge sums of money were spent on building the infrastructure that would permit economic exploitation, racial segregation was introduced at all levels of the new society and continued armed resistance was suppressed with unremitting force.[5] Yet Mussolini merely pursued – with greater determination and greater indifference to international opinion – a policy that had long antecedents. Like his predecessors, he was wedded to the belief that national wealth would flow from agricultural colonization rather than through international trade and, like them, he saw the acquisition of empire as the answer to the problem of poverty and the loss of Italian labour through emigration.

But the empire was a rapidly built edifice and its collapse was as dramatic as its construction. Italy entered the Second World War on the side of Germany with the expectation that it would make substantial territorial gains across Africa and the Middle East through its support of its more powerful ally.[6] In reality, its growing empire had folded like a house of cards within two years of the start of the war. By 1941 British troops had moved into most of Italy's former territories in North and East Africa and the fascist dream of creating a vast empire stretching from the Mediterranean across Egypt down to Ethiopia had come to an end. In the immediate post-war period the lengthy process of decolonization began and proceeded relatively rapidly; by the early 1950s, for example, the Italian population of Eritrea's capital city, Asmara, which had exceeded 100,000, had fallen to around 17,000; by the mid-1970s that figure stood at around 1,000; by 1981 the number of Italians living in

Marcelo Svirsky and Simone Bignall (Edinburgh: Edinburgh University Press, 2012), pp. 155–77.

[5] The work of Ian Campbell, based principally on Ethiopian testimonies, demonstrates the degree of inhumanity of which the regime was capable. See *The Addis Ababa Massacre: Italy's National Shame* (Oxford: Oxford University Press, 2017).

[6] For an account of the full extent of Italian imperial ambitions at the start of the Second World War, see Nir Arielli, *Fascist Italy and the Middle East 1933–40* (Basingstoke and New York: Palgrave Macmillan, 2013), pp. 169–73.

the whole of Ethiopia (including at that time Eritrea) was around 1,500.[7] Italy's disengagement from its colonies was never seriously contested, except by forces to the far right. The history of the transition from fascism to democracy is also a history of Italy's changing geographical relationship to the rest of the world – broadly speaking, from expansion beyond Europe to integration within Europe.[8]

Written Accounts of Italian Colonialism and Its Legacy

Italian colonial involvement in numerous countries and the legacy of that involvement are, then, issues of enormous significance: one can, for example, understand little of modern Italian culture without some knowledge of the origins and development of fascism; in turn, one can understand little of Italian fascism without taking into account its plan for imperial development; and one can understand little of contemporary Italy without some knowledge of the enduring impact of Italy's role as a colonial power. There are many ways in which one can gain a deeper understanding of the dynamics and conse-quences of Italian expansionist policies in the late nineteenth century and in the early part of the twentieth. One means is to look in depth at the corpus of written and visual material that accompanied the drive towards empire and to analyse how this corpus is constructed rhetorically and how it was intended to mould the ideas of its readers or viewers.

Considering the rapidity of territorial expansion in the interwar years and the desire of Mussolini's regime to forge a colonial consciousness among Italians, it comes as little surprise that a huge amount of writing on the colonial world was produced in the 1920s and 1930s. This material can be categorized, more or less, along the following lines: there are the official publications which presented an image of the progress of colonization in Italy's overseas territories and which endeavoured to popularize a vision of how life there could be lived; there are the many reflections on aspects of colonial society that were written by those involved at different levels

---

[7] See Angelo Del Boca, *Gli italiani in Africa orientale, vol. IV, Nostalgia delle colonie* (Rome-Bari: Laterza, 1984), pp. 3–75 (esp. pp. 30–34). On Italian withdrawal from Libya, see Pamela Ballinger, 'Colonial Twilight: Italian Settlers and the Long Decolonization of Libya', *Journal of Contemporary History*, 51.4 (2015), 813–38.

[8] On the subject as a whole, see Ben-Ghiat and Fuller, *Italian Colonialism* and Jacqueline Andall and Derek Duncan, eds, *Italian Colonialism: Legacy and Memory* (Oxford and New York: Peter Lang, 2005). See also *Quel che resta dell'impero*, ed. by Valeria Deplano and Alessandro Pes (Milan: Mimesis, 2014). On transnational resistance to Italian colonialism, see Neelam Srivastava, *Italian Colonialism and Resistances to Empire, 1930–1970* (London: Palgrave Macmillan, 2018).

within its administration; there is the body of work that was produced by the journalists of the period and the smaller number of works that attempted to establish a nascent form of colonial literature. An essential element of the book, newspaper and magazine culture of the time were the reams of photographs that were taken on every aspect of Italy's territories overseas.[9]

The writing on the legacy of the Italian empire is of a different nature and the corpus of representations that one can examine, though by no means small, is less extensive. There is, to begin with, the post-war writing of high-ranking Italian soldiers and officials, almost all of whom wrote with a sense of bitterness and betrayal at the collapse of Italy's imperial ambitions. In addition, there is the publication of journals, fictional and non-fictional writing by the inhabitants of Italy's former colonies.[10] There are literary evocations of episodes from the colonial past, such as Ennio Flaiano's well-known *Tempo di uccidere* (1947) or the series of novels of life in Libya by Alessandro Spina, contained within the collection *I confini dell'ombra: in terra d'oltremare* (2007).[11] The military occupation of parts of East Africa has been represented in writing drawing upon archival research and oral history: for example, the texts by Angelo Angelastro and by Marco Consentino, Domenico Dodaro and Luigi Panella.[12] Former Italian residents of Asmara, such as Erminia Dell'Oro or Nicky Di Paolo (see below), have written fictional accounts of their experiences in Africa and of the transnational community to which they belonged. Well-known writers like Gabriella Ghermandi (see below) or Igiaba Scego, with personal links to the Horn of Africa, have uncovered moments from the history of Italian involvement in East Africa and drawn attention to its continuing relevance in Italy's multicultural present.[13]

---

[9] On this corpus see Charles Burdett, 'Nomos, Identity and Otherness: Ciro Poggiali's Diario AOI 1936–37 and the Representation of the Italian Colonial World', *Papers of the British School at Rome*, 79 (2011), 329–49. The present chapter refers to a number of articles that I have previously published on these issues.

[10] See Burdett, 'Memories of Italian East Africa', *Journal of Romance Studies*, 1.3 (2001), 69–84.

[11] Ennio Flaiano, *Tempo di uccidere* (Milan: Longanesi, 1947); Alessandro Spina, *I confini dell'ombra: in terra d'oltremare* (Brescia: Morcelliana, 2006).

[12] See, for example, Angelo Angelastro's *Il bel tempo di Tripoli* (Rome: Edizioni e/o, 2015) and Marco Consentino, Domenico Dodaro and Luigi Panella, *I fantasmi dell'impero* (Palermo: Sellerio, 2017).

[13] See, for example, Scego's novel *Adua* (Florence: Giunti, 2015). For an analysis of the literary work in Italian by authors of Somali origin, see Simone Brioni, *The Somali Within: Language, Race and Belonging in 'Minor' Italian Literature* (Oxford: Legenda, 2015). For a recent article on *Adua*, see Lucy Rand, 'Transgenerational Shame in Postcolonial Italy: Igiaba Scego's *Adua*', *Journal of Postcolonial Writing*, 56.1 (2020), 4–17.

There are many ways in which this written material can be addressed. Perhaps the most straightforward approach is to isolate and comment on the work of an individual who represented Italy's self-appointed role in Africa or who has written on its long-lasting implications. An approach of this kind can give a very clear picture of the sort of person who participated, at whatever level, in the colonial enterprise or whose formative experiences were in Italy's colonies; the approach can reveal aspects of the life story of an individual, their way of seeing themselves and their role within the newly created space of empire or within countries struggling with the legacy of empire; it can indicate the desires and ambitions of a person as well as their attitudes towards the prevailing organization of society. Such an approach shows the individual's mode of expression, his or her use of language to capture a view of reality or how the world is represented within a given perspective.

A potential problem, however, of concentrating on the work of one individual or another is that you run the risk of exaggerating the degree to which their views were independent. It often proves the case that, at least during the years of the Italian empire, the perception recorded by a writer or photographer simply repeated what was an officially sanctioned position. Another way of conducting analysis is to proceed from the insights of postcolonial criticism and examine how specific writers' works are related to the wider cultural complex of which they were or are a part.[14] The advantage of taking an approach of this kind is that it avoids the danger of implying that individuals are free, unproblematically, to step out from the ideologies of their time and to view reality in a perspective that is unencumbered by the constraints of their cultural formation. It is, in other words, an approach that allows one to see how the language and structure of collective constructions of reality assert themselves in any piece of writing, however original it may claim to be. If one approaches the extensive corpus of writing on empire and its legacy as a means of understanding collectively organized interpretations of the social world, then one can see with greater clarity the cultural geography of the regime and its lasting effects, the continuation across time of certain ways of thinking and the changing dynamics of cultural and social interchange.[15]

---

[14] For an introduction to the study of postcolonial criticism, see Bill Ashcroft, Gareth Griffiths and Helen Tiffin, eds, *Post-Colonial Studies: The Key Concepts* (London and New York: Routledge, 2000); Ania Loomba, *Colonialism/Postcolonialism*, 2nd edn (London and New York: Routledge, 2005); Robert Young, *Empire, Colony, Postcolony: A Short History* (Chichester: Wiley-Blackwell, 2015). With a specific focus on Italy, see Cristina Lombardi-Diop and Caterina Romeo, eds, *Postcolonial Italy: Challenging National Homogeneity* (Basingstoke and New York: Palgrave Macmillan, 2012).

[15] I am grateful to Alessandro Ruggiero and to Francesca Amendola at the Italian Cultural Institute in Addis Ababa, who hosted both myself and Gianmarco

If we approach the body of representations of empire and its legacy, looking for what it tells us about collective modes of thought and behaviour, then one of the most interesting questions that we can ask is what it reveals about the operation of a complex network of ideas and imaginings about time.[16] Focusing on those writings that were produced during the period of imperial expansion, one can see the working of a whole series of ideas concerning: the development of empire in tandem with the consolidation of the nation state; the aspiration towards a model of modernity; the echo of earlier periods in time; the anticipation of enhanced global significance; and the imagining of an imperial future. One can also see how the production of imagined temporalities can function as a powerful means of gathering support on one hand and of justifying oppression on the other. One can see how ideas concerning time formed part of a hierarchical vision of cultural difference, reinforcing the putative superiority of the colonial power and legitimating policies of segregation.

Among the most important questions that one can ask of post-war representations of the Italian presence in Africa is how, in this body of work, the experience of time is thought about and imagined. One can examine how works belonging to a clearly defined corpus consider the lasting impact of empire on those societies which were the object of the expansionist policies of the first half of the twentieth century; one can look at the way these works characterize the physical remnants of the Italian presence in Africa, most notably in the architecture of cities like Tripoli, Asmara and Addis Ababa; one can consider how the increasing transculturation of the Italian communities which remained in the north and east of Africa after the end of empire is represented. Above all, one can consider how this body of work conveys the power of past injustices to haunt the present.

The dimensions of the questions regarding time that we can ask of the body of writing on the Italian empire and its afterlife are imposing, not least because of the many pathways that they open into the past but also, and perhaps especially, because of the extent to which such questions impinge upon the present. In the context of a present that is shaped by the proximity and interlayering of cultures, insight into the legacy of colonialism is a matter

---

Mancosu while pursuing work on the legacy of the Italian empire for the project 'Transnationalizing Modern Languages'.

[16] For a discussion of how to approach questions relating to temporality with particular reference to the postcolonial, see Russell West-Pavlov, *Temporalities* (London and New York: Routledge, 2012); Johannes Fabian, *Time and the Other: How Anthropology Makes Its Object*, 2nd edn (New York: Columbia University Press, 2014); Achille Mbembe, *On the Postcolony* (Berkeley: University of California Press, 2001).

of crucial importance. In seeking to address phenomena that are witnessed with regularity – whether that is the growth in far-right political parties, the backlash against immigration or the increase in instances of racially motivated violence – knowledge of the consequences of past actions is essential. What follows aims to suggest some of the ways in which one can take further the inquiry into the temporalities of Italian colonialism and to indicate some of the reading strategies that can be adopted in addressing representations that concern, either directly or indirectly, the enduring effects of expansionism.

The Creation of a New Order

Perhaps one of the most effective means by which we can isolate various narratives concerning time within the history of Italian imperialism is to see the whole expansionist project as a peculiarly accelerated attempt to create a new type of reality. Many recent studies have argued that one of the core elements of Italian fascism consisted in the attempt to refashion not only the collective social world but the internal experience of the individual.[17] If this is so, then it is undeniably the case that a violent and dramatic process of world creation took place in Italy's overseas territories during the 20 years of fascist rule and it is equally true that an essential element in the creation of this new imperial reality was the organization of its perception. Rather than seeing so much of the writing that was produced on Libya or on Italian East Africa in the 1920s and 1930s as simply stressing the material presence of Italy's colonial world, it is more appropriate to adopt a different critical perspective. One can see the pages of descriptive prose on the creation of new infrastructure, on the building of towns and cities, on the use of mechanized industry not just as providing proof of the reality of empire, but as demonstrating an advance towards modernity that was occurring beyond habitual temporal constraints. The appearance of the environment that was brought rapidly into existence first through the massive exertion of military force and subsequently through the deployment of a vast workforce of Italian and African labour was made to seem as though it was little short of miraculous.[18]

By focusing on the way in which the passage of time is evoked, it becomes clear that the material as a whole conveys a narrative that is essentially

---

[17] For an example of this kind of work, see Roger Griffin, *Modernism and Fascism: The Sense of a Beginning under Mussolini and Hitler* (Basingstoke: Palgrave Macmillan, 2007).

[18] For a discussion of the tropes that accompanied Italian expansionism, see Mia Fuller, *Moderns Abroad: Architecture, Cities and Italian Imperialism* (London and New York: Routledge, 2007), pp. 39–62.

anticipatory in character: by virtue of its precipitously changing physical environment, the empire was presented as a mirror of national life under fascism and as a site where the power of the state, together with the forceful imposition of the structures of modern world, could be experienced to the full. The awe-inspiring transformation of the landscape of the colonies encouraged a faith in the inevitability of the material advantages that would accrue from territorial aggrandizement as well as a belief in the ultimate purpose of the expansionist path on which the nation had embarked. The visual and verbal images of the colonial world invited their viewer not only to look upon what had actually been achieved, but to anticipate the coming of a new type of society.

The utopianism that can be seen throughout this material is accompanied by another series of temporal associations, but these associations point backwards rather than forwards; though much of the book and magazine culture of the time anticipated a world to come, it was haunted to a remarkable degree by nostalgia for the ancient past. In Libya, as in mainland Italy, the remains of Roman buildings and monuments were meticulously restored and in all parts of the empire, as in Italy itself, attributes of Roman architecture were sedulously imitated. The promotion of the belief that modern Italy was *visibly* haunted by the example of Rome and that for centuries the inheritance of antiquity had been discarded or repressed served to fuel the conviction that Italians were involved in a concentrated process of time and that it was their duty to regain what was 'rightfully' theirs.

It is by looking at the recurrence of familiar concepts, at the similarity of modes of perception and at the use of the same literary constructs that one can witness a pattern of approaches to temporality emerging with startling clarity. But the most important question to ask is how this vision of temporality was used as a means of coercing the subject communities of Italian colonialism. A crucial object of inquiry, in other words, concerns the way in which the inhabitants of North and East Africa were positioned in relation to the vision that lay at the heart of Italian imperialism. In the 1930s, as the expansionist drive of the regime gathered momentum, as Italy consolidated its hold over Libya and prepared for the invasion of Ethiopia, the representation of the indigenous cultures of those parts of Africa over which Italy claimed the right to govern served as a means of emphasizing the new world that fascist Italy claimed it was in the process of creating.

All Italian representations in the interwar years of the indigenous community of Libya, its culture and its religion were in some way concerned with time. As Italian officials or observers either travelled through the country or sought to make sense of their experiences there and the role of the colonial mission of which they were in some capacity a part, they reflected upon the degree of 'civilization' which in their view the Arab-Berber population of Libya had attained, they speculated on the notion of progress that animated the indigenous society and they thought about the connection between the sacred and the profane as they considered the rituals and daily practices that defined the collective life that they saw in Tripoli and Benghazi and in the towns and villages of the interior. Italian commentators painted a picture of a community that was, putatively, in the grip of a belief system that promoted immobility over progress, acceptance of the world as it was over the desire for change.[19] For example, the influential colonial official Angelo Piccioli developed in his writings an interpretation of Arab-Berber society in Libya as reaching its peak with the building of the most impressive mosques of Tripoli but then failing to find the intellectual dynamism to go beyond past achievements and becoming satisfied with the repetition of the same forms, patterns and figurations. Recounting his journey to Ghadames, in the interior, he encouraged his reader to believe that he had entered a space where the spirit of Islam, unsusceptible to the changes that dictated the restless evolution of European nations, could be felt in its most concentrated form.[20]

All commentators who wrote on Libya and East Africa in the 1920s and 1930s asserted that the coming of fascism represented both an immediate rupture with the political tradition that had preceded it and the certainty that it would reshape society so fundamentally that the nation's and the colonies' sense of time would be altered forever. If the indigenous communities in Tripolitania or Cyrenaica had, supposedly, lost a sense of dynamism, then fascism, by contrast, brought with it a wholly new means of conceptualizing time. In the publications of the interwar period, one witnesses how Italy's overseas territories become involved – at the very least rhetorically – in a messianic understanding of time: in place of the notion of time as an undifferentiated continuum, one finds a narrative of decline and renewal, and in place of an acceptance of things as they are, one finds the collective desire to move to a common goal.

The brutality with which fascist Italy sought to expand its empire and to suppress resistance to the new colonial order that it aimed to establish has been extensively documented and it is an issue that continually needs to be

---

[19] Angelo Piccioli, *La porta magica del Sahara* (Tripoli: Libreria Editrice Minerva, 1931).

[20] On the work of Piccioli, see Loredana Polezzi, 'Aristocrats, Geographers, Reporters ... Travelling through "Italian Africa" in the 1930s', in *Cultural Encounters: European Travel Writing in the 1930s*, ed. by Charles Burdett and Derek Duncan (New York and Oxford: Berghahn Books, 2003), pp. 187–204.

addressed from a range of perspectives.[21] One means, however, of gaining a deeper understanding of the motivation behind the violence that characterized the most advanced stages of Italian expansionism is to look at the utopianism, with its promise to create a magnificent future, that underlay the drive to create a vast empire across Africa and the Middle East. In much of the writing of those who participated at a high level in the administration of Italy's colonies and in that of those who observed its workings at close quarters, the use of inhumane methods was fully justified in the transformation of Italy's overseas territories into the mirror of national life under fascism. The people who wrote with such eloquence on the infrastructure and architecture of the colonies, on the need to convince the indigenous population of the wisdom of cooperating with the imperial power, were the same people who wrote, without any sense of contradiction, about the 'pacification' of Cyrenaica and about the ferocious suppression of resistance to Italian rule in Ethiopia. In the writing of a figure like Graziani, commander of Italian forces in Libya and subsequently the first Viceroy of Ethiopia, the systematic use of violence was fully justified if the imminent accession to the new reality promised by fascism was to be achieved. The brutal endeavour to impose an ideal society and a new notion of time depended on a fanatical belief in the right to impose one vision of society over another.[22]

The Legacy of Empire

The historian Angelo Del Boca has defined the Italian empire as a creation that was born late and died early; in other words, Italy was attempting to expand its colonial possessions at a time when the empires of other Western European countries were already beginning to show the signs of what would be their inevitable dissolution, while the weakness of the foundations of the Italian empire was revealed by the very rapidity of its collapse.[23] When one considers the nature of the ambition that lay behind Italian aggrandizement in the early part of the twentieth century, it is perhaps not surprising that the attempt to refashion the very nature of consciousness, to instil a belief in an

---

[21] For a recent analysis of documentation of the brutality that accompanied the war in Libya before the advent of fascism, see Pierre Schill, *Réveiller l'archive d'une guerre coloniale* (Ivry-sur-Seine: CreaphisEditions, 2018).

[22] For a longer discussion on the manipulation of time in the discourse of Italian expansionism, see Charles Burdett, 'Italian Fascism, Messianic Eschatology and the Representation of Libya', *Politics, Religion and Ideology*, 11.1 (2010), 3–25.

[23] Angelo Del Boca, 'Impero', in *I luoghi della memoria: simboli e miti dell'Italia unita*, ed. by Mario Isnenghi (Rome: Laterza, 1996), pp. 417–37.

Figure 13.1 – Example of the Italian presence in Addis Ababa.
Photograph by Gianmarco Mancosu, 2015.

altered conception of time and to encourage the transference of a sense of identity from the individual to the collective should have folded so quickly. The examination of the consequences of the way in which an imperial temporality was constructed does not, of course, end with the shattering of the reality of empire: the debris of utopia is material (see Figures 13.1 and 13.2) and it can be observed in the physical presence that Italy has left in large parts of northern and eastern Africa, but that debris is also psychological and it can be seen in the way in which the past continues to play a role in how people think about their environment, their relationship with other people and the very nature of their self-experience.

One of the most significant elements of the writing on the legacy of empire is its concern with the interlocking of a range of temporalities. There are many ways in which one can see how deeply the texts are concerned with the workings of time: an analysis of this feature of the writing will concentrate on both what occurs at the surface of the texts and what takes place less evidently and, in many cases, more ambiguously. If, for example, we concentrate on the chronological sequence of events, then we see that the writing has a great deal to reveal. Indeed, many of the works mentioned earlier on the legacy of empire can be read as a source of information on the arc of the Italian presence in

Figure 13.2 – The Piazza district of Addis Ababa.
Photograph by Gianmarco Mancosu, 2015.

East Africa. Erminia Dell'Oro's *Asmara addio* (Pordenone: Edizioni Studio Tesi, 1988) and Nicky Di Paolo's *Hakim: quasi quasi torno in Eritrea* (Milan: Wichtig Editore, 1994), for example, refer to the history of the first Italian settlers in Eritrea, to the invasion of Ethiopia in 1935, the entry into the Second World War, the rapid collapse of the imperial ambitions of fascist Italy and the slow decline of the Italian community in Eritrea in the wake of the war.[24] Both writers chronicle the period of the British administration of Eritrea from 1941 to 1950 and subsequently the Eritrean war of independence in the wake of Haile Selassie's annexation of the country in 1962. Di Paolo's work, in particular, while focused on the period after the end of the British administration and on the early years of the Eritrean struggle for independence, ranges across the whole history of Italy's involvement in the Horn of Africa. Gabriella Ghermandi's text of 2007, *Regina di fiori e di perle* (Rome, Donzelli) begins later, towards the end of the 1980s, and evokes the atmosphere in Ethiopia in the final years of Mengistu's military dictatorship (1977–91), while through the

[24] For a longer discussion of the work of these writers see, Charles Burdett, 'Transnational Time: Reading Post-War Representations of the Italian Presence in East Africa', *Italian Studies*, 73.3 (2018), 274–88.

stories that are told to Mahlet – the work's central protagonist – it moves back in time to recover the history of the Italian occupation of Ethiopia as it was experienced by those who lived through its different phases.

All of these novels can be read for the information that they convey on the dramatically changing reality of Eritrea and Ethiopia, on the period of peace which followed the Second World War, on the consequences of the Italian occupation of Ethiopia, on the effects of Ethiopia's attempted annexation of Eritrea, and on the spaces of interaction between members of different communities. But an essential part of any reading has to be concerned with the manner in which the writing leads us to develop insights into the way in which deep-laid processes are not simply observed as they unfold across time but operate through people's very mode of perception and cognition. If we approach the texts following this reading strategy, we are inevitably led to question how a social order, with all its inequalities and all its inherent precariousness, is constructed and maintained, and we are also led to question how elements of collapsed social systems return to play upon the psychology of an individual or on the imaginary of a group. We are led to question, in other words, how an agency, thought to belong to the past, continues – with varying moments of intensity – to haunt the present.

In many places, Dell'Oro's *Asmara addio* reveals how the central character, Malena, is imbricated within the social structures that surround her and how perceived changes in the social environment lead to changes of mood and of self-understanding. In describing the gradual dissolution of the Italian community in Eritrea through the eyes of her fictional protagonist, Dell'Oro is not only enumerating a series of emotions and sensations, she is attempting to capture how those affective states reveal the progression of much wider societal developments; or rather, she evokes how one mode of societal organization succeeds another and how the collapse of a recognized social structure carries with it an alteration of collective consciousness. Throughout *Asmara addio*, the sense of a society that is disappearing with bewildering effects on its members is strong and in those passages towards the end of the novel – in the midst of the Eritrean-Ethiopian war – where Malena witnesses the disintegration of the social fabric around her, it is consistently portrayed through the language of haunting – with all the concomitant suggestions of the uncanny, the disquieting and the anxious.

The writing makes us aware of the instability of the individual subject within shifting symbolic or social orders and it encourages us to consider the architecture of concepts and practices that sustains any societal construction. If we ask how Nicky Di Paolo's *Hakim* leads to an enhanced understanding of transnational time, we can say that the work concentrates on the intersection of three national temporalities: first, the aftermath of Italian colonialism;

second, the development of Eritrean national sentiment; and third, the resistance to Ethiopian imperialism. As a work of fiction, the novel communicates the experience of the development of each of these time frames through the way in which the characters perceive one another, through their attempts to understand the sets of cultural norms and practices that define their lives, and through the mutual witnessing of their participation in a chain of events that will lead the principal Eritrean characters of the story towards oblivion. Di Paolo's novel is framed as a work of mourning as the fictional narrator, Marco Delandi, moves between the reality of the present and the evocation of the past. Similarly, the ontological status of the characters changes as the time of the narrative alters; at one moment, they are the agents of the action of the story, at another they are the memories within the mind and emotional history of the narrator-author. Through the act of memory, the novel foregrounds the cultural hybridity of the narrator, the nature of transcultural interchange within Eritrea and the transnational subjectivity of each of the characters.

Posing questions concerning time in the fiction of writers like Dell'Oro or Di Paolo leads to a clear sense of the precariousness of individual identity and its dependence on the impermanent structures that lie outside the self. But questioning how time operates in works that address the legacy of empire also alerts us to how the subject can be haunted by surmounted models of society, aware of the injustices in their framing of categories of race, gender or class, and sensitive to the voices – whether they belong to the living or the dead – of those who have experienced the full force of an inimical social configuration. This means of approaching a text can be exemplified by referring to the mode of narration of Gabriella Ghermandi's *Regina di fiori e di perle*, a text in which the notion of haunting is embedded in the very framework of the story.

The first-person narrator of the novel, Mahlet, grows up in Debre Zeit, close to Addis Ababa, and displays from a young age a gift for listening to the stories of the lives of others. It is this gift that marks her out, in the eyes of Yacob, a relative of advanced years, as suited to the task of gathering the testimonies of those who lived through the Italian occupation of Ethiopia. It is through the encounters that he prepares for her that she hears the stories of the generation of Ethiopians who experienced the invasion of their country. The relationship between Yacob and Mahlet is central to the text and, to begin with, it is based on the telling of the events of the past; yet the novel is anything but a simple accumulation of stories and the relation between the two should be seen less as a device that enables the delivery and reception of stories and more as one that facilitates a discourse on the nature of storytelling. The conversation between the two, though its beginnings are straightforward, becomes increasingly complex and, above all, it continues *after* the death of Yacob: his figuration returns to visit Mahlet in her dreams and she, attempting to make sense of the nature of his communication, struggles with an imperfect understanding of her role as witness, listener, reader and narrator.

The dramatization of the nature of storytelling is important, but no less important is the process of self-realization that Mahlet undergoes. The novel implies throughout that to become meaningful, stories need to be constructed, lived through the psychology of their listener. Many of the stories that are told recount the horror of the Italian occupation of Ethiopia at the very apex of fascism and their effect is to haunt Mahlet with images of the violent imposition of an implacable social order. The vicarious experience of the lives of others and the assumption of the role of narrator of other people's stories inevitably alters Mahlet's sense of selfhood. She becomes aware of how private memory can become public, of how the sustained social violence enacted by the application of the race laws, though a feature of the colonial past, continues to stalk the present in the persistence of attitudes governed by reliance on racial stereotypes. She also becomes aware of how intergenerational transmission is neither direct nor linear and that the full complexity of transnational time is graspable only through narrative.[25]

Questions concerning temporality are at the very basis of the study of the interweaving of the national within the transnational and of how inequalities of power continue to operate within a present that is shot through with the manifold legacies of the past. In societies that have witnessed the effects of colonialism, the transnational assumes a range of specific meanings all of which can be explored further by examining representations that are literary, non-literary and visual in character. The analysis sketched above refers only to the Italian presence in Eritrea and in Ethiopia and it refers only to a limited selection of texts. However, the corpus to which these texts belong can be used as a means of analysing the working of social structures, how these structures imprison individuals through their operation and through their direction of habits of perception and interpretation. The corpus, as a whole, allows us to see how social processes move through time and how modes of apprehension are subject to alteration.

---

[25] For further comment on *Regina di fiori e di perle*, see the chapter by Jennifer Burns in this volume. For a recent work of fiction on the Italian occupation of Ethiopia, see Ethiopian-American writer Maaza Mengiste's novel *The Shadow King* (New York: W. W. Norton and Company, 2019). For an analysis of the representation of the occupation in Ethiopian literature, see Sara Marzagora, 'Nationalism: The Italian Occupation in Amharic Literature and Political Thought', in *The Horn of Africa and Italy: Colonial, Postcolonial and Transnational Cultural Encounters*, ed. by Simone Brioni and Shimelis Bonsa Gulema (Oxford and New York: Peter Lang, 2018), pp. 141–67.

It is perhaps not surprising that literary evocations of empire offer some of the most complex inquiries into the functioning of time. Indeed, it is true to say that through the conventionalities of literary communication, we see characters caught up in a web of transnational temporalities with effects that have a profound impact on their grasp of the realities that surround them. One might even go further and suggest that it is within the representation of haunting that the instability of temporal distinctions is at its most intense. We do not have to look far to find representations of something that is presumed to be past or surmounted continuing to exert an insidious or unacknowledged presence, or to discover the intrusion of the spectral within the real or the sense of reality losing its everyday contours and time beginning to seem – to adapt the language of Derrida – *out of joint*.[26] Within the fiction of writers like Dell'Oro, Di Paolo or Ghermandi, the principal characters witness the persistence of voices from the past, shifts in the sense of their own subjectivity, the feeling of their autonomy being compromised. The intensity of the awareness of temporal dislocation that the texts represent leads the reader to question the experience of transnational time, its modalities, its challenges to the experience of personhood and its continual merging of the past, present and future.

[26] See Jacques Derrida, *Spectres of Marx*, trans. by Peggy Kamuf (New York and London: Routledge, 1994).

14

Transnational Italian Comics

Graphic Journalism across Memories and Cultures*

Barbara Spadaro

Drawing is a primary visual language, essential for communication and expression. In our globalizing world, we communicate more and more in a visual way.[1]

Being able to decipher a story that's coming at you in words and images is crucial. It's part of functioning in society today.[2]

Comics is a narrative medium that combines words and images.[3] This combination enables multiple forms of storytelling which make comics one of the most dynamic media of our times. A wealth of authors of different backgrounds are currently experimenting with forms, themes and platforms

---

* My thanks to Michele Foschini and Lorenzo Bolzoni at Bao Publishing and to Takoua Ben Mohamed and Beccogiallo for permission to use images in this chapter.

[1] https://drawingthetimes.com/about/ [accessed 22 November 2019].

[2] Hillary Chute, *Why Comics? From Underground to Everywhere* (New York: Harper, 2017), p. 23.

[3] 'There is a peculiar grammatical glitch in the word Comics: is it or are they a singular or a plural phenomenon?' J. W. T. Mitchell, 'Comics as Media: Afterword', *Critical Inquiry*, 40.3 (2014), 255–65 (p. 256). In line with Scott McCloud's influential definition of Comics ('plural in form, used with a singular verb', *Understanding Comics* (New York: Harper Perennial: 1994), p. 9), many anglophone scholars support the usage of a singular verb when referring to the medium. However, in the wider world of comics authors, readers and practitioners, comics is used both in singular and plural form. In Italian the medium *fumetto* requires the singular verb and exists also in the plural *fumetti*. This chapter reflects the fluid usage of the term within the wider, plurilingual comics world.

for comics, and this is taking the medium well beyond the adventures of exotic characters and superheroes traditionally associated with comic strips and commercial magazines. Over the last few decades, the rise of the graphic novel and of graphic journalism has shown the potential of the medium to enter new spaces in the cultural industry, to enable new forms of storytelling and to attract new communities of authors and readers. In 1992 Art Spiegelman became the first comic book author to receive a Pulitzer Prize for his *Maus: A Survivor's Tale* – the first comic about a family of Holocaust survivors and the first to become a global phenomenon. Since then, the language of comics has attracted new readers, publishers and authors: graphic novels are featured in reviews, libraries and bookstores, and regularly shortlisted for prestigious awards such as the Man Booker Prize in the UK and the Premio Strega in Italy. Newspapers and media platforms increasingly feature graphic reportage and animations to engage readers with facts and stories from around the world. Comics are also increasingly adopted in research and education projects to facilitate knowledge exchange among participants and reach out to wider audiences. Museums, art galleries and institutions curate comics exhibitions and cultural events. To acknowledge this dynamism of comics across media, the term 'graphic narratives' has recently been proposed by scholars of the expanding field of comics studies.[4]

Crossing boundaries between texts and images, languages and cultures, testimony and fiction, comics have always been much more than just 'funnies' or the chronicles of deeds of superheroes that have long been associated with the medium, particularly in the anglophone world. In this respect, Hillary Chute points out that the English term 'comics' is biased, evoking the early humoristic genre that became popular in the nineteenth century in newspaper strips and commercial magazines.[5] The Italian term *fumetto* (which literally translates with 'little puff of smoke') sounds much less connotative than 'comics', and encompasses a wealth of forms and genres of graphic narratives developed by Italian authors and publishers over time – from the short *striscia* [strip] to the book-length *romanzo a fumetti* and the non-fictional *fumetto di realtà*. However, English terms such as 'graphic novel', 'graphic journalism', 'webcomics' and 'blog' (*a fumetti*) are also now fully adopted in Italian, highlighting the dominance of English across different comics scenes in the twenty-first century. Furthermore, social media and web platforms have enabled new forms of graphic storytelling such as blogs and webcomics,

---

[4] Hillary Chute and Patrick Jagoda, 'Introduction', *Critical Inquiry*, special issue 'Comics and Media', 40.3 (2014), 1–10.

[5] Chute, *Why Comics?*, p. 11

which have been transforming the practices of self-production and circulation of comics across underground and commercial scenes.[6]

As comics and authors push national, linguistic and formal borders, the Italian comics scene of the twenty-first century thrives in multiple, transnational directions. Rather than mapping the full spectrum of this movement, this chapter focuses on graphic journalism as one of the most dynamic genres of comics since the 2000s, and on two authors who show the centrality of memory and translation in the development of the Italian *fumetto*: Zerocalcare and Takoua Ben Mohamed. The two authors have pushed the boundaries of comic book genres, experimenting with different formats of comics (the vignette, the short story, the graphic reportage) and with an expanding range of media (printed books, graphic blogs, social media, digital platforms). Their work represents specific examples of the mobility of (Italian) memory and culture and their constant process of translation. Why is the comics medium particularly suited to convey this mobility? What do we mean by transnational and transcultural processes? Which are the narrative strategies developed by comics authors? Why understand them as forms of translation? The chapter aims to answer these questions by exploring Zerocalcare's *Kobane Calling* and Takoua Ben Mohamed's graphic journalism. Firstly, because their comics emerge from transnational trajectories: whether in terms of migration, travel, imaginaries or political participation – or indeed a combination of the four – these comics show that Italian culture is produced inside and outside Italy, in many languages and by people of different backgrounds. Second, these comics show the variety of Italian cultures and subcultures – whether local, political, religious or generational – in the backgrounds of the authors. Both Zerocalcare and Ben Mohamed identify with a series of local and transnational communities, and their comics convey the multiple acts of translation with which they navigate the world. 'We are all practising members of our own cultures, subcultures and micro-subcultures (our private imagination), each looking for suitable translations', says Shaun Tan, one of the most imaginative and acclaimed visual artists of our times. 'Illustrated books are very good at crossing divides'.[7] This chapter examines how comics enable acts of translation – and indeed transformation – of memory and culture.

First, what do we mean by memory? Memory is a creative process that connects past, present and future shaping the processes of identification

---

[6] Lorenzo Ghetti, 'Dal digitale all'universale. Ragionare sul fumetto online per discutere il fumetto tradizionale', *Hamelin*, 42 (2016), 43–53.

[7] Harriet Earle and Shaun Tan, 'Strange Migrations: An Essay/Interview with Shaun Tan', *Journal of Postcolonial Writing*, 52.4 (2016), 385–98 (p. 386).

of individuals – in other words, their ideas of identity and belonging. An essential component of culture, memory changes over time and depending on its sociocultural context: memory and culture are always on the move. One way to understand this mobility is to look at how memory 'travels' through a series of mental, medial and social processes.[8] For example, to look at how certain forms of memory – written records, say, such as fieldwork notes or letters, photographs, artworks, recorded interviews, but also the immaterial, sensorial memories of an individual – are 'translated' into a medium, in this case a comic book, in order to engage the cognitive and narrative process of new potential carriers of the memory. Scholars in memory studies have described this movement as a relentless process of mediation and remediation of memory content that unfolds not only *across* but also *beyond* cultures:[9] a transcultural process that challenges and transcends old (i.e., eighteenth-century) separatist and homogenizing ideas of cultures.[10] This mobility is constitutive of memory and culture: it is a constant, vital process that enables their expression, communication and transformation at multiple levels. In a mobile and multilingual world, this testifies to what Loredana Polezzi calls 'the translational fabric of cultural practice (and also of everyday life)'.[11] Combining words and images, comics enable multimodal forms of mediation-translation of memories that illuminate the transcultural nature of the cognitive and narrative processes of our times.[12]

This chapter explores the processes of mediation-translation of memory in the graphic journalism of Zerocalcare and Takoua Ben Mohamed. It also introduces other groundbreaking figures of a globalizing comics scene in which the two named authors are increasingly acknowledged. The first section outlines instances of graphic journalism as a genre that extends the boundaries of comics and media to represent the full complexity of the experiences

[8] Astrid Erll and Ann Rigney, eds, *Mediation, Remediation, and the Dynamics of Cultural Memory* (Berlin and New York: Walter de Gruyter, 2009).

[9] Astrid Erll, 'Travelling Memory', *Parallax*, 17.4 (2011), 4–18; Astrid Erll, 'Media and the Dynamics of Memory: From Cultural Paradigms to Transcultural Mediation', in *Handbook of Culture and Memory*, ed. by Brady Wagoner (Oxford and New York: Oxford University Press, 2018), pp. 305–24.

[10] Wolfgang Welsch, 'Transculturality – the Puzzling Form of Cultures Today', in *Spaces of Culture: City, Nation, World*, ed. Mike Featherstone and Scott Lash (London: Sage, 1999), pp. 194–213.

[11] Loredana Polezzi, 'Translation', in *Translating Cultures: A Glossary* (Liverpool: Liverpool University Press, forthcoming).

[12] Barbara Spadaro, 'The Transcultural Comics of Takoua Ben Mohamed: Memory and Translation *a Fumetti*', *Modern Italy*, Special Issue: 'Transcultural Italy', ed. by Brigid Maher and Rita Wilson, 25.2 (2020), 177–197.

of cultural translation of authors who travel across languages and cultures. In this context, the graphic journalism of Takoua Ben Mohamed represents an example of translation of the memories of Muslim women in Italy into a series of multilingual comics. The second part of the chapter explores Zerocalcare's *Kobane Calling*,[13] a recent book-length graphic reportage from Syria that stems from the transformation of the Italian underground comics scene, its transnational networks and transcultural memory processes.

Graphic Journalism across Media and Languages

I was furious at American journalists, and the American style of journalism in which I had been trained. I realized that you could write 'facts' about something and still not tell what is really going on.[14]

Graphic journalism is an expanding genre of comics, initiated by authors committed to reporting on the complexities of the world. The 'slow journalism' of Joe Sacco is one of the most influential attempts to develop news reporting in comics to subvert the consumption of facts, people and places, and to translate stories across cultural and social borders. Sacco's books reporting from conflict zones intend to represent the multidimensionality of encounters on the ground and to raise awareness of the processes of translation embedded in the production of any account from a distant reality. The visual and verbal intensity of the style aims to engage the readers in slow-looking, participatory reading practices.[15] By pushing the boundaries of comics as an entertaining, easy-reading medium and those of the news report as a factual, linear genre, Sacco has developed graphic journalism as a narrative form that acknowledges the process of listening, bewilderment and translation embedded in the reporter's experience of the world. This creative and intellectual tension is shared by many other comic authors who resist the consumption of 'facts', stories and places in the accelerated media ecologies of our times.

Graphic journalism increasingly conveys the political and aesthetic stands of authors and independent media from across the world, including Italy. In Ravenna, for example, the *Komikazen Festival Internazionale del fumetto di realtà*, curated by Gianluca Costantini and Elettra Stamboulis between 2005 and 2016, represented a seminal hub of the transnational circuits and

---

[13] Zerocalcare, *Kobane Calling* (Chivasso: Bao, 2016).

[14] Joe Sacco and W. J. T. Mitchell, 'Public Conversation', *Critical Inquiry*, 40.3 (2014), 53–70 (p. 54).

[15] Sacco and Mitchell, 'Public Conversation'. A classic example is Joe Sacco, *Palestine* (Seattle: Fantagraphics Books, 2001).

publishing ventures for graphic news in Europe. Costantini considers himself a human rights activist and his work aims to enhance the visibility of events and actors marginalized by Europe's visual and political culture. His graphic *reportages* ['news reports' in French and Italian] are often assemblages of images, texts, drawings, photographs that experiment with the multidimensionality of the comic framework and invite reading in all directions. Over two decades of collaboration with printed and digital media, Costantini and Stamboulis have published their work in underground art magazines, mainstream platforms such as *Le Monde Diplomatique* and, more recently, in a book that celebrates their influential work.[16]

Graphic narratives are increasingly developed by independent media as a tool to subvert the Anglocentrism and polarization of the media industries. The platforms Graphic News (started by the Italian comic book artist Pietro Scarnera) and Drawing the Times (founded by the Dutch graphic journalist Eva Hilhorst) are committed to 'inform, entertain, engage and challenge readers on global issues and local stories'; the Tunisian platform of investigative journalism Inkyfada integrates graphic narratives in its research on storytelling and participatory reading experiences, whilst PositiveNegatives focuses on social and humanitarian issues.[17] These examples demonstrate the increasing political relevance of visual storytelling as a tool to establish encounters and empathy and to resist the dehumanizing impetus of mainstream media discourses.[18] They also help us to understand some of the key instances that underlie the production of Takoua Ben Mohamed and Zerocalcare. What are the creative strategies developed by these authors?

The Graphic Journalism of Takoua Ben Mohamed

Takoua Ben Mohamed came to Italy in the 1990s as a child refugee fleeing the Tunisian regime and started to draw comics to communicate with the multilingual classmates and Italian teachers of her school in the eastern periphery of Rome. Comics helped her to make contact with people, establish empathy, raise questions, exchange Arabic and Italian words, and later to represent the experience of the Muslim girls and women of her circles. An exemplar of a young, urban and networked generation that produces and shares

---

[16] Gianluca Costantini, *Fedele alla linea* (Padua: Beccogiallo 2017).

[17] Graphic News, https://www.graphic-news.com/info/?lang=en; Drawing the Times, https://drawingthetimes.com; Inkyfada, https://inkyfada.com/fr/a-propos/; PositiveNegatives, https://positivenegatives.org/ [accessed 22 November 2019].

[18] Kathy Burrell and Kathrin Horschelmann, 'Perilous Journeys: Visualising the Racialised "Refugee Crisis"', *Antipode*, 1 (2019), 45–66.

millions of digital images everyday as forms of self-narration,[19] Ben Mohamed tried different forms of digital self-publishing while pursuing her studies in animation. Her work stemmed from an urgent need to communicate the experience of living between different cultures and to change the representation of Muslims in the mainstream media. Rather than building on the established tradition of the Italian *fumetto*, the Franco-Belgian *bande dessinée* or Tunisian satirical cartoons – all unfamiliar in the social and cultural environment of her upbringing – Ben Mohamed's style translates memories of the US and Japanese Manga TV series screened on Italian commercial TV in the 1990s, such as Matt Groening's *The Simpsons*. Because her work is more intent on changing the representation of Muslim women in Western media than on developing formal or aesthetic aspects of comics, Ben Mohamed identifies herself as a journalist rather than a comic book artist. Her graphic narratives have taken a variety of different forms: digital platforms, exhibitions, 'blog a fumetti', until the book-length narrative featured in her first printed volume, *Sotto il velo* (2016), and the recent memoir *La Rivoluzione dei gelsomini* (2018). Through all these projects Ben Mohamed has developed her own style of visual storytelling and a distinctive profile as media professional and social media influencer. Her trajectory highlights the expanding circuits of production and consumption of comics in Italy, whilst her ability to engage very diversified audiences demonstrates the potential of comics as a tool for self-expression, communication and education beyond language barriers and drawing skills.[20]

Il fumetto intercultura, Takoua Ben Mohamed's first project, began at a community event in the Centocelle Mosque in Rome, where she started making comics on the everyday experience of Muslim women wearing the *hijab* in Italy. The development of the project tracks changes in the self-perception of young Muslims in Italy after the Arab revolutions in North Africa and the Middle East[21] and parallel shifts in Italian imaginaries of the Islamic world.[22] Some of the stories feature characters of Chinese, Roma and African background, to report on the racist and cultural stereotypes that shape the everyday experience and self-perception of young people in Italy,

---

[19] Nicholas Mirzoeff, *How to See the World* (London: Pelican, 2015).

[20] Barbara Spadaro, 'The Transcultural Comics of Takoua Ben Mohamed: Memory and Translation *a fumetti*', *Modern Italy*, 25.2 (2020), 177–97.

[21] Ivana Acocella, Renata Pepicelli and Katia Cigliuti, eds, *Giovani musulmane in Italia: percorsi biografici e pratiche quotidiane* (Bologna: il Mulino, 2015); Renata Pepicelli, *Il velo nell'Islam. Storia, politica, estetica* (Rome: Carocci, 2012).

[22] Charles Burdett, *Italy, Islam and the Islamic World: Representations and Reflections from 9/11 to the Arab Uprisings* (Oxford: Peter Lang, 2016).

and to encompass the variety of social and cultural tensions around ideas of Italian citizenship and belonging. For example, the vignette 'The most absurd questions about the veil' (Figure 14.1: 'Le domande più assurde sul velo') illustrates the experience of being the object of projections, prejudices, sometimes just the naïve curiosity of non-Muslims towards Islamic culture, and the complex feelings raised by these constant interrogations. The vignette features a girl in *hijab* who metamorphoses into a three-headed creature as a series of mundane questions are thrown at her from all directions, filling the whole space of the panel. By emphasizing the girl's exasperation and the strength required to resist the overwhelming flood of questions, this comic conveys feelings of resistance to an environment charged with explosive tensions.

By translating into comics the everyday clashes produced by the visibility of Islamic culture in Italy, Ben Mohamed has produced a tool of self-awareness and communication for both Muslim and non-Muslim audiences, opening new spaces for exchange and identification. First published on Facebook and later on a dedicated platform, the project *Il fumetto intercultura* has expanded into a series of small exhibitions and workshops for intercultural education that travel across Italy and beyond via multiple circuits of cultural activists, academics and journalists – from Islamic networks to academic projects such as the exhibition 'Beyond Borders: Transnational Italy'.[23]

Ben Mohamed's distinctive style is driven by a constant search for immediacy to facilitate empathy and the reader's identification with the characters of her stories. At the same time, a continuous dynamic of embodiment and disembodiment with the protagonist of most of the stories, the *hijab*-wearing 'personaggino', explores the clashes and contradictions of her multiple belongings.[24] Whilst the early comics that she produced for community events aimed to convey the memories of Muslims in the West, other projects progressively expressed Ben Mohamed's individual positioning, questioning and feelings towards her multilingual and multicultural background. This process of (self-)identification is apparent through the languages and memories featured in the comics. One of the early stories

---

[23] *Beyond Borders: Transnational Italy/Oltre i confini: Italia transnazionale* is the interactive exhibition of the 'Transnationalizing Modern Languages' (TML) research project, which has featured the comics of Takoua Ben Mohamed in Rome, London, New York, Melbourne, Addis Ababa and at the Italian Cultural Institute of Tunis (2016–18).

[24] Barbara Spadaro, 'Hijab, corpi e spazi transculturali: un graphic blog di Takoua Ben Mohamed', *Roots/Routes: Research on Visual Culture*, 6.22 (2016), http://www.roots-routes.org/?p=18736 [accessed 25 September 2019].

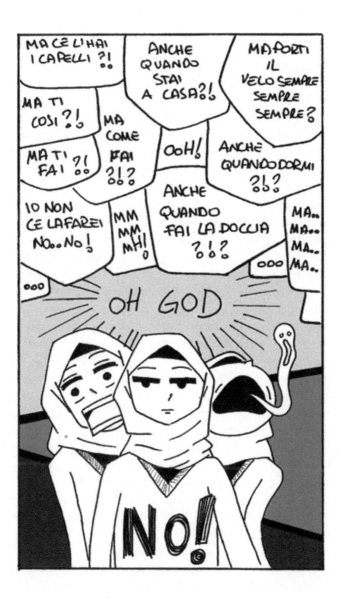

Figure 14. 1 – Takoua Ben Mohamed, 'Le domande più assurde sul velo'.
Courtesy of the author and BeccoGiallo Editore, Italy.

of *Il fumetto intercultura,* 'In the bus stop [*sic*]', sets out to represent an episode of linguaphobia that would potentially be familiar to any Muslim woman.[25] Two women in *hijab* speak Arabic at a bus stop and become the object of a series of speculative and racist comments from two white men. The latter are blind to the fact that despite the Muslim outfits, the women may, in fact, speak and understand their language all too well. At the end of the story it is revealed that they do, causing great embarrassment to the male characters. To emphasize the universal nature of this experience for Muslim women, Ben Mohamed put the dialogue between the two female characters in Modern Standard Arabic rather than in the dialects actually spoken in everyday life – such as the Moroccan of the women who reported the episode to her or the Tunisian that she herself speaks. In this comic, the Modern Standard Arabic translates the experience of two specific women into a story that may be shared regardless of nationality or background by any Muslim woman and, thanks to the immediacy of the comic book medium, also by non-Arabic readers who may embrace this story as their own. It would be possible to see this process as an example of remediation of memory content; yet to acknowledge the full complexity of a multimodal process enabled by the visual and written devices of a multilingual comic, we should consider its translational dimension.

Ben Mohamed's comics feature her multiple linguistic and cultural repertoires, which include Tunisian, broken English and French, and references to the multiple pop (sub)cultures of her generation. Whilst the Modern Standard Arabic of 'In the bus stop' was meant to encompass the experience of any Muslim woman in Europe regardless of nationality or background, the Roman slang increasingly featured in her work identifies a *tunisina de' Roma* [a Tunisian from Rome], as she puts it in Roman vernacular. Her first book features 'la mia vita con il velo per le strade di Roma' [my life with the veil in the streets of Rome; back cover].[26] The book illustrates the protagonist's search for self-determination through a series of everyday situations common to any young woman of her age, such as shopping and interactions with neighbours, potential employers and people in the street. In going out into the street in her *hijab*, the young woman experiences judgements and unwanted comments from a variety of people, including religious fundamentalists, and also white secular men and women of various social and ideological backgrounds.

In the background of the panels, bunches of anonymous and evil-eyed figures emanate strings of BLABLABLA from their large mouths to represent

---

[25] https://ilfumettointercultura.wordpress.com/2016/04/06/in-the-bus-stop/ [accessed 17 October 2019].

[26] Takoua Ben Mohamed, *Sotto il velo* (Padua: Beccogiallo, 2016).

the gazing and unwanted comments that underlie the life of the protagonist and her search for self-determination. These recurrent background figures, which act as narrative devices for this book-length project, are an example of Ben Mohamed's ability to maintain the simplicity of her narrative style while exploring the multimodal language of comics. The caricatural devices of comics underline the desire, curiosity and frustrations in the everyday encounters represented in the stories. The self-reflective attitude adopted by the protagonist throughout the book highlights the relational nature of processes of identification that combine mutual stereotypes, memories, emotions and experiences. This is an early and recurrent theme in Ben Mohamed's work, and it informs the way in which she represents transculturality: a series of encounters, translations, clashes and mutual reflections that challenge exclusive ideas of cultural and national belonging (for Muslims and non-Muslims, Italians and Tunisians), expose their performative nature and affect their reconfiguration. *Sotto il velo* shows the development of the unidentifiable Manga characters in *hijab* of the early stories into Takoua, the cartoon alter ego of the author. This process of (self-)identification begins by presenting the book as a fictionalized version of the memories of the author, and is accomplished by featuring the language that she speaks.

Sotto il velo is constructed as a fictional autobiography in which Ben Mohamed represents her own prejudices, desires, disappointments and *scleri* [emotional turmoil, in Roman slang]. The vernacular nature of comics allows Ben Mohamed to introduce an element that she considers important in the self-perception of Muslims of her generation in Italy, namely their accents and slang, which show their rootedness in the specific urban and regional contexts of their upbringing. *Sotto il velo* features the spoken language of the author and the vernacular expressions that identify her as a *tunisina de' Roma* and a Muslim woman sensitive to global issues such as the burkini controversy, the rise of ISIS and mounting Islamophobia. This book still responds to the documentary urgency of the author's earlier projects: it still visualizes challenges and translates memories of Muslims and non-Muslims into comics. Yet it does so by foregrounding an individual rather than collective self – one that is located in Rome and embodied in Takoua, and that draws from the personal memories, emotions and the full linguistic repertoire of the author as she responds to global issues. The episode entitled 'Black fashion style (*ma non per tutti*)' [Black fashion style – (*not for everybody though*)] uses a couple of very Roman expressions such as 'Aoo – paro una de l'Isis!' [Hey – I look like I belong to ISIS!] to expose and subvert the pervasiveness of representations of young Muslims as foreign fighters in Syria (Figures 14.2 and 14.3). The translanguaging with English in the title references the global circuits of fashion, mirroring – indeed ironically reversing – the global circulation of

Figure 14.2 – Takoua Ben Mohamed, *Sotto il velo*. Courtesy of the author and BeccoGiallo Editore, Italy.

images of ISIS fighters. As these elements short-circuit into the subjectivity of the author, they provoke an eruption of Roman slang and facial expressions.

Sotto il velo marks the definitive embodiment of the *personaggino*, or the full development of Ben Mohamed's comic book alter ego. Whilst explicitly drawing from the personal experiences of the author, the book captures

Figure 14.3 – Takoua Ben Mohamed, *Sotto il velo*. Courtesy of the author and BeccoGiallo Editore, Italy.

aspects that are relevant to the trajectories of (Muslim) women of her generation confronted with the intersecting challenges of gender, religious, cultural and linguistic heteronormativity. The book represents different aspects of the struggle of young women for independence and self-determination – for example, how they intersect in a job market which requires single, childless, physically attractive, flexible workers with no religious connotation. While episodes such as *Colloquio – lo sclero di ogni donna* [Job interview – the emotional turmoil of any woman] foreground these aspects, many other episodes – and indeed the conclusion of the book – underline the value of education, motivation and intellectual development in the personal and professional trajectory of the author. The latter are recurrent themes in Ben Mohamed's production as she intensifies the development of her work as a form of self-narration, whether through the educational and cultural events of the *Il fumetto intercultura* project, her subsequent blog and book, or her more recent graphic memoir.[27] This creative and professional trajectory towards the memoir illuminates an important development of the contemporary Italian comics scene, namely the multiplication of graphic narratives by authors of diverse backgrounds that document, often for the first time, transnational trajectories marginalized by the history of Italy. Zerocalcare, the second author featured in this chapter, traces a different but equally illuminating trajectory across the borders between memoir and graphic journalism.

Rebibbia Calling Kobane: Proximity, Distance and Transcultural Memory
Kobane Calling is an example of graphic reportage and of the productive nature of memory and translation. This is the first book-length project (out of two shorter reportages published in the magazine *Internazionale* in 2015) by an author active in Italy's underground and punk scene since the early 2000s and whose blog *a fumetti* – https://www.zerocalcare.it, opened in 2011 – is now considered the manifesto of a generation. Inspired by French graphic bloggers' autobiographies with a breadth of social and generational portraits,[28] the blog – and the books subsequently published, gathering the stories – has progressively conveyed the development of an author profoundly grounded in the scene of the *centri sociali* [independent cultural centres] and occupied spaces of Rome. Zerocalcare and this background – particularly his home neighbourhood of Rebibbia, a Roman suburb commonly identified with the local prison – are in fact inseparable. Many devices in the work of this author – notably his ability to combine different registers of Italian and Roman jargon – make this clear. More than a backdrop, Rebibbia appears in the stories as a spirit character in the form of a mammoth, which embodies with subversive irony and pride the only archaeological glory excavated in Rebibbia – a mammoth skeleton from the Pleistocene. Representing at once family and community, Rebibbia is the bulwark of Zerocalcare's social and

---

[27] Takoua Ben Mohamed, *La rivoluzione dei gelsomini* (Padua: Beccogiallo, 2018).
[28] Sara Pavan, *Il potere sovversivo della carta. Dieci anni di fumetti autoprodotti in Italia* (Milan: Agenzia X, 2014), p. 133.

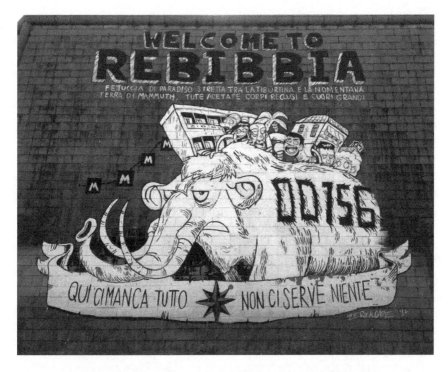

Figure 14.4 – Zerocalcare's mammoth mural in Rebibbia, Rome.
Photograph by the author.

emotional self, and this feeling of belonging is questioned throughout *Kobane Calling* (Figure 14.4).

The book has been translated into English and has fuelled the author's popularity outside as well as inside Italy. Zerocalcare has recently been celebrated with a major bilingual (Italian and English) exhibition at the Museum of the Arts of the Twenty-First Century (MAXXI) in Rome. The exhibition catalogue acknowledges an author who has visualized in comics the experience of a generation growing up in the wealthy decades of the 1980s and subsequently faced with the dissolution of the Western narratives of social and cultural progress.[29] His popularity has been attributed to nostalgia for the positive emotions attached to pop icons of his generation: the heroes of *Star Wars* and Disney, science fiction, TV series, Japanese Manga and anime, as well as the European philosophers featured in the national curriculum of

---

[29] Zerocalcare and Michele Foschini, *Zerocalcare: Scavare fossati nutrire coccodrilli: 10 novembre 2018–10 marzo 2019* (Chivasso: Bao, 2018).

his generation.[30] This gallery of positive icons represents a form of resistance to the uncertainties of the present and the loss of the future for those Italians confronted with the grim reality of neoliberalism and the marginalization of their social and political values. Zerocalcare's work constitutes an act of translation of the memories of this generation into comics.

Kobane Calling represents an interesting turning point in the self-reflective process of the author as a carrier of this generational memory, which in this graphic reportage is acknowledged as Western and situated, yet mobile. Exploring his own bewilderment by using his creative tools, Zerocalcare represents the possibility of navigating the feelings of uncertainty and marginalization projected by this generation – and by an expanding community of readers – on the present and the future in a globalizing world. The narrative strategies developed in *Kobane Calling* allow us to understand transcultural mobility as a productive process of memory and translation that is highly imaginative and emotional and invests the author at multiple levels. The multimodality of the comic book medium enables the representation of the verbal, visual and aural devices of these translation processes.

As mentioned, the graphic journalism *à la* Joe Sacco explores the tensions between supposedly factual, objectified realities and the inevitably subjective, fragmented, imaginative nature of visual storytelling. *Kobane Calling* makes this point explicit: the subtitle *Facce, parole, scarabocchi da Rebibbia al confine turco-siriano* [Faces, words and scribbles from Rebibbia to the Turkish-Syrian border] indicates from the outset that this book explores a set of political and emotional tensions rather than pretending to explain objectively specific facts or places. However, the book has been criticized by specialists for an excessive emphasis, within the narrative, on the subjective frame of reference of its author – particularly in the recurrent references to Rebibbia and pop culture – to the detriment of the informative purpose of a reportage from a distant and marginalized context.[31] Such reviews reveal that in a variety of approaches to graphic journalism in Italy some would still prefer linear, depersonalized accounts of objectified realities. Instead, by foregrounding the self-reflective processes of the author, *Kobane Calling* develops a narrative complexity that demonstrates the new and exciting directions taken by graphic journalism.

The urge for testimony in *Kobane Calling* rises from a collective, long-standing engagement with the transnational networks that support

---

[30] Oscar Glioti in Zerocalcare and Michele Foschini, *Zerocalcare: Scavare fossati nutrire coccodrilli: 10 novembre 2018–10 marzo 2019* (Chivasso: Bao, 2018), p. 17.

[31] Andrea Bramini, 'Non chiamatelo giornalismo. *Kobane Calling* di Zerocalcare', *Lo Spazio Bianco*, https://www.lospaziobianco.it/chiamatelo-giornalismo-kobane-calling-zerocalcare/ [accessed 17 October 2019].

the Kurdish resistance in Rojava. Zerocalcare has travelled twice to the Kurdish territories with the *Staffetta solidale per Kobane*, a humanitarian and informative convoy organized with the Kurdish community and the *centri sociali* in Rome in support of the men and women resisting at once the Islamic State and the international attempts to crush the independent revolutionary process of the PKK (the Kurdistan Workers' Party). Visiting the war context, the author is confronted with the incomparable biographies of men and women of Rojava, the complexity of a global conflict, the naivety of his sentiments of solidarity, the privilege and isolation of being a European passport holder. This provokes feelings of proximity and distance that are acknowledged and explored throughout the narrative with the tools of the comic book medium. The strategies used to visualize the experience of the multilingual local context offer an example: firstly, a disclaimer page acknowledges the chaotic mechanics of translation on the ground, whose representation the author must negotiate for narrative purposes.[32] Then, throughout the book, the lettering in the balloons visualizes Zerocalcare's perception of the soundscape, the language-switching of the people around him. Balloons of scribbles convey experiences of fragility and curiosity, of being silenced and alienated, but also the understanding and empathy established beyond the command of spoken words (Figures 14.5–14.6).

The use of trademark metaphors and references to a universe that is familiar to his reader is a translational strategy that makes intelligible to Western audiences a context radically different and misrepresented at home, if not invisible. Adopting funny spatial parallels and the metaphors and pop icons typical of his repertoire, Zerocalcare mobilizes a cultural memory that may help to convey some of the most challenging realities encountered between Rome and Rojava. Hence cartoons and TV icons embody ISIS troops and other sinister characters, Kurdish food avatars protect the identity of informants, and the distance between the camp and the actual war front *è tipo Rebibbia-Santa Maria del Soccorso, so' tre fermate di metro* [sic; Roman slang: it's more or less the distance between Rebibbia and Santa Maria del Soccorso, three metro stops].

A chapter set in the Kurdish cultural centre in Rome features the Stargate (the sci-fi icon of space-and-time travel) to represent the simultaneity, interconnection and alienation of the globalized present: on one side of a dodgy wall, the familiar street life of Testaccio with its mundane rhythm and thoughts; on the other, people fighting a war in Syria via satellites and mobile phones. The next panel is a close-up in which Zerocalcare's mind is reset to a different moment in time as he feels transported to

---

[32] Zerocalcare, *Kobane Calling*, p. 22.

Figure 14.5 – Zerocalcare, *Kobane Calling.*
Copyright Michele Rech 2016 and Bao Publishing.

IL CENTRO DI TUTTE LE CONTRADDIZIONI E I CONFLITTI DEL MONDO GLOBALIZZATO.

DOVE GLI AMERICANI BOMBARDANO MA NON TROPPO, LA TURCHIA STA NELLA NATO MA IN REALTÀ AIUTA L'ISIS CONTRO I CURDI, C'È UNA SOCIETÀ MUSULMANA CHE HA FATTO DELLA LIBERAZIONE DELLA DONNA LA SUA BANDIERA E CHE COMBATTE DA SOLA UN'ALTRA SOCIETA MUSULMANA CHE HA FATTO DELL'OPPRESSIONE DI GENERE E RELIGIONE LA SUA.

E LA POVERTÀ IL PROGRESSO L'ECONOMIA IN CRESCITA LA REPRESSIONE LE DONNE GLI UOMINI I RUOLI LA RELIGIONE IL PETROLIO...

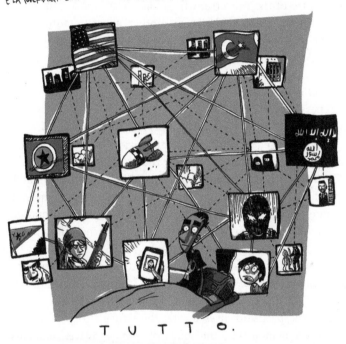

T U T T O.

HAI PRESENTE QUEL PEZZO DI MAX PEZZALI? "SIAMO AL CENTRO DEL MONDO / CI SIAMO DENTRO ANCHE NOI / DOVE SUCCEDE TUTTO ..."

ECCO. QUI CAPISCO CHE SIGNIFICA DAVVERO.

E MI ADDORMENTO COME UN CIOCCO, SENZA MELATONINA TISANE, VALERIANA...

30

Figure 14.6 – Zerocalcare, *Kobane Calling*.
Copyright Michele Rech 2016 and Bao Publishing.

Kurdistan, 'three tube stops from the war', while his memories emerge from a transparent panel.[33]

The recurrent appearance of the mammoth-Rebibbia marks heights of contradictory feelings of fear, proximity, admiration, identification, nostalgia and frustration with the two radically different contexts of Rebibbia and Rojava. The author explores these emotions, dialoguing with the sceptical mammoth – who obsessively questions whether Zerocalcare is ready to leave Rebibbia for Rojava. Zerocalcare eventually realizes that the feeling of being at the centre of the universe, which has always made him identify Rebibbia as 'home', may correspond also to another, albeit unfamiliar place. In other words, he realizes that his universe has expanded beyond the binary opposition home/Rojava posed by the mammoth and his exclusive concept of selfhood and belonging. Instead, Zerocalcare appreciates new possibilities for being inspired and connected, new possibilities for being 'at home' with an expanded awareness of the world.

The forty-year revolutionary process undertaken by women and men in Kurdistan to build an equal and democratic society and their resistance for Kobane is, of course, incomparable with the experience of Zerocalcare and he is aware that his readers might have difficulty in fully understanding it. Hence the book experiments with translational strategies as the multi-modality of comics allows the author to combine visual, written and aural elements. Two chapters, for example, inscribe the visual narrative into the lyrics of two very specific songs, 'L'Oltretorrente' ['Beyond the torrent'] and 'La preghiera dei Banditi' [The bandits' prayer], written in 2006 by the combat rock band Atarassia Grop. These songs translate, respectively, the memory of the resistance of Parma, in 1922, against the advent of fascism, and that of the hardship of the partisans' lives during the struggle for the liberation of Italy. Both chapters demonstrate the ability of comics to layer moments of time and to convey multisensorial mnemonic processes, starting from those of the author. Furthermore, by choosing two contemporary songs from his background rather than other 'authentic' and perhaps monumentalized songs of the Italian Resistance, Zerocalcare draws from the media and the practices of anti-fascist memory of his generation to establish a transcultural connection with two other memories of resistance: that of Kobane and that of the early Italian resistance of 1922–43. Elsewhere, the author marks the coincidence of the 2015 terrorist attack at the Amara Kurdish centre – a hub of international solidarity for Rojava – with the anniversary of Carlo Giuliani's death at the G8 in Genova in 2001.[34] This is a further attempt to translate two memories

---

[33] Zerocalcare, *Kobane Calling*, pp. 51–52.

[34] On the Genova G8 see Jansen in this volume.

marginalized by nationalist narratives into a wider transcultural mnemonic framework.

More than a factual reportage, *Kobane Calling* is thus a powerful example of the potential of comics to translate memory and culture in a globalizing world.

Conclusion

Comics have an extraordinary potential for communication and narration in a globalizing, multilingual world. By opening different paths of engagement with visual and written content, comics enable a fluid, multimodal process of meaning-making which resonates with the cultural and cognitive processes of memory and translation. This flexibility explains the increasing popularity of graphic narratives, the rise of new generations of authors and the expanding development of comics as a transcultural medium.

An expanding genre of visual storytelling, graphic journalism expresses the ambitions of an increasing number of authors and media professionals to represent the multilayered nature of transcultural contacts, to challenge simplistic ideas of proximity and distance, and to mirror the complex processes of identification occurring in a globalizing world. The two authors explored in this chapter – Zerocalcare and Takoua Ben Mohamed – develop different styles and narrative strategies to represent their processes of identification across social, linguistic and national borders. Yet by translating memories and cultures into comics, they both contribute to the incessant reconfiguration of Italian culture and its media. Their graphic journalism exposes the transnational and transcultural mobility of modern Italian culture.

This chapter has explored the productive, constitutive nature of translation for memory and culture. As new authors, readers and practitioners continue to expand the transnational Italian comics scene in multiple directions, graphic narratives convey some of the most imaginative processes of cultural translation of our times.

Part Four

Subjectivity

15

Dante and the Transnational Turn

Tristan Kay

In the context of literary and cultural studies, the transnational turn has challenged what Paul Jay terms the 'nationalist paradigm':[1] the ways in which teaching and research have been shaped, rather narrowly and restrictively, by modern nation states and their associated languages. While convenient on a practical and administrative level, such a model can easily imply that national cultures and identities, whether English or French, German or Italian, are sealed and self-contained entities which fit neatly within territorial boundaries. The traditional separation of modern languages into discrete departments and disciplines (French studies, Hispanic studies, Italian studies, German studies) risks overstating the importance of the nation state in shaping cultural realities and overlooking the ways in which different national traditions intersect and cross-fertilize one another. Critics have paid particular attention to the inadequacy of this model in the context of modern-day globalization: the transnational movement of people, capital, commodities, languages and cultural products that has rendered national boundaries ever more porous in social, cultural, political and economic terms. Scholars have attempted to show how different facets of globalization have impacted so decisively upon cultural production that the very notion of 'national' cultures and canons, as once understood, no longer holds. Thus, at the heart of transnationalism is an attempt to move beyond a nineteenth-century notion of the monolingual nation state, one which still implicitly shapes the organizational and pedagogical structures of many modern languages departments, and to forge instead a critical

---

[1] Paul Jay, *Global Matters: The Transnational Turn in Literary Studies* (Ithaca: Cornell University Press, 2010), p. 1.

methodology that can respond to the transnational realities and complexities of the modern world.

By contrast, few figures in world literature are more strongly associated with the nation and literary nationalism than Dante Alighieri (1265–1321). Dante is often cited as the 'father' of the Italian language and, along with Petrarch and Boccaccio, as one of the 'three crowns': the pioneering originators of Italian literary culture. During the Risorgimento, Dante was evoked as a model patriot and a prophet of Italian unification. Later, Italian fascists were drawn to him as a source of fervent national pride and identified intimations of the coming of Mussolini in the *Commedia*'s foretelling of the advent of a strong imperial ruler. A vast monument in Rome called the Danteum, drawing connections between the poet, his endorsement of Empire and the fascist state, was approved by Mussolini but never built. Dante remains a cornerstone of the Italian school curriculum and, despite his stern criticisms of the medieval Church, has at times been co-opted by the Vatican. Hundreds of institutions around the world associated with the promotion of the culture and language of the Italian nation bear the poet's name. In Italian cities, his poetry is still recited and dissected in public lectures or *lecturae* – a format dating back to fourteenth-century Florence. Dante retains, moreover, a strong presence in departments of Italian studies throughout the world, with the *Commedia* regarded as the national classic *par excellence* and the unquestioned core of a traditional Italian studies curriculum. The Florentine is, in other words, a poet of unparalleled national canonicity, whose work has been at the heart of different phases and forms of Italian nation-building.

What, then, could such a poet have to do with the transnational turn in cultural and literary studies? On first inspection, the study of Dante appears antithetical to this critical and methodological tendency. While a transnationalizing approach seeks to examine how cultural products are understood more profitably in the ways they reflect mobility and exchange across different languages and cultures, and thus question the value of the nation state as a category of understanding and inquiry, Dante as a cultural and historical figure has often been used to reassert the importance of the nation. While the transnational turn has tended to draw attention to the non-canonical and to more marginal texts, voices and genres, which resist conventional 'national' categorization, Dante's *Commedia* is as canonical and privileged as any text in the Western world. Where the transnational turn is associated by Jay with a shift in academic attention from 'sameness' to 'difference', inspired not only by the processes of globalization but also by a number of liberalizing social movements associated with the 1960s,[2] the European, Christian, white,

---

[2] See Jay, *Global Matters*, p. 17.

male, hyper-canonical Dante might easily be seen as the very incarnation of the hegemonic and normative discourses that transnationalizing scholarship seeks to call into question.

In this essay, however, I shall attempt to problematize the image of Dante as a monumental figure of national literary culture and consider how the transnational paradigm can in fact resonate in intriguing ways with several aspects of his work, his cultural context and his later reception.[3] I shall begin by reflecting upon the very applicability of the term 'transnational' to a poet whose work predates the modern nation state. I shall then focus upon three points of interest: (1) the multilingualism and the different forms of cultural and literary translation associated with Dante and his cultural milieu; (2) the question of mobility and citizenship in late medieval Europe and the porous and dynamic qualities of a medieval city state such as Florence; and (3) the transnational dimension of Dante's modern reception.

The Transnational and the Pre-National

As noted above, transnationalism often associates a 'nationalist paradigm' that frequently remains implicit in literary studies with what is an increasingly anachronistic notion of the nation state. If identities today are increasingly hybrid, with movement across international borders commonplace and cultural contact often instantaneous, the model of the strongly demarcated nation state that flourished throughout western Europe in the nineteenth century placed great emphasis upon the inalienable association of national territory, language, culture and populace. As explored by Yasemin Yildiz, this conception of the nation state is fundamentally a monolingual one, aimed at shaping nations as homogenous social and cultural entities and based on a 'reified conception of language'.[4] According to Yildiz, this persistent notion of the nation state has 'obscured multilingual practices across history'.[5] With the advent of the monolingual paradigm, she writes, 'the notion of

---

[3] As Emma Bond notes, there has generally been little inclination to 'perform a temporal stretching out of the existing Italian cultural canon, and to re-evaluate past writers in Italian, both canonical and "ex-centric" alike, in trans-national terms [...] And yet such figures, whose own biographical trajectories conceivably took them outside their own cultural and linguistic contexts, but whose writings crucially also continue to inspire further transnational narratives, are not uncommon within the canon'. 'Towards a Trans-national Turn in Italian Studies?', *Italian Studies*, 69 (2014), 415–24 (p. 418).

[4] Yasmin Yildiz, *Beyond the Mother Tongue: The Postmonolingual Condition* (New York: Fordham University Press, 2011), p. 7.

[5] Yildiz, *Beyond the Mother Tongue*, p. 2.

monolingualism rapidly displaced previously unquestioned practices of living and writing in multiple languages'.[6]

Across Western Europe, this understanding of the nation and its relationship to language and national culture has played a key role in shaping schooling, universities and cultural canons. The intellectual roots of more traditional French, German and Italian departments, as clearly delimited and essentially monolingual entities, can be located in the nineteenth century, their literary curricula shaped by the historical, ideological and political proclivities of that particular era.[7] One of the first objectives of the unifiers of Italy in the nineteenth century was to establish a national language in what was a linguistically and politically fragmented peninsula. What we today call Italian is, of course, a language based upon the literary Tuscan of the 'three crowns', as standardized by Pietro Bembo in the sixteenth century. The value of this language for the nationalists was clear: firstly, it would serve to instil a greater sense of coherence and fraternity among the Italian populace, of whom only some 2.5 percent spoke Italian in 1861;[8] secondly, it would help instil in 'Italians' a strong association of nation, language and cultural patrimony, each clearly defined and demarcated.

At times, Dante's own writing can be seen to foreshadow the modern European nation state, and especially Italy, in a manner that has proved suggestive for his modern readers. In Canto VI of his *Purgatorio*, for example, the poet offers a famous invective on 'serva Italia',[9] decrying the peninsula's political turbulence and subordination and its lack of strong imperial governance. In his linguistic and poetic treatise, the *De vulgari eloquentia*, meanwhile, Dante divides Europe into linguistic and geographical territories which anticipate some of the states and languages of modern Europe. Having first delineated the Greek and Germanic languages, he then speaks of the tripartite Romance vernacular, comprising the languages of *oc* (Occitan), *oïl* (French) and *sì* (Italian), the latter spoken by the 'Latini' in the region known today as Italy.[10] However, for all Dante's modern association with the Italian nation and different forms of cultural nationalism, the very notion of 'Italy'

---

[6] Yildiz, *Beyond the Mother Tongue*, p. 6.

[7] See Jay, *Global Matters*, pp. 24–25, citing Bill Readings, *The University in Ruins* (Cambridge, MA: Harvard University Press, 1997).

[8] See Tullio De Mauro, *Storia linguistica dell'Italia unita* (Bari: Laterza, 1963), pp. 33–34.

[9] Dante Alighieri, *Purgatorio* VI, 76. Citations from the *Commedia* are taken from Dante Alighieri, *La Commedia secondo l'antica vulgata* (Florence: Le Lettere, 1994).

[10] Dante Alighieri, *De vulgari eloquentia* I, viii. Citations from the *De vulgari eloquentia* are taken from Dante Alighieri, *De vulgari eloquentia*, ed. and trans. by Steven Botterill (Cambridge: Cambridge University Press, 1996).

at the turn of the fourteenth century requires immediate interrogation. It is well known that the peninsula at this point in history, many centuries before unification in 1861, was defined not by homogeneity and cohesion but by social, political and linguistic fragmentation. Unlike the centralized kingdom of France, the Italian territory comprised a significant number of autonomous city states or communes, variously falling under the competing jurisdictions of the papacy and the Holy Roman Empire, and there was considerable volatility both within and between these political entities.

Thus, as well as occasionally prefiguring national states and identities, Dante's writing more often reminds us that the poet is the product of a radically different, 'pre-national' reality, one that diverges from the modern world both in its more universalist and its more localist tendencies. As witnessed continually in his *Commedia*, Dante as a medieval Christian conceives of all humans as beings created in God's image, their regional and political forms of identification seen as wholly contingent from the perspective of eternity. Dante engages continually with worldly realities in his masterpiece, but views them through the prisms of Christian cosmology and eschatology. Such universalism also extends into the realm of politics. In his *Monarchia* and *Convivio*, as well as his *Commedia*, Dante defends what he regards as the divinely willed authority of a Roman emperor to rule over all of Christendom, in light of humanity's common political purpose. (The Holy Roman Empire was in a period of interregnum at the turn of the fourteenth century, and those who claimed to occupy the position of emperor, located in Germany, were not accepted as legitimate by the papacy.) By the time Dante writes his *Commedia*, he regards narrower forms of political allegiance, such as an overbearing attachment to city, lineage or political party, as foolish and destructive. In the *De vulgari*, meanwhile, as well as first mapping the history of language from a universal, Christian perspective, it is intriguing that Dante describes the three Romance vernaculars referenced above not as entirely distinctive linguistic entities but as three branches of an inclusive, supra-regional Romance language. As well as anticipating modern nation states, the work thus implies a fraternity of Romance languages and cultures, notwithstanding political tensions between them, that transcends modern national contours.

Dante thus offers examples of affiliation and identification of far broader application than those associated with the modern nation state. Yet, on the other hand, his *Commedia* also presents us with countless examples of the intense hostility and sharply divergent identities that existed between Italian communes, some of them, such as Florence and Fiesole, only several miles apart. Furthermore, Dante describes in the *De vulgari* the extreme fragmentation that exists within the Italian language, an idiom that can be divided into 'at least fourteen vernaculars'.[11] These universalist and localist impulses in Dante's thinking and in his wider culture are encapsulated in the two forms of language in which he writes and which he theorizes with great acuity. Latin was understood to be an immutable form of language, subject to grammatical laws and common to peoples across space and time. It was the language of cultural authority, associated with texts considered to be of universal and unchanging importance. The vernacular, meanwhile, was understood to be a 'natural' form of language, particular to a given community and shaped by the vagaries of usage, place and time.

Dante's oeuvre thus offers examples of, on the one hand, forms of allegiance and identity that *transcend* modern borders and territories and, on the other, evidence of the many social, political and linguistic fault lines that existed *within* a terrain that we now conceive of as a single nation state. One can be struck, simultaneously, by both the vastness and the smallness of the late medieval experience and understanding of reality. In this context, we may only speak of 'Italy', the nation with which Dante is today so intimately associated, in the most cautious of terms. John Larner, in his history of the peninsula in the age of Dante and Petrarch, traces the use of the ancient word 'Italia' in the later Middle Ages, such as in political leaders' appeals for 'Italian' unity against invading forces from the north. Yet this was a word, he reminds us, entirely unfamiliar to most citizens; one used only occasionally by a literate elite. Larner ultimately remarks that 'Italy was nothing more than a sentiment [...] or a literary idea. The reality was not unity, but a mass of divided cities, lordships, and towns, dominated by particularist sentiments and local interests'.[12] In short, if there was a loosely bound cultural, linguistic and geographical entity known as 'Italia' in the later Middle Ages, its coherence was faint and subordinate to many other forms of political, territorial, civic, cultural, linguistic and religious identification and organization.

As such, we must assert that the term 'transnational', dependent upon the idea of the modern nation state, is unsuited to late medieval culture. Dante's was a *pre-national* culture, one that occasionally foreshadows but fundamentally predates the existence of modern nations. Nonetheless, it is often through the monolingual prism of the modern nation state that undergraduates first access Dante and late medieval Italian culture. By approaching the poet within the context of an 'Italian studies' degree (or else, especially in the United States, as a representative of 'Italy' within a course on the classics of

[11] Dante, *De vulgari eloquentia* I, x, 9.

[12] John Larner, *Italy in the Age of Dante and Petrarch* (London: Longman, 1980), p. 3.

'world' literature), students are often given an impression of a national solidity (especially in the case of a poet whose 'national' connotations are now so numerous) that is every bit as inadequate in the context of medieval or early modern culture as it is in the study of the modern globalized world. In both cases, the notion of a container culture can lead us to an unwelcome levelling of the complexity of a culture and its particular political, social and linguistic realities. Thus, while the term 'transnational' sits uneasily, at best, with the study of Dante and the culture of the late medieval Italian peninsula, I would argue that many of the critical and methodological insights associated with the transnational turn are nevertheless important and suggestive. Critical endeavours that highlight the mobility and interaction of languages, cultures and traditions, that explore how these interactions shaped subjectivities, and that consider how critical approaches have often been constrained by the confines of the modern nation state, are as valuable in the context of the study of medieval as of modern cultures.

A striking example of how the insights associated with transnationalism can be brought to bear on the study of medieval culture comes in the recent *Europe: A Literary History, 1348–1418*, edited by David Wallace.[13] Wallace's magisterial two-volume history departs from many existing histories of European literatures, which have overwhelmingly been *national* histories, by offering a literary history which emphatically disavows the nation state as a category of inquiry. As Wallace puts it in his introduction:

> The notion of national literary history that still, remarkably, predominates today owes little to medieval understandings of *natio* and much to nineteenth-century historiography – where the literary product of a particular place, such as Palermo, Toledo or Toulouse, is declared constitutive of a larger entity known, or later known, as Italy, Spain or France.[14]

Thus, rather than containing chapters on Italian, Spanish or French literature from the period in question, Wallace focuses upon cities, grouped together into 'sequences' by itineraries (reflecting routes of trade, pilgrimage, language, cultural exchange and more), which frequently cross the borders between modern nations. Sequence V, for instance, runs from Avignon to Naples, and 'reminds us that much of the literature flowing down the spine of Italy was,

---

[13] See David Wallace, ed., *Europe: A Literary History*, 2 vols (Oxford: Oxford University Press, 2016).

[14] Wallace, 'Introduction', in *Europe: A Literary History* (Oxford: Oxford University Press, 2016), I, p. xxviii.

like much of the artwork, French-inspired'.[15] Sequence VI, meanwhile, begins with Palermo and connects the Sicilian city to Muslim and Jewish communities in the Iberian peninsula and in North Africa. By underlining how the cities of the Italian peninsula were shaped by contact with other sites, cultures and languages, the work powerfully underlines the inadequacy of critical approaches to medieval Europe that are implicitly shaped by the borders of the modern nation state. While Wallace does not use the term 'transnational', the methodology that underpins his volumes, and his concern with re-evaluating the boundaries that are often understood to shape and delimit national cultures, resonate powerfully with the critical paradigms associated with recent critical work in this field.

Medieval Multilingualism

If one of the key thrusts of transnationalizing criticism has been to critique a perceived overdetermination of the nation state as a lens through which to examine and understand different forms of cultural production, another has been to explore the ways in which languages are not confined to given territories but move, adapt and respond to social, cultural and political pressures. As noted above, the powerful linking of language and nation state is a development largely associated with the nineteenth century. Prior to this privileging of monolingualism, linguistic practices were often much more fluid and dynamic,[16] and few medieval authors offer richer meditations on language than Dante.[17] Indeed, the poet's modern identification as 'father' of the Italian language, invoked to reinforce the relationship between language and nation state, can mask the breadth of his thinking on a number of languages and their interrelation. While later appropriated as a totem of monolingualism, Dante's literary production and his cultural and linguistic formation were in fact fundamentally multilingual. They are multilingual, firstly, insofar as Dante, like any late medieval Italian intellectual, had to negotiate the diglossia of Latin and the vernacular. At the time when Dante

---

[15] Wallace, 'Introduction', I, p. xxviii.

[16] 'Exclusive first language allegiance [...] was not the most desired of linguistic identities or imagined communities in the late medieval period'. Mary Davidson, *Medievalism, Multilingualism, and Chaucer* (Basingstoke: Palgrave, 2010), p. 137. Cited in Yildiz, *Beyond the Mother Tongue*, p. 6.

[17] Mirko Tavoni describes how the *De vulgari* reveals an 'acute and lucid level of cultural awareness and understanding of the salient structural aspects of his contemporary linguistic reality'. 'Linguistic Italy', in *Dante in Context*, ed. by Zygmunt G. Barański and Lino Pertile (Cambridge: Cambridge University Press, 2016), pp. 243–59 (p. 258).

wrote his *Commedia*, Latin remained the dominant and prestigious written language of the learned elite. As well as forming the bedrock of medieval education, it was the language of public record, of law, of the Church, of intellectual discourse, and was the required *lingua franca* in many established and emerging mercantile and diplomatic professions. In contrast with Latin stood the unstandardized vernacular, the everyday spoken language of the people, acquired not through formal instruction but through everyday use. Dante produced works in both Latin and the vernacular and, in a move of decisive importance for the development of European literary culture, would come to challenge the assumed cultural primacy of Latin, not least by writing his magnum opus, the *Commedia*, in his Florentine mother tongue.

Yet Dante's culture and intellectual formation was also multilingual insofar as he was shaped not only by the language and literary culture of Florence, or even by the many Italian vernaculars, but by the three principal branches of the Romance vernacular he set out in the *De vulgari* – what we today would term Italian, Occitan and French – and their associated cultural traditions. While this unfinished Latin treatise in part seeks to locate and codify an 'illustrious' supra-regional Italian vernacular (an endeavour Dante ultimately abandons, seemingly cognizant of the inherently mutable quality of all vernaculars), it is striking that the examples he gives of different poetic genres and forms are drawn from Occitan and Old French authors as well as from Italians. Thus, the treatise presupposes that its reader (and the vernacular poet of Dante's time) is capable of operating not only in Latin and his or her local Italian vernacular, but also in the vernaculars of *oc* and *oïl*. Indeed, while Dante seeks to promote the Italian vernacular as a serious literary language, Occitan and Old French, which predated it as prestigious literary vernaculars, are presented not as 'foreign languages', but as pre-eminent Romance languages to be deployed in different literary genres, accessible to citizens of 'Italy' and 'France' alike. A number of prose writers from the Italian peninsula did, in fact, choose to write important works in Old French, while some Italian lyric poets chose to write in Occitan. The Italian lyric tradition, born in the cultural melting pot of Frederick II's imperial court in thirteenth-century Sicily,[18] was in effect a transplantation of the Occitan poetry of the troubadours, which flourished a century prior. Dante himself wrote a trilingual lyric entitled 'Ai faux ris', whose verses alternate between Latin, Italian and Old French. In the *Commedia*, meanwhile, he not only encounters a series of French poets in the afterlife, but also allows the

---

[18] On the multilingual and multicultural character of twelfth- and thirteenth-century Sicily, see Karla Malette, *The Kingdom of Sicily, 1100–1250* (Philadelphia: University of Pennsylvania Press, 2005).

troubadour Arnaut Daniel to speak in Occitan. Multilingualism, then, and an understanding of languages that transcends territorial considerations and confines, is a topic every bit as pertinent in 'pre-monolingual' late medieval culture as it is in Yildiz's 'post-monolingual' globalized world. Dante's writings not only encompass numerous languages but also engage continually with cultural traditions and genres associated with locations beyond the Italian peninsula, and especially with the territory today known as France. Thus, as well as in classical and medieval Latin works, his cultural formation has roots in a number of vernacular languages and cultures which he skilfully negotiates and synthesizes in an oeuvre which constantly seeks innovative and hybrid forms of expression.[19]

Dante's cultural environment was, moreover, one where translation – a key category of enquiry in transnational studies – was widespread. A key form of literary production in the Italian peninsula from the thirteenth century was vernacularization.[20] With a view to disseminating knowledge to a broader public, writers (usually anonymous) would transfer authoritative religious and secular texts of different genres from Latin to the local vernacular. In Dante's immediate milieu, for example, Brunetto Latini translated works and speeches by Cicero into the vernacular, while Taddeo Alderotti, a Florentine who taught medicine and logic at the University of Bologna in the late Duecento, translated into Italian a Latin version of Aristotle's *Ethics*. Indeed, the broader rediscovery of Aristotle in the West was an eminently transcultural operation, mediated across languages, cultures and territories, in both the medieval Islamic and Christian worlds. As well as the vernacularization of important Latin and Greek authors, Dante's world hosted the translation or adaptation of texts into Italian from other vernaculars. These ranged from Italian rewritings of French romances to a widely circulated Italian version of Brunetto's French encyclopaedia the *Trésor*, sometimes attributed to Bono

---

[19] On the experimental and syncretic quality of Dante's writing, see for example: Zygmunt G. Barański, 'Dante Alighieri: Experimentation and (Self-)exegesis', in *The Cambridge History of Literary Criticism: Volume II: The Middle Ages*, ed. by Alistair Minnis and Ian Johnson (Cambridge: Cambridge University Press, 2005), pp. 561–82. Syncretism and hybridism are terms frequently deployed by critics in relation to Dante's innovative handling of genre. Compare Vertovec on the 'fluidity of constructed styles and everyday practices' typical of transnational forms of cultural production: 'These are often described in terms of syncretism, creolization, bricolage, cultural translation and hybridity'. *Transnationalism* (Aldershot: Routledge, 2009), p. 7.

[20] On the culture of vernacularization in Dante's Italy, see especially Alison Cornish, *Vernacular Translation in Dante's Italy: Illiterate Literature* (Cambridge: Cambridge University Press, 2010).

Giamboni. The first works attributed to Dante himself, the *Fiore* and *Detto d'Amore*, are Tuscan appropriations of the thirteenth-century French text the *Roman de la Rose*, whose narrative was adapted not only into the poet's literary vernacular but also into the Italian poetic form of the sonnet sequence. As well as a highly fluid and dextrous approach to different languages, then, Dante's culture hosted a rich and sophisticated culture of translation, with authors adopting different strategies and imaginatively adapting source texts to the cultural and generic norms of the target language.

Mobility and Citizenship

Contemporary perspectives on transnationalism foreground the radically increased mobility associated with the globalized world which, along with novel modes of communication, has created new and hybrid forms of identification and expression. A walled Italian city state, such as Dante's Florence, by contrast, may ostensibly suggest a small and enclosed world, but its compact dimensions can distract us from the many kinds of mobility and cultural exchange, across significant distances and linguistic borders, which it experienced and facilitated.

As well as its local artisanal economy, Florence was a major financial and mercantile hub in the later Middle Ages, with links to many parts of Europe through both trade and banking. Wealthy foreign clients, for instance, entrusted Florentine bankers with significant sums of money and asked them to generate profits. As such, Florence was at the heart of a circulation of wealth across different political jurisdictions – a 'transnational' flow of capital *avant la lettre*. Moreover, the city traded in commodities from across Europe and the Mediterranean, from England to North Africa. As John Najemy writes: 'If it sometimes seems that Florence had two different economies – an international economy of traders, bankers, and merchants who were more often than not in London, Avignon, Naples, or the Levant, and a local economy of cloth manufacturers, artisans, shopkeepers, and labourers – they were nonetheless intimately linked'.[21] Florence's place in an extensive economic network reflects the dynamics of politics in this period. Just as Vertovec writes of the 'multiple ties and interactions linking people or institutions across the borders of nation-states' associated with the globalized contemporary world,[22] medieval historian William Caferro uses the example of the French-born ruler Charles of Valois, whose political interests and family connections ran from Aragon and Valencia to Sicily and

---

[21] John Najemy, *A History of Florence: 1200–1575* (Oxford: Blackwell, 2006), p. 117.
[22] Vertovec, *Transnationalism*, p. 3.

Constantinople, to illustrate 'the international nature of politics' in the late medieval period.[23] Medieval politics and economics, like medieval literary culture, thus continually unfolded across multiple territories and kingdoms, whose own boundaries were often nebulous and mutable.

Another important form of mobility experienced by many medieval Italians was pilgrimage, a venture which impacted strongly upon imagery and expression in literary works and the visual arts alike. Christians from different parts of society embarked upon pilgrimages, especially to the Holy Land, Rome and Santiago de Compostela, as a demonstration of religious devotion and a retreat from day-to-day worldly preoccupations. Florence itself was on the pilgrimage route to Rome from the north in Dante's time, and so the city hosted numerous visitors around the turn of the fourteenth century. In his collection of early love poems, the *Vita nova*, Dante describes speaking of his love for Beatrice with two pilgrims who find themselves in the city en route to Rome, and uses the etymology of *peregrino* to reflect upon the spiritual and historical implications of the word, whose classical etymology suggests strangeness and foreignness.[24] Indeed, the metaphor of pilgrimage – widely exploited in medieval religious literature – underpins the entire *Commedia*, with Dante's journey figured as a spiritual quest from the earthly to the heavenly city, an adventure from the familiar into a land that is new and other. Conquest is another form of transcultural experience exploited by Dante. In one of the climactic cantos of the *Paradiso*, for example, he evokes a paradigmatic cross-cultural encounter in comparing his sensation upon reaching the Empyrean to that of the conquering barbarians arriving in the city of Rome, stupefied by the magnificence of its monuments.[25]

Mobility was enforced as well as sought by many citizens of medieval Italian communes. Such was the volatility of the politics of the peninsula at this time that power in many cities was wrested back and forth between rival factions. The two main factions in this period were the Guelph and Ghibelline parties, who defended the political interests of the papacy and empire respectively. Such political instability meant that exile was a common feature of life in medieval Italian cities, especially for figures of cultural and intellectual importance, such as Dante, who were often also embroiled in civic affairs. Exile was fraught with dangers: the Florentine poet Guido

---

[23] William Caferro, 'Empire, Italy, and Florence', in *Dante in Context*, ed. by Zygmunt G. Barański and Lino Pertile (Cambridge: Cambridge University Press, 2016), pp. 9–29 (p. 13).

[24] Dante Alighieri, *Vita nova* XL, in *Vita nuova*, ed. by Domenico De Robertis, in *Opere minori*, 2 vols (Milan and Naples: Ricciardi, 1979), I, i, 1–247.

[25] Dante, *Paradiso* XXXI, 31–51.

Cavalcanti, for instance, died of malaria in the Tuscan Maremma in 1300, shortly after his banishment. However, exile also allowed for different forms of intercultural contact. Guelph politician and intellectual luminary Brunetto Latini, for example, travelled to Paris, having been exiled from Florence during the period of Ghibelline rule that followed the 1260 Battle of Montaperti. This sojourn not only acquainted Brunetto with Paris's rich intellectual culture but also inspired him to write his *Trésor* in Old French. Brunetto's return to Florence in 1269 saw him resume his political career as well as his role as cultural figurehead in the city, where he played an important role in mediating French, as well as Ciceronian, language and culture into the city.

In Dante's own case, his exile from Florence in 1302 (under accusation of political corruption, following a coup by a rival Guelph faction) led to two decades of peregrinations within the Italian peninsula. His experience of its different regions and dialects fertilized his fascination with language and informed not only his insightful discussion of Italian vernaculars in the *De vulgari* but also the broad lexical range of the 'plurilingual' *Commedia*, notable for its boldly inclusive approach to language and register. All three of Italy's 'crowns', in fact, experienced considerable mobility. Giovanni Boccaccio spent some 13 years in Naples, initially sent by his father to study law, and took his first steps as a writer in the context of the city's vibrant Angevin court. Petrarch, meanwhile, was shaped more decisively by the 'cosmopolitan culture' of the French city of Avignon, 'where the most powerful, influential, and learned men of Europe gathered',[26] than by any single location in the Italian peninsula. In her recent book on Petrarch and the literary culture of nineteenth-century France, Jennifer Rushworth explores the complex forms of appropriation of the poet by the Avignonese and, in ruminating on the poet's transnational credentials, is prompted to ask the provocative question: 'Was Petrarch French?'[27]

Late medieval Italian culture thus presents us with many interesting examples of the movement of individuals, commodities, monies, languages and cultural traditions between regions which, from the vantage point of modernity, we can too easily think of as sealed and discrete container cultures. The mercantile commune of Florence, in particular, was a site of continual comings and goings. As Kenneth Clarke puts it, the city was 'in constant negotiation by those who were both in the *here* of the city and in the *there* of absence, whether

[26] K. P. Clarke, 'Florence', in *Europe: A Literary History*, 2 vols, ed. by David Wallace (Oxford: Oxford University Press, 2016), vol. I, 687–707 (p. 690).

[27] Jennifer Rushworth, *Petrarch and the Literary Culture of Nineteenth-Century France* (Woodbridge: Boydell and Brewer, 2017), p. 233.

it be because of exile, trade, diplomacy, or pilgrimage'.[28] Clarke's words here resonate suggestively with the language of transnationalism. Steven Vertovec, for example, speaks of the emergence of the 'dual or multiple identifications' associated with 'diaspora consciousness' in a globalized world: the sense of being 'home away from home' or 'here and there'.[29] Such terms could just as easily apply to the medieval exile. Doris Sommer, meanwhile, suggestively writes that 'By now strangeness is the norm in big cities worldwide, where urban life is recovering the *heterogeneousness and dynamic qualities that once defined the medieval metropolis*'.[30] One must appreciate, in other words, that the small unit of political administration, the medieval city state, finds itself located within and shaped by a much larger political, economic, religious and cultural ecosystem that stretched from England and Germany to North Africa and Constantinople. Far from being sealed and homogenous, the late medieval Italian peninsula was porous and dynamic – 'a diverse and heterogeneous entity, with a variety of cultural and ethnic influences'.[31] As such, it is easy to appreciate Vertovec's contention that 'transnationalism [...] certainly preceded the nation'.[32] As Sommer's words above suggest, the qualities associated with transnationalism attest to a *recovery* of the 'heterogeneousness and dynamic qualities' of the pre-modern, pre-national urban world.

Transnational Reception

My essay has so far reflected upon some of the ways in which forms of mobility, multilingualism and intercultural exchange associated with trans-nationalism can also be identified in the vibrant culture of late medieval Italy, a world where modern assumptions concerning monolingualism and nation states as container cultures are not yet established. In this final section, I shall reflect briefly upon the transnational elements of Dante's modern reception. There is, naturally, a rich history of cultural engagement with Dante's work within the Italian peninsula, but the poet's reception over the last two centuries, in particular, has been truly global in scope.

The sheer breadth of Dante's modern reception can be witnessed, for instance, in the 20 essays found in the 2011 volume *Metamorphosing Dante:*

---

[28] Clarke, 'Florence', p. 687.

[29] Vertovec, *Transnationalism*, p. 6.

[30] Doris Sommer, 'Language, Culture, and Society', in *Introduction to Scholarship in Modern Languages and Literatures*, ed. by David G. Nicholls (New York: MLA, 2007), pp. 3–19 (p. 3); emphasis mine. Cited in Jay, *Global Matters*, p. 16.

[31] Caferro, 'Empire, Italy, and Florence', p. 13.

[32] Vertovec, *Transnationalism*, p. 3.

Appropriations, Manipulations, Rewritings.[33] These studies highlight the productive reception of Dante's work in an array of modern contexts – that is, the way in which Dante's *Commedia* is not passively 'received' by modern communities but serves as a spark for new creative operations and allows for the transposition of the medieval poem's tensions onto contemporary realities. One is immediately struck by the transnational scope of this collection, which moves from the use of Dante in twentieth-century English, German and Irish literature to the appropriation of the poet in twentieth-century American gay poetry. Furthermore, the collection contains a number of studies of intermedial responses to the poet, from the queer cinema of Derek Jarman to the transfer drawings of Robert Rauschenberg. Similarly, a recent conference at the University of Leeds, '*L'ombra sua torna*: Dante, the Twentieth Century, and Beyond' (2017), hosted a range of interventions on modern cultural responses to the poet's work, from the powerful postcolonial rewriting by Aimé Cesaire in *And the Dogs Were Silent* to Roland Barthes's sophisticated but neglected engagement with the poet and modern Persian translations of the *Commedia* and their negotiation of the *Inferno*'s represen-tation of Muhammad.

Two important and original in-depth studies from recent years that bring to light the transnational dimension of Dante's reception through the centuries are Nick Havely's *Dante's British Public: Readers and Texts, from the Fourteenth Century to the Present* and Dennis Looney's *Freedom Readers: The African American Reception of Dante Alighieri and the 'Divine Comedy'.*[34] Havely's monograph takes a long view of the British reception and appropriation of Dante, addressing a plethora of case studies, many of them previously unexamined, to showcase different forms of Anglo-Italian cultural contact and the broadening appeal of the poet's work through the centuries. A striking aspect of Havely's study, especially pertinent to the idea of trans-nationalism, is that it not only uses Dante to explore the contact between two nation states but also focuses on itinerant British readers, collectors and translators, in locations such as Mumbai, Cape Town and Berlin, to highlight the complex ways in which British readers have accessed and dissemi-nated the poet's work. Havely also explores the intersection of imperial

---

[33] Fabio Camilletti, Manuele Gragnolati and Fabian Lampart, eds, *Metamorphosing Dante: Appropriations, Manipulations, Rewritings* (Vienna: Turia and Kant, 2011). The volume followed a 2009 conference at the Berlin Institute for Cultural Inquiry.

[34] Nick Havely, *Dante's British Public: Readers and Texts, from the Fourteenth Century to the Present* (Oxford: Oxford University Press, 2014); Dennis Looney, *Freedom Readers: The African American Reception of Dante Alighieri and the 'Divine Comedy'* (South Bend: Notre Dame University Press, 2011).

history and Dante reception, considering the peregrinations of valuable Dante manuscripts that accompanied British colonialists around the world to signal the cultural prestige of the Empire. Looney's work, meanwhile, explores how African-American authors have read and responded to Dante's work, from the 1820s to the present day, encompassing Romantic, modernist, novelistic and filmic appropriations. Most compellingly, Looney reveals how these rewritings of the *Commedia* have reimagined the poem as a slave narrative that raises questions of segregation and migration and highlights how certain African-American authors have taken inspiration from Dante's refinement of a new kind of poetic vernacular in formulating their own forms of expression.

Confronting such a rich multiplicity of modern responses to Dante is of interest not only in allowing us to trace and catalogue textual influences and residues of the poet's writing in the modern world. It is also important to note how staggeringly variegated the poet's reception is, and how his writing has been refracted through different locations, realities and subjectivities. Far from being a stifling monument to cultural nationalism or Christian orthodoxy, Dante's *Commedia*, translated into new languages in every corner of the globe, has served as an infinitely flexible text through which to interrogate a gamut of social, cultural and historical questions. As the editors of *Metamorphosing Dante* put it in the introduction to their volume, the continual engagement with Dante in the twentieth and twenty-first centuries attests to 'Dante's ability to help the contemporary world understand itself'.[35] In some cases, the totalizing scope of the theocentric *Commedia*, and its unqualified notions of truth, justice and salvation, are invoked as unattainable concepts in modern, secular authors' more fragmented realities. In other cases, however, Dante offers a more productive model for writers and artists around the world in confronting and articulating aspects of modernity.

Conclusion

It is quite understandable that a pre-modern, extensively studied author such as Dante has not been the focus of transnationalizing scholarship within the field of Italian studies. Other texts and genres, especially from recent decades, respond in more explicit ways to questions of transnationalism, globalization, cultural translation and mobility. Indeed, I began this essay by drawing attention to the ways in which Dante might easily be regarded as a totem of precisely the kind of cultural nationalism and canonicity that such

---

[35] Camilletti, Gragnolati and Lampart, 'Metamorphosing Dante', in *Metamorphosing Dante: Appropriations, Manipulations, Rewritings* (Vienna: Turia and Kant, 2011), pp. 9–18 (p. 11).

scholarship seeks to resist and move beyond. Nonetheless, future research and teaching within the field would benefit from a greater attentiveness to the ways in which the framework of transnationalism can be germane even to the most canonical of authors. By limiting Dante (and, indeed, his fellow *corone*, Petrarch and Boccaccio) to an association with a national container culture, we can obscure the intercultural complexities of his writing. I hope to have highlighted in this essay how his poetry is the product of a heterogeneous and multilingual cultural reality, and how its reception has seen a monument of Italian literary culture endlessly transformed, reappropriated and reimagined across territorial and linguistic borders. Given this complex picture, and the inadequacy of the nation state as a prism through which fully to understand Dante, there also remains work to be done on how the poet has been used and abused in shaping different forms of Italian national identity,[36] within and beyond the peninsula, and the processes through which this pre-national author became the anointed poet of the nation. I would suggest, then, in conclusion, that Dante's poetry and its reception not only offer us numerous insights into diverse strands of medieval culture, history and society but, alongside more contemporary forms of cultural production, can contribute to a broader reflection on questions of nationalism and transnationalism, and the ways in which cultures do not represent hermetic entities but rather interact and cross-fertilize one another across space and time.

---

[36] For ideas of 'use' and 'abuse' of Dante in the context of fascism, see Stefano Albertini, 'Dante in camicia nera: uso e abuso del divino poeta nell'Italia fascista', *The Italianist*, 16.1 (1996), 117–42.

16

Conscience, Consciousness, the Unconscious

The Italian Subject and Psychoanalysis

Fabio Camilletti and Alessandra Diazzi

Introduction

This chapter sets out to examine how Italian literature has assimilated – and at the same time questioned – the notion of subjectivity postulated by Freud. By so doing, we aim on the one hand to investigate Italy's response to the transnational dissemination of psychoanalysis, a hybrid discourse that transcends disciplinary and geographical boundaries and is characterized by a moving and undefinable nature. On the other hand, we hope to demonstrate that, although Italy seemingly resisted the spread of psychoanalytic culture, this aversion did not jeopardize the diffusion of the discipline in the country. Rather, the work of appropriation carried out by Italian culture in order to metabolize the new understanding of subjectivity contributed to transnationalizing psychoanalysis itself, through a radical revision *all'italiana* of its teachings.

Sigmund Freud, the founding father of psychoanalysis, is today considered 'the Copernicus of the psyche', to the extent that, according to John Forrester, ignoring his teaching in psychology is comparable to 'going back to pre-Copernican beliefs' in science.[1] Freud's revolution impacted the notion of subjectivity in particular. His discoveries changed forever the meaning we attribute to the word 'I' as well as the understanding of the subject in Western psychology and philosophy. Psychoanalysis is conventionally understood to have been born in the Austrian Empire, in 1899, with the publication of *The Interpretation of Dreams*. In Freud's words, the theory

---

[1] John Forrester, *Dispatches from the Freud Wars: Psychoanalysis and Its Passions* (Cambridge, MA: Harvard University Press, 1997), p. 2.

postulated an 'I' (the Ego, *das Ich*) that is no longer 'master in its own house'.[2] Contrary to the view of subjectivity rooted in Descartes's identification of the subject with the conscious, rational self, Freud focused instead on those phenomena – such as dreams, slips of the tongue and involuntary actions – that are situated outside of the rationalizing control of the psyche. Moreover, Freud's argumentation did not refer to the philosophical tradition that originated with Aristotle, based on a formalized reasoning system and rooted in a strong belief in the scientific method. Rather, Freudianism stemmed from the junction of medicine, Jewish-German thought and literature – with the consequence that he often gave literary names to his discoveries, such as the Oedipus complex. Eventually, Freud would directly challenge the long-lasting philosophical legacy of Socrates and Plato by arguing, in *Beyond the Pleasure Principle* (1920), that the human mind does not always (nor necessarily) operate for its own good and well-being: together with the principle of self-preservation, there exists a 'death-drive' (*Todestrieb*) that pushes individuals towards self-destruction and which should be accepted as a substantial component of the human mind.

The relationship between Italian culture and psychoanalysis has often been narrated in terms of resistance: in different moments and for different reasons, the main ideological trends that have been hegemonic in Italy from the early twentieth century to the 1960s – Catholicism, but also fascism, Croce's historicist idealism and the dialectical materialism of Marxism – firmly opposed psychoanalysis and the threat it posed to the Cartesian model of subjectivity.[3] However, as we will argue, psychoanalysis penetrated Italian culture by other means, primarily through literature. After all, although since Aristotle philosophy has been considered the most suitable field for questions about the nature of the subject, about the exploration of interiority and about the apperception of the external world, recent scholarship has stressed the pivotal role played by literature in the shaping of subjectivity from a culturally oriented viewpoint. In *The Invention of Literary Subjectivity*, Michel Zink takes French literature as the starting point for the study of the history of the self, investigating the birth, development and

---

[2] Sigmund Freud, 'A Difficulty in the Path of Psycho-Analysis' (1917), in *The Standard Edition of the Complete Psychological Works*, trans. by James Strachey, 24 vols (London: Hogarth Press, 1968), XVII, pp. 140–43 (p. 143).

[3] For an overview of the reception of psychoanalysis in Italy see Michel David, *La psicoanalisi nella cultura italiana* (Turin: Boringhieri, 1966); Pierluigi Barrotta, Laura Lepschy and Emma Bond, eds, *Freud and Italian Culture* (Oxford: Peter Lang, 2009); Lesley Caldwell and Francesco Capello, eds, *Journal of Romance Studies*, 3.10, special issue: 'Psychoanalysis and Italian Studies' (Winter 2010).

metamorphoses of the idea of the subject across the centuries.[4] Similarly, in *Shakespeare's Perjured Eye*, Joel Fineman claims that, in his poetry, Shakespeare gives birth to the archetype of the lyrical 'I', shaping an idea of subjectivity that would influence further developments in the conceptualization of the subject and its perception of external phenomena.[5] It is once again literature that, in Philip Shaw and Peter Stockwell's *Subjectivity and Literature from the Romantics to the Present Day*, acts as the testing ground for the investigation of the multifarious nature of the subject, proving – or challenging – modern and contemporary philosophical theories of subjectivity through the aid of fictional voices.[6] Such a close relationship between literature and the history of subjectivity is particularly revealing in Italy, where, as noted by Pierpaolo Antonello, literary texts had an unparalleled role in the construction of the nation's public discourse and, above all, of the nation's identity.[7]

Accordingly, in this chapter, we will use literature to investigate how Italian culture dealt with the 'dethroned Ego' proposed by psychoanalysis. In so doing, we will discuss a reception history that is intrinsically 'transnational', in that psychoanalysis both has transnational origins and has enjoyed a transnational circulation since its first appearance. As a discipline, psychoanalysis situated itself from the start at the crossroads of different cultures and can in fact be conceived as a melting pot of multifarious influences. The talking cure was 'created in Vienna (a declining capital of a declining empire) by a Bohemian-born Austrian Jewish medical doctor who occupied a relatively marginal position in the academic and professional fields of his country'.[8] It was then influenced in its development by Ashkenazi thought, French psychiatry and philosophy, German Romanticism and Eastern philosophies. In addition, just a few years after its birth, psychoanalysis 'transcended national and cultural boundaries and was practiced and discussed in countries [...] culturally and geographically removed from the new republic of Austria'.[9] As

[4] Michel Zink, *The Invention of Literary Subjectivity* (Baltimore: The Johns Hopkins University Press, 1998).

[5] Joel Fineman, *Shakespeare's Perjured Eye: The Invention of Poetic Subjectivity in the Sonnets* (Berkeley: University of California Press, 1986).

[6] Philip Shaw and Peter Stockwell, *Subjectivity and Literature from the Romantics to the Present Day* (London and New York: Pinter Publishers, 1991).

[7] Pierpaolo Antonello, *Dimenticare Pasolini: L'intellettuale nell'Italia contemporanea* (Milan and Udine: Mimesis, 2012), p. 49.

[8] Joy Damousi and Mariano Ben Plotkin, 'Introduction', in *The Transnational Unconscious: Essays in the History of Psychoanalysis and Transnationalism* (London: Palgrave Macmillan, 2009), pp. 1–16 (p. 2).

[9] Damousi and Plotkin, 'Introduction', p. 2.

a result, psychoanalysis is an embodiment, *ante litteram*, of what we would define today as a paradigmatic example of transnational culture or, in other words, a form of knowledge that challenges – from both a geographical and psychological angle – a monolithic understanding of the notion of 'identity'.

The controversial reception of psychoanalysis in Italian culture is linked, at least in part, precisely to this hybrid character of the discipline and to the foreign flavour associated with it. In Italy, psychoanalysis was perceived as an exotic practice, 'an exquisitely "gothic" activity' that 'fit[s] to introverted and twisted Anglo-Germanic and Frankish souls [and] contrasts sharply with the Renaissance brightness and sunny Mediterranean extroversion of Italian culture'.[10] At the same time, a nation that for centuries had faced a difficult and at times dramatic process of national identity construction seemed to regard with suspicion psychoanalysis's dismantlement of a stable and unitary 'I'. That destabilization was perceived as a threat to both the private and the political understanding of the subject which dominated Italian culture.

The Plague and the Antibody

Besides exceeding the boundaries of the national, psychoanalysis also crosses disciplinary borders. Not only is psychoanalysis a hybrid form of knowledge, half way between science (e.g., medicine, psychiatry) and the humanities (e.g., philosophy, literature), but it also constantly interacts with other cultural fields – such as anthropology, sociology, philosophy and, broadly speaking, the arts – influencing them and in turn being influenced by their discourses. As a result, psychoanalysis' transnational dimension goes hand in hand with its interdisciplinary character. This is due to the varied nature of psychoanalysis which is at once:

> secondo le definizioni datene dallo stesso padre fondatore, un metodo di indagine dei fenomeni psichici e psicopatologici, un procedimento terapeutico delle nevrosi e una teoria metapsicologica. Soltanto la compresenza delle tre componenti indicate dà vita alla psicanalisi in quanto tale e dunque, all'inverso, nessuna delle componenti può prendere isolatamente il nome di psicanalisi.[11]

---

[10] Sergio Benvenuto, 'Italy and Psychoanalysis', *Journal of European Psychoanalysis*, 5 (Spring–Autumn 1997), para. 1 of 8, http://www.psychomedia.it/jep/number5/benvenuto.htm [accessed 1 September 2018].

[11] Elio Gioanola, 'Psicanalisi e critica letteraria', in *Freud and Italian Culture*, ed. by Pierluigi Barrotta, Laura Lepschy and Emma Bond (Oxford: Peter Lang, 2009), pp. 9–30 (p. 9). All translations are by the editors of the present volume.

[according to the definitions provided by its own founding father, a method of enquiry into psychological and psychopathological phenomena, a therapeutic procedure regarding neurosis and a metapsychological theory. Only the presence of all three components constitutes psychoanalysis as such, which means that, on the other hand, none of them, taken on its own, can be called psychoanalysis]

Exceeding the physical borders of clinics, psychoanalysis thus embodies a form of knowledge that impacts several intellectual discourses and translates itself not only in a therapeutic dimension but also into critical, philosophical and, more generally, cultural praxes.[12] As a result, the Copernican revolution of the subject which the Freudian discipline represents raises questions which go well beyond the sphere of psychology and threaten the dominion of rationality and reason.

At the end of his life, in the attempt to provide a retrospective overview of the discipline that he had founded, Freud illustrates the main principles of his doctrine in *An Outline of Psychoanalysis* (published posthumously in 1940). From a psychoanalytic perspective, Freud maintains, the human psyche is structured around three organizing forces, the Id, the Ego and the Super-Ego. Whereas the Ego and the Super-Ego embody regulatory principles that control the subject's behaviour, the stimuli s/he responds to and the mechanisms by which s/he reaches their satisfaction, the Id is the instinctual and unregulated side of the psyche, led by the pleasure principle. In other words, whereas the Ego and the Super-Ego belong to the conscious sphere, the Id encompasses the unconscious drives that, while remaining hidden, influence one's agency and ultimately provide the underlying trigger of human behaviour. In other words, Descartes's thinking entity is replaced by a self who is only in partial control of his/her own thoughts and whose truth emerges – or emerges *especially* – when s/he *does not think*. To further complicate this scenario, one must bear in mind that the Id witnesses the continuous tension between the pleasure principle (Eros) and the death drive (Thanatos), where the latter is understood as 'an urge in organic life to restore an earlier state of things' or, in other words, an inorganic state in which any vital activity is completely annihilated.[13]

Although elements of Freud's theory were already present in the philosophical, medical and psychological debates of the eighteenth and nineteenth

---

[12] We use the terms 'form of knowledge' (*savoir*) and 'discursive practice' (*pratique du discours*) with reference to Michel Foucault's works, and more specifically to *The Archaeology of Knowledge*, trans. by A. M. Sheridan Smith (London: Tavistock, 1972).

[13] Gunnar Karlson, *Psychoanalysis in a New Light* (Cambridge: Cambridge University Press, 2010), p. 147.

centuries,[14] Freud was doubtless right in defining this challenge to a positive view of the human mind as the most revolutionary and disturbing premise of his newborn discipline. It was exactly this understanding of the psyche as profoundly affected by the unconscious sphere and ultimately orientated towards self-destruction that made it an uncanny host in Italy. In the early twentieth century, psychoanalysis faced the same prejudice that, a hundred years before, had affected the Italian reception of Romanticism and of the inward turn associated with it, both of which were also regarded as a dangerous challenge to the cult of reason.[15] The negative assessment of Romanticism and psychoanalysis was conceptualized in the same cultural-geographical terms: northern/central Europe *vs* the Mediterranean, irrationalism *vs* rationalism, introversion *vs* extroversion. This last opposition, as we will see, is particularly telling as far as subjectivity is concerned.

The *difference*[16] in the Italian assimilation of Freud's revolution in the sphere of subjectivity (when compared to other linguistic and cultural domains) becomes patent if we consider the very first literary encounter of Italian culture with psychoanalysis: Italo Svevo's novel *La coscienza di Zeno* (1923). Unanimously defined by scholars as a 'psychoanalytic novel', the book is presented as a manuscript written by the protagonist and narrator, Zeno, as he engages in a review of his present and past life at the request of his psychoanalyst. Not by chance, the book was conceived in Trieste, the 'most transnational' of Italian cities and the one that embodied (and still embodies, in some respects) an uncanny manifestation of 'otherness' within the borders of the country, due both to its geographical position and to its history.[17] At the time of the publication of Svevo's novel, the Triestine environment was characterized by a peculiar cultural syncretism, an exceptional cosmopolitanism, a hybrid border identity and, at the same time, a profound nationalist

---

[14] See Alessandra Aloisi and Fabio Camilletti, eds, *The Archaeology of the Unconscious: Italian Perspectives* (London: Routledge, 2019).

[15] See Fabio Camilletti, '"Timore" e "terrore" nella polemica classico-romantica: l'Italia e il ripudio del gotico', *Italian Studies*, 69.2 (2014), 231–45; Fabio Camilletti, 'Italians and the Irrational', in *Echoing Voices in Italian Literature: Tradition and Translation in the 20th Century*, ed. by Teresa Franco and Cecilia Piantanida (Newcastle upon Tyne: Cambridge Scholars, 2018), pp. 159–79.

[16] See Roberto Esposito, *Living Thought: The Origins and Actuality of Italian Philosophy*, trans. by Zakiya Hanafi (Stanford: Stanford University Press, 2012), p. 1.

[17] Dominating the Gulf of Trieste, the city is located at the northernmost point of the Adriatic, a few miles away from Slovenia (to the east) and Croatia (to the south). From 1381 to 1918 it was part of Habsburg territory and became its principal seaport in the nineteenth century. At the end of the First World War, Trieste was annexed to Italy as a territorial reward for siding with the Allied powers during the conflict.

sentiment regarding the Italian motherland. As a result, in the first half of the century the city acted as a 'door' through which Northern European influences started seeping into the country. Psychoanalysis was one of the foreign imports that reached Italy via Trieste, and *La coscienza di Zeno* was one of the earliest examples of the way in which Freudian discourse was (un)welcomed in Italian culture.[18]

As scholarship has widely demonstrated, however, the very first Italian psychoanalytic novel is also a text that actually took a robustly resisting stance against the discipline of psychoanalysis, marking its distance through a sophisticated game of irony.[19] Whilst presenting itself as one of the first literary channels through which Freud's discipline could be disseminated across the country, Svevo's book also functioned as a first 'antibody' against a *savoir* that clashed with some of the crucial features of Italy's accepted national character.[20] In order to show how the novel embodies an early resistance against Freud's challenge to subjectivity, we will focus here on three main elements: the book's hybrid genre, the choice of title and the difficulties this posed for subsequent English translations of the volume, and Zeno's reflection upon the language in which he is writing as a first-person narrator.[21]

Let us start with the issue of genre. When presenting the book to the English-speaking public, seven years after its Italian publication, translator Beryl De Zoete opted for the title *Confessions of Zeno*.[22] In so doing, she gave her audience a firm indication with regard to the ambiguous nature of the book, which, in the preface, presented itself either as a *novella*, an *autobiografia* or a collection of *memorie*. This ambiguity was deliberately designed to superimpose each genre over the other, with the clear intent of puzzling the reader.[23] By foregrounding *confessions* and placing this keyword in plain

---

[18] On the role of Trieste in the dissemination of psychoanalysis in Italy see Giorgio Voghera, *Gli anni della psicoanalisi* (Pordenone: Edizione Studio Tesi, 1980), p. 3.

[19] See Aaron Esman, 'Italo Svevo and the First Psychoanalytic Novel', *International Journal of Psychoanalysis*, 82 (2001), 1225–33.

[20] See Silvana Patriarca's discussion of this notion in *Italian Vices: Nation and Character from the Risorgimento to the Republic* (New York: Cambridge University Press, 2010).

[21] For a systematic analysis of *La coscienza di Zeno*'s resistance against the dethroning of the conscious subject see Alessandra Diazzi, 'Is There an Unconscious in this Text? On Italo Svevo's *La coscienza di Zeno*', in *The Archaeology of the Unconscious: Italian Perspectives*, ed. by Alessandra Aloisi and Fabio Camilletti (London: Routledge, 2019), pp. 235–56.

[22] Italo Svevo, *Confessions of Zeno* (London: Alfred A. Knopf, 1930).

[23] Italo Svevo, *La coscienza di Zeno* (Milan: Feltrinelli, 2002), p. 3.

view at a paratextual level, the translation aimed, instead, to propose a predetermined interpretation of Zeno's writings, making explicit reference to the well-defined genre of the memoir. As acknowledged by another of Svevo's translators, William Weaver, the implications of such a choice went beyond the question of literary genre:[24] it betrayed the translator's discomfort with the ambiguity of the Italian term *coscienza*, which could be translated into English either as 'conscience' or as 'consciousness'. The choice between the two words was not irrelevant. As Sandor Goodhart puts it, the difference between 'consciousness' and 'conscience' is, on the one hand, 'a matter of perception or awareness' and, on the other, 'a matter of moral authority, the degree to which I am constrained or governed by a voice which speaks to me of what I should or should not do'.[25] In strictly Freudian terms, 'conscience' would coincide with the Super-Ego. Therefore, De Zoete's choice, voluntarily or not, appears to mitigate and possibly downsize the profound ambiguity entailed by the model of subjectivity presented in Svevo's text.

The emphasis on the dimension of *coscienza* in Svevo's novel produces at least two major, paradoxical consequences. These are at the heart of the book's operation and are particularly relevant for the way in which it copes with a discourse – that of psychoanalysis – that is perceived, in the Italian-speaking domain, as a quintessentially *foreign* one. First, it is at least unexpected for a book that is explicitly inspired by psychoanalysis and is presented as the journal of an analytic treatment to put such emphasis on the term *coscienza*, rather than placing the unconscious – the psychoanalytic buzzword *par excellence* – in the spotlight. Secondly, a book that allegedly 'entails a programmatic subversion of the traditional model of a fixed and individuated subjectivity' effectively places itself under the aegis of rationalism and consciousness, by employing a term that is strongly related to Cartesian and rationalist understandings of subjectivity.[26] Labelling the book as a *confession* and a *memoir* can be interpreted as a way of softening these contradictions, ultimately inserting Svevo's hybrid book within a genre traditionally associated with an Ego-led speaking voice.

What the English translator could not convey to her readers, however, is that Svevo's ambiguous title introduces a fundamental surplus of meaning.

---

[24] See William Weaver, 'Translator's Introduction', in Italo Svevo, *Zeno's Conscience* (New York: Vintage International, 2001), pp. xiii–xxv (p. xxv).

[25] Sandor Goodhart, *'Conscience,* Conscience, Consciousness', in *Remembering for the Future*, ed. by John K. Roth, Elisabeth Maxwell, Margot Levy and Wendy Whitworth (London: Palgrave Macmillan, 2001), pp. 98–113 (p. 98).

[26] Deborah Anderson, 'An Ethics of Nicotine: Writing a Subjectivity of Process in Italo Svevo's *La coscienza di Zeno'*, *Forum Italicum*, 2.39 (2005), 441–60 (p. 442).

The presence of *coscienza* on the threshold of Svevo's text can actually be interpreted as a fundamental, though dissimulated, interpretative key. The term stands out as an essential clue, which enables us to interpret the book as an early example of a peculiarly Italian approach to – and a resistance against – Freud's Copernican revolution of subjectivity. The fact that conscience should be taken as a key for reading and interpreting Zeno's pages is confirmed in the last chapter of the book, 'Psico-analisi'. Here, Zeno suggests to his readers that everything they have read up to that point was the fruit of a conscious elaboration of truths and lies. In other words, the narrator reveals that his recollection of memories followed a controlled creative process rather than an attempt to investigate the most hidden recesses of his psyche. Interestingly, this is presented as a linguistic matter. The Triestine narrator, who speaks dialect as his first language, reveals the impossibility of loosening the constraints of consciousness when forced to exercise a rational control over his discourse in order to express himself in Italian, a language which is not his mother tongue: 'Il dottore [...] ignora cosa significhi scrivere in italiano per noi che parliamo e non sappiamo scrivere il dialetto. Una confessione per iscritto è sempre menzognera. Con ogni nostra parola toscana noi mentiamo!' [The doctor does not know what it means to write in Italian for those of us who speak but don't know how to write in dialect. A written confession is always mendacious. With every word we write in Tuscan we are lying!][27] Through this confession, Svevo establishes dialect as the genuine language of the psyche, whereas Italian is presented as the discourse of the egoic subject. In doing so, he suggests an understanding of the unconscious as a melting pot of both domestic and foreign influences. National identity, on the other hand, somehow suppresses this dimension, imposing a unified language spoken by a unitary, and therefore lying, subject. As a result, *La coscienza di Zeno* articulates and exemplifies how, as soon as psychoanalysis made its appearance in the country, Italy erected a *cordon sanitaire* against its uncanny knowledge and against the discipline's 'dethroning' of Ego-oriented subjectivity. The latter is not intended in exclusively individual terms: Zeno is meant to embody a character split between a neurotic soul, shaped by the Triestine environment and its Northern European influences, and the typically Italian and Mediterranean tendency to 'extroversion', to put it in Benvenuto's terms, already quoted above.[28]

---

[27] Italo Svevo, *La coscienza di Zeno* (Milan: Mursia, 1986), p. 434.
[28] See above, p. 312.

Inwardness and Outwardness

Far from remaining an *unicum*, *La coscienza di Zeno* marked a well-defined path in the peculiar way Italian literature would conceptualize the struggle between conscious and unconscious drives. After Svevo's work, it is difficult to find another example in Italian literature of a novel presenting such an explicit analytical structure.[29] However, Ottiero Ottieri is probably the Italian author who most extensively employed psychoanalysis throughout his literary production. A substantial engagement with the discipline is not the only link between these two writers. They also share, in fact, a view of the unconscious/consciousness pair that relies on sociopolitical, rather than exclusively psychological, factors.

In 1954, Ottiero Ottieri published *Memorie dell'incoscienza*, a representation of the years of fascism narrated through the vicissitudes of an Italian family. Through the book's evocative title, we can assume that Ottieri meant to recall, whether explicitly or not, Svevo's *La coscienza di Zeno*. Despite the differences between the two works, the term *(in)coscienza* enables us to detect an ideal connection, rooted in the rejection of 'unconsciousness' and in the primacy of extroversion over introversion which lies at the core of the two books' models of subjectivity.

Ottieri's use of the term *incoscienza*, as the author himself explains, originates from the psychoanalytic notion of the unconscious, and refers to a condition in which the irrational aspects of personality dominate over consciousness and rationality:

> L'incoscienza, qui, dovrebbe venire da inconscio (nel senso della moderna psicologia del profondo), della cui azione quotidiana è il frutto; e sta a indicare non tanto la spericolatezza, quanto una assoluta immaturità psicologica, un male senza colpa, eppure capace delle conseguenze più disastrose [...] La coscienza è una faticosa conquista che gli individui e le classi sociali si guadagnano faticosamente (o non si guadagnano affatto) storicamente.[30]

> [Here, 'incoscienza' is meant to come from 'unconscious' (in the sense attributed to it by modern depth psychology), as it is the product of its everyday activities. What it indicates is not so much heedlessness, but rather the total lack of psychological maturity, a sinfulness beyond

---

[29] An exception to this is Giuseppe Berto, *Il male oscuro* (Milan: Rizzoli, 1964).

[30] Ottiero Ottieri, *Memorie dell'incoscienza*, 2nd edn (Milan: Bompiani, 1967), p. 215.

guilt, that is nevertheless capable of producing the most disastrous consequences (...) 'Coscienza' is a demanding goal which, historically, individuals as well as social classes attain through hard work (or not at all)]

Rather than presenting individual 'memories from the unconscious', however, the book suggests broadening the term on a relational, social and, ultimately, historical scale. As Ottieri himself makes clear, the novel narrates individual and historical events which are set in motion by the influence of the unconscious sphere:

In questo libro, il fascismo, l'impulso suicida, l'affetto tra sorella e fratello, i vari meschini modi di vedere il mondo in alcuni personaggi, sono mossi direttamente dai fili di un inconscio individuale e collettivo.[31]

[In this book, fascism, suicidal instinct, love between sister and brother, or the small-minded way in which some characters see the world are all motivated by the pulling of the strings of the individual and the collective unconscious]

As a result, in a book that aims to provide 'una risposta parziale e comunque necessaria all'inspiegabile e convinta fede di molti giovani alla fede fascista' [a partial yet necessary answer to the inexplicable and unshakeable faith placed in fascism by many young people], fascism is explained as a collective relapse into a state of preconscious subjectivity, dominated by the prevailing of irrational drives.

The notion of the unconscious therefore takes on a negative connotation, in that it provokes 'disastrose conseguenze' [disastrous consequences] on a social scale. The idea of the unconscious as the trigger for irresponsible, dramatic events implies the necessity for the politically responsible subject to attain full control over it, moving towards a perception of the acquisition of consciousness as a civil responsibility. Ottieri presents the unconscious as a 'territory' to be 'reclaimed' by the conscious sphere, according to a movement of progressive rationalization that is, first of all, a political goal. The restraints of subjectivity and the subject's condition of self-awareness are, in fact, perceived as the fundamental premises for civil commitment, whereas the eclipse of a structured self implies the loss of social freedom and of political rights.

The association between an Ego-led subject and civil responsibility

---

[31] Ottieri, *Memorie dell'incoscienza*, p. 249.

is also evident in Ottieri's later book *Il campo di concentrazione* (1972), a journal of his psychiatric treatment while he was hospitalized in a private clinic in Switzerland. Here, Ottieri explicitly states the impossibility of being socially and politically engaged when a stable and fixed identity is affected by a serious condition of neurosis. A state of reduced consciousness, caused by illness, leads the subject to lose his/her social and relational nature. As a result, he finds himself trapped in an extreme state of solipsism: 'La mia energia è tutta ripiegata in se stessa, rovesciata in dentro, verso la "realtà interiore" dello "psichismo"' [My energy is entirely folded in on itself, bent inwards, towards the 'interior reality' of 'psychism'].[32] Ottieri carries this view further by opposing the pathological subject to the figure of the philosopher Antonio Gramsci, symbolically taken as the role model of the engaged intellectual in Italy: 'Gramsci in carcere non parlava di sé, studiava e faceva cultura. Io faccio e disfaccio solo me stesso – non più cultura – come rimasto solo al mondo' [In prison, Gramsci did not talk about himself, he studied and produced culture. I only make and unmake myself – not culture, not any more – as if I were alone in the world].[33] As a result, for Ottieri the subject affected by psychological disorders must be seen as a prisoner deprived of freedom and rights. The loss of rational thinking and of the Ego's control over personality are explicitly compared to the state of detention in a total institution: 'Che cosa è meglio? La depressione o il carcere? Il carcere [...] Vivo nell'ergastolo della psiche' [What is preferable? Depression or imprisonment? Imprisonment (...) I am experiencing a life-sentence of the psyche'].[34] The author interprets neurosis as a metamorphosis that takes him from a form of extroverted subjectivity to a state of introverted isolation and which, rather than being narrowly related to the individual's private well-being, is conceived as a lack of social engagement. Ottieri describes himself as a patient who longs for psychiatric drugs and analytical treatment, portraying these as the aids that may restore his ability to be a public, rather than an exclusively private, subject: 'L'analista vuole costruire in me una personalità integra e libera [...] L'analista vuole che torni uno scrittore' [My analyst wants to build me a personality that is whole and free (...) My analyst wants me to be a writer once again].[35] *Il campo di concentrazione* thus ultimately establishes an equivalence between a fully functioning and structured subject and the possibility of political and public agency, just as *Memorie dell'incoscienza*

---

[32] Ottiero Ottieri, *Il campo di concentrazione* (Milan: Bompiani, 1972), p. 23.
[33] Ottieri, *Campo di concentrazione*, p. 14.
[34] Ottieri, *Campo di concentrazione*, pp. 15, 104.
[35] Ottieri, *Campo di concentrazione*, pp. 13, 258.

interpreted the supremacy of the unconscious over the conscious sphere in collective and historical terms. As Svevo had already suggested decades earlier, subjectivity is ultimately a matter that pertains primarily to the social, public and national terrain.

The Unconscious and the Political

Ottieri's view of the collapse of an Ego-oriented subjectivity as the eclipse of civil commitment should be read in parallel with the work of the Italian New Avant-garde's most radical wing and, in particular, that of one of its pre-eminent members, Edoardo Sanguineti. For Sanguineti, the dethronement of the Ego did not imply a fall into irrationalism and therefore (as it was for Ottieri) into fascism; rather, it was the only condition of possibility for freeing the subject from the constraint of bourgeois values.[36]

As Alfredo Giuliani noted as early as 1961 in his preface to the anthology *I Novissimi*, Italian Avant-garde poets generally adopted a model of 'schizoid' expressive style, aimed at mimicking the apperception of reality on the part of a subject with a 'disturbed sense of the self and an extreme perplexity about one's identity'.[37] In particular, for Sanguineti this linguistic strategy was the primary means to portray and interpret the condition of alienation and exploitation of individuals living under capitalist modes of production. The role of schizoid language was to reproduce – and to denounce – the condition of the individual subjugated by dominant social structures, thereby portraying alienation (from a Marxist point of view) both as a condition of disease and as the condition of possibility for challenging the social order.

What we need to note, here, is that although Sanguineti's position is drastically opposed to that of Ottieri, both interpret the eclipse of rational thinking as a primarily social and historically inherited condition, rather than as the symptom of an individual discomfort. Within a social, cultural and literary context that was still under the influence of what Jennifer Burns has defined as a 'monolithic notion of commitment',[38] Sanguineti proposed a 'legit' rethinking of the subject's psyche. As a result, he cast an extroverted

---

[36] This position was most notably expressed in his poem *Laborintus*, published in 1956. See Edoardo Sanguineti, *Laborintus: Laszo Varga, 27 poesie* (Varese: Magenta, 1956).

[37] Sue E. Estroff, 'Self, Identity, and Subjective Experiences of Schizophrenia: In Search of the Subject', *Schizophrenia Bulletin*, 2.15 (1989), 189–96 (p. 189).

[38] Jennifer Burns, *Fragments of 'Impegno': Interpretations of Commitment in Contemporary Italian Narrative, 1980–2000* (Leeds: Northern Universities Presses, 2001), p. 1.

gaze on the most intimate dimension of the human being – a gesture which must not be read as a *riflusso*, a return to the private, but rather as a subversive stance. Irrationality is not celebrated for the sake of the triumph of the 'Es' [Id], but is rather seen as a necessary phase in the process of historical development.

The ideological appropriation of the schizoid subject is closely related to Sanguineti's interpretation of Freud's theory of subjectivity and, in particular, of the deconstruction to which the rationally oriented 'I' is exposed after the introduction of the notion of unconscious:

L'io va in pezzi con la scoperta dell'inconscio [...] se riparto da Freud – che aveva capito che là dove c'era l'Es bisognava porre l'Io – devo rifare i conti sul soggetto.[39]

[The 'I' shatters with the discovery of the unconscious (...) if I restart from Freud – who had understood that where we found the Id we must place the Ego – I must find new ways to come to terms with the subject]

What interests Sanguineti about the collapse of the Ego is the ideological repercussions of this process. The author interprets the crisis of the 'I' brought to light by Freud in social terms, understanding it as a challenge to bourgeois identity. By undermining the dominion of a monolithic self, Sanguineti argues, psychoanalysis may challenge 'l'Io penso' [the I think] that coincides, on the social level, with the 'proiezione borghese di un io regolatore' [the bourgeois projection of a regulating 'I'].[40] The sabotage of subjectivity undertaken by Freud takes on ideological and political significance, in that it corresponds to the collapse of the social constructs that bourgeois ideology imposes on individuals: 'Nasce la psicoanalisi e il soggetto che la borghesia aveva costituito con la carta d'identità è liquidato' [Psychoanalysis is born, and the subject which had been built by the bourgeoisie with its identity cards, is undone].[41] The Freudian motto, 'where Id was, there Ego shall be' (*Wo Es war, soll Ich werden*), thus takes on an ideological nuance, with the Id becoming an essential stronghold of ideological resistance against an Ego that is the result of the bourgeois exploitation – and ideological colonization – of the subject. Through literature, Sanguineti theorizes an equivalence between a disorganized subjectivity and political disorder, almost twenty

[39] Antonio Gnoli, ed., *Sanguineti's Song: Conversazioni immorali* (Milan: Feltrinelli, 2006), p. 17.

[40] Gnoli, *Sanguineti's Song*, p. 15.

[41] Gnoli, *Sanguineti's Song*, p. 148.

years before the publication of Deleuze and Guattari's *Capitalism and Schizophrenia*.[42]

The work undertaken in Sanguineti's *Laborintus* in many respects heralds the ideological appropriation of the deviant subject that pervades Italy's counterculture, from the early 1960s to the anti-authoritarian movements that emerged after 1968 and aimed to give voice to 'new subjects, who were expected to express what until then had remained censured and excluded'.[43] Within this time span, the most relevant figure for the history of psychoanalysis in Italy is certainly Franco Basaglia, the psychiatrist who reformed the country's mental care institutions and championed the total closure of asylums (which were abolished in 1978).[44] Marginalized subjects thus found in protest a means of empowerment, transforming themselves, their discourses, their bodies and their identities into fields of political battle. Once again, psychoanalysis was being appropriated through discourses that were primarily political. And it was resiliently adapted to extrovert modalities of action.

The Italian psychoanalyst Elvio Fachinelli is one of the most original representatives of this tendency, both within the national context and worldwide. Aiming to propose a new, subversive, form of psychoanalysis, Fachinelli started from a radical rethinking of subjectivity, which aimed in particular to reinterpret the Freudian motto *Wo Es war, soll Ich Werden*. Instead of seeing it as a call for the subject to *subentrare* into the domain of the unconscious (in an act of possibly partial substitution), Fachinelli states that the subject should *entrare*, that is fully enter, its space.[45] By so doing, the subject can reach an ecstatic condition which enables the self to soften the constraints of a socially, historically and culturally imposed fixed structure. As a result, Fachinelli firmly rejects the idea that psychoanalysis aims to reinstate the Ego as master in his own house, supporting, on the contrary, an analysis that may help the self to dismiss its boundaries, absorbing Otherness within itself. This process is seen as the sunset of a 'masculine' understanding of subjectivity, in order to embrace a 'feminine' modality of conceptualizing one's own identity.

[42] Gilles Delueze and Felix Guattari, *Anti-Oedipus: Capitalism and Schizophrenia*, trans. by Robert Hurley, Mark Seem and Helen R. Lane (London: Athlone, 1984).

[43] Paola Di Cori, 'Listening and Silencing', in *Speaking Out and Silencing*, ed. by Anna Cento Bull and Adalgisa Giorgio (London: Legenda, 2006), pp. 30–41 (p. 32).

[44] See John Foot, *The Man Who Closed the Asylums: Franco Basaglia and the Revolution in Mental Health Care* (London: Verso, 2015).

[45] Sergio Benvenuto, 'Finale al femminile', *Aut Aut*, 325 (October–December 2011), 89–102.

Not incidentally, Fachinelli's theory of the subject was profoundly influenced by Italian feminism, which in turn had undertaken a substantial rethinking of the theory and the praxes of psychoanalysis. The 'female subject and a new female cogito' are in fact essential aspects of a variegated feminist movement that, although influenced by foreign – and especially French – movements, 'remains distinctively Italian',[46] including in its political uses of the notion of the unconscious. Italian feminists identified in the unconscious the site wherein the subjugation of women is most deeply engrained. For them, patriarchal domination has been unconsciously introjected and it is therefore maintained, or even reiterated, as an ambiguous form of compulsion. Manuela Fraire claims:

> Il modo in cui l'inconscio entra nell'oppressione femminile è per talune la più grande scoperta del femminismo degli anni settanta: esso costituisce un elemento in più che caratterizza e distingue l'oppressione femminile rispetto alla condizione degli altri soggetti oppressi.[47]

> [For some women, the way in which the unconscious becomes part of female oppression is the greatest discovery of 1970s feminism: it is an additional element that characterizes and distinguishes female oppression from that of other oppressed subjects]

Italian feminists conceived the unconscious as an intrinsically political dimension, in that its 'decolonization' from masculine fantasies would coincide with the first fundamental step towards self-determination. In order to achieve this goal, the groups of *pratica dell'inconscio* [consciousness raising groups], founded in Milan in the early 1970s, promoted an original reinterpretation of collective analysis inspired by political praxes that had originated in France. This form of women-led group analysis was based on the assumption that work done on the dimension of the self would not liberate the preconscious dimension from masculine control. Nor would it be effective in debunking the legacy of the Ego, perceived as the by-product of centuries of patriarchal domination and ultimately controlled by a colonized unconscious. As a result, the groups believed that an 'unconscious production which is

---

[46] Sandra Bono and Paola Kemp, eds, *Italian Feminist Thought: A Reader* (Oxford: Blackwell, 1991), p. 2.

[47] Manuela Fraire, *Lessico politico delle donne: Teorie del femminismo* (Rome: Franco Angeli, 2002), p. 78.

collective' without 'end[ing] up in the private sphere' did exist.[48] This public dimension of the psyche was the fundamental point of departure to refound a feminine, and feminist, subjectivity, which had both private and political implications. At the same time, group analysis aimed to decouple the deep exploration of the self from a solipsistic dimension through a form of therapy that acted on a relational form of subjectivity, as though women as a collective subject had to be healed from a historically inherited disease.

Conclusion

'Transnationalism', Damousi and Plotkin argue, 'encourages a move away from traditional analytic paradigms to those which are framed by intersection and interdisciplinarity, challenging accepted categories such as center and periphery'. Applying this challenge to the domain of the psyche, we can see the subversion of subjectivity as a refusal of the idea of the Ego as the stable centre of personality and of the unconscious mind as a peripheral territory to be colonized by conscience.[49] The assimilation of psychoanalysis into national culture since the early twentieth century has acted here as a lens through which we have aimed to identify some specificities in the Italian approach to the discipline. At the same time, assuming that 'the transnationalization of a system of thought can only be understood as a historical process that occurs as a result of movements between sites, places and cultures but that, at the same time, is linked to local conditions', we hope this chapter has contributed to shed light on the crucial role Italy had in transnationalizing psychoanalysis.[50]

From *La coscienza di Zeno* onwards, it is possible to observe in the country a resistance against those unconscious forces and external sources that threaten the rational and unitary understanding of the 'I'. This process is not to be understood exclusively on a psychological level; rather, it should be read, first and foremost, as a sociopolitical phenomenon. The unconscious/consciousness dichotomy takes on a collective meaning in the resistant appropriation of psychoanalysis within Italian culture, embodying, in turn, the tension between regional identities and national unity (*La coscienza di Zeno*); the opposition between political agency and lack of civil responsibility (*Memorie dell'incoscienza*); the conflict between the relapse into the private and political commitment (*Il campo di concentrazione*); the fight between

---

[48] Practice of the Unconscious Group, Milan, 1986, 'Practice of the Unconscious and Women's Movement', in *Italian Feminist Thought: A Reader*, ed. by Sandra Bono and Paola Kemp (Oxford: Blackwell, 1991), pp. 83–94 (p. 83).

[49] Damousi and Plotkin, *Transnational Unconscious*, p. 6.

[50] Damousi and Plotkin, *Transnational Unconscious*, p. 8.

a bourgeois, institutionalized and structured identity and a deviant, revolutionary, subject (*Laborintus*, as well as the revolution carried out by Basaglia's democratic psychiatry and by the feminist movement).

According to Roberto Esposito, 'Italian thought' finds one of its more radical traits in its intersectional positioning: while placing itself as an element of 'difference' and as an 'exceptionality' within the broader framework of global thought, it manages nonetheless to address, however obliquely, and to reorient global debates, despite (and often thanks to) its deliberate marginality. The examples presented here, although necessarily limited, confirm this view. Though it may present itself as intrinsically alien to, or strenuously resisting against, allegedly 'foreign' strains of thought – and particularly those falling in the broad cauldron of 'unreason', where psychoanalytic discoveries were often relegated – Italian-speaking culture managed to incorporate, manipulate and profoundly reorient psychoanalysis through specific paradigms. First of all, through its deterritorialized dimension, where 'territory' is to be understood, first, geographically – given the degree of 'foreignness' and, above all, hybridity associated with psychoanalysis – and, secondly, epistemologically – considering that psychoanalysis, as a discipline, constantly blurs the boundaries between subjects (e.g., medicine, psychiatry, philosophy, psychology). At the same time, Italy has domesticated psychoanalysis according to two further, specific mechanisms, which Esposito terms the 'immanentization of antagonism' and the 'mundanization of the subject'.[51] The first expression relates to the idea that 'conflict is inherent to a reality that cannot be transcended in a different dimension'; the second to the fact that, 'from the time of its Renaissance beginnings, Italian philosophy can be said to have been constructed outside th[e] argumentative machine' that postulates 'the unity of the subject' as based 'on a separation between itself and its own biological substrate – or in metaphysical terms, between body and soul – crucial to the entire Western tradition'.[52] In other words, while explicitly conceptualizing 'unreason' as otherness from its 'rational' standpoint, Italian-speaking culture nonetheless introjects and metamorphoses it according to its 'extrovert' vocation, constantly renegotiating it in a political dimension. This goes against the dominant idea of Italy's allegedly constitutive hostility towards intellectual discourses coming from the 'outside' – an interpretation that has pervaded the vocabulary of *Italianistica* as a discipline, in Italy and abroad, to the extent of becoming almost invisible. We should think, instead, of 'Italophony' as a sphere of resilience and as an intellectual laboratory engaged in the transnational circulation of ideas.

---

[51] Esposito, *Living Thought*, p. 24.
[52] Esposito, *Living Thought*, p. 29.

17

Speaking in Class

Accented Voices
in Transnational Italian Cinema

Derek Duncan

To survive linguistically and emotionally the contradictions of everyday life, multilingual subjects draw on the formal semiotic and aesthetic resources afforded by various symbolic systems to reframe these contradictions and create alternative worlds of their own. (Claire Kramsch)

Migratory aesthetics is an aesthetic of geographical mobility beyond the nation state and its linguistic uniformity. (Mieke Bal)

Parliamo di noi rispetto a quella roba lì. (Valerio Mastandrea)

Sam Mendes's blockbuster *Spectre* (2015), the second feature he directed in the James Bond series, is set partly in the spectacular urban spaces of Rome's historic centre. Filming was initially held up as the production team struggled to identify suitable locations for shooting the external scenes. On the one hand, it proved difficult to find areas of the city centre uncontaminated by rubbish and graffiti. On the other, the team had to deal with attempts to limit their access to certain sites because of anxieties that the film crew's presence might further damage the city's cultural heritage. Protests were largely assuaged by an enormous street cleaning operation that got on top of a problem that had completely defeated Rome's local authorities. As well as funding the pristine version of the Eternal City required for the film, the producers paid an estimated one million euros in location fees not to mention covering additional municipal staffing costs. They also made a substantial contribution to the local economy through their presence, as well as indirectly promoting Rome as an object of tourist desire through the film itself. Rome was a key part of the film's marketing strategy, one of a series of sublime spectacles including the Austrian Alps and the Sahara which featured prominently in the film as apposite sets of cosmopolitan glamour.

Spectre offers a way of thinking about transnational cinema which emphasizes film's place in multinational economic production and exchange. Although its director is British, as was ostensibly the production company Eon, the film is less an example of national cinema than the product of global capital. Its British star Daniel Craig featured alongside an unusually international supporting cast which included Monica Bellucci, Christoph Waltz, Léa Seydoux and Dave Bautista, further displacing the film from a securely mononational frame. *Spectre* addresses an international commercial market. Sony, Columbia Pictures and 20th Century Fox Home Entertainment managed its international distribution and exhibition (both theatrical and on DVD), indicating again the truly global dimensions of the film as a cultural product.[1]

The term 'transnational' has also been used to designate films which in some way express and reflect contemporary global movements of people and the cultures that inevitably travel with them. Rather than offering further proof of multinational capital's indifference to the impenetrability of national borders, this other transnational cinema makes the inequities of geopolitical power a recurrent concern. Sometimes, but not necessarily, these films are directed by people who themselves have moved across cultural and political borders.[2] They interrogate formations of cultural identity put under pressure by increased global mobility and interconnectedness. They may document or critique the migrant experience, often reflecting negatively on the host country, but sometimes also offering more celebratory accounts of cross-cultural encounters.

However transnational cinema is understood, it challenges long-standing and powerful ideas about the particularity of 'national cinema'. These ideas shape in a descriptive sense the body of cinematic work produced by a single

---

[1] The full and extremely lengthy cast and technical credit list gives a powerful insight into the global dimensions of the film's production. See http://www.imdb.com/title/tt2379713/fullcredits?ref_=tt_ov_st_sm [accessed 30 October 2019].

[2] The work of Hamid Naficy has been particularly influential in thinking about the aesthetics and cinematographic practices of film-makers living outside their homeland. See *An Accented Cinema: Exilic and Diasporic Film-Making* (Princeton: Princeton University Press, 2001). For a discussion of the work of the limited number of non-Italian-born film-makers working in Italy, see Àine O'Healy, 'An Accented Gaze: Italy's Transmigrant Filmmakers', in *A Companion to Italian Cinema*, ed. by Frank Burke (Chichester: John Wiley & Sons, 2017), pp. 484–99.

nation but, more saliently, provide a malleable technology through which to lay claim to the specificity of a national culture by asserting its difference from other cultures. In counterpoint, the transversal study of film culture, looking at circuits of production, circulation and reception, as well as the close thematic or formal analysis of individual films, moves beyond an isolationist view of the national paradigm.[3] Transnational understandings of film culture in its diversity offer fundamental insights into the connectedness and porosity of cultures, economies and national identities, as well as the transformative power of cultural models as they travel. In the case of *Spectre*, the essential Britishness of James Bond as a cultural icon functions as a transnational commodity. The saleability of Bond on the global market does not undermine his iconic national status, but offers an alternative albeit complementary mechanism for understanding how the national and the transnational are both constructed and intersecting.

My focus is on the type of cinema, however, which shows a preoccupation with human mobility at a historical moment when demographic displacement, both forced and elected, is a highly charged political, social and cultural concern. While it is extremely illuminating to look at films produced in different locations across the globe dealing with this topic, it is equally valid to limit critical analysis to films made in a single nation, not least as a way of testing exactly what that singularity might mean. It is less paradoxical than it might initially seem to talk about transnational cinema in a national context, because the transnational is always determined by the multiple specificities of place, not by their absence. The transnational is a global phenomenon experienced also at a local level. This essay will analyse in some detail *La mia classe* (2013), a little-known Italian film which dramatizes how transnational mobility may be experienced at a very local, human level. The analysis of the film which is set in an Italian language class for adult learners looks particularly at how the accented voice of the migrant is an essential aspect of its aesthetic strategies, directed towards the interrogation, and finally expansion, of what constitutes national subjectivity caught in a transnational frame.

Human movement, it needs to be stressed, is never unfettered, and is shaped by particular histories and opportunities. Italian films about late twentieth- and twenty-first-century global mobility have on occasion brought to the fore the specificity of Italy's place in such patterns of displacement. Gianni Amelio's *Lamerica* (1993) addresses the often-forgotten history of

---

[3] For a concise but rich account of Italian cinema in a transnational industrial context see Laura Rascaroli, 'Italian Cinema in the Post-National Age', in *The Italian Cinema Book*, ed. by Peter Bondanella (London: British Film Institute, 2013), pp. 285–94.

Italian colonialism and historical links with Albania. This memory of colonialism is tightly bound up with Italy's own history of mass emigration. The grammatical imprecision of the film's title recalls the United States as the object of migrant aspiration, but stands in too for the economic necessity and ambition which saw millions of Italians move to South America, Northern Europe, Australia and elsewhere in search of a more secure life. The film also touches on the historical divide between the north and south of Italy, and internal histories of economic disadvantage, racism and discrimination which play into responses to migration to Italy today.[4] The entanglements of such apparently disparate phenomena are brought together again in Emanuele Crialese's *Terraferma* (2011), set on the tiny island of Linosa, a hundred miles south of Sicily. In *Terraferma*, a local family gives refuge to a pregnant Eritrean woman and her son after saving them from a shipwrecked vessel that had set sail from the Libyan coast. The film recalls Italy's colonial presence in East Africa and Libya, as well as exploring the economic tensions between the rich north and less affluent south. The presence of wealthy tourists from Northern Europe on Linosa creates different tensions in the local community and dramatizes questions of citizenship and national belonging that have been defining aspects of Italian films dealing with transnational mobility since the early 1990s. Film-makers have characteristically invented dramas of co-habitation examining both what it means for migrants to live in Italy, and what their presence means for Italians.[5] This last element underpins the statement by the actor Valerio Mastandrea used as an epigraph for this essay, when he asserts that when we speak about the other, we are really speaking about ourselves.[6]

This type of indirect self-reflection means that films ostensibly about migration to Italy may, on a deeper level, offer a critique of Italy's anxieties over questions of national identity, cultural memory, and its place in Europe

---

[4] The intersections of these different historical and cultural factors are analysed with great insight in Rhiannon Noel Welch, 'Contact, Contagion, Immunization: Gianni Amelio's *Lamerica* (1994)', in *Italian Mobilities*, ed. by Ruth Ben-Ghiat and Stephanie Malia Hom (New York: Routledge, 2015), pp. 68–87.

[5] The emotional and psychological tenor of these dramas varies a lot. Many are explorations in very personal, domestic settings of the anxieties that migration to Italy has caused. For a discussion of a number of these films see Derek Duncan, 'Double Time: Facing the Future in Migration's Past', *California Italian Studies*, 2.1 (2011), https://escholarship.org/uc/item/38q389mk [accessed 13 May 2020].

[6] For a very useful analysis of this phenomenon in a range of Italian films about migration see Giovanna Faleschini Lerner, 'From the Other Side of the Mediterranean: Hospitality in Italian Migration Cinema', *California Italian Studies*, 1.1 (2010), https://escholarship.org/uc/item/45h010h5 [accessed 13 May 2020].

and the global economy. The identification and analysis of such anxieties is not straightforward. Àine O'Healy, who has written extensively on films about migration, warns of the pitfalls of interpreting film texts at face value, not least since most Italian films about migration have adopted a realist storytelling mode encouraging the spectator to accept uncritically the truth of what is on screen. In an essay on the representation of the Mediterranean crossing, she argues for the importance and value of seeking out 'the elisions and inconsistencies in the cinematic narration which point to some of the unspoken tensions and broader political dilemmas underpinning Italian attitudes toward Mediterranean mobility'.[7] To point this out is not to dismiss films as mere fictions or misrepresentations, but rather to acknowledge that texts require interpretation and a careful interrogation of the strategies through which meaning is produced.

The film I will analyse in the rest of this essay invites the kind of attentiveness to 'elisions and inconsistencies' that O'Healy mentions as it attempts both to document an aspect of contemporary experience in Italy while simultaneously reminding the audience that it is a self-consciously crafted cinematographic work of representation. As such it asks the spectator to question *how* they see as much as *what* they see on screen. Daniele Gaglianone's *La mia classe*, a low-budget semi-documentary film set on the outskirts of Rome, features Mastandrea, already well-known to Italian audiences as a political activist as well as a prominent film actor. Although this film was presented at the Venice Film Festival and as such entered the international art cinema circuit of exhibition, it has not been widely distributed.[8] I decided to use it as the primary subject of this essay because it explores the lives of a group of people living in Rome who come from a wide range of different countries. Their reasons for migrating are varied, and their mixed emotional responses to Italy and to the places they left challenge the tendency to homogenize the figure of the migrant and the experience of migration. Crucially, the film moves some way from telling a story that only uses non-Italians as a prism through which to reflect on the nation itself, and allows its characters some autonomy in

---

[7] Àine O'Healy, 'Mediterranean Passages: Abjection and Belonging in Contemporary Italian Cinema', *California Italian Studies*, 1.1 (2010), 1–19 (p. 2). Her path-breaking monograph on Italian cinema of migration offers a theoretically informed and densely contextualized analysis of the topic: Àine O'Healy, *Migrant Anxieties: Italian Cinema in a Transnational Frame* (Bloomington: Indiana University Press, 2019).

[8] The English Press Book prepared for Venice gives some useful insight into how Gaglianone saw the project and information on the students who take part: http://www.venice-days.it/public/documenti1/BOOK_MYCLASS_inglese_eng9220820132147310.pdf [accessed 30 September 2019].

narrating their own lives. My main reason, however, was determined by the primacy it gives the Italian language as a vehicle for communication but also, more interestingly, as a medium intimating cultural change and new forms of political aggregation. *La mia classe* is about a group of multi-lingual migrants in Rome for whom Italian has become the *lingua franca* of daily life, and Italian is spoken, almost exclusively, throughout the film. It is, however, Italian with an accent as each non-native speaker interferes with the national linguistic landscape by adding their own audible imprint or inflection. Yet the film does not fall into the familiar, often comedic trap of representing the foreigner through a stereotypically marked voice. Its accentedness is more subtle and challenging as it takes issue with cinema's arguably artificial linguistic homogeneity, a feature that defines national cinema yet is often taken for granted. From a very common-sense perspective, French films are, for example, 'in French'. Languages other than the recognized national language are routinely dubbed or subtitled for the national audience, a practice which actively promotes the idea of the nation as a monolingual construct.[9] Films which reflect the plurilingual reality of migration come into conflict with these normative industrial standards at odds with the real experience of border-crossing and cultural encounter.[10] A key question for transnational film-making becomes how it manages the multiple languages of human mobility. In what follows I will argue that a key, if not defining, feature of transnational cinema is precisely the transformative pressure it puts on economies of monolingual practice.

La mia classe

La mia classe features Valerio Mastandrea in the role of an Italian language teacher working in a school on the outskirts of Rome. Non-Italian, non-professional actors play his students. The actors were recruited from local schools offering evening Italian language classes. Fully identified in the credits, they play characters with what seem to be identical names leading the audience to assume an equivalence between actor and character: they

[9] David Gramling has effectively argued that the concept of monolingualism was constructed as part of the modern nation state. See *The Invention of Monolingualism* (New York: Bloomsbury, 2016). In the case of Italy, attention should also be paid to how cinema manages dialect in relation to the national language. In recent years, dialect has been used more extensively in films, accompanied sometimes, but not by any means always, by Italian subtitles.

[10] For a discussion of some of these issues see Tijana Mamula and Lisa Patti, eds, *The Multilingual Screen: New Directions on Cinema and Linguistic Difference* (New York: Bloomsbury, 2016).

appear to be playing themselves. This creates an immediate ontological disparity between pupils and teacher as Mastandrea is clearly acting in a fictional role. The film plays throughout with the uncertain border between fiction and reality, so the audience is unsure about what kind of film they are actually watching, and about how to interpret what they see. The spectator is never sure if they should approach *La mia classe* as a documentary or a feature film. The uncertainty is emphasized from the beginning of the first narrative sequence, which sees the film crew fitting the actors with mics and doing sound checks. The actors, who could be real students, laugh and chat about what is about to happen. Mastandrea is on hand, and out of character, to reassure them. He then assumes the role of the teacher, and at this point, the fictional narrative of the film begins. Here, the spectator may be reminded of the work of the early twentieth-century dramatist Luigi Pirandello, and how he used the theatre to explore the unstable layers of perception and reality.

I will go on to discuss more closely how the film plays with different planes of reality, a common strategy in what Luca Caminati has called 'new narrative non-fiction' in Italian cinema.[11] Caminati identifies a significant body of recent politically motivated film-making which combines incisive social critique and critical self-reflection on film's capacity to document reality. These films, which have the formal appearance of documentary, slide easily between fiction and non-fiction, and do not inform the audience about a given situation in a straightforward manner, but force them to engage more actively with the moving image. What Caminati refers to as a 'destabilizing spectatorial act' (124) characterizes, I would suggest, the experience of watching *La mia classe*. The film demands an intellectual as well as affective response from its audience, intermittently reminding them that what is on screen is (mostly) a fiction, and asking them to question their relationship with what they see. I will go on to argue that, like the films Caminati discusses, what *La mia classe* achieves is profoundly important on both a political and stylistic level for understanding what the transnational, as a critical category of analysis, might do in offering a critique of both globalization and cultural nationalism. In what follows, I will pick up on these tensions between identity and mobility in *La mia classe*, where the acquisition of competency in the Italian language itself is the symptomatic territory on which these issues are worked through.

[11] Luca Caminati, 'Narrative Non-Fictions in Contemporary Italian Cinema: Francesco Munzi's *Saimir* (2002), Giorgio Diritti's *Il vento fa il suo giro* (2005) and Pietro Marcello's *La bocca del lupo* (2009)', *Studies in Documentary Film*, 5.2–3 (2011), 121–31.

The type of language class where the film is set is now common in Italy, particularly since applicants for long-term residence permits are required to demonstrate proficiency in Italian as one of the essential criteria for residence. The students in *La mia classe* (none of them EU citizens) are working to obtain a diploma which would facilitate their right to reside in Italy. The Italian language becomes the medium through which this entitlement is fought for and, they hope, won. As the narrative unfolds, the right to remain and language proficiency become entangled in an increasingly complex and precarious spiral of power.

Unlike *Spectre*, which is notable for its use of multiple locations across the globe, the transnational geography of *La mia classe* is highly circumscribed. The film is set almost entirely in the language classroom, with occasional shots of the school corridors and the building's exterior. One very short sequence looking out from the school towards Tor Pignattara establishes the school's highly symbolic location in a part of Rome long associated with migration from Italy's south and now home to a highly diverse multi-ethnic population. There is a brief hospital scene where we see Mastandrea receive chemotherapy, and a longer sequence shot in an unidentified park in which one of the students is taken into custody by policemen. As I will later discuss, his subsequent suicide in police detention is crucial to understanding the politics and aesthetics of the film. After class, the students habitually have a drink outside a local bar, which replicates the secure intimacy of the school room. These are the limits of the film's diegetic world, and while the students talk about their lives in Italy and in their countries of origin, these other places are not represented. Curiously, the pupils do not appear to engage at all with digital forms of communication which in the last 20 or so years have increasingly offered people on the move opportunities to keep in touch, eroding the pain of distance commonly believed to characterize the migrant experience.

In class, the students assume a jovial and mutually supportive group identity brought together through the experience of learning Italian. They speak Italian with varying levels of accuracy and fluency, and in a variety of what are heard as foreign accents, the sounds of which implicitly contest a rigidly bounded notion of identity brokered through language. The space of the classroom is constructed and made meaningful by the network of relationships formed there. While the classroom is obviously in Italy, it is certainly not a microcosm of the nation; it is, as I will go on to suggest, a very specific place constructed as a negative mirror of society as a whole. Foucault referred to such places as heterotopias and, in this case, I would suggest that the classroom might be understood in terms of what he calls a 'heterotopia of deviation', a heterotopia 'in which individuals whose behaviour is deviant in relation to the required mean or norm are placed'.[12] The students are deviant precisely because they are not Italian, and as the narrative develops, their 'deviance' dramatizes the limits of the film crew's benevolent hospitality which, as I will argue, has no purchase beyond the classroom, and only a very circumscribed articulation within it.

In class, Mastandrea is an encouraging pedagogue and with gentle good humour he corrects the mistakes of grammar, lexis and pronunciation that the students make. As the only native speaker in the room, his benign authority is unrivalled. On the one hand, he embodies hospitality, yet at the same time he is an adjunct to the state's power to determine who may reside in the multicultural space of the nation as he prepares his pupils for the exam. The teacher habitually addresses the class standing in front of a map of Italy, usefully framing the national project of language acquisition. Role-play and particularly storytelling are the key strategies that Mastandrea uses in class. The pupils devise the figure of Maria, choosing what they see as a universal name to imagine the life of a hard-working, single mother of two. The story-telling becomes the site of cultural exchange as well as language development when, for example, two students discuss what it means for a married couple to be 'separated' in their native Bangladesh. A simple exercise on Italian prepositions in which the teacher asks the class to explain the difference in meaning between being 'in una casa', 'a casa' and 'di casa' rapidly becomes a conversation on feelings about home and belonging. The superficial comedy of the quite lengthy sequence in which the pupils act out job interviews prompts conversations about low wages and exploitative employers, as well as the constant threat of unemployment and the consequent loss of legal resident status. The political solidarity achieved through this conversation makes Italian a language of shared resistance, and the scene might be fruit-fully understood in terms of Sandro Mezzadra and Brett Neilson's notion of the 'labor of translation' in their analysis of contemporary global capitalism.[13] They affirm the potentially radical effects of forging a common language across borders in which everyone speaks in translation, and in which the practice of translation allows for the emergence of a new collective, yet heterogeneous voice at odds with the hard borders of the nation state. Language learning is never a formal exercise but becomes the site of intercultural exchange and a means of speaking back to the nation. In effect, the students assume a pedagogical authority in relation to the spectator.

[12] Michel Foucault and Jay Miskowiec, 'Of Other Spaces: Utopias and Heterotopias', *Diacritics*, 16.1 (1986), 22–27 (p. 25).

[13] Sandro Mezzadra and Brett Neilson, *Border as Method, or The Multiplication of Labor* (Durham, NC and London: Duke University Press, 2013), pp. 274–76.

La mia classe expands the range of sounds through which the Italian language is articulated, and simultaneously these sounds extend the range of what Italian might be used to say. Italian is the language in which the students express, and recognize, their collective experience. It is unequivocally the vehicle of aspiration and protest in the film, operating as the medium of transnational exchange, a receptacle for the reception and expression of other cultural possibilities. Translation is never about the simple movement from one language to another as the linguistic diversity of the non-homogenous migrant body disallows any simple sense of binary equivalence or division. The Italian language becomes an expansive space of cultural reciprocity, the medium of what Paul Ricoeur calls 'linguistic hospitality' where speakers of different languages learn to be open to encounters offering the promise but never the guarantee of mutual understanding.[14]

Migratory Aesthetics

On a thematic level, *La mia classe* records global patterns of movement and settlement. Yet transnational cinema has not been defined solely by content but also by the aesthetic strategies through which that content is managed. Mieke Bal coined the term 'migratory aesthetics' to refer to the formal choices of works of art which express both geographical movement, and the sense of relationality formed by the spectator's affective response. For Bal, the term 'migratory' engages not just those who migrate but anyone touched in some way by the increasingly commonplace experience of global mobility. She doesn't offer a precise definition of 'migratory aesthetics' other than to claim its openness to innovation in both content and form. This openness informs her own work as a documentary film-maker and installation artist in which she expresses an ongoing interest in language diversity as a defining element of cultural transformation, and in making explicit the relationship between producer and subject in ways reminiscent, I would suggest, of Gaglianone's film.

Bal's suggestion, which I placed as an epigraph to this essay, that 'migratory aesthetics' challenge the 'linguistic uniformity' of the nation clearly resonates with the brief outline I have already given of *La mia classe* where Italian becomes the space of cultural difference rather than uniformity. In answer to her own provocative question, 'What do documentaries document?' Bal affirms that what they document most valuably does not lie in their manifest content, but rather 'resides in the performance of the relationship between

---

[14] Paul Ricoeur, *On Translation*, trans. by Eileen Brennan (London: Routledge, 2006), pp. 23–24.

makers and subjects'.[15] To foreground actively this 'double-relationality' is particularly relevant to migratory creative practice as it shifts attention from the migrants as objects of knowledge to critical reflection on how knowledge about them is produced. As I have noted, the opening scene of *La mia classe* shows initial sound checks before the fictional lesson begins. The visible presence of Gaglianone and the production team in the film reminds the spectator that what they are seeing is the result of a variously negotiated relationship between the film-maker and the subjects of the film, a relationship which conventionally does not appear on screen. Throughout the film, the team appears in front of as well as behind the camera, speaking to the out-of-character actors, self-consciously allowing the spectator to hear as well as see their sometimes heated conversations, but more tellingly, and with great honesty, revealing, as becomes most apparent at the end of the film, the provisional nature of the hospitality offered to the inhabitants of the heterotopic classroom.

As the film goes on, role-play and storytelling become blurred as fiction appears gradually to spill over into reality raising questions about identity, the claim of authenticity and changing perceptions of the real. In a familiar language learning scenario, students bring an object to class as a prompt from which to tell their own stories. Good luck charms, scented tea and a camera recall networks of transnational attachment. A number of students bring photographs of family or friends which frame the sense of loss or sometimes exile felt by the group, but also recall the excitement of departure. The increasingly intimate nature of the narratives is moving, and the camera cuts systematically between storyteller and other members of the class whose faces, in close-up, register the unvoiced lineaments of emotional identification across national difference. These close-ups offer a model of empathetic listening to the film's spectator.

The emotional intensity of the narrative increases when the teacher is diagnosed with a serious illness. The students discover this by chance in a move which implicates them in the fabric of the film's fictional world. It is the character of the teacher not Mastandrea who is ill. The scene in which the spectator sees Mastandrea's reaction to their discomfort forms an affective, but also political, nodal point in the film. Its ontological status is, however, completely unclear. The previous scene ends with a close-up of a dejected Mastandrea, alone at the end of a lesson, and then fades to show him sitting behind his desk in medium close-up at the front of the class. The words on

---

[15] Mieke Bal, 'Documenting What? Auto-Theory and Migratory Aesthetics', in *A Companion to Documentary Film*, ed. by Alexandra Juhasz and Alisa Lebow (Chichester: John Wiley & Sons, 2015), pp. 124–44 (130).

the blackboard are always significant parts of the film's *mise-en-scène*. *Salute, morire* and *identità* remind the spectator of the immediate drama which is unfolding. The camera cuts between the teacher and, in turn, the disconsolate faces of three of his students. As the camera draws back, however, it reveals an empty classroom, leaving the audience uncertain how to interpret the stories which follow. Shadi, an Egyptian student who had already spoken to the class about family memories associated with the scent of hibiscus tea, provides the backstory to his presence in Italy. Caught up in the political protests that swept the Arab world in 2010, Shadi fled Egypt after witnessing the killing of his closest friend. He tells his story in a single shot held in extreme close-up, the camera documenting in capillary detail the silences and emotional responses of his body as it accompanies his story. The intensity and corporeal performance of the storytelling continues as five more of the students recount their part in contemporary histories of global conflict. The most detailed narrative is given by Easther in a stark account of her journey across the Sahara from Nigeria. Again, this contrasts with the anticipation felt on the day of her departure captured in a family photograph taken to mark the occasion. She describes the constant threat of police violence, the thirst that forced her to drink her own urine and the support of her travelling companion, Adidì, who showed her how to fake the signs of menstruation to avoid rape. Adidì later died crossing the desert, his head in her lap; Easther is unable to weep for his loss. At the end of her story, told in faltering Italian, she falls silent and the camera holds onto those seconds of silence, the spectator caught in a moment of transnational aporia facing the incommensurability of that experience and the possibilities of Italian to convey it. The friability of the Italian language under the pressure of experience intensifies. Nazim switches to accented English to reveal his determination to speak: 'It is difficult, but I must try'. The final narrative of this sequence consists of a 20-second single shot of Bassirou. He looks indirectly in the direction of the camera saying nothing, the only sounds heard are the minimal movements of his body as he shifts uneasily under the camera's gaze.

The direct address to camera, characteristic of conventional documentary, quite apart from the content of each student's story, invites the spectator to assume that what they hear is a true account – the account of events which really did happen to the person speaking. As such the narratives are received as testimony, and the narrators as bearers of trauma. In telling their stories in Italian, the speakers are responding to what Bal calls the 'ethical requirement of cultural translation'.[16] Italian becomes the vehicle through which a 'migratory aesthetics' of difference and alterity is made palpable

---

[16] Bal, 'Documenting What?', p. 130.

as each student expresses themself with different degrees of fluency and grammatical accuracy. Speaking Italian seems to be the gesture of a dutiful guest and also pedagogue as they speak to render their experience intelligible. Yet a critical interpretation of their testimony needs to be pushed further. As I have mentioned, conventional cinema has been adept at managing linguistically divergent voices in ways which enforce the presumption of monolingualism. The management of linguistic diversity in *La mia classe* complicates this closed economy. The students could have delivered their narratives in languages in which they were ostensibly more fluent, with Italian subtitles confirming the address to the Italian spectator. This solution might have created the illusion of an unmediated, authentic migrant voice, but it would have done nothing aesthetically to disturb the conventional logic of monolingualism which insists on the containment of linguistic and cultural difference. In *La mia classe*, accented voices and bodies redefine the repertoire of the Italian language. More particularly, the silence of Bassirou, Nazim's interjection in English and Easther's faltering narrative are crucial in the creation of what Bal, drawing on the work of the translation theorist Lawrence Venuti, calls the 'remainder' – the residue which translation does not succeed in domesticating or making disappear. This 'remainder' here is the voiced recurrence of the transnational body which, interestingly, are disciplined and silenced by the SDH (subtitles for the deaf and hard of hearing) by translating the grammatical and lexical imprecisions of the speakers into unmarked standard Italian.

Early in the film, Shadi tells his teacher that his residence permit has expired. Although he can't sit the language exam without it, the teacher is happy for him to carry on attending class, underlining the exceptional hospitality of that space. As I have mentioned, Shadi is later arrested, vulnerable in the public space of a park, where the arresting policemen initially mistake his scented tea for drugs. Unable to face deportation, Shadi hangs himself in his cell. Yet a short scene in which a member of the production team is seen rehearsing the suicide with Shadi alerts the spectator in advance that this event is part of the film's fictional world. When the teacher announces Shadi's death in class, there is an outburst of laughter as one of the students confuses the scripted suicide with reality, thinking that he really is dead.

La mia classe never allows the spectator the comfort of a single mode of interpretation. Less securely fictional, but integral to the film, is the parallel plot involving Issa, whose right to reside depends on the retention of his internationally recognized 'humanitarian protection' status. Like Shadi, he receives a letter telling him that this status has been revoked and he will be sent back to the Ivory Coast. The immediate effect is that he can no longer work on the film, unlike Shadi whose story is ostensibly part of the plot. The production crew, while sympathetic, find their performance of hospitality compromised. The heterotopia of the classroom is revealed to be indeed 'deviant', a space in which, as one of the students remarks, they are all equally under threat as provisional residents of the nation. On a practical level, this threat endangers the completion of the film but, more disturbingly, endangers the promise of benign hospitality on which the film is premised. The students challenge Gaglianone about what is happening to Issa in a scene which delineates the inequality in the performance of charitable relationality. All the producers do is give Issa some money, but his absence haunts the final section of the film juxtaposed with a shot of Mastandrea in hospital receiving chemotherapy which cuts to a short scene of the other students and film crew celebrating on the beach.

The film in fact stages its beginning and end through Issa. An unexplained sequence right at the start of the film sees Mastandrea walking towards camera along the corridor of a dilapidated building. The camera tracks him as he turns and retreats down the darkening corridor. The sound of footsteps on the stone floor intensifies as Mastandrea disappears before the camera picks up the figures of two policemen striding towards a barely perceptible figure crouching in a corner. The figure turns out to be Issa and the film ends with the same scene shot from a different angle as the policemen stride towards the camera rather than appearing as dark silhouettes shot from behind. Although the scenes focus on Issa, it is the morphing of Mastandrea into the forces of the law that makes the spectator reflect on the politics of the transnational encounter. The entire film is constructed around this invitation to the spectator to investigate the uneven logics of power in the film as it unpicks the film crew's well-intentioned gestures of hospitality. It also allows an exploration of new aesthetic possibilities that the encounter instigates. Gaglianone's film is above all a critical reflection on the aesthetic practices of transnational cinema, yet these practices are inseparable from the critique of national hospitality and belonging whose limits it documents.

Final Remarks

As a brief postscript to the film, it might be useful to reflect on the questions of citizenship which the film raises, not least because it may be the area in which a sense of national entitlement is most vigorously felt. The political philosopher Étienne Balibar contrasts the increasingly free flow of 'good, funds, and information' in a multinational economy with human mobility, 'the object of heavier and heavier limitations'. He makes this observation in the course of an argument exposing the contradictions of the democratic modern state and its strategies to segregate and discriminate against non-national subjects. He suggests that citizenship and its entitlements need to be rethought 'so that social rights with a transnational character can be guaranteed'.[17] Balibar's proposition annuls the idea of the multilingual and multi-ethnic classroom as a 'heterotopia of deviation' and the discipline of learning Italian as anything other than a pragmatic accomplishment. His proposal to extend citizenship beyond national entitlement challenges the logic of cultural nationalism which films about migration may inadvertently reiterate in their investigation of the conditions of settlement once the harrowing journey to Italy has been completed and the border successfully crossed. *La mia classe* does not offer solutions or resolutions to the ethical questions and legal dramas it instantiates. The spectator is not told what happens to Issa and the other students, but neither are they given any indication of the outcome of the teacher's medical treatment. The film, however, gets made, and in that sense the project is concluded. Yet, most abidingly, what the film offers the spectator is an understanding of human mobility that national borders, in all their articulations including linguistic ones, are never quite able to manage or contain.

---

[17] Étienne Balibar, *We, The People of Europe? Reflections on Transnational Citizenship*, trans. by James Swenson (Princeton: Princeton University Press, 2004), p. 113.

18

Transnational Subjectivities and Victimhood in Italy after the 2001 Genoa G8 Summit

Monica Jansen

Transnational readings of subjectivity have been developed in fields such as postcolonial and migration studies. These readings have envisioned the formation of hybrid, 'in-between' forms of postnational citizenship. They have also addressed the question of inclusive and exclusive national, cultural and ethnic identities. In the context of Italian studies, two texts that present themselves as postcolonial and transnational 'manifestos' may serve here as an example. In 'The Italian Postcolonial: A Manifesto', Cristina Lombardi-Diop and Caterina Romeo argue that 'it is precisely through a postcolonial approach, inclusive of the multiple processes of extraterritorial conquest, expansion, and migration, that one can comprehend the complex, transnational history of Italy's cultural identity'.[1] Emma Bond, in her mapping of a 'trans-national turn' in Italian studies, shows how Italy's 'peripheral status within Europe' and the fact that the country represents 'a historical palimpsestic context of motion' mean that it could function as a 'hyphenated "trans-" or in-between space', particularly apt for queering 'fixed notions of a national time and space'.[2] This broader 'trans-national' perspective on Italian culture, according to Bond, can also be theorized as a bodily experience of transnational subjectivity:

> It is precisely this attention to the dialectic relation between place and perspective that must be enacted as twin poles of a hyphenated

---

[1] Cristina Lombardi-Diop and Caterina Romeo, 'The Italian Postcolonial: A Manifesto', *Italian Studies*, 3 (2014), 425–33 (p. 429).

[2] Emma Bond, 'Towards a Trans-national Turn in Italian Studies?', *Italian Studies*, 3 (2014), 415–24 (p. 417).

trans-national, and that can shed light on other trans-embodiments. Indeed, the body, as privileged site of lived subjectivity, yet also as a means of experiencing the local and the global simultaneously, becomes an important hinge of meaning within a mapping of the trans-national.[3]

These aspirational perspectives on the hybridization of identities and the formation of a postcolonial and transnational citizenship will be put to the test in this chapter with a special focus on the cultural memory of the anti-G8 summit protests held in Genoa in 2001. What started as the joyful performance of a multicultural, transnational and transgenerational no-global 'multitude', gathered at Genoa to protest peacefully against the G8 summit, was soon transformed in a transgenerational and transnational traumatic bodily experience of violent repression. The G8 counter summit started on 19 July with the 'migrants' march' and continued on the 20th with the occupation of thematic squares (*piazze tematiche*) in the yellow zone (*zona gialla*), where the protesters with their carnivalesque banners, music and costumes mocked the G8 establishment.[4] The non-violent marches of different social movements gathered at the Genoa Social Forum (GSF) were, however, soon replaced by the urban guerrillas of the black bloc, who played the role of 'tricksters'[5] and, with their attempt to force access to the fenced red zone (*zona rossa*) of the city centre, provided the police with the pretext to exercise violence against all protesters. This resulted in an escalation of violence. Instead of becoming a transnational 'in-between' space to share ideas and practices capable of presenting alternatives against globalization, Genoa became a conflict zone re-enacting the dialectics of fascism and anti-fascism in Italy. The bodies of the international protesters assembled in Genoa from 19 to 22 July in order to contest global neoliberalism were exposed to police violence legitimized by the so-called 'state of exception'.[6] The simultaneous bodily experience of the local and the global did not, in this case, lead to the realization of the proposed no-global alternative of *un altro mondo è possibile* [another world is possible], embodied by a new generation overcoming binary oppositions.[7] Instead, it contributed

---

[3] Bond, 'Towards a Trans-national Turn', p. 416.

[4] Emanuela Guano, *Creative Urbanity: An Italian Middle Class in the Shade of Revitalization* (Philadelphia: University of Pennsylvania Press, 2017), pp. 67–68.

[5] Guano, *Creative Urbanity*, p. 70.

[6] Giorgio Agamben, *State of Exception*, trans. by Kevin Attell (Chicago: University of Chicago Press, 2005).

[7] The collective documentary *Un mondo diverso è possibile* (dir. Francesco Maselli

to reinforce the subjectivity of youth and victimhood that informs Italy's traumatic history of 'divided memory'.[8] The link between resistance and victimhood was strengthened by the killing of protester Carlo Giuliani on 20 July, transforming the images of his action and of his dead body into icons of anti-globalism and of a new generation of political subjectivity grounded in precarity.

The postmemory quality of these counter-narratives transforms trauma into a form of future-oriented agency, as can be extrapolated from the model that Marianne Hirsch established in her seminal article on Holocaust photographs. Hirsch's assumption that 'the work of postmemory defines the familial inheritance and transmission of cultural trauma' does not restrict postmemory to an identity position: Hirsch prefers to see it instead 'as an intersubjective transgenerational space of remembrance, linked specifically to cultural or collective trauma'.[9] The counter-narratives produced to memorialize the 'fatti di Genova' (the Genoa events)[10] analysed in this chapter show how the traumatic impact of Italy's divided memory plays a crucial role in the bodily experience of the transnational subjectivity of a generation that experienced the events of the G8 in 2001 as a 'watershed'. On the one hand, they show the complexity of layered local memories of conflict and, on the other, they hypothesize an idea of collectivity based on 'other' grounds, found in affects rather than in ideologies, and situated in the in-between space of transnational mobilities.

The public memory of Genoa's G8 is highly mediated and continuously remediated, transformed and amplified by the accumulation of testimonies and juridical evidence. It is constructed through the images transmitted by mainstream media as well as deconstructed by the counter-images and counter-narrations produced by participants and sympathizers of the movement's anti-summit. The blurring of the boundaries between fiction and non-fiction and the appeal to an ethics of memory, which are an integral part of these narratives, are symptomatic of what has been called the turn

---

et al.; Luna Rossa Cinematografica, 2001), which was the most widely distributed document of its kind, echoed the movement's slogan in its optimistic title, despite the fact that the crew was among the first to shoot the state-sanctioned violence at the Diaz school. Melody Niwot, 'Narrating Genoa: Documentaries of the Italian G8 Protests of 2001 and the Persistence and Politics of Memory', *History and Memory*, 2 (2011), 66–92 (p. 83).

[8] John Foot, *Italy's Divided Memory* (New York: Palgrave Macmillan, 2009).

[9] Marianne Hirsch, 'Surviving Images: Holocaust Photographs and the Work of Postmemory', *The Yale Journal of Criticism*, 14.1 (2001), 5–37 (pp. 9–10).

[10] See the Wikipedia entry 'Fatti del G8 di Genova', https://it.wikipedia.org/wiki/Fatti_del_G8_di_Genova#cite_note-140 [accessed 1 November 2019].

towards 'new realism' in contemporary fiction and critical thought, after postmodernism.[11] This makes counter-narratives of Genoa 2001 paradigmatic for broader readings of the conflict between narrations of victimhood and of precarious resistance against a world order that, from this perspective, can be identified with neoliberalism.

This chapter will first discuss Genoa 2001 as a watershed in terms of the relationship between cultural memory, biopolitics and aesthetics, and analyse cultural production relating to the G8 in terms of iconicity, counter-narration, cultural trauma and affect. Secondly, it will focus on the construction of a transnational and transgenerational subjectivity as it appears in three works – Christian Mirra's graphic novel *Quella notte alla Diaz* (2010), Carlo Bachschmidt's documentary *Black Block* (2011) and Daniele Vicari's film *Diaz – Don't Clean Up This Blood* (2012) – focusing on some of the most tragic events of Genoa 2001: the raid on the Armando Diaz school and the torture carried out in the Bolzaneto barracks. Thirdly, this chapter will reflect on the formulation of an alternative subjectivity which goes beyond the notion of victimhood and on how this can be analysed in transnational and transgenerational terms. In this respect, the Genoa G8 'movement of movements' can be seen as a watershed moment which marks the emergence of cultures and performances of subjectivity that have gone on to characterize a number of contemporary social movements,[12] from student protests against austerity to the Occupy movement, to Extinction Rebellion.

The Genoa 2001 Watershed

Genoa 2001: 'Divided Memory'

The genealogy of a new Italian transgenerational and transnational subjectivity can be traced back to the tragic events of the no-global protests against the G8 summit held in Genoa in July 2001. From the point of view of the participants in the protest (who were equipped with audiovisual devices and able to document the events), between 20 and 22 July Genoa was the playground of a brutal police force pitted against defenceless protesters. On the opposite side, mainstream media, using selected iconic

[11] See the manifesto launched by philosopher Maurizio Ferraris on 8 August 2011, almost ten years after the Genoa events: *Manifesto of New Realism* (New York: SUNY Press, 2014).

[12] See Jeffrey S. Juris, 'Embodying Protest: Culture and Performance within Social Movements', in *Anthropology, Theatre, and Development: The Transformative Potential of Performance*, ed. by Alex Flynn and Jonas Tinius (New York: Palgrave Macmillan, 2015), pp. 82–104.

photographs,[13] presented the events as a case of preorganized aggression on the part of violent protesters, belonging to the so-called 'black blocs', against the public order. The various episodes of what has gone down in history as the 'battle of Genoa'[14] led to one death – that of 23-year-old Carlo Giuliani, who was shot by *carabiniere* Mario Placanica while he was attacking a police van with a fire extinguisher. The events also resulted in a high number of injuries caused by the aggression and torture inflicted by the police on protesters, in particular during the raid against the Armando Diaz school (21 July), where the GSF had established its temporary headquarters, and the subsequent detention of affiliates of the movement in the Bolzaneto barracks (22 July). The G8 events represent an 'open wound' which is the object of an annual moment of remembrance held at the (contested) memorial stone which was placed in Piazza Alimonda in 2013.[15] The stone is inscribed with the words 'Carlo Giuliani ragazzo, 20 luglio 2001', a phrase that has itself become iconic, as illustrated for instance by its adoption as the title of Francesca Comencini's 2002 documentary film.[16]

The archive formed by the many video testimonies of the G8 events and by the artistic production related to them[17] makes it possible to speak of a

---

[13] Particularly significant is the reception history of two press photographs taken by Dylan Martinez for the Reuters agency, one of Carlo Giuliani as an 'aggressor' and one of his dead body; on this topic see David D. Perlmutter and Gretchen L. Wagner, 'The Anatomy of a Photojournalistic Icon: Marginalization of Dissent in the Selection and Framing of "a Death in Genoa"', *Visual Communication*, 1 (2004), 91–108; Antigoni Memou, '"When It Bleeds, It Leads": Death and Press Photography in the Anti-Capitalist Protests in Genoa 2001', *Third Text*, 3 (2010), 341–51.

[14] Guano, *Creative Urbanity*, p. 61.

[15] Piazza Alimonda is described as a 'grassroot memorial' in *Grassroot Memorials: The Politics of Memorializing Traumatic Death*, ed. by Peter Jan Margry and Cristina Sánchez-Carretero (New York and Oxford: Berghahn, 2011), pp. 304–19. Comparable initiatives are the naming of the Carlo-Giuliani-Platz in Bern and the Carlo-Giuliani-Park in Berlin (in 2011). The memorial stone in Piazza Alimonda is the object of continuous contestation by groups representing the police force and right-wing parties.

[16] Francesca Comencini, *Carlo Giuliani, ragazzo* (2002). On this film see Mauro Sassi, '*Carlo Giuliani, ragazzo*: A Counter-Hegemonic Italian Documentary', *Studies in Documentary Film*, 2–3 (2011), pp. 169–81.

[17] On the relationship between archive and memory, Assmann writes: 'The archive is a pure potential, a possible source of information, nothing more. It is dependent on others to actualize and realize this potential, to transform it from the status of virtual information to that of palpable objects that can be transmitted and received by future individuals who, in witnessing the witnesses, will themselves learn and know and remember'. Aleida Assmann, 'History, Memory, and the Genre of Testimony', *Poetics Today*, 2 (2006), 261–73 (p. 271).

'transgenerational memory'[18] of Genoa 2001. That archive makes an appeal to a 'moral community' of 'secondary witnesses' who commit themselves to 'listen to the testimony with empathy' and to restore its voice in a future (re)telling of history.[19] However, the G8 events remain a divisive experience of perpetrated violence which cannot be reduced to one version of perpetrator history. In this sense, in the case of Genoa, the experience of memory and factual history cannot act as complementary modes.[20] Instead, testimonies also aim to document the symptoms of trauma through the witnesses' bodily experience – appealing to 'experiential and indexical (or "symptomatic") truth' rather than to 'representational truth'.[21]

Historian John Foot uses the formula of 'divided memory' to indicate the form that memories of conflict take in post-unification Italy.[22] This divisive and simultaneously complementary nature of Italy's memories of conflict has recently been ritualized by historian Alessandro Portelli into a *Calendario civile*, a civic calendar meant to run in parallel to the religious one and to provide the basis for a community of responsible citizens. In this calendar, 21 July – associated with 'Fatti del G8 di Genova' [Events of the Genoa G8] – is included as a date that has emerged from below and is part of a memory still in its making.[23]

With its complex, divided and divisive nature, the memory of the G8 episodes of violence inserts itself into Italy's recent history of political conflict and victimhood as well as into a global history of war and economic inequalities. It is a memory which is divided precisely because it is historically layered.[24] Furthermore, its polarized imaginary was contemporaneously negotiated by the mainstream media (which launched a campaign of fear and failed to provide a public counter-narrative),[25] by the anti-G8 summit movement's counter-narration (both during and after 2001) and

[18] Assmann, 'History, Memory', p. 271.

[19] Assmann, 'History, Memory', p. 269.

[20] Assmann, 'History, Memory', p. 263.

[21] Assmann, 'History, Memory', pp. 269–70.

[22] Foot, *Italy's Divided Memory*.

[23] *Calendario civile. Per una memoria laica, popolare e democratica degli italiani*, ed. by Alessandro Portelli (Rome: Donzelli, 2017). A presentation of the project can be found on the editor's website, https://www.donzelli.it/libro/9788868435776 [accessed 1 November 2019].

[24] On the construction of the G8's collective memory, see: Niwot, 'Narrating Genoa'; Claudia Capelli, 'From Documentary Truth to Historical Evidence: The Images of the Genoa G8 Protests and the Construction of Public Memory', *Journal of Italian Cinema & Media Studies*, 3 (2015), 319–35.

[25] Guano, *Creative Urbanity*, pp. 66–67.

by the textual and visual evidence produced by multiple juridical testimo-nies.[26] The collective body of counter-narratives relating to the events, in particular, led to the emergence of a new transgenerational subjectivity, figuring at the same time as a victim and as a 'mnemonic agent'[27] in a narrative of violent repression, which generated a national as well as a global loss of trust in the Italian state.[28]

The failure of the Italian state to act, institutionally, as a supreme guarantor transforms the Italian Republic into a 'Republic of sorrow' built on victimhood, as discussed by historian Giovanni De Luna who, however, also warns against the 'absolute' truths of competing groups of victims.[29] In the case of the 'justice and truth' sought for the G8 incidents, both the organizations associated with protesters and the representatives of the police forces claim their rights in the name of victimhood. This coexistence of irreconcilable truths can be linked to the debate on the 'turn to the victim' which historians have discussed in connection to the postmemory narratives produced by the relatives of victims of terrorist violence during Italy's 'years of lead' (*anni di piombo*).[30] These transgenerational testimonials have shown how trauma can be overcome by future-oriented forms of ethical memory based on participatory citizenship.[31] Though often contested,[32] the outcomes of the encounters organized between victims, guardians and agents of terrorist violence recorded in collective works such as *Il libro dell'incontro* constitute a model of compromise that does not annul dissent. Italian criminologist Adolfo Ceretti suggests that all parties involved should agree to forgive, acknowledging that the irreducibility

---

[26] The Committee for Truth and Justice for Genoa (Comitato Verità e Giustizia) was founded in 2001 by a group of witnesses of the incidents in order to raise money for the victims' defence and to provide updates on the judiciary investigations. See the Committee's website, http://www.veritagiustizia.it [accessed 1 November 2019], as well as Supporto Legale (www.supportolegale.org) [accessed 1 November 2019], run by the Genoa Legal Forum, a group of Italian and international lawyers working on the Genoa trials.

[27] See Stefania Vicari, 'The Interpretative Dimension of Transformative Events: Outrage Management and Collective Action Framing after the 2001 Anti-G8 Summit in Genoa', *Social Movement Studies*, 5 (2015), 596–614 (pp. 610–11).

[28] Guano, *Creative Urbanity*, p. 77.

[29] Giovanni De Luna, *La Repubblica del dolore* (Milan: Feltrinelli, 2011), p. 96.

[30] Ruth Glynn, 'The "Turn to the Victim" in Italian Culture: Victim-Centred Narratives of the *anni di piombo*', *Modern Italy*, 4 (2013), 373–90; Sciltian Gastaldi and David M. Ward, eds, *Era mio padre. Italian Terrorism of the Anni di Piombo in the Postmemorials of Victims' Relatives* (Oxford: Peter Lang, 2018).

[31] Anna Cento Bull and Philip Cooke, eds, *Ending Terrorism in Italy* (London: Routledge, 2013), pp. 219–20.

[32] For a critique, see Gastaldi and Ward, *Era mio padre*.

of the conflict will not be resolved and that each party will stay inscribed within their own past, language and narrative.[33] Similar initiatives have been undertaken to elaborate the traumatic facts of Genoa 2001.[34] This conciliatory paradox is also reflected in what historian Anna Cento Bull describes as the impossibility of reconciliation in contemporary Italy, if not in the form of a compromise between different models of conflict solving.[35] This notion of a memorial compromise also comes close to Foot's description of the historical approach to divided memories:

> Recognizing plural and divided memories in this way is the opposite of accepting a bland conservatory revisionism. In the revisionist project, the dead are all the same and the intended goal is national reconciliation. Bringing out divided memories allows for a deeper understanding of history. The dead – and the living – are never all the same.[36]

Genoa 2001: 'State of Exception'

The opposed political imaginaries of Genoa 2001 clearly show how Italy's recent past is haunted by a divided memory and how this resists a transnational conception of subjectivity. The icon of the G8 anti-summit's victim and 'rebel',[37] embodied by 'Carlo Giuliani, ragazzo', also stands for a new kind of generational 'fragile resistance'[38] against the violation of political subjectivity. Portelli, who undertook an oral history project on 'Generations

[33] Adolfo Ceretti, 'Lotta armata, vittime, conflitti e dissidi. Un'ultima ricognizione', in *Il libro dell'incontro. Vittime e responsabili della lotta armata a confronto*, ed. by Guido Bertagna, Adolfo Ceretti and Claudia Mazzucato (Milan: Il Saggiatore, 2015), pp. 375–400 (p. 398).

[34] Adriano Zamperini and Marialuisa Menegatto, *Cittadinanza ferita e trauma psicopolitico. Dopo il G8 di Genova: il lavoro della memoria e la ricostruzione di relazioni sociali* (Naples: Liguori, 2011).

[35] Anna Cento Bull, 'The Italian Transition and National (Non)reconciliation', *Journal of Modern Italian Studies*, 3 (2008), 405–21.

[36] Foot, *Italy's Divided Memory*, p. 18.

[37] See Francesco Barilli and Manuel De Carli, *Carlo Giuliani. Il ribelle di Genova* (Padua: BeccoGiallo, 2011); the book has been translated into French as *Bello ciao: G8, Gênes 2001* (2012), and into German as *Carlo Vive – G8, Genua 2001* (2016). On this graphic novel see Inge Lanslots, 'Gli ingranaggi della memoria del G8 2001 in *Carlo Giuliani. Il ribelle di Genova*', *Forum Italicum*, 1 (2017), 112–32.

[38] The reference is to the both 'fragile' and 'resistant' written messages left by citizens for Carlo Giuliani at the gate of the Nostra Signora del Rimedio Church in Piazza Alimonda; these were subsequently collected by Fabio Caffarena and Carlo Stiaccini in the volume *Fragili, resistenti* (Milan: Terre di Mezzo, 2005).

in Genoa, July 2001', suggests that the use of the word *ragazzo* with reference to Giuliani reinforces the sense that Carlo was just one of many, 'not a hero, not even a militant – just a *ragazzo*'. Furthermore, according to Portelli, 'the inclusiveness of the word suggests that, although not only young people participated, the identity of the movement and the meaning of the Genoa experience is defined by this age group, the *ragazzi* who lost their political naiveté in the streets, the schools, the barracks, the jails of Genoa, where they discovered the violence of the State'.[39] 'Generation' as a keyword in the Genoa narratives also defines political subjectivity in increasingly transnational terms. As argued by Sidney Tarrow, young protesters are more inclined to a global or continental consciousness than their elders, but this does not necessarily lead to the conclusion that 'the assumption of global identities is general enough to have produced an international cadre of cosmopolitans'. According to Tarrow, it is possible, however, to claim with confidence that 'we are witnessing to an increasing degree the formation of a broad spectrum of activists who face both inward and outward and combine domestic and transnational contention'.[40]

The conceptual framework elaborated by the philosophy of biopolitics has also turned out to be very useful for analysing the mechanisms of sovereign power enacted by the Italian government during the repression of the anti-G8 summit protests. Biopolitics, summarized by Andrea Righi as the area of investigation that studies the 'modes by which the biological dimension and life (including also our human social life) come under the control of power apparatuses',[41] can also provide a perspective from which to analyse the formation of a new, transnational and resistant, generational subjectivity.

According to philosopher Roberto Esposito, a specific trait of Italian biopolitics and its transnational dissemination in non-specialist venues is 'that this philosophical inclination did not come about in opposition to, but rather as a reflection of, a strong commitment to militant activism' and therefore can be considered as 'thought in action' rather than as a 'method of contemporary knowledge'.[42] This means that thinking about subjectivity is conceived here as an integral part of the practice of a 'community'. Esposito's reflection starts

[39] Alessandro Portelli, 'Generations in Genoa, July 2001', *Forum for Anthropology and Culture*, 4 (2007), 346–67 (pp. 352–53).

[40] Sidney Tarrow, 'The Dualities of Transnational Contention: "Two Activist Solitudes" or a New World Altogether?', *Mobilization: An International Journal*, 1 (2005), 53–72 (pp. 56–58).

[41] Andrea Righi, *Biopolitics and Social Change in Italy: From Gramsci to Pasolini to Negri* (New York: Palgrave Macmillan, 2011), p. 1.

[42] Roberto Esposito, *Living Thought: The Origins and Actuality of Italian Philosophy*, trans. by Zakiya Hanafi (Stanford: Stanford University Press, 2012), p. 263.

from the concept of 'biopower', originally conceived by Michel Foucault as consisting of 'several devices of control and protection resorting, at times, to violence on the basis of the discrimination between the *us* of a community and the *other* excluded by it, which is thought of as something dangerous'.[43] In this exclusivist version, biopower thus acts in the interest of the category of 'immunity', which is central to the ideology of what Esposito calls a negative biopolitics or a 'thanatopolitics'.[44]

In the case of the repression of the anti-G8 protests in Genoa, the (ab)use of biopower by the police against the threat embodied by the international community of prevalently young protesters, perceived as being the enemy, obeyed the logic of thanatopolitics and therefore followed the 'sovereign principle', no longer acting 'as the order that creates the law [...] but on the contrary, as what shuts the law down, inaugurating a state of exception that is legally entitled to suspend the law'.[45] This state of exception has been identified, in particular, with the use of torture and of fascist slogans and methods by the police force within the closed space of the Bolzaneto barracks. In that space, the detainees, reduced to 'bare life',[46] could be disposed of with impunity. However, according to Esposito, it is also possible to conceive of an affirmative interpretation of biopolitics, when the transformative ambivalence of the terms 'community' and 'immunity' is made productive. In *Living Thought* Esposito develops an Italian 'affirmative biopolitics' that views life as modes or substance, both 'impersonal and singular', which 'escape from the prescriptive and exclusionary dialectic between subjectification and subjection'.[47] This 'affirmative biopolitics' could be compared to Judith Butler's reflections on Western supremacy in the wake of the terrorist attacks on the Twin Towers in New York. In *Precarious Life* Butler conceives of 'vulnerability' as a category that opens up towards a condition of interdependency and that cannot be foreclosed by any act of sovereignty. The injury inflicted on 'First World privilege [...] offers a chance to start to imagine a world in which that violence might be minimized, in which an inevitable interdependency becomes acknowledged as the basis for global political

[43]　Righi, *Biopolitics and Social Change*, p. 3.

[44]　Roberto Esposito, 'From the Unpolitical to Biopolitics', *Annali d'Italianistica*, 29 (2011), 205–13 (p. 212).

[45]　Esposito, *Living Thought*, pp. 262, 268.

[46]　Guano, *Creative Urbanity*, pp. 74, 78, quotes Giorgio Agamben's *Homo Sacer: Sovereign State and Bare Life*, trans. by Daniel Heller-Roazen (Stanford: Stanford University Press, 1988) and *State of Exception*. Amnesty International classified the police detention and treatment of protesters during Genoa's G8 as the worst violation of human rights in a Western country since the Second World War.

[47]　Esposito, *Living Thought*, pp. 269, 277.

community'.[48] In this light, transgenerational and transnational subjectivity is not only the disposition to act locally and globally but also to experience life as precarious and interdependent, as singular and as part of a community. So, while the G8 events have a local dimension, which is very much linked to the Italian context and its sociopolitical history, they also act as a 'prefiguration' or a moment of emergence of interconnected movements which are, however, configured differently at local and global level.[49]

Post-Genoa Narratives and their 'After-Affects'

The facts of Genoa 2001 can, like 9/11, be seen as a watershed not only on a sociopolitical, philosophical and experiential level, but also on the level of cultural production. The memorandum *New Italian Epic*, published in 2009 by the Italian writers' collective Wu Ming, states that Genoa 2001 can be seen, together with the attack on the Twin Towers, as a double key moment in the perception of the relationship between literature and society.[50] Following their lead, David Ward describes the impact of these two key events on Italian post-postmodern literature:

> In such a post Genoa, post 9/11 new world, into which reality had brusquely intervened in the form of terrorist attacks on a previously unheard of scale and of police wielding cudgels, it seemed that postmodern irony, playfulness and concern for text had little to say, was incongruous and even complicit.[51]

[48] Judith Butler, *Precarious Life: The Powers of Mourning and Violence* (London and New York: Verso, 2004), pp. xii–xiii.

[49] For instance, the episodes of violence that occurred during anti-austerity protests on 15 October 2011 in Rome have been connected not only to the contemporary Occupy/Indignados manifestations but also to the events of the Genoa G8, with the result that, in Italy, Occupy has not taken the same form or gained the same presence as in other countries. See Stefania Milan, 'The Italian Anomaly', *Index on Censorship*, 42.1 (2013), 12–15.

[50] Wu Ming, *New Italian Epic. Letteratura, sguardo obliquo, ritorno al futuro* (Turin: Einaudi, 2009), p. viii. One of the members of the collective, Wu Ming 1, also theorized the mythopoetic or myth-making potential of the 'Tute Bianche' [White Overalls], a more extremist fringe of the non-violent movements that tried to physically violate the fence cordoning off the red zone during the Genoa G8 protests. Wu Ming 1, 'Tute Bianche: The Practical Side of Myth-Making (in Catastrophic Times)', *Autonomedia. Radical Media, Politics and Culture*, 15 August 2002, http://dev.autonomedia.org/node/1160 [accessed 1 October 2019].

[51] David Ward, *Contemporary Italian Narrative and 1970s Terrorism: Stranger than Fact* (Madison, CT: Palgrave MacMillan, 2017), pp. 36–37.

Since 9/11, we have seen the growth of an international debate on the end of postmodernism and on the need for new, committed forms of realism. What emerges from these discussions on the uses of literature and film is a shift from political ideas towards affects, or even 'after-affects', which, according to Pieter Vermeulen, turn the novel into 'one site where the reorganization of human life that is underway in the early twenty-first century is being registered as an affect that remains to be captured'.[52] This trend also shows a preference for ambivalent, post-dialectic concepts such as 'cruel optimism', theorized by Lauren Berlant in order to conceptualize a new 'affective realism' which manifests the 'attrition of a fantasy, a collectively invested form of life, of good life'.[53]

The foregrounding of affective ambivalence that cuts across the immunity dichotomy theorized in Esposito's affirmative biopolitics (discussed above) is key to a number of postmemory narratives dedicated to the police incursion – on 21 July, at about 11p.m. – in the Diaz school, which hosted the Indymedia centre as well as several GSF members and journalists, and to the arrest and torture of 75 Diaz school protesters who were taken to the Bolzaneto barracks. These episodes are the only ones that were not documented by audiovisual devices, and testimonial narrations concerning what happened took almost ten years to emerge in fictional form.

Quella notte alla Diaz: The Transnational Work of a Divided Memory

The first among these narrations is Christian Mirra's testimonial graphic novel *Quella notte alla Diaz*.[54] The story is structured as the 'chronicle' of the night raid of the Diaz school and is divided into three parts, before, during and after the event. Each part reflects related 'affects': from the euphoria of collective protest to the tragedy of the 'Chilean night',[55] to the elegy of post-traumatic physical and juridical rehabilitation. The combination of images and words, as they unfold in the sequence of the panels, visualizes the material experiences and the sounds associated with the main character's

---

[52] Pieter Vermeulen, *Contemporary Literature and the End of the Novel* (Basingstoke: Palgrave Macmillan, 2015), p. 152.

[53] Lauren Berlant, *Cruel Optimism* (Durham, NC and London: Duke University Press, 2011), pp. 8, 11.

[54] Christian Mirra, *Quella notta alla Diaz. Una cronaca del G8 a Genova* (Parma: Guanda, 2010).

[55] The title of the second part, 'La notte cilena', refers to the transnational imaginary activated by European and US newspapers reporting Italy's brutality, which links the repression in Genoa to that of a 'Chilean', 'Argentine', 'East European' or 'Cuban' dictatorship (Guano, *Creative Urbanity*, pp. 77–78).

growing fear, pain and anger. Significantly, the comic book is cut in half by a single panel which zooms in on the victim's screaming face, disfigured by the violence perpetrated by the police. The images also transfigure the perpetrators allegorically into monstrous animals. This is clearly a non-conciliatory narrative which displays, with the help of experiential truth, the bodily symptoms of the victim's trauma: the very first frame shows the first-person narrator waking up in hospital with stitches in his face, asking himself what happened. The image is combined with the header 'Genova, 22 luglio 2001'. The healing process narrated in Part 3 is visualized initially through Christian's broken glasses and severely wounded eye, which result in blurred vision of his whereabouts during his hospital detention. Factual evidence, inserted into the graphic novel through quotations and commentaries, also shows that truth and justice for the victims of the atrocities are still missing.

The state of exception that legitimized the events at the Diaz school and Bolzaneto barracks is not presented as limited to those two episodes. To reinforce the idea of the historical recurrence in Italy of a negative biopolitics embodied in the opposition between demonstrators and public order, Mirra also establishes a link between the G8 events and the violence which occurred in Naples during no-global manifestations prior to the Genoa summit. These are narrated in Part 1, 'La manifestazione' [the march]. The utopian vision which first fostered Christian's desire to be part of the transnational no-global community of *ragazzi* gathered in Genoa, and later sustained his determination not to be traumatized by police violence, is embodied by the fantasy of a flying dragon.[56] In real life, he is assisted in his recovery by the affect and empathy of family and friends, who act as a 'moral community'[57] as well as an intergenerational community.[58] Trauma management by the state, on the other hand, is shown to be ineffective in its attempts at juridical repair and also in recognizing the victim's rights and status, resulting in the impossibility of reconciliation. The two closing panels show black crows and a fascist-style monument. At its top stand policemen wearing anti-riot helmets, while the names of those police officers who got a promotion after the Genoa events are inscribed on its base.

With its first-person, experiential narrative, this graphic novel inscribes itself firmly among the narratives of Italy's 'divided memories'. Yet it could also be analysed as an example of the transnational work of graphic narratives,

---

[56] See Inge Lanslots, 'La trasmissione della memoria del G8 2001: Due percorsi grafici dell'irruzione nella Diaz-Pertini-Pascoli', *Narrativa-Nouvelle série*, 35–36 (2014), 207–19.

[57] Assmann, 'History, Memory', p. 269.

[58] Portelli, 'Generations in Genoa', p. 349.

with the reader's dynamic interaction and movement between frames or 'medial boundaries' mirroring the movement across 'national and cultural boundaries'.[59] According to Shane Denson, the multistable frame typical of comic books makes it possible to envision a sort of 'transnational multistability – a flickering of the border frames of nations as imagined communities, a multivalent dynamic by which national borders are both questioned and reinforced, alternately and unceasingly, in the exchanges between real and imagined geographies as they take shape in and around the medium of comics'.[60] In this view, the visual and even audible expression of the bodily experience of state violence in *Quella notte alla Diaz* signals the contrast with the alternative vision voiced by the slogan *un altro mondo è possibile* – a vision that has to be searched for outside of Italy, within an affective transnational community of interconnected youth, as depicted in the opening images of the comic's preamble or 'retcon'.[61] It is particularly significant, in this perspective, that Mirra is now living and working as a graphic artist in Spain.

Black Block and *Diaz*: 'After-Affects' of the Crisis of Democracy

Claudia Capelli has divided the visual representations of Genoa 2001 into different phases: from the 2001–02 documentaries, with their 'collective narrative' and their 'need to communicate a truth', to the images which were used as 'legal evidence' during the trials and therefore 'acquired that status of "truth" that had been previously denied to them', to, finally, the 'attempt at the construction of a reconciliatory narrative'.[62] However, for those demonstrators who are firmly convinced that the police and the Italian government intentionally traumatized the movement, 'the trauma belongs exclusively to the movement's counter-memory, and reconciliation is not yet a viable path'.[63]

Unlike Mirra's personal and individual account, Bachschmidt's documentary *Black Block* and Vicari's docudrama *Diaz – Don't Clean Up*

---

[59] Shane Denson, 'Afterword: Framing, Unframing, Reframing: Retconning the Transnational Work of Comics', in *Transnational Perspectives on Graphic Narratives: Comics at the Crossroads*, ed. by Shane Denson, Christina Meyer and Daniel Stein (Bloomsbury, 2013), pp. 271–84 (p. 271).

[60] Denson, 'Afterword', p. 279.

[61] The technique of retcon 'retrofits the series with continuity by means of a revisionary view of past events' (Denson, 'Afterword', p. 277).

[62] Capelli also notes the importance 'of images as particular media of memory, which often become the primary markers of historical events especially for the creation of cultural traumas' ('From Documentary Truth to Historical Evidence', p. 320).

[63] Capelli, 'From Documentary Truth to Historical Evidence', pp. 326, 327, 330, 331.

This Blood[64] are based on testimonies by protesters from different countries, some of which have acquired an iconic status comparable to that of Carlo Giuliani. Bachschmidt conceived his documentary while, as a member of the Genoa Legal Forum, he assisted Vicari with the research for *Diaz*. In these two cultural products, affect is filtered through the 'after-affects' of the G8 events: trauma is visualized through the bodily experience of pain, anger, humiliation, followed by psychical and physical recovery, while the viewer, as a 'secondary witness',[65] is asked to empathize with all of these experiences. Bachschmidt explicitly stated that his documentary aims to perform a therapeutic exercise in public.[66] Through the eyes of 31-year-old activist Muli, from Berlin, the director-interviewer (who remains invisible) shows how the reconstruction of hope can be imagined as a form of trauma management within ordinary life practices of community and solidarity.[67] In the case of Vicari's *Diaz*, both the director and the producer have declared their intention of making the events of Genoa 2001 part of Italy's shared memory.[68] Vicari, however, has also stated that his film does not aim to offer a political explanation of what happened,[69] but rather he wished to turn the events into a metaphor of the contemporary crisis of democracy.[70] He has confirmed, too, that his intention was to produce an emotional rendering of the beatings which took place in the Diaz school and the Bolzaneto barracks, by adopting the personalized view of Alma Koch – in reality the German activist Lena Zühlke, whose testimony has been used in a number of documentaries on the Genoa G8. Through this strategy, his film succeeds in producing a fictional representation of a first-hand, embodied experience of that part of the events

---

[64] Carlo A. Bachschmidt, *Black Block* (Rome: Fandango, 2011; DVD + book); Daniele Vicari, *Diaz, Don't Clean Up This Blood* (Rome: Fandango, 2012).

[65] Assmann, 'History, Memory', p. 269.

[66] Bachschmidt, *Black Block*, p. 9.

[67] For an analysis of *Black Block* see Monica Jansen, 'Documentare il G8 a Genova dieci anni dopo: lo sguardo "fuori campo" in *Black Block* e in *Solo limoni*', in *Un nuovo cinema politico italiano? Vol. II: Il passato sociopolitico, il potere istituzionale, la marginalizzazione*, ed. by William Hope, Silvana Serra and Luciana d'Arcangeli (Leicester: Troubador, 2014), pp. 98–110.

[68] Capelli, 'From Documentary Truth to Historical Evidence', p. 329.

[69] This critique was moved against him by Lorenzo Guadagnucci, the journalist impersonated in the film by Elio Germano. See Lorenzo Guadagnucci, '"Diaz", morte accidentale di una democrazia', in *MicroMega*, 16 April 2012, available at http://temi.repubblica.it/micromega-online/diaz-morte-accidentale-di-una-democrazia/ [accessed 1 November 2019].

[70] See Monica Jansen, '*Diaz* di Vicari: il personale è globale', *Narrativa-Nouvelle série*, 35–36 (2014), 195–205.

that had remained invisible in media representations and had therefore also been excluded from institutional commemoration and remembrance.

Diaz was well received at the 2012 Berlin Film Festival and the docudrama has provided an occasion for victims worldwide to see their trauma represented for the first time. However, critical responses to Vicari's work have also shown the diversification which is to be found in the transnational dimension of the cultural memory of the Genoa G8, both between different European countries and between Europe and the US. The title with which the film was distributed in France in 2013, *Diaz. Un crime d'État*, emphasizes an ethical reading, while in the UK the collective dimension of the Genoa G8's traumatic experience seems to be mediated first of all by the personal experience of activist and journalist Mark Covell, who was beaten at the Diaz school. In the US, finally, the Genoa G8 is framed within the broader context of the international anti-global movements against consumerism.[71] Furthermore, Vicari's own reading of the Genoa G8 as a metaphor for the delegitimization of the democratic system, in the end, confirms the predominance of a national interpretative framework, which identifies transgenerational subjectivity with the victimhood of 'bare life' and the nation of Italy with a transnational 'laboratory' of biopolitics and of radical thought.

Conclusion: New Mobilities after Genoa 2001

In these post-G8 2001 narratives, the alternative to globalized capitalism and to Italy's concurrent 'immobilism' is imagined in terms of a transnational subjectivity which, in turn, is conceived as based on generational 'interconnectedness'. The post-Genoa generation identifies itself as precarious, not only in terms of its relationship with the state and its apparatuses, but also in terms of economic conditions. The events of Genoa 2001 can be read not just in association with the epochal, traumatic experience of 9/11, but also with the ontological tensions brought about by the increasingly 'flexible' nature of working conditions and identified with the concept of 'precarity'. In Italy, this divisive experience of social and economic subjectivization – which came into being, at a national level, as the result of a number of job reforms aiming to liberalize the labour market – has generated an increase in the transnational mobility of, predominantly, young individuals. This new wave of emigration has come to equal the numbers of immigrants moving to Italy and, as a result, the country has become a migratory

---

[71] See the documentary by Erik Gandini, *Surplus: Terrorized into Being Consumers* (Atmo Media Network, 2003).

'crossroad'.[72] The collectivity or 'multitude' that took shape in the wake of the GSF, coalescing around shared opposition to neoliberal capitalism, has found further embodiment in transnational social movements focusing on the issue of precarity, as shown for instance by international Euro May Day demonstrations. One of these events, held in Milan in 2004, gave birth to 'San Precario', the Saint of precarious workers and lives.[73] Butler's appeal, after 9/11, for precarious life to be understood in terms of interdependency and shared vulnerability could thus be extended to the transnational subjectivity of a new generation in the making, as shown by the many developments undergone by the two main movements present within the Genoa G8 anti-summit, the ecopacifist and the anti-capitalist groups, which eventually merged to form the various 'souls' of the GSF.[74] In this perspective, the notions of hybridization and interconnectedness, studied in fields such as migration and mobility studies,[75] offer new, conscious ways to locate privileged sites where the twin poles of the local and the global can meet outside the boundaries of the national paradigm of victimhood and move, instead, towards a transgenerational subjectivity inspired by affective realism.

[72] Enrico Pugliese, *Quelli che se ne vanno: La nuova emigrazione italiana* (Bologna: Il Mulino, 2018), p. 122.

[73] On this topic, see Nicole Doerr and Alice Mattoni, 'Public Spaces and Alternative Media Practices in Europe: The Case of the EuroMayDay Parade against Precarity', in *Media and Revolt. Strategies and Performances from the 1960s to the Present*, ed. by Kathrin Fahlenbrach, Erling Sivertsen and Rolf Werenskjold (New York and Oxford: Berghahn, 2014), pp. 386–405; Marcello Tarì and Ilaria Vanni, 'On the Life and Deeds of San Precario, Patron Saint of Precarious Workers and Lives', *The Fibreculture Journal*, 5 (2005), http://five.fibreculturejournal.org/fcj-023-on-the-life-and-deeds-of-san-precario-patron-saint-of-precarious-workers-and-lives/ [accessed 1 November 2019].

[74] Herbert Reiter (with Massimiliano Andretta, Donatella della Porta and Lorenzo Mosca), 'The Global Justice Movement in Italy', in *The Global Justice Movement*, ed. by Donatella della Porta (Boulder: Paradigm Publishers, 2007), p. 56.

[75] See Thomas Nail, *The Figure of the Migrant* (Stanford: Stanford University Press, 2015), p. 235: 'The migrant is the political figure of our time [...] From this new starting point, it reinterprets political theory as a politics of movement: a kinopolitics'.

19

Queer Translanguagers versus Inclusive Language

Translingual Practices and Queer Italian Studies

Serena Bassi

> You tell your older brother when you've masturbated for the first time and he calls you a 'pervert'. You look the word up in the dictionary and see the word 'homosexual' – he knows.
>
> (A Gay Male Group, 'Notes on Gay Male Consciousness-Raising', 1973)[1]

The above epigraph tells the story of a gay liberation activist whose search for an alternative sexual identity was abruptly interrupted by a dictionary definition. The text was written collectively in the early 1970s after a meeting of a London-based consciousness-raising group in which one of the members recalled fearing moral condemnation from his family as he was approaching puberty. Eventually, condemnation did come, but via the monolingual English dictionary, for which 'homosexual' was a synonym of 'pervert'. Whilst some readers may think of the above quote as a linguistic trace of a bygone past, in November 2018 the *New York Times* reported that the President of the United States Donald Trump had been working on a legal definition of 'gender' that would likely have similar stigmatizing effects. The definition, which was intended as an addition to Title IX legislation, cast gender 'as either male or female, unchangeable, and determined by the genitals that a person is born with'. The essentialist redefinition prompted the journalist reporting on it to speak of an emergent right-wing political project to 'write transgender people

---

[1] Karla Jay and Allen Young, *Out of the Closets: Voices of Gay Liberation* (New York: NYU Press), p. 293.

out of existence'.[2] By drawing attention to the symbolic violence exercised by the monolingual dictionary and the law, these two stories foreground the vexed relationship between sexuality, social injustice, official terminologies and national processes of linguistic standardization.

Just like English and other national languages, modern standard Italian may also function as a heteronormative and cisnormative construct.[3] In particular, the way in which the morphological and grammatical structures of Italian and other dominant Romance languages, like French and Spanish, reify a binary understanding of gender[4] has long been problematized by feminist and queer linguists,[5] especially in the context of Italian's circulation as a widely taught 'foreign language' in university departments of modern languages across the world. While the gender-neutral pronoun 'they' (as in the sentence, 'You'll see Alex tonight: they and I are going to the party') was picked up as 2015 'Word of the Year' by Anglophone lexicographers to provide an official alternative to the standard he/she singular pronouns, a similar debate centred upon grammar, representation and queer inclusion has been taking place within Italophone language studies in the past few years. For example, a recent special issue of the online journal *gender/sexuality/italy* dedicated to gender and language proposed a set of linguistic strategies that ranged from recommending the use of asterisks instead of standard word endings to finding one neutral vowel for all gendered adjectives in Italian.[6]

---

[2] Christoph Hanssmann, 'Trump's Anti-Trans Memo Opens Door to Escalating State Surveillance', *Truthout*, 27 October 2018, https://truthout.org/articles/trumps-anti-trans-memo-opens-door-to-escalating-state-surveillance/ [accessed 10 December 2019].

[3] A cogent example of the symbolic violence that 'correct' and 'fluent' Italian exercises is the widely used collocation 'la famiglia naturale', which refers to the kinship structure consisting of one woman, one man and their children, and problematically naturalizes and universalizes a specifically modern and Western social formation.

[4] Kris Knisely, 'Language Learning and the Gendered Self: The Case of French and Masculinity in a US Context', *Gender and Language*, 10.2 (2016), 216–39; Charlotte Ross, 'Qu@*ring the Italian Language', *Queer Italia Network Blog*, 12 January 2017, https://queeritalia.com/2017/01/12/queeringitalian/ [accessed 10 December 2019].

[5] Alma Sabatini, *Raccomandazioni per un uso non sessista della lingua* (Florence: Accademia della Crusca, 1987); Eva Nossem, 'Potere e autorità nei dizionari', *gender/sexuality/italy*, 2 (2015), https://www.gendersexualityitaly.com/potere-e-autorita/ [accessed 10 December 2019]; Cecilia Robustelli, *Sindaco e sindaca: il linguaggio di genere* (Florence: Accademia della Crusca, 2017).

[6] Chiara Nardone, 'Asimmetrie semantiche di genere: un'analisi sull'italiano del corpus itWaC', *gender/sexuality/italy*, 3 (2016), https://www.gendersexualityitaly.com/1-asimmetrie-semantiche-di-genere-unanalisi-sullitaliano-del-corpus-itwac/ [accessed 10 December 2019].

Even though they reached different conclusions, all contributions moved from the assumption that modern Italian is intrinsically sexist, heteronormative and cisnormative, and advocated substituting existing linguistic standards with revised standards, which contributors cast as part of an emerging 'inclusive language'.[7]

As the preceding chapters in this volume have made clear, the transnational turn in modern languages has allowed us to reconsider the very process of discipline formation in Italian studies and ask: What do we study when we study something we conventionally call 'Italian culture'? The transnational turn has also enabled a nuanced and self-reflexive conversation about the Italian language itself, its global circulation and the way it is thought about and taught. In particular, research areas like translation studies, critical multilingualism studies and applied linguistics have focused our attention on the metalinguistic discourses through which languages are turned into objects of knowledge and desire to be sold – through 'foreign language' classes, or in film, music and other popular media – in global cognitive markets.[8] As part of these scholarly conversations, processes of linguistic standardization themselves and the nationalist and monolingual attachments that underpin them have come under increasing scrutiny. In this context, the phrase 'language ideologies' draws attention to the often invisible processes of differentiation through which we have historically come to identify a group of linguistic signs as a unitary, distinct and autonomous semiotic system (i.e., as a national language).[9] Since the ascendance of the so-called 'monolingual paradigm' in the nineteenth century, the dominant language ideologies of Western societies have been versions of Romantic-era ethnolinguistic nationalism.[10]

Current dominant language ideologies allow us to perform a variety of social actions: they make it possible for us to differentiate between a 'native speaker' of a particular language and a 'non-native speaker', to hold the

[7] Ilaria Marotta and Salvatore Monaco, 'Un linguaggio più inclusivo? Rischi e asterischi nella lingua italiana' *gender/sexuality/italy*, 3 (2016), https://www.gendersexualityitaly.com/4-un-linguaggio-piu-inclusivo-rischi-e-asterischi-nella-lingua-italiana/ [accessed 10 December 2019].

[8] Alastair Pennycook, 'The Myth of English as International Language', in *Disinventing and Reconstituting Languages*, ed. by Sinfree Makoni and Alastair Pennycook (Amsterdam: Multilingual Matters, 2007), pp. 90–115.

[9] Sue Gal and Judith Irvine, 'Language Ideology and Linguistic Differentiation', in *Regimes of Language: Ideologies, Polities, and Identities*, ed. by Paul V. Kroskrity (Santa Fe: School of America Research Press, 2000), pp. 35–83.

[10] Thomas Bonfiglio, *Mother Tongues and Nations: The Invention of the Native Speaker* (New York: De Gruyter, 2010).

opinion that language learners speaking with a regionally marked accent are 'surprising' or 'amusing', to attribute different status and value to standard and non-standard varieties of the same national language, to view a literary text written in a particular language as standing in for a thing we call 'national culture', and to maintain that certain words and phrases are ontologically untranslatable from one language into another. In other words, language ideologies allow us to distinguish and differentiate between languages, speakers and texts in ways that reflect dominant belief systems about communication, community, nation and ethnicity. There is also another meaning of the phrase 'language ideology' which is rarely explored but is particularly useful to tackle Italian's supposed ontological status as a sexist, homophobic and transphobic language. Language ideologies allow us to cast languages as having a fixed ideological import – as carriers of the 'national genius', the manifestation of a particular 'national vice' or the product of an imagined 'national essence'. This essay will offer an alternative to 'authoritative' terminologies and standardized languages, whilst simultaneously critiquing essentialist metadiscourse on language that risks affording ontological status to a particular, standardized and nationalized version of Italian and may thereby unwittingly erase 'actually existing' linguistic varieties. In fact, constructing languages as formations with a fixed ideological import may foreclose our ability to see the creative ways in which speakers of multiple dialects and sociolects are already intervening in dominant narratives about gender and sexuality through their particular use of existing linguistic repertoires and, at the same time, resisting linguistic standardization.

In particular, the essay will focus on one example of creative subcultural intervention on language in twentieth-century Italian cultural history. In what follows, I will address the pivotal role of the so-called 'youth proletarian movement' – born out of what is known as the *movimento del '77* – in intervening in and against the very idea of a correct, standard and fluent national language, as well as against heteronormativity and cisnormativity. At present, linguistic experiments disrupting gender and sexual normativity are a largely uncovered archive in Italian studies, despite the recognized importance of experimental literature subverting language in Italian cultural production throughout the twentieth century.[11] As a number of historians and critical theorists argue, of the Euro-American protest movements that began to organize in the late 1960s, the Italian was the most long-lasting, spreading

---

[11] See for example: Serena Daly, 'Futurist War Noises: Confronting and Coping with the Sounds of the First World War', *California Italian Studies*, 4.1 (2014), https://escholarship.org/uc/item/8fx1p115 [accessed 10 December 2019]; Maurizio Calvesi, *Avanguardia di massa. Compaiono gli indiani metropolitani* (Milan: Feltrinelli, 2018).

from universities into factories and then out again into society as a whole, stretching all the way to the late 1970s.[12] In the years between 1975 and 1979, these movements experienced an important and widely studied surge that has particular implications for my interrogation of politicized linguistic experiments. In Rome, Bologna, Turin, Naples, Milan and other cities, young people organized themselves into 'proletarian youth groups', squatted in buildings and reclaimed the right to access urban leisure practices for free.[13]

At the height of the movement in 1977, tens of thousands of young people were involved in mass protests and street battles with the police.[14] However, tactically more significant than seeking direct confrontation with the state, was perhaps the movement's attempt to take over the urban linguistic landscape through free radios, theatre performances held during mass protests, slogans and chants, posters, political graffiti and improvised poetic interventions on city walls.[15] These grass-roots interventions into public space used a set of semiotic guerrilla tactics that performed a carnivalesque disruption of everyday life and staged the unravelling of language, something of a deliberate linguistic regression to childhood.[16] In these practices, the challenge to moral respectability intertwined with that to grammatical correctness, as both notions were seen as repressive lynchpins of bourgeois culture. As we will see in the next section, these moments of linguistic experimentation also operated as sites through which terms and terminologies of the then globalizing youth movements could circulate across national and linguistic borders.

L'unica giustizia è quella frocetaria: Queerness as Translingual Practice

Even though 'Anglonormative' accounts of resistance against heteronormativity and cisnormativity tend largely to privilege urban contexts in the United States and Great Britain, gay liberation and transgender liberation have long

---

[12] Paul Ginsborg, *History of Contemporary Italy* (London: Palgrave, 2003).

[13] The political practice of *autoriduzione* entailed reclaiming unrestricted access to consumption and leisure in the contemporary city by entering public spaces like cinemas or means of transport like trains or buses in large groups; it was theorized as a way of taking back what late capital owes the exploited youth proletariat. On *autoriduzione* and similar political practices, see Robert Lumley, *States of Emergency: Cultures of Revolt in Italy from 1968 to 1978* (London: Verso, 1995).

[14] Lumley, *States of Emergency*.

[15] Danilo Mariscalco, *Dai laboratori alle masse: Pratiche artistiche e comunicazione nel movimento del '77* (Verona: Ombre corte, 2014).

[16] Umberto Eco, *Sette anni di desiderio* (Milan: Bompiani 1983), p. 59; Marco Belpoliti, *Settanta* (Turin: Einaudi, 2010), pp. 321–22.

been complex and uneven transnational phenomena.[17] In particular, in the second half of the twentieth century, after the Compton Riots in 1966 in San Francisco and the Stonewall Riots in 1969 in New York, an internationalist vision of a worldwide gay and transgender movement began to travel globally as communities of gender and sexual dissidents – activists, writers, artists, performers and translators – imagined a future outside what we today call heteronormativity and cisnormativity. A remarkable 'traffic in meaning'[18] between these communities produced a plethora of new terminologies that rethought sex, gender, sexuality and social inequalities, as well as fostering new strategies for translating meaning across languages and cultural contexts.

If in today's Italy gay and queer lifestyles, subcultural languages and cultural products form a recognizable and profitable niche in the mainstream cultural markets, it is partly thanks to the often unremunerated translation of key gay liberation texts, such as Dennis Altman's *Homosexual Oppression and Liberation* among many others, which first imported concepts like that of an autonomous and separate 'gay culture'[19] and phrases like 'coming out of the closet' into Italian.[20] In the 1960s and 1970s, when the Italian gay movement began to form, a number of anti-psychiatry essays, homoerotic poems, gay-themed novels, political manifestos and pamphlets, posters and leaflets celebrating sexual liberation, travelled to Italy thanks to what the linguist Roman Jakobson famously categorized as 'translation proper',[21] that is a distinct cultural and social practice that produces a 'target text' in a given national language out of a 'source text' written in another. For example, the key texts of the Anglo-American women's movement and the Gay Liberation Front were interlingually translated chiefly by unpaid 'movement translators' and published in a number of anthologies by feminist and queer collectives and small radical publishing houses, such as La Salamandra and Arcana Editrice, and, less frequently, by large publishers too.[22]

---

[17] Martin Manalansan, *Global Divas: Filippino Gay Men in the Diaspora* (Durham: Duke University Press 2003); Tom Boellstorff, *The Gay Archipelago: Sexuality and Nation in Indonesia* (Princeton: Princeton University Press 2005).

[18] Mary Louise Pratt, 'The Traffic in Meaning: Translation, Contagion, Infiltration', *Profession* (2002), 25–36.

[19] Jim Downes, *Stand by Me: The Forgotten History of Gay Liberation* (Toronto: Basic Books, 2016).

[20] Charlotte Ross, 'Queering Spaces in Turin', in *Beyond the Piazza: Public and Private Spaces in Modern Italian Culture*, ed. by Simona Storchi (Brussels: Peter Lang, 2017), pp. 129–47.

[21] Roman Jakobson, 'On Linguistic Aspects of Translation', in *On Translation*, ed. by Reuben A. Brower (Cambridge, MA: Harvard University Press, 1959), pp. 232–39 (p. 233).

[22] A landmark case study within translation history more widely, the Italian translation of the North American feminist health manual *Our Bodies, Ourselves*, offers a

However, in order to make sense of the redeployment in Italian and in local languages of theories, tropes and vocabularies that had initially travelled through interlingual translation but eventually developed a life of their own in the target culture and language, the notion of 'translation proper' is not sufficient. In fact, as translation theorists have shown, translation does not only produce a discrete target text out of an easily identifiable source text. Rather, contemporary regimes of translation may also involve significant rearrangement and displacement of a number of sources at once, or the travel of lexical items across languages. These kinds of reconfiguration of meaning across national borders are often referred to as 'translanguaging' or 'translingual practice', and have been widely explored by scholars in applied linguistics and in postcolonial literary studies.[23] Rather than producing an orderly bilingual text in which two separate languages are clearly recognizable, translingual practices may create seemingly monolingual texts that sound jarring because multiple codes and conflicting meanings are in fact housed within them. Importantly, translingualism demands that we rethink translation as a 'social relation'[24] that may be inscribed in a number of texts and cultural products rather than as a spatially determined cultural practice that takes us unproblematically from a clearly defined 'source' to an equally recognizable 'destination'.[25]

By reimagining translation as a set of translingual practices, we may become cognizant of the fact that when travelling theories, tropes and terminologies are redeployed in monolingual contexts in an already domesticated form, a labour of translation is occurring that may not be visible.

---

complex example of a text that was published by a major publisher (Einaudi), but – thanks to the intervention of the feminist collective that wrote the original text, the Boston Women Health Book Collective – some aspects of the production of the translated text were left under the control of chapters of the Italian Women's Liberation Movement. See Katy Davies, *The Making of Our Bodies Ourselves* (Durham, NC: Duke University Press, 2007).

[23] Key scholarly studies on translanguaging in these fields are: Suresh Canagarajah, *Translingual Practice: Global Englishes and Cosmopolitan Relations* (New York: Routledge, 2013); Lydia Liu, *Translingual Practice: Literature, National Culture, and Translated Modernity: China, 1900–1937* (Palo Alto: Stanford University Press, 1995); David Gramling, *The Invention of Monolingualism* (London: Bloomsbury, 2016); Rebecca Walkowitz, *Born Translated* (New York: Columbia University Press, 2017).

[24] Naoki Sakai, *Translation and Subjectivity: On Japan and Cultural Nationalism* (Minneapolis and London: University of Minnesota Press, 1997), p. 3.

[25] Maria Tymoczko, 'Western Metaphorical Discourses Implicit in Translation Studies', in *Thinking through Translation with Metaphors*, ed. by James St. André (Manchester: St. Jerome, 2010), pp. 109–43.

Without such labour, the newly travelled concepts would not be intelligible, recognizable or relatable at the point of arrival. In Italy in the 1970s, the slogans of the youth proletarian movement engaged in precisely this labour of translation by mixing youth sociolects, local dialect and foreign loanwords together, while also making reference to current and historical events, as well as Marxist, anarchist and feminist theories. The gay liberation chants that queer militants and their allies shouted during youth proletarian demonstrations and festivals are a case in point; and because of the diverse archives that these slogans drew from, they require various levels of multilingual and cultural competence for full comprehension. The crucial role that the semiotic guerrilla warfare tactic of creative *détournement* played in the youth proletarian movements is especially evident in the gay liberation movement's queer slogans, which were often parodies of existing 'straight' slogans.

In order to provide examples of the linguistic experiments that the gay and trans liberation movement engaged in during the 1970s, the following table[26] juxtaposes five popular 'straight' radical left slogans to their correspondent queer 'anti-slogans' that were circulating in the youth proletarian movements:[27]

'Tutti i tribunali salteranno in aria, l'unica giustizia è quella proletaria!' [All courts will blow up, the only justice is proletarian justice]	'Tutti i maschi salteranno in aria, l'unica giustizia è quella frocetaria!' [All males will blow up, the only justice is faggot-arian justice]
'Lotta di lunga durata, lotta di popolo armata, lotta continua sarà!' [Long-lasting struggle, armed people's struggle, continuing struggle]	'Frocia di lunga durata, frocia di popolo armata, frocia continua sarà!' [Long-lasting faggot, armed people's faggot, continuing faggot]
'El pueblo unido, jamás será vencido!' [The people, united, will never be defeated]	'El pueblo unido è meglio travestito!' [The people, united, is better cross-dressed]
'Uniti si, ma contro la DC!' [United indeed, but against the Christian Democracy Party]	'Isteriche si, ma contro la DC!' [Hysterical indeed, but against the Christian Democracy Party]

---

[26] Beppe Ramina, *Ha più diritti Sodoma di Marx?* (Bologna: Quaderni di Critica Omosessuale, 1994), pp. 97–99.

[27] The English translations of the Italian slogans are my own.

'Tremate, tremate, le streghe son tornate!' [Tremble, tremble, the witches are back]

'Tremate, tremate, le checche son armate!' [Tremble, tremble, the poofters are armed]

Another chant that Italian gay liberationists would use during both gay and 'mixed' demonstrations – 'La gioia, la gioia, la gioia la si inventa: frocia si nasce, gay lo si diventa!' [Joy is invented: you are born a faggot, but you become gay] – altered and adapted Simone De Beauvoir's famous formula – 'On ne naît pas femme: on le devient' [You are not born a woman, you become one] – to evoke the moment of rapture in the life of gay liberationists when they begin deliberately reclaiming an 'abject' identity for themselves ('gay lo si diventa'), having being called homophobic names from a young age ('frocia si nasce'). A close reading of these slogans shows that they operate on two separate but interrelated levels. Their most obvious political targets are, of course, anti-gay sentiments, heteronormative cis-masculinities ('tutti i maschi') and the logics of heteronormative society more broadly ('l'unica giustizia è quella frocetaria'). However, equally central to these queer linguistic experiments is an attack against the notions of 'correct language' that lie at the core of dominant nationalist language ideologies. Because they simultaneously deride and contest heteronormative society and normative ideas about language, the camp slogans cited above can help us start a conversation about the borders of the ideology we commonly call 'Italian', and even begin to question our epistemological approach towards language in Italian studies.

What makes these slogans useful as a way into a conversation on the Italian language as an object of enquiry is the way in which they simultaneously contest *and* reproduce dominant language ideologies. For example, in the final slogan quoted above – 'La gioia, la gioia, la gioia la si inventa: frocia si nasce, gay lo si diventa!' – the social stigma associated with male homosexuality is represented by the regionally marked derogative term *frocia* [faggot]. By contrast, the English-language word 'gay' – a foreign loan word, in this case – stands in for the act of proudly reclaiming 'homosexual' as a positive, progressive identity. The dichotomy between 'local' and 'foreign' languages may appear to reinforce the problematic way in which dominant language ideologies associate dialects – in the Italian context, southern dialects especially – with origin, local cultures, tradition, conservatism and, in this case, homophobia, whilst English is conflated with mobility, cosmopolitanism, egalitarianism and progress.[28]

---

[28] Pennycook, 'The Myth of English as International Language'.

However, if, in the above example, the linguistic practice of code-mixing reproduced the dominant language ideologies that construct a binary opposition between 'backward' local languages and 'progressive' global ones, in other contexts gay liberation slang openly contested those same language ideologies. Gay slang's main strategy to do so was precisely to imagine the relationship between the emerging international term 'gay' and the stigmatizing regional slur *frocio* in new ways. For example, in the second slogan in the table above, the queer slang phrase 'giustizia frocetaria' – an ironic appropriation of the Marxian stock phrase 'giustizia proletaria' or 'proletarian justice' – resignifies the homophobic slur *frocio* by implicitly making reference to the notion of 'gay militancy', which was pivotal to the transnational gay liberation movements at the time.[29] In the underground publications of the gay movement and in its key texts,[30] the notion of 'gay militancy' and of a 'gay revolutionary project' was at the centre of debates on the place of the 'sexual revolution' in the context of a larger project of social transformation, and on the intersections between economic exploitation and gendered oppression. Through the newly coined phrase 'giustizia frocetaria', the slogan quoted above foregrounds gay men's experience of being criminalized by the state, and implicitly suggests that gay men and the politically organized working class are both targeted by different manifestations of the same 'bourgeois justice'. At the same time as debates in the gay liberation movement about the political import of the 'sexual revolution' culminated in the forging of the new political identity of the 'gay revolutionary' or 'gay rev', the parodic phrase 'giustizia frocietaria' registered and encoded these debates through the implicit comparison between 'faggots' and 'proletarians'.

To further address the relationship between the local slur *frocio* and the cosmopolitan category 'gay' discussed above, the newly coined phrase 'giustizia frocietaria' fuses the meanings of the two signs together, thereby contesting the language ideologies that keep the two terms separate and differentiated. Since the neologism *frocetario* is best understood as an Italian adaptation of the English-language phrase 'gay rev' via a strategic appropriation of the local term *frocio*, something of a 'translingual' exchange is being performed through these slogans. To explain the concept of 'translingualism' as it pertains to these queer slogans, we may also return to the slogan 'La gioia, la gioia, la gioia la si inventa: frocia si nasce, gay lo si diventa!'; here, the apparent opposition of the terms *frocio* and 'gay' is complicated by the

---

[29] Emily Hobson, *Lavender and Red: Liberation and Solidarity in the Gay and Lesbian Left* (Berkeley: University of California Press, 2016).

[30] See for example: Mario Mieli, *Elementi di critica omosessuale* (Turin: Einaudi, 1977).

suggestion that 'joy' is not simply an emotion as it is normally understood, but something of a cultural formation that can and should be 'invented'. Moreover, in the slogan, the notion of an 'invented joy' holds the promise of changing a subject that had been defined by others as abject into one that turns that definition on its head, reclaims it and transforms it.

Through the use of the term 'invention' and through its proximity to the term 'gay', *gioia* exceeds its meaning in standard Italian by alluding to a specifically 'queer joy' that can only be invented by those who are targeted by homophobia. Whilst today the word 'gay' has been incorporated into the Italian language as a loanword and is routinely employed to mean 'homosexual', in the first phase of the Italian gay and trans liberation movement the word circulated chiefly in subcultural milieus and would have sounded 'foreign' and unfamiliar to the broader public, thereby opening up a space for a process of resemanticization of the English word in the Italian context. Thus, at the same time as *frocio* and other local labels are being resematicized *via-à-vis* 'gay' and the notion of 'gay militancy', 'gay' itself is being 'invented' through these slogans.

Improper Objects: The Stakes of Transnational (Queer) Italian Studies

The kinds of queer translingual practices that I have analysed above can offer Italianists a compelling archive which will enable them to complicate dominant Anglophone ideas of what 'inclusive languages' should sound like. The communication strategies of *il movimento del 1977* demand to be interrogated through a transnational approach because the movement was part of a larger global youth movement and participated in its transnational traffic in meaning. Moreover, the transnational reach of the youth movements in general and of the gay liberation movement specifically had an aesthetic consequence: it made it possible for language to be experimentally reinvented as a postnational formation that critiqued national divisions and nationalized linguistic correctness.

As I mentioned in the introduction to this essay, critical multilingualism studies and translation studies together challenge us to think about what modern languages may stand to gain from rethinking languages themselves transnationally and to move from a monolingual approach to knowledge as the unmarked given of language studies to a focus on the intrinsic multilingualism of texts and utterances that may pass as monolingual. However, an important part of this endeavour as modern languages scholars is asking what political point our insistence on linguistic multiplicity is making exactly, rather than acritically celebrating the coexistence of more than one language in the same social space as always already a victory for 'multicultural diversity'. David Gramling employs a powerful metaphor to encourage us to think more carefully about our epistemological approach to language and linguistic diversity:

> A recent Coca-Cola commercial featuring a multilingual version of 'America the Beautiful' appears to be celebrating language diversity and multi-ethnic, multi-heritage U.S. citizenship. And yet, when the symbolic subject of the video, the children, dive to the bottom of a pool collectively, their arms reach out for the same thing: a Coke bottle cap. Such is the structure of glossodiverse monolingualism: the pursuit of identical monetized meanings in multiple codes. What use is multilingualism for the world if all of its multiple-language speakers are pursuing the same bottle of Coke?[31]

This essay began by raising a similar concern: when we look for one transparent, properly standardized and nationalized 'inclusive language' that seeks to imitate existing Anglophone strategies, do we risk reducing the struggle against heteronormative and cisnormative language, metaphorically, to the same bottle of Coke?

By retrieving grass-roots translation strategies such as the ones analysed above, I am attempting to make the case for an improper, non-standard and intrinsically post-monolingual object of enquiry for Italian studies. The queer chants examined above can be read as attempts to domesticate in the Italian context the notion of 'queer militancy' that had been circulating in the transnational gay and lesbian left since the late 1960s.[32] In the Italian case, the new militant identity emerged by means of a twofold strategic appropriation: that of stigmatizing expressions like *frocio* [faggot] and *checca* [poofter] and also of the internationalizing term 'gay'. In the slogans I have discussed, both standard Italian and subcultural 'gay English' are being translated into something else in the process of producing a new queer sociolect. In my analysis, I have tried to make visible an otherwise invisible process of translation that rendered the familiar unfamiliar, the standard non-standard. Instead of clarifying and fixing meaning, these queer slogans confuse it through ongoing movement from one linguistic variety to another. As a result, the very meaning of 'sexuality' becomes unfixed here, as non-conforming sexual identity categories like 'gay' and *frocio* hint at once at a set of other signifiers like class, justice and revolution.

---

[31] David Gramling, *The Invention of Monolingualism*, p. 194.
[32] See Hobson, *Lavender and Red*.

In the path-breaking essay 'Thinking Sex', which is considered one of the first contributions to modern queer theory, Gayle Rubin argued that a new theory of sexual oppression should not concentrate on the representation of 'same-sex desire' in history, nor focus on the experiences of gay men and lesbians. Instead, queer critical endeavours would interrogate the production of different kinds of gendered, sexualized, classed and racialized 'moral deviants' at different historical junctures.[33] Along similar lines, in 'Against proper objects', Judith Butler asks us to think critically about the way Anglophone academia separates, orders hierarchically and organizes knowledge about 'minority identity'. The specific target of Butler's critique is the tendency in queer studies to analyse 'sexuality' in isolation from other vectors of power such as 'gender', 'race' and 'class', in order to stake a claim to an autonomous field of study unmistakably centred upon sex. Whilst, as Butler concedes, this strategy may have helped LGBT studies and queer studies gain academic legitimacy, one of its by-products has been the reification of 'same-sex desire' as a transhistorical category. Drawing our scholarly attention away from these problematic categories, Butler reimagines queer studies as focusing on a set of messy, intersectional and improper objects of enquiry.[34] In this chapter, I have suggested that the study of improper queer objects may also happen through a focus on 'translation improper', that is, on the translingual practices that defy prescriptive notions of 'translation proper' and undergird processes of globalization.

Building simultaneously on Rubin's and Butler's seminal texts and on critiques of the reification of translation, I want to suggest that 'same-sex desire', 'homosexuality' or even 'queer identity' should not become 'proper' objects of Italian studies – that is, objects of academic enquiry overdetermined by subject matter as well as national origin. It is certainly true, as has been remarked, that representations of homoerotic desire and non-conforming gender performances have a constitutive role in the Italian canon and that these are often neglected by scholars.[35] Nonetheless, as I have attempted to show through my analysis of samples taken from the archive of 1970s linguistic experiments, the 'queerness' of queer representations, languages

---

[33] Gayle Rubin, 'Thinking Sex: Notes for a Radical Theory of the Politics of Sexuality', in *Pleasure and Danger: Exploring Female Sexuality*, ed. by Carole Vance (London: Routledge & Kegan Paul, 1984), pp. 300–09.

[34] Judith Butler, 'Against Proper Objects: Introduction', *Differences: A Journal of Feminist Cultural Studies*, 6.2 (1998), 1–26.

[35] Gary Cestaro, *Queer Italia: Same-Sex Desire in Italian Literature and Film* (London: Palgrave, 2004).

and narratives is best attended to by locating non-conforming sexualities and desires in a broader history of translingual and transnational circulation.

As David Gramling reminds us, the 'monolingual paradigm' does not preach the superiority of one language over others. Rather, monolingualism's main moral tenet can be said to be the idea that you can say everything in every language, that is, the 'principle of transposability'. It is thanks to that principle that we can have sexuality studies within, for example, Italian, Russian and American studies and expect them to be organized through fairly similar, or at least comparable, concepts. In the examples I have analysed here, 'sexuality' is a highly permeable formation that translingually reconstitutes meaning as it compares sexuality with a variety of other signs like 'justice', 'revolution' and 'the global youth proletariat'. When queer studies aspires to becoming a 'proper object' within a field of modern languages that is made up of separate national silos, it may focus its intellectual enquiry on proper subjects with proper languages, proper nations and proper literary canons. By contrast, this essay has attempted to reimagine queer studies within a transnationalizing model of modern languages, with its individual constituencies operating as a set of queer laboratories co-conspiring against linguistic standardization. Rather than using sexuality to bolster existing ideas of the Italian language, a more transnational variety of queer Italian studies may focus on improper objects of enquiry and on the undoing of standard language that is at the heart of queer cultural politics.

Index